A Place Called School

John I. Goodlad

McGraw-Hill
New York   Chicago   San Francis
London   Madrid   Mexico City   Milan
San Juan   Seoul   Singapore   Sydney   onto

Copyright © 2004, 1984 by John I. Goodlad. All rights reserved. Printed in the United States of America. Except as permitted under the United States Copyright Act of 1976, no part of this publication may be reproduced or distributed in any form or by any means, or stored in a database or retrieval system, without the prior written permission of the publisher.

9 10 11 12 13   DOH/DOH   15 14 13

ISBN 978-0-07-143590-1
ISBN 0-07-143590-5

McGraw-Hill books are available at special quantity discounts to use as premiums and sales promotions, or for use in corporate training programs. For more information, please write to the Director of Special Sales, Professional Publishing, McGraw-Hill, Two Penn Plaza, New York, NY 10121-2298. Or contact your local bookstore.

This book is acid-free paper

Library of Congress Cataloging-in-Publication Data

Goodlad, John I.
    A place called school / John I. Goodlad.—20th anniversary ed.
        p. cm.
Includes bibliographical references and index.
    ISBN 0-07-143590-5 (Pbk. : alk. paper)
    1. Public schools—United States. I. Title.

    LA217.G654   2004
    371.01—dc22

                                                         2003025745

To
those individuals—
more than 27,000 in number—
who provided the data
on which this book is based

Contents

Chapter 10
Beyond the Schools We Have   321

Afterword   363

Foreword

Back to
A Place Called School

Theodore R. Sizer

In August of 1981, United States Secretary of Education Terrel Bell appointed the National Commission on Excellence in Education and requested that it report on the quality of schooling in America to the newly elected Reagan administration and to the American people.[1] The Commission, led by David Gardner, then president-elect of the University of California, was a distinguished group. Its specific charge was to respond to the "widespread public perception that something is seriously remiss in our educational system."[2] The group was to assess the nature of this condition and recommend to the Secretary, the President, and the public how to address it.

During these same months, John Goodlad and his colleagues based at the University of California at Los Angeles were hip deep in one of the largest and most sophisticated studies of American schooling ever undertaken. This Study of Schooling probed deeply into the workings of schools, depending far less on expert testimony or extrapolations about the goodness of schools and children from the latter's scores on brief paper-and-pencil tests and far more on painstakingly structured and sustained visits to a carefully selected group of schools, watching, recording, comparing, and assessing. The scale of the research project gave its conclusions great weight. As the dedication of the summary volume by Goodlad cites, "more than 27,000" individuals provided data.[3] Goodlad's team was advised by an outside group with impeccable scholarly credentials and was supported by fourteen of the country's largest and most discriminating private foundations. This was a Rolls-Royce of educational inquiries.

Reprinted with permission from Kenneth A. Sirotnik and Roger Soder (eds.), *The Beat of a Different Drummer: Essays on Educational Renewal in Honor of John I. Goodlad* (New York: Peter Lang, 1999), pp. 103–118.

Not surprisingly, Commission Chairman Gardner turned to Professor Goodlad for help. The Study staff met with the Commission and offered access to all of its then-gathered material. Contact thereafter apparently was fleeting. The Commission's report, *A Nation at Risk: The Imperative for Educational Reform*, was issued in May 1983. Goodlad's public report, *A Place Called School: Prospects for the Future*, was published by McGraw-Hill in 1984. To a remarkable extent, the former reflected little either of the analysis of or the conclusions of the latter.

What had the staff of the Study of Schooling put before the Commission, what had the Commission heard, and what did the commissioners choose to make of it? The outsider today can speculate only by matching what the report recommended with what ultimately appeared in *A Place Called School*.[4] The book outlines several interwoven themes. From the vantage point of the late 1990s, several stand out starkly. They bear repetition.

The Study team found "a strange, rather indefinable sameness" among schools, "seating arrangements, materials being used, teachers' roles, students' roles, teaching methods."[5] There were differences, too; one of the Study's high schools was, the researchers felt, to be "near collapse."[6]

What emerged for Goodlad was a critical distinction. "*Schools* differ; *schooling* is everywhere very much the same. Schools differ in the way they conduct their business and in the way the people relate in them to one another in conducting that business. But the business of schooling is everywhere very much the same."[7]

This pattern of schooling was not expressly a representation of clearly stated district and state policies. "My major conclusion from perusing most state guides to education in schools," Goodlad wrote, "is that this entire area is a conceptual swamp."[8] "Comprehensive lists of goals are hard to find. Instead, one finds long lists of goals and objectives for the separate subject fields and, recently in many states and districts, lists of proficiencies students are to acquire for high school graduation or grade-to-grade promotion. And in my own visits to many schools, I find little evidence of goals consciously shared by the teachers and precious little dialogue about what their schools are for."[9] "There appears to be a formidable discrepancy between the goals for schooling . . . [articulated at a school] and curricular provision for their attainment."[10] The well-intentioned mindlessness within schools that had been so devastatingly portrayed by Charles Silberman in his popular *Crisis in the Classroom* a decade earlier was clearly still a fact of educational life.[11]

A disjunction between school and society—between the schools' curricular regimens and the youngsters' real worlds—emerged in the Study's inquiries. Goodlad saw "a picture of rather well-intentioned teachers going about their business somewhat detached from and not quite connecting with the 'other lives' of their students. What the students saw as primary concerns in their daily lives, teachers viewed as dissonance in conducting school. . . . Somewhere, I suspect, down in the elementary school, probably in the fifth and sixth grades, a subtle shift occurs. The curriculum—subjects, topics, textbooks, workbooks, and the rest—comes between teacher and student. Young humans come to be viewed only as students, valued primarily for their academic aptitude and industry rather than as individual persons preoccupied with the physical, social, and personal needs unique to their circumstances and stage in life."[12] Clearly, the disjunction between school and society, carefully documented by James Coleman and his colleagues in their 1974 *Youth: Transition to Adulthood* report to President Nixon's Science Advisory Committee, was still alive and well.[13]

Goodlad saw the inadequacies of schooling increasing as the students grew older.[14] He has been often heard to remark that the best-schooled American youngster is a kindergartner and the least a high school senior.[15] He was harsh with Americans' toleration of the distance between widely articulated ends and the reality of means. "The gap between the rhetoric of individual flexibility, originality, and creativity in our educational goals, and the cultivation of these in our schools reveals a great hypocrisy."[16] "Securing the grades necessary to a high school graduation certificate appears to be more important than the actual content of schooling and the classes taken."[17] Credentials were more important than content, especially that "content" implicit in each young person's informed capabilities and the respectful commitment to use these well.

In a variety of ways, Goodlad identified the boredom experienced by students in school, especially by adolescents. "Too few of the kinds of engagements we want young people to have with knowledge occur in the classroom setting." He elaborated: "it appears that large numbers of secondary teachers resort to practices designed to keep students passive and under control just at the time when adolescents should be taking more charge of their education."[18]

Goodlad summarized:

> the modal classroom configurations which we observed looked like this: the teacher explaining or lecturing to the total class or a single student, occasionally asking questions requiring factual answers; the teacher, when not lecturing, observing or monitoring students working individually at their desks; students listening or appearing to listen to the teacher and occasionally responding to the teacher's questions; students working individually at their desks on reading or writing assignments; and all with little emotion, from interpersonal warmth to expressions of hostility.[19]

The Study team "observed that, on the average, about 75% of class time was spent on instruction and that nearly 70% of this was 'talk'—usually teacher to students. Teachers out-talked the class of students by a ratio of about three to one. . . . The bulk of this teacher talk was instructing in the sense of telling. Barely 5% of this instructional time was designed to create students' anticipation of needing to respond. Not even 1% required some kind of open response involving reasoning or perhaps an opinion from students."[20] The error of this approach was highlighted by Goodlad, citing research extending back to the Eight-Year Study and Project Talent: "facts students are able to recall in classroom examinations are up to 80% forgotten just two years later."[21]

These sorts of findings have been uncovered over and over since the 1970s. The appalling waste of time and imagination in most American classrooms was nicely recounted by Mihaly Csikszentmihalyi and Reed Larson in *Being Adolescent*. In a typical mid-1980s high school classroom, they wrote, "at least half the time the student is not really thinking about anything even remotely related to the lecture or to the subject matter."[22] There was little engagement, little spark, little connection between the ideas of the classroom and the position of the student.

Goodlad had much to say about the world of teachers. "To reach out positively and supportively to 27 youngsters for five hours or so each day in an elementary-school classroom is demanding and exhausting. To respond similarly to four to six successive classes of 25 or more students each at the secondary level may be impossible."[23] He wrote of the isolation and fragmentation of much of the teacher's regimen, and of the autonomy that the individual classroom provided. The latter was popular with teachers. He challenged the dominant metaphor for teachers' workplaces: "Schools and classrooms cannot be understood or accurately and usefully described by the relatively simplistic input-output factory model so often used; they are better understood as little villages in which individuals interact on a part-time basis within a relatively constrained and confining environment."[24]

Goodlad's study team examined student grouping practices and found that "effective instructional practices were found to be more characteristic of high than of low classes. Students in the lower tracks were the least likely to experience the types of instruction most highly associated with achievement."[25] When tracking was eliminated, "most of the mixed classes resembled the high more than the low track classes in nearly all of the areas studied."[26] Goodlad concluded that

> popular assumptions and myths regarding headedness and handedness, good and poor students, fast and slow learners, and the like are generally accepted and at the outset built into classroom organization. Instead of creating circumstances that minimize and compensate for initial disad-

vantages in learning, teachers unwittingly create conditions that increase the difficulty of eliminating disadvantage. . . . Tracking . . . is perceived to be a logical and expedient way to take account of wide differences in students' academic attainments. In effect, however, it serves as an organizational device for hiding awareness of the problem rather than an educative means for correcting it.[27]

Such are samples of the argument and findings of A Study of Schooling. Many had been, or soon were to be, reinforced, extended, or challenged by the work of other researchers.[28] All are nuanced, careful, and thorough, yielding a picture that is devastatingly recognizable to those who know schools well. The picture is necessarily complex. "The realization of this complexity is a first step away from myths and simplistic notions of roads to improvement such as more discipline by teachers and proficiency tests for grade-to-grade promotion. . . . I do in fact doubt that schooling, as presently conceived and conducted, is capable of providing large segments of young people with the education they and this democracy require."[29] He concluded, "The agenda suggested by the data presented will not be carried out by a little tinkering."[30]

A Place Called School was a volume of 361 pages, plus 19 pages of notes and references. *A Nation at Risk* was a report of 36 pages—in large type and with generous margins—plus 25 pages of appendices. Both had similar audiences: the serious public, educators, and policymakers. Their strategies for dissemination, however, were strikingly different.

Goodlad called on his readers to read long and hard, a rigorous exercise that, in his view, was absolutely necessary work. *A Place Called School* was deliberately light on detailed recommendations; these were to follow state by state, district by district, school by school, college by college, with the Study's critique providing a solid platform. Goodlad clearly wanted his readers to *think differently* about learning and schooling as a prelude to action.

On the other hand, Gardner and his colleagues clearly wanted to create a thunderclap, thus to get people's attention. And the people's attention would be caught by artful language and simple, familiar, understandable remedies. The Commission's report was to be an opening salvo for sustained reform and, while not a definitive blueprint, to provide at least a framework for action, a list of recommendations from which (say) a governor could launch his or her state's reform effort. The Commission wanted the country to move toward resolute action, *now*.

The rhetoric of *A Nation at Risk* is memorable. "Our Nation is at risk. Our once unchallenged preeminence in commerce, industry, science and technological innovation is being overtaken. . . . If an unfriendly power had attempted to impose on America the mediocre educational performance that exists today, we might have viewed it as an act of war. . . . Our concern . . . goes well beyond matters such as industry and commerce. It includes the intellectual, moral, and spiritual strengths of our people which knot together the very fabric of our society."[31]

This apocalyptic language worked. It got the attention of the nation, and even of the astonished president who had no idea of the bold message that the Commission of his administration might put before the people.[32] Goodlad received excellent reviews in important places. Gardner got on Page One.

The Commission focused on the effects of weak schooling rather than the causes of weak schooling. It produced a barrage of specific data including test scores, course enrollments, comparisons with foreign nations, and specific complaints from business and government employers about school graduates. It painted these universally mediocre indexes against a background of a new, global labor market. The commissioners quoted Paul Hurd: "We are raising a new generation of Americans that is scientifically and technologically illiterate" and John Slaughter who "warned of 'a growing chasm between a small scientific and technological elite and a citizenry ill-informed, indeed uninformed, on issues with a science component.'"[33]

The Commission identified a "national sense of frustration . . . a dimming of personal expectations and a fear of losing a shared vision for America."[34] The commissioners painted a need for what they termed a Learning Society and argued that "for too many people education means doing the minimum work necessary for the moment, then coasting through life on what may have been learned in its first quarter . . . (w)here there should have been a continuum of learning, we have none, but instead an often incoherent, outdated patchwork quilt."[35]

The Commission was no less disturbed than was Goodlad on the sloppiness in defining the purpose for the schools. The commissioners outlined four sets of "Findings." Regarding "content . . . the very 'stuff' of education," they asserted that "secondary school curricula have been homogenized, diluted, and diffused to the point that they have no longer a central purpose." Regarding "expectations," they found these to be shoddy. Regarding "time," they found too little spent on the serious matters of schooling, especially in contrast with that allocated for academic education in competing industrial nations. Finally, regarding teaching, they despaired over the weak academic background of teachers-in-training, the excessive emphasis in that training on "educational methods," poor salaries, limited professional influence over text selection, and great shortages in certain academic fields.[36]

The silences are revealing. There were no "findings" whatever about the realities of classrooms, about the boredom of students, and the disjunction between their world and that offered them up in school, about the very design and daily functioning of schools and the waste that such produces or of the lack of connection between what is known about learning and current widespread practice—that is, about the guts of Goodlad's findings.

There were five omnibus recommendations. For "Content," there were to be "Five New Basics . . . (1) 4 years of English; (2) 3 years of mathematics; (3) 3 years of science; (4) 3 years of social studies; and (5) one-half year of computer science," with two years of foreign language strongly recommended.[37] "Schools, colleges, and universities [should] adopt more rigorous and measurable standards . . . for academic performance and student conduct."[38] There was to be "significantly more time devoted to learning the New Basics."[39] Several discrete initiatives would "improve the preparation of teachers," these having to do with matters of standards, salaries, contracts, career ladders, and incentives.[40] Finally, there were recommendations for "Leadership and Fiscal Support," none suggesting a significant change in the balance of power among traditional stakeholders but expecting deep, new, and coordinated commitments from each.[41]

Was all this the "tinkering" that Goodlad urged us to avoid? Perhaps. But one person's tinkering is another's belief of what is practically doable. Clearly, the Commission believed that there had to be renewed—even unprecedented—commitments made to achieve America's needed "learning society." So did Goodlad. The differences between the two are found in the nature and scope of those commitments, and these differences may reflect more than merely choice among tactics.

Crudely put, while both Goodlad and Gardner accepted the notion of formal education—important things happening for and to children in places called schools—Goodlad, as the result of his research, recommended significant rethinking and redesign of those schools while Gardner's Commission wanted those schools, essentially structured as at present, simply to be pushed much harder. Goodlad wanted new sorts of schools. Gardner wanted the sorts of schools we currently had to do a better job. Goodlad clearly believed that without significant change inside those places called school, serious improvements were impossible. Gardner believed that an aroused public and polity could make the existing system work.

In the short run, the Commission was remarkably successful in its quest for renewed public and political concern for education. After the release of its report, every state in one form or another created commissions or task forces to respond to its call. Presidents and governors met. State "standards" and "curricular frameworks" spewed forth lists that may have largely dodged many of the deep problems of purpose that so troubled Goodlad's researchers, but at least they gave a semblance of consistency of purpose, largely in the form of curricula. The New Basics, already familiar in every high school in the country, were re-embraced. The system was ordered to shape up, and given how difficult this was to be in practice, administrators' heads rolled with striking frequency. By the mid-1990s, the nation was awash in new tests. There was talk of longer school years. The rhetoric of toughness and rigor ruled.

America appeared to be taking its "risk" seriously—a substantial accomplishment for a small commission that had been, in fact, expected to start and end in obscurity. Gardner's tactics were brilliant. The Commission had effectively sounded a call for educational reform, with concise eloquence, in acceptably familiar ways that were not too hard. The country took heed.

Why did *A Nation at Risk* spawn such a reaction? While it is tricky to write contemporary history, several explanations seem worth taking seriously.

First, the stage for fundamental reconsideration of public education had been set. The triggers were the launching of Sputnik in 1957 and the reformist surge of the Eighty-Ninth Congress and its passage of a Civil Rights Act and the Elementary and Secondary Education Act (ESEA). The former authorized the influential study of equality of educational opportunity led by James Coleman, the first sweeping study ever of education in terms of the performance of the students rather than the provision of opportunities for those students. ESEA, and its cousins found in legislation related to the so-called War on Poverty, gave national muscle to the new attention to underschooled Americans and to the inequities and incompetencies of the system.[42]

Over the next twenty years, a series of critiques and studies accelerated the pounding absorbed by the existing system. The raft of angry testimonials such as Jonathan Kozol's *Death at an Early Age* and equally angry social science studies such as Samuel Bowles's and Herbert Gintis's *Schooling in Capitalist America*, all products of the late 1960s and early 1970s, fueled the erosion of public confidence in the schools that it knew.[43] The National Assessment of Educational Progress (NAEP), a federal "thermometer" of the work of American schoolchildren launched in 1970, built on the example of the equal educational opportunity study by providing data about the performance of the system rather than merely its provision, and the NAEP results sustained the slowly growing distrust on the part of an influential public of the efficacy of the system of schools Americans provided for their children. For example, tuition tax credits—the indirect but consequential support of families choosing private schools—was a small, but interesting part of the agenda of the first Nixon administration. National attention increasingly focused on evidence of students' performance, and a major study of the meaning of the "slipping" scores on the Scholastic Aptitude Test of the College Board was conducted during the late 1970s by a commission chaired by former United States Secretary of Labor Willard Wirtz.[44]

Soon the traditionally mawkish sentiments about public education so familiar during the 1950s began to fade, and with them the post–World War II knee-jerk practice of pouring resources into the expansion of a school system whose existing design was unquestioned. The time for a trumpet call to reform had arrived. By the early 1980s, if it had not existed, the National Commission on Excellence in Education would have had to be invented.

One can say the same about A Study of Schooling. The foundations that elected to support Goodlad were as much influenced by the accelerating challenge to the educational *status quo* as any other prominent American institution. The time for agonizing reappraisal was at hand, and the public appeared to be prepared.

And yet, one wonders. While political, foundation, and business leaders, and the lions of the press were disturbed, how deep was their distress and, equally, the distress of the public?

One hazards a guess that the distress was not very deep by looking in two places: the ideas formulated by the collective, albeit usually self-appointed, leadership for the public schools; and the scale of financial resources energetically allocated by local, state, and federal governments for fundamental reform.

In neither case was there vigorous response, in the 1980s or the 1990s, with the single and interesting exception of the ultimate fallout of the Education for All Handicapped Americans Act passed and signed during the Nixon administration. There is no question that the ordinary American school pays attention differently—that is, more responsively—to the children in its midst with special physical or emotional needs in the 1990s than had been the case in the 1970s; and the notable rise in school-level educational expenditures for children who have special needs since the mid-1980s can largely be attributed to that focused and stubbornly led initiative.

However, the exception proves the rule. Beyond this legislation, the *ancien régime* persisted. One can only conclude that the public and the polity, for whatever reasons, were largely satisfied with the existing shape and routines of the familiar place called school, even though they worried about them rhetorically. What David Tyack and Larry Cuban call the "grammar" of schooling—the detailed ways and means of providing deliberate education—remained intact.[45]

What John Goodlad was addressing was this very grammar—the ideas, practices, and routines of schooling and the attitudes that lay behind them. Goodlad might have had generous cheerleaders, but the establishment, beyond its rhetoric, was only weakly behind him. On the other hand, the National Commission essentially reinforced the existing apparatus, only urging it to do much, much better. It did not recommend an initiative comparable with its rhetoric—a 1980s version for education of the 1960s war on poverty. Far from it; and the Commission probably read the country's attitudes correctly.

America wanted a new dawn to an old day. If Americans were to reinvigorate their schools, they would do so by rallying the existing army rather than recruiting any sort of new one. Even the privatizing of education, which seemed an interesting prospect to many Reagan supporters, sparked no widespread positive response. That idea, and its varied kin, for the moment went nowhere.

A second reason for the impact of *A Nation at Risk*, and the state and district steps following upon its release, was its challenge *to*, but not challenge *of*, the existing educational hierarchy. In the jargon of the time, the powers-that-be were to gather the existing stakeholders and energize them to push for new levels of excellence.

There is a paradox here, as professional educators and the bureaucracies in which they had sat for generations were under extraordinary rhetorical assault. They were frequently and unflatteringly referred to as a "blob" in the way of reform, yet by the mid 1990s had recouped most of their lost power, and, with the stick of testing, had added to it. Reagan himself pledged to disband the Department of Education, even as it grew in scale and scope over his eight-year tenure. Business leaders called for new sorts of management requiring new sorts of administrators, but no prominent business schools started substantial, focused programs for school administrators.

From all the talk, one might have expected a fundamental shift in the way public education was governed and financed. This was not to be. The momentum of existing practice was believed to be too strong to provide new arrangements with much chance for success. The sanctity of the symbols of school—graduation at age eighteen, homecoming, taking American history in the eleventh grade, Friday night football, sorting wealthier kids from less wealthy kids and kids of color, and the like—were deeply embedded in the ways the American middle class shaped its experience. Alternatives to this, however ingenious and rational, had, not surprisingly, little political traction.

The National Commission apparently sensed this reality. The commissioners recommended "that citizens across the Nation hold educators and elected officials responsible for providing the leadership necessary to achieve these reforms."[46] The Commission did not recommend changing just who these officers might be or whether power among them might be redistributed, much less even mention these possibilities. The commissioners read the political tea leaves and left the existing power relationships much as they were. Not surprisingly, the existing power groups grasped eagerly onto the report. These groups had the authority to move quickly, and move they did. The report extended their power, rather than clipping it.

Finally, there was no national, respected, and tough-minded base to rally the ideas and aspirations of the diverse constituencies within education to the cause of the kinds of reform implicit in A Study of Schooling. Public education lacked an influential community of independent academics and policymakers that characterized higher visibility professions such as those in law and medicine.

On the contrary, the university-based concentrations of people concerned with the schools were largely gathered into underfunded, overregulated (by the states), and overenrolled colleges of education, which for many institutions were at once cash cows for their university writ large and objects of scorn by the better-funded members of sister faculties. Limited persuasive and probing research was forwarded within them, and what did emerge was usually highly circumscribed and all too often shrouded in an intramural jargon that insured its limited effect.

Not surprisingly, education professors closed in on themselves, and their national associations, again while numerous, remained relatively remote from influential counterparts in related areas, neither influencing nor drawing from them in consequential ways. The political and material costs of this insularity, while difficult precisely to measure, were substantial. Nationally, there were few highly respected academics drawing on deep and wide research on learning and schooling who could insist that the National Commission pay very respectful attention to what Goodlad was saying, even if this meant shaping the Commission's ultimate report in ways that did not largely reflect the limited and limiting conventional wisdom of the times. They could have spurred the Commission to dramatic and compelling recommendations as bold as its rhetoric of the risks the nation confronted.

The National Commission's report provoked great activity, sustained for over a decade. The national problem of inadequate schooling—and inadequate learning—is now widely acknowledged. Homilies about how nice teachers are and the wonders of this year's football team are now permanently joined by harsh demands for high standards and a better academic "product."

The conventional remedies suggested by the Commission will run their course, leading to a resurgence of frustration. The existing system, even if threatened, cannot carry the load of national needs without fundamental rethinking and consequent redesign. All the testing currently in vogue will narrow instruction to what it takes to get good grades on mass-produced, machine-graded tests and will tell us once again that poor kids score less well than rich kids. It will also suggest that, if conventionally taught, neither poor nor rich youngsters will demonstrate the deep and sustained understanding of important ideas that truly matters to a nation profoundly at risk. In time, inevitably, there will be agonizing reappraisals.

It is at this point that A Study of Schooling will gain the leverage it deserves. The frustration of the moment could lead to a reanalysis of what and how young people in our time learn, and that reanalysis could inform a surge of constructive interest in a new and more effective form of schooling than the one that Americans have used for almost one hundred years. That Goodlad's data were collected twenty years ago will make little difference because the patterns he chronicles and critiques are still sweepingly familiar. The breathtaking waste of time and treasure tolerated in many schools is no less with us today than when today's middle schoolers' mothers were twelfth graders. There is a sad, almost eerie relevance to the detailed specifics of Goodlad's critique.

A Nation at Risk was crucial for its moment. *A Place Called School* is crucial for the longer haul. Gardner dramatically attracted and focused the attention of the nation. Goodlad suggested what that nation must ponder as it shapes new and better schools.

If Americans stay the course of reform, if they are encouraged to do the hard work of thinking deeply about the issues of learning and schooling, history will mark well the special—and necessarily consecutive—contributions of both grand efforts of the early 1980s.

Goodlad needed Gardner. And as the times ripen, Gardner will need Goodlad.

Notes

[1] National Commission on Excellence in Education, *A Nation at Risk: The Imperative for Educational Reform* (Washington. D.C.: U.S. Government Printing Office, 1983), see introductory frontmatter.

[2] National Commission on Excellence in Education, *A Nation at Risk*, p. 1.

[3] John I. Goodlad, *A Place Called School* (New York: McGraw-Hill, 1984), p. iii.

[4] A set of internal documents produced by the Commission rests at the John Hey Library at Brown University. However, no detailed record of the internal discussion related directly to Goodlad's contribution appears there.

[5] Goodlad, *A Place Called School*, p. 27.

[6] Goodlad, *A Place Called School*, p. 28.

[7] Goodlad, *A Place Called School*, p. 264.

[8] Goodlad, *A Place Called School*, p. 48.

[9] Goodlad, *A Place Called School*, p. 50.

[10] Goodlad, *A Place Called School*, p. 280, parentheses in the original.

[11] Charles E. Silberman, *Crisis in the Classroom: The Remaking of American Education* (New York: Random House, 1970).

[12] Goodlad, *A Place Called School*, p. 80.

[13] United States President's Science Advisory Committee Panel on Youth, *Youth: Transition to Adulthood* (Chicago: University of Chicago Press, 1974), Part IV especially.

[14] Goodlad, *A Place Called School*, pp. 165, 166.

[15] Personal recollection of this essay's author.

[16] Goodlad, *A Place Called School*, p. 241.

[17] Goodlad, *A Place Called School*, p. 191.

[18] Goodlad, *A Place Called School*, p. 192.

[19] Goodlad, *A Place Called School*, p. 230.

[20] Goodlad, *A Place Called School*, p. 229.

[21] Goodlad, *A Place Called School*, p. 231.

[22] Mihaly Csikszentmihalyi and Reed Larson, *Being Adolescent: Conflict and Growth in the Teenage Years* (New York: Basic Books, 1984), p. 257.

[23] Goodlad, *A Place Called School*, p. 112.

[24] Goodlad, *A Place Called School*, p. 113.

[25] Goodlad, *A Place Called School*, p. 155.

[26] Goodlad, *A Place Called School*, p. 156.

[27] Goodlad, *A Place Called School*, pp. 164, 297.

[28] See, for example, a potpourri of studies around themes raised in Goodlad's book, *A Place Called School*; Seymour B. Sarason, *The Culture of the School and the Problem of Change* (Boston: Allyn and Bacon, 1971, revised in 1997 by Teachers College Press); Mary Haywood Metz, *Classrooms and Corridors: The Crisis of Authority in Desegregated Secondary Schools* (Berkeley: University of California Press, 1978); Sara Lawrence Lightfoot, *The Good High School: Portraits of Character and Culture* (New York: Basic Books, 1983); Howard Gardner, *Frames of Mind: The Theory of Multiple Intelligences* (New York: Basic Books, 1983); Arthur G. Powell, Eleanor Farrar, and David K. Cohen, *The Shopping Mall High School: Winners and Losers in the Educational Marketplace* (Boston: Houghton Mifflin, 1986); Tracy Kidder, *Among Schoolchildren* (Boston: Houghton Mifflin, 1989); Milbrey McLaughlin, Joan E. Talbert, and Nina Bascia, eds., *The Contexts of Teaching in Secondary Schools: Teachers' Realities* (New York: Teachers College Press, 1990); Paul T. Hill, Gail E. Foster, Tamar Gendler, *High Schools with Character* (Santa Monica, Calif.: RAND Corporation, 1990); David Perkins, *Smart Schools: From Training Memories to Educating Minds* (New York: Free Press, 1992); Mike Rose, *Possible Lives: The Promise of Public Education in America* (Boston: Houghton Mifflin, 1995); Deborah Meier, *The Power of Their Ideas: Lessons for America from a Small School in Harlem* (Boston: Beacon Press, 1995); Linda Darling-Hammond, *The Right to Learn: A Blueprint for Creating Schools That Work* (San Francisco: Jossey-Bass, 1997). The subtitles alone tell much of the publishers' judgments about what the serious reading public might choose to read about schooling.

[29] Goodlad, *A Place Called School*, pp. 81, 91.

[30] Goodlad, *A Place Called School*, p. 358.

[31] *A Nation at Risk*, pp. 5, 6.

[32] Terrel H. Bell, *The Thirteenth Man: A Reagan Cabinet Memoir* (New York: Free Press, 1988).

[33] *A Nation at Risk*, p. 10.

[34] *A Nation at Risk*, pp. 11, 12.

[35] *A Nation at Risk*, p. 14.

[36] *A Nation at Risk*, pp. 18–23.

[37] *A Nation at Risk*, p. 24.

[38] *A Nation at Risk*, p. 27.

[39] *A Nation at Risk*, p. 29.

[40] *A Nation at Risk*, pp. 30–31.

[41] *A Nation at Risk*, pp. 32–33.

[42] James S. Coleman et al., *Equality of Educational Opportunity* (two volumes) (Washington, D.C.: U.S. Government Printing Office, 1966). The most careful contemporary analysis of this study is Frederick Mosteller and Daniel Patrick Moynihan, eds., *On Equality of Educational Opportunity* (New York:. Random House, 1972).

[43] Jonathan Kozol, *Death at an Early Age* (Boston: Houghton Mifflin, 1967). Samuel Bowles and Herbert Gintis, *Schooling in Capitalist America: Educational Reform and the Contradictions of Economic Life* (New York: Basic Books, 1976).

[44] College Entrance Examination Board, Advisory Panel on the Scholastic Aptitude Test Score Decline, *On Further Examination: A Report of the Advisory Panel on the Scholastic Aptitude Test Score Decline* (New York: College Entrance Examination Board, 1977).

[45] David Tyack and Larry Cuban, *Tinkering Toward Utopia: A Century of Public School Reform* (Cambridge: Harvard University Press, 1995), chapter 4.

[46] *A Nation at Risk*, p. 32.

Preface

In his Foreword to this 20th-anniversary edition of *A Place Called School*, Theodore Sizer elegantly and succinctly summarizes the essence of what he describes as two grand educational efforts of the early 1980s. One was the work of the National Commission on Excellence in Education, reported in *A Nation at Risk*, responding to the "widespread public perception that something is seriously remiss in our educational system." The other was what he perceives to have been one of "the largest and most sophisticated studies of American schooling ever undertaken," the study reported in what follows here.

One of the major differences he sees between the two is that the former focused on the effects of weak schooling, the latter on causes. Sizer credits the commission with creating a thunderclap, artfully designed to arouse public attention to its recommendations, largely calling for the school we had—and still have—to do a better job. By contrast, he wrote, *A Place Called School* addressed the "grammar" of schooling—the ideas, practices, and routines and the attitudes lying behind them—and proposed fundamental shifts. But, he neatly notes, "America wanted a new dawn to an old day." Now, twenty years later, awash in a reform era of testing and individual and institutional accountability, is the nation still waiting?

Ted Sizer did not intentionally write the Foreword to this reissue of *A Place Called School*. Entitled "Back to *A Place Called School*," it first appeared in *The Beat of a Different Drummer* (1999), a series of essays on educational renewal edited by Kenneth A. Sirotnik and Roger Soder. Not a word has been changed, nor from the first edition of the volume reporting the study he discusses.

Roger Soder's reminder a year ago that *A Place Called School* was still in print but should be brought once more to public attention sent me to a rereading of Ted's essay. At its end, he looks to a time when the conventional remedies of the current school reform era run their course and are followed by "agonizing reappraisals." The quoted paragraph that follows ended my doubts about a reissue, confirmed my decision to seek permission to use Ted's piece—unchanged—and convinced me to write an Afterword that would draw from and expand on the themes crafted in the Foreword:

> It is at this point that A Study of Schooling will gain the leverage it deserves. The frustration of the moment could lead to a reanalysis of

what and how young people in our time learn, and that reanalysis could inform a surge of constructive interest in a new and more effective form of schooling than the one that Americans have used for almost one hundred years. That Goodlad's data were collected twenty years ago will make little difference because the patterns he chronicles and critiques are still sweepingly familiar. The breathtaking waste of time and treasure tolerated in many schools is no less with us today than when today's middle schoolers' mothers were twelfth-graders. There is a sad, almost eerie relevance to the detailed specifics of Goodlad's critique.

The study and the writing of *A Place Called School*, extending from the late 1970s into the early 1980s, proved to be a deep, rewarding, exhausting series of learning experiences. The study drew thousands of buckets of data from a purposively representative sample in the stream of schooling in the United States of America. The scope of these data becomes clear in the extensive list of technical reports and other source materials drawn upon in the writing, provided in Appendix A of the first edition. Many people listed in the personnel roster, Appendix B, were part-time, most during the final phase of data collecting. Both appendixes, along with the Preface and much of the other front matter of that edition, have been removed from this one in order to create room for the Foreword and Afterword. The dedication to the 27,000 individuals—parents, students, teachers, and school administrators who provided the data—remains.

Once again, I thank the fourteen foundations and agencies that funded the initiative and those individuals whose roles warranted special recognition in the copy of the book sent to them years ago, which, I hope, still serves as a memento of what we collectively accomplished. Sadly, many of these individuals, including four of the six who graced the membership of our outstanding external advisory committee, are no longer with us.

My guess is that most authors are as weary of their product as I was when I finished reading the page proofs—the last chance to make minor changes. I had begun the manuscript when some of the data were still coming in and some of the technical reports not yet completed. For many months, time for writing had to be added to that taken up by an array of other responsibilities for which, thankfully, I had the help of able colleagues.

In retrospect, I think that my decision to allocate all rights to that edition—copyright, royalties, and the rest—to the Institute for Development of Educational Activities (|I|D|E|A|) was an act more of self-preservation than of generosity. I am pleased, however, that the royalties did help to keep |I|D|E|A| alive during the difficult period of its separation from the Kettering Foundation and its establishment as a nonprofit educational improvement agency. In an interesting way, this assignment of rights separated me somewhat from the book and, I think, increased my ability to look at it more objectively, as a piece of the fabric of schooling during the years of considerable educational turbulence that followed. It even helped me shrug off the question of well-meaning interrogators who asked how I felt about the probability that *A Place Called School* would overshadow anything I had done before or would do afterward. Now, writing the Afterword with which this reissue ends provides an opportunity to look hard at the two decades that have transpired since 1984.

The cover of this 20th-anniversary edition notes that I am the author also of a book entitled *Romances with Schools*. The two, although very different in their approaches to schooling, modes of inquiry, narrative style, and more, are in many ways complementary companion pieces. As stated above, *A Place Called School* draws and analyzes an enormous amount of data from the nation's stream of schooling. It is a thick description of schools at a point in time. *Romances with Schools* recounts a journey—a personal educational odyssey—extending over seven and a half decades and an ocean of schooling that includes Canada and visits abroad, as well as the United States. I endeavor to be the camera recording the scenes while simultaneously being in the pictures.

Romances with Schools cozies up to a few schools—in higher as well as elementary and secondary education—and then backs off into their changing context during successive eras of a large slice of the twentieth century. Concluding chapters trace the public disaffection with the schooling enterprise that began well before *A Nation at Risk* was published and note that, should this cancer spread to encompass the local school, still high in public affection, this nation will be in very deep trouble.

After finishing *Romances with Schools* and rereading *A Place Called School*, particularly the concluding two chapters, I decided that the Afterword to the latter should concentrate again on the "grammar" of schooling, which is, as Ted Sizer points out, the central focus of the whole. I place this focus within a few dominant contextual themes and hope that the serious reader wanting to explore these further will turn to *Romances with Schools: A Life of Education*.

ACKNOWLEDGMENTS

Thanks, Roger, for jump-starting this anniversary edition of *A Place Called School*. My thanks and appreciation for bringing it off go to Ted Sizer for enthusiastically agreeing to my using his "Back to *A Place Called School*" as its Foreword; Peter Lang Publishing, Inc., for granting permission to reproduce Ted's essay; the good people at McGraw-Hill Companies, particularly Philip

Ruppel, Barbara Gilson, and Andrew Littell, for their support and dedication to the necessary work; and (one more time) Paula McMannon for keeping me afloat throughout.

As stated above, my thanks to those many people and agencies that contributed to the study appear in the first pages of the initial edition. To those readers who remember how I ended that Acknowledgments section and still ask me if Lynn and I have yet responded to a sybaritic drummer and enjoyed that promised but chimeric summer, absent my writing and filled with self-indulgent pleasures, the answer is NO. And, with respect to its realization in the future, the answer is, as Eliza of *My Fair Lady* would say, "not bloody likely."

John I. Goodlad
January 2004

A Place
Called School

Chapter 1

Can We Have Effective Schools?

The problems confronting American schools are substantial; the resources available to them are in most instances severely limited; the stakes are high, and it is by no means preordained that all will go well for many of them in the end.

Preface to issue on
America's Schools: Public and Private
Daedalus (Summer 1981), p. v.

American schools are in trouble. In fact, the problems of schooling are of such crippling proportions that many schools may not survive. It is possible that our entire public education system is nearing collapse. We will continue to have schools, no doubt, but the basis of their support and their relationships to families, communities, and states could be quite different from what we have known.

To survive, an institution requires from its clients substantial faith in its usefulness and a measure of satisfaction with its performance. For our schools, this is a complex matter. The primary clients of American public schools—parents and their school-age children—have become a minority group. Declining birth rates and increased aging of our population during the 1970s increased the proportion of citizens not directly involved with the schools. And there appears to be a rather direct relationship between these changed demographics and the growing difficulty of securing tax

1

dollars for schools. Tax levies in several parts of the country are failing even as these words are being written. More than one district is in the process of closing down its schools. Our public system of schooling requires for its survival, to say nothing of its good health, the support of many not currently using it, and that support is in doubt.

To the extent that the attainment of a democratic society depends on the existence of schools equally accessible to everyone, we are all their clients. It is not easy, however, to convince a majority of our citizens that this relationship exists and that schools require their support because of it. It is especially difficult to convince them if they perceive the schools to be deficient in regard to their traditional functions. Unfortunately, the ability of schools to do their traditional jobs of assuring literacy and eradicating ignorance is at the center of current criticism, which is intense.

A basic premise underlying what follows is that this nation has not outgrown its need for schools. If schools should suddenly cease to exist, we would find it necessary to reinvent them. Another premise is that the schools we need now are not necessarily the schools we have known. And a third premise is that the current wave of criticism lacks the diagnosis required for the reconstruction of schooling. This criticism is in part psychologically motivated—a product of a general lack of faith in ourselves and our institutions—and is not adequately focused.

What we need, then, is a better understanding of our public schools and the specific problems that beset them. Only with this understanding can we begin to address the problems with some assurance of creating better schools. As a nation, we have a history of capitalizing on this kind of focused diagnosis and the constructive criticism emerging from it. A few initial successes would renew our sense of confidence in both ourselves and our schools. This book seeks to assist the reader in acquiring this understanding of some representative schools, an awareness of the problems they have, and a sense of priorities for school reform.

It is not the fact of recent criticism of schools that leads one to contemplate seriously the demise of the educational system. Periodically, it is more fashionable to kick the schools than to praise them, and previous attacks have produced a litany of criticism. As recently as the early 1950s, a back-to-basics movement was fueled by books with such doleful and fearsome titles as *Why Johnny Can't Read*, *Crisis in Education*, and *Educational Wastelands*. No, it is not the fact of recent criticism, but the nature and depth of the concern it reflects that raises troubling uncertainties about the future of public schooling. The attacks of the 1950s tended to be not so much against the system of schooling as on the competence of those who staff schools—and especially on the administrators and those who train teachers. When Charles Silberman, as recently as 1970, wrote about "mindlessness" in the schools, he had in mind those who administer and teach. [1]

During the 1970s, however, public criticism included the institution, not just those who run it. Schools shared in our loss of faith—in government, the judicial system, the professions, and even ourselves. Uncertainty swiftly arose about the inherent *power* of schools and, indeed, education. Robert M. Hutchins sensed the climate of the times before it became widely apparent. Pondering the school's sudden fall from grace, he wondered what had happened to the institution that so recently had been "the foundation of our freedom, the guarantee of our future, the cause of our prosperity and power, and bastion of our security, the bright and shining beacon . . . the source of our enlightenment, the public school."[2]

Hutchins wrote tongue-in-cheek and thus illuminated the unreality of our past expectations. He was writing just a few years after the 88th Congress appeared to be making real for all what had previously been at best a compelling dream for most.

This "Education Congress" passed legislation supporting vocational and technical education, teaching handicapped children, preventing juvenile delinquency, medical education, college and community libraries, graduate schools, technical institutes, public community colleges, student loans, student counseling, schools in federally impacted areas, educational media, educational research, humanpower development, and instruction in science, mathematics, and foreign languages. Through the Equal Educational Opportunities Program of the Civil Rights Act of 1964, the 88th Congress provided special assistance to public school districts seeking to effect desegregation and instructed the commissioner of education to report on the lack of availability of equal educational opportunities for individuals by reason of race, color, religion, or national origin. And through the Economic Opportunity Act of 1964, this Congress also provided assistance to students from low-income families in their pursuit of higher education, opportunities for persons over the age of 18 to secure basic programs in reading and writing, and encouragement to school districts to provide early learning opportunities for disadvantaged children to offset the assumed disabling effects of their restrictive environment.

The 89th Congress extended most of these commitments in the astonishing and unprecedented Elementary and Secondary Education Act of 1965. Title I was designed to assist school districts with their momentous tasks of helping children from low-income families in school and giving them there the kind of education thought to be needed. Title II provided for the purchase of books—in both public and private nonprofit elementary and secondary schools. Titles III and IV provided funds for linking the educational resources of communities and for comprehensive programs of research, development, and dissemination of knowledge through the collaborative efforts of universities, public schools, private nonprofit education agencies, and state departments of education. Title V put money directly into state departments of education for strengthening their increasingly compelling leadership responsibilities. To effect all of this, the budget of the Office of Education was increased by $1,255,000,000 for fiscal 1966.

The 88th and 89th Congresses enacted legislation to support education virtually from cradle to grave. But that was not all. Prodded by President Lyndon B. Johnson, Congress sought to use the schools to address pressing social problems of poverty, unemployment, urban decay, crime, violence, and racial discrimination.

The seeds of disillusionment had now been sown. Education no doubt contributes to the resolution of such problems in the long run but provides little demonstrable evidence of success over the short haul. The effects of education in general cannot be determined within the time span of a congressman's term of office. It is a grave error to look for results as one might look for an early groundbreaking following the allocation of funds to a building or a bridge. But many people did look for quick, visible results nonetheless, and expected that the benefits would be felt before the decade of the 1960s came to an end. And why not? The power is in education and schooling; large outlays of money would unleash it.

Imagine the dismay, then, when early reports did not confirm this assumption. The much-publicized results of Coleman's analysis of schools (1966) created uneasiness.[3] Differences between schools in regard to the resources allocated to them account for only a small part of the inequalities in school test scores, he concluded. What children bring from their homes and encounter there among children from other homes, not teachers and their practices, is what contributes most to their academic attainments. Not good instructional materials, equipment, curricula, and pedagogy in school, but whether or not there are well-educated, reasonably affluent parents at home accounts most for the margins of difference in students' achievement. What a dismal hypothesis for educators and all those who have expected so much from our schools! Might there be cracks in the pillars of schooling?

Many persons in the mid-1960s, as in some earlier periods, had a vision of a self-renewing society in which education, supported by government, plays a major role. "In the ever-renewing society what matters is a system or framework within which continuous innovation, renewal, and rebirth can occur."[4] This belief continues to be sustained by a segment of our society. But the euphoria surrounding the governmental role and, in particular, the power of schools to effect or contribute significantly to renewal gradually began to be displaced by doubt, growing stronger in the 1970s. Consequently, the conclusions of Christopher Jencks (1973) regarding the importance of schools were received by many people as facts, not hypotheses.[5]

Jencks went so far as to conclude that school reform could do little to reduce the extent of cognitive inequality among students. And he saw differences in schools as irrelevant in explaining differences in attainment among individuals. These are explained, rather, by socioeconomic status and IQ. Variations in performance, then, are caused by forces outside of school, not inside schools.[6] What the child brings into the classroom largely determines his or her performance there. The Coleman hypothesis was confirmed, apparently.

I shall not enter here into the arguments, pro and con, regarding the Coleman and Jencks theses. The educational and sociological literature is replete with debate on them, particularly Coleman's. Coleman's data have been reworked many times. It should be noted, however, that these analyses have generally ignored achievement differences *within schools* or linked these differences with classroom processes. It is likely that good teaching makes differences, but these can easily get washed out in analyses that average the data *across* schools. Also, even if Coleman was correct in his interpretation, some critics argue, he surveyed only what is and not what *could be*. Suppose we were to compare run-of-the-mill schools with schools in which everything we know about desirable conditions and practices had been implemented. Would Coleman's conclusion still apply? If not, hope lies in the vigorous reconstruction of schools.

The quarrel with Jencks has been less with his findings than with his interpretations. Jencks's focus was on factors affecting inequality among individuals in regard to ultimate financial returns. He concluded that the equalization of expenditures for schools across school districts does little to reduce the inequality in such outcomes. This comes as no great surprise. But he appears to be straying well beyond his data in drawing his pessimistic conclusions about the potential impact of school reform on cognitive development.

Fortunately, most educational researchers and reformers accepted the Coleman and Jencks conclusions only as hypotheses and were not traumatized into abandoning the search for more insight into schools and better ways of conducting them. Indeed, the work of these two men provided a fresh impetus for this search. On the other hand, many less careful readers took the conclusions of Coleman and Jencks to mean that schools have little or no effect on student learning. Some even went so far as to suggest that children who go to school are no better off in this regard than children who do not. And it seems clear that these widely publicized conclusions and interpretations have contributed significantly to a growing spirit of gloom and doom regarding our schools. Once findings in any field have been heralded as fact in newspaper headlines, it is virtually impossible to reverse the public view that they are indeed fact, and in this case the supposed scientific findings fit nicely into a growing belief about the ineffectiveness of schools. Beginning in the second half of the 1960s, this belief grew to major proportions in the 1970s.

There is little doubt in my mind that this mood of disillusionment came to affect the attitudes of students toward their studies, particularly among middle-class adolescents. With the incomes of their parents continuing to expand and with jobs still plentiful for those in their socioeconomic class, the future appeared sufficiently secure with or without a college education. With their peer-group culture, fed by television attuned to the buying power of the young, extolling the here and now, the long-term gains of education were less than compelling. And if long-term gains from schooling were questionable anyway, why exert one's self at school? Besides, there always was some college that would take you. Teachers of the time were well aware of these less-than-subtle changes in student attitudes.

The datum that appeared most to give substance to the mood of disenchantment with schooling was a decline in some standardized achievement test scores, particularly the SAT taken by many high school juniors and seniors seeking admission to the better colleges and universities. Analysts and critics looked to conventional, simple explanations, much as those who write daily analyses of the stock market look for simple explanations to account for zigs and zags. The reasons given for falling test scores ranged from "progressive" teaching practices of the 1960s, to incompetent administrators, to poorly prepared teachers, and to those in teachers' colleges who prepare teachers. A half century ago, the Commission on the Relation of School and College, looking across the nation, wrote of secondary schools and those who run them as follows:

> They had failed to convey a sincere appreciation of the American heritage; they did not prepare students to the limits of their abilities; they neither guided nor motivated their pupils effectively; and their curricula were a hodgepodge of lifeless materials unrelated to the real concerns of young people. [7]

As the preceding examples suggest, the indictments of the 1970s usually were less diagnostic and more simplistic. They seldom pointed to specific deficiencies, and they tended to shift from villain to villain. At the same time, they often generalized vaguely about the overall decay of the school system.

Not surprisingly, the reforms proposed were piecemeal. Indeed, it is fair to say that few reforms were proposed. Rather, pressures were exerted on teachers and, ultimately, students to do better, particularly in the "basic subjects." States set up procedures for holding teachers accountable for raising reading and mathematics scores from year to year. Some required students to pass proficiency tests in order to graduate from high school, sometimes even to pass from grade to grade.

The apparent assumption that teachers and students only had to concentrate on the 3 Rs and try harder in order for all to be well is a familiar one. But it ignored an array of conditions surrounding the conduct of schooling which, if not entirely new, were far more intense and widespread than was recognized.

First, the two traditionally stable institutions, the household and the church, which had done much of the educating for centuries, were themselves in seriously weakened condition by the 1970s. Strained in performing their own functions, they could only hope that the school would stand strong in performing its function—and perhaps pick up some of what they found increasingly difficult to do. A minority of families now attended church together. Sunday school had lost much of its appeal to the young. By the end of the decade, a quarter of the mothers with children under the age of seven were working; approximately 55% of all mothers of school-age children held a job. For large numbers of children and youths, no parent was there to greet them at the end of the school day. Almost 45% of children born today can expect to be living with only one parent before they reach 18 years of age. It is difficult to estimate the impact of these developments on our young people and the increased burden they place on our schools.

Second, and closely related, the almost unquestioned supportive relationship between home and school that characterized earlier periods deteriorated substantially. The child spanked in school one hundred or even fifty years ago often was spanked again at home. The child spanked in school in 1975 frequently became the pivotal figure in a suit against the school brought by his parents. Principals and teachers could no longer assume that they stood *in loco parentis*. Obviously, the collaborative strength of school and home working together toward common goals of child rearing and educating was weakened. Not so obviously, the willingness of school personnel to engage in activities that took their students out of the routines of seat-based instruction also was reduced. Even a slight accident on a field trip could trigger a lawsuit.

Third, the economics of providing for such essentials as food, clothing, and shelter joined other factors in changing the nature of communities. Small local markets, specialized shops, and gasoline stations where once one met and chatted with neighbors were replaced by supermarkets where one ignored or stared blankly at strangers from other communities. The decline in the ratio of single family homes to apartments and, later, condominiums changed the whole nature of neighborhoods. We continued to use the words "community" and "neighborhood," but the fit between the words and reality became increasingly loose and obscure. Children and youths often knew none or only a few of the families of their classmates. Much of the former power of "being known" by families who knew one's own family was lost to the child-rearing process. When I was growing up, my parents already knew before I got home about my transgressions on the way home from school. What are the implications of this change for the moral education of the young? What additional problems are thrust upon the school by all these changes in communities and decline in our sense of community?

Fourth, a political coalition that had fought extremely successfully for financial and moral support of public education was largely in disarray by the 1970s. The decline in little more than a decade was precipitous. Stephen Bailey's description of who attended the 1955 White House Conference on Education suggests the scope of this coalition of legislators, school board members, parent groups, school administrators, teachers, business leaders, and others:

> One third of the delegates were educators and two thirds were lay citizens. Each state and territory was allowed to send delegates in proportion to population, with an assured minimum of ten delegates. Two hundred eighty-three national organizations interested in education were also invited to send representatives. President Eisenhower was honorary chairman of the steering committee. The more than thirty working members of the steering committee represented an impressive cross-section of American civic, economic, news media, cultural, and political leadership. Although many of the policy dividends of this unprecedented, broad-gauged national conference took a decade or more to be realized, the importance of the 1955 White House Conference on Education as a symbol of public concern about, and support for, education is without parallel in our nation's history.[8]

As Bailey points out, many of the material goals of this conference took ten years or more to be realized. Then, no doubt, the contrast between its idealistic expectations and the short-term consequences of federal commitments to schooling contributed significantly to the coalition's unravelling. At any rate, we frequently saw school boards and their superintendents working at cross-purposes during the 1970s. We rarely found legislators, parents, educators, and business leaders working in concert toward common goals. It no longer was stylish to work for the schools. The consequences for the schools' welfare now and, unless a new coalition can be built, in the future are inestimable.

Fifth, educators themselves became badly divided. The manner in which collective bargaining evolved set administrators against teachers. Superintendents' efforts to build an undivided administrative team frequently separated principals from their teachers. Yet a bond of trust and mutual support between the principal and teachers of a school appears to be basic to school improvement. Teachers of English, mathematics, science, social studies, and the like at the secondary level and various specialists at all levels regard themselves as teachers of subjects of their specializations first and as educators second. They belong to professional organizations that reinforce these affiliations rather than concern for the entire educative process. There is an enormous schism, often verging on distrust, between those who run the schools and those in universities who study the schools. Education is a badly segmented profession. Undoubtedly, this makes it exceedingly difficult for the necessarily collaborative effort of school improvement to occur.

Sixth, the very success of our society in moving impressively toward universal elementary and secondary schooling has vastly complicated the tasks of the high school. At the turn of this century, it shared with private schools in the education of a small, elite student population preparing, for the most part, for higher education. Today, it educates an extraordinarily diverse student body from families varying widely in their expectations for education. Many of the boys and girls graduating from elementary schools and moving up into junior and senior high schools are not clients in any sense of the word. They go to school until the age of 16 or more because society requires it—and, of course, their friends are there. Many high school teachers simply were not prepared for what they encountered in their students.

Seventh, closely related, today's young people are securing their education, to use the word loosely, from sources other than home, church, and school. Television is such a source, one of great but still little-understood power. The total array of educating forces and their impact are as yet little studied and little understood. Much of what is learned by our children comes to them with no mediation, interpretation, or even discussion by the traditional configuration of educating agencies. There has been little rethinking of the school's role in the new configuration.

To summarize, the very zenith in expectations for schools was reached just as the conditions surrounding them, such as those described, were becoming least propitious and most demanding. The expectations, as Diane Ravitch stated them, were that more education for more people would:

- Reduce inequality among individuals and groups by eliminating illiteracy and cultural deprivation.

- Improve the economy and economic opportunity by raising the nation's supply of intelligence and skill.
- Spread capacity for personal fulfillment by developing talents, skills, and creative energies.
- Prove to be an uplifting influence in the nation's cultural life by broadly diffusing the fruits of liberal education.
- Reduce alienation and mistrust while building a new sense of community among people of similar education and similar values.
- Reduce prejudice and misunderstanding by fostering contact among diverse groups.
- Improve the quality of civic and political life.[9]

By the beginning of the 1980s, many people doubted the school's capacity to contribute to these democratic ideals. Some had little interest in schools' "fostering contact among diverse groups," for example. Others were opposed to schools' being used for such a function. The argument that parents should choose their children's school appealed to increasingly large numbers of people for a variety of reasons. Proponents of the so-called voucher plan sought support for the concept of putting most of the money required to operate public schools directly into the hands of parents, who would then select among alternative schools, which would be in many ways more private than public. In the 1981 Gallup Poll on public schools, 49% of those sampled said that the increasing number of nonpublic schools is a good thing; 30% said that it is a bad thing. Even when only public school parents were surveyed, 44% said the increase is a good thing, as compared with 36% who said it is a bad thing.[10]

What indeed had happened in so short a time to "the foundation of our freedom . . . the source of our enlightenment, the public school"? And what will happen to it in the future?

HOW BAD—OR GOOD—ARE OUR SCHOOLS?

Put on one pair of glasses and our schools appear to be the worst of places. Put on another and they appear to be the best. The rosy picture emerges when we associate schooling with the rapid evolution of this country to a position of global eminence. In that rise the role of elementary and secondary education often has been regarded as causal, not just an accompaniment to our abundance of resources and use of them in building economic power. And faith in schooling has gone hand in hand with belief in unlimited opportunity for anyone with the will to seek it.

Two assumptions in particular about the virtues of the American public education system were taken for granted until recently. First, the primary schools socialized immigrants of diverse backgrounds into the norms, values, and beliefs of a democratic society. Second, the role of the schools—in which they were considered to be highly successful—was to prepare all the young to carry out a responsible adult social, working life. Schools were to transmit much of the dominant culture and imbue commitment to that culture. Attendance of the young at school assured the necessary learnings and commitments and became in itself "a good."

A negative view of schooling strengthened during recent decades with growing awareness of barriers to individual attainment growing out of racial and economic backgrounds. The conduct of schooling frequently was seen as part of, rather than ameliorative of, discrimination and inequality. Critics argued that the public educational system has served to socialize large numbers of people into uncritical acceptance of the status quo. The expansion of schooling upwards, downwards, and sideways has provided fresh opportunities to move up the occupational ladder. But, say the critics, every major increase in educational opportunity has favored initially those already favored by family circumstances. Lower status groups are included in the expansion of schooling in proportion to their number in the population only after upper and middle status groups have been accommodated.[11] Schools have functioned, goes the argument of those who would repaint the rosy picture of schooling, to lock young people into the relative social and economic status of their birth.[12]

There is, then, substantial disagreement over the merits of schooling as it has functioned even before one turns to the ongoing debate over the efficiency and effectiveness of the system in teaching the young. The long-standing belief that universal schooling is an unmitigated blessing has suffered considerable erosion. Nonetheless, most parents still regard more schooling, whether general or vocational, as good and desirable. Schools provide access to knowledge not readily attainable elsewhere, especially in fields such as mathematics and the natural sciences.[13] The differences in knowledge possessed by those with more schooling become particularly apparent among college graduates.[14] There is evidence to suggest, also, that increased educational attainment brings with it increased individual belief in many of the values we espouse for our society—civil liberties, freedom of information, freedom from legal restraints, the value of privacy, etc. But the relationship appears to diminish with age.[15] Perhaps there are not in adult society institutions comparable to schools that continue to reinforce belief in these idealistic values in the face of conflicting values and practices in the practical arenas of public affairs.

Admiration of our educational system coming from abroad focuses most on two elements which are not always a source of domestic pride and satisfaction. The first is what frequently is referred to as the American experiment in mass or universal schooling. The second is the innovation that has characterized this expansion, well exemplified by the development of junior high schools and community colleges to meet special needs.

The recent record in increasing the proportion of youths graduating from high schools is particularly impressive. In 1950, only about half of all white and a quarter of all black students graduated from secondary schools. In 1979, the figures were 85% for whites and 75% for blacks.[16] Also, more young adults have been completing their high school education. In 1970, 75% of adults aged 25 to 29 had finished secondary education. By 1979, this figure had climbed to 86%.[17]

It is ironic that while more people were coming to participate in the educational system, criticism of it was on the rise. Still, expansion did bring with it some problems. Teachers frequently have perceived themselves as confronting difficult problems of teaching less motivated students: "some of our classrooms are loaded with youths who have no wish to be there, whose aim is not to learn but to escape from learning."[18] During the 1950s and 1960s, the school system had a difficult time expanding rapidly enough to take care of increased enrollments. At one time during the late 1950s, the rate of growth of the city of Los Angeles was so rapid that the equivalent of a new school to house 500 elementary school students was required each Monday morning. During this period of expanding enrollments, 70% of the elementary schools in this country had no libraries; many schools had an average of one-half book per child. It is easy to forget the strains placed upon our schools as we tried to provide more schooling for increasingly large numbers of boys and girls.

Many of these children lacked the kind of home support frequently characterizing the educational effort when much smaller percentages attended and completed high school. The federal government attempted to pick up some of the slack. Approximately $5 of every $6.50 added to the budget of the Office of Education for fiscal 1966 went to assist school districts with their tasks of keeping children from low-income families in school and providing education for them there. The lion's share of federal support has been in this area for each successive year. Unfortunately, the benefits that began to show a decade or more after this upsurge in federal support appeared after many people had become convinced that much of it was misspent, especially the funds directed to projects regarded as innovative. Not unexpectedly, the gains were greatest when the commitments were relatively long-term and stable, as with Head Start.[19]

We should have anticipated that, given the circumstances surrounding schooling, achievement test scores would begin to fall off before educators learned to cope with the new problems. The shortage of teachers from the mid-1950s into the early 1960s was acute. School districts played fast and loose with standards in seeking to staff classrooms. Many districts were on double shift; classrooms were crowded. Reformers were promoting new curricula and new ways of grouping students, organizing classrooms, and teaching. Curricular options were provided to take care of students with uncommon backgrounds and interests. As never before, schools were thrust into the public arena as agents of social change.

Instead of placing in perspective the not-surprising decline in achievement test scores, critics heralded them as one more sign of a collapsing school system. The new criticisms of the schools, rising quickly in the 1970s, fit rather comfortably with growing concern over changing economic conditions and busing to desegregate schools. Doubts about the effectiveness of schools were fueled by widely publicized findings and opinions such as those of Coleman and Jencks referred to earlier.

Actually, many of the facts regarding students' achievement were obscured by inflamed rhetoric regarding declined school effectiveness. In a survey of reading abilities first conducted in 1970-71 and repeated in 1974-75 and again in 1979-80, the National Assessment of Educational Progress found that the reading skills of 9-year-olds improved steadily over the decade, increasing by 3.9 percentage points between 1971 and 1980. The average performance of 9-year-old black students rose by 9.9%. Reading skills of 13- and 17-year-olds remained stable during the same period.[20] But a combination of student marks in secondary school increasing each year and average scores on the well-known Scholastic Aptitude Test simultaneously declining fueled a furor. And the SAT scores did decline, from averages of 466 on the verbal and 492 on the mathematics component in 1966-67 to 434 and 472, respectively, in 1974-75.[21] Critics blamed teachers for easing up on standards and "socially promoting" students with severe deficiencies in achievement.

Analyses of what contributed to the SAT-score decline are inconclusive. The argument that increased numbers of minority students began taking the test and contributed to the drop in average score appears not to be supported by the evidence.[22] A somewhat stronger argument is that more and more students started using their junior year averages in seeking admission to college, choosing to forego the opportunity of repeating the tests as seniors. After examining the data used to support these and other arguments, Edson concluded, "it cannot be conclusively shown that changes in the composition of the test-taking population have caused the decline in SAT scores. On the other hand, it would be incorrect to rule out the possibility that such changes may contribute to the score decline."[23]

The explanations commanding the most attention at the beginning of the 1980s focused on conditions in and around the schools, particularly at the secondary level—difficulty of enforcing discipline, court-ordered busing, declining resources, poor or disinterested teachers, new demands on teachers' time, "modern educational ideas," reduced attention to reading and writing, narrowly technical courses, too many electives, inadequate teacher education programs, and lack of parental support. Critics catch on to whichever of these appeals to their present biases. The range of explanations, the lack of supporting data, and the assorted array of proposals leave us at a loss with respect to appropriate corrective action.

Perhaps the most serious bar to understanding or improving our schools is the inadequate measures we use in seeking to determine their health. We use test scores, such as those on the SAT, as though they tell us something about the *condition* of schools. They tell us even less about schools than a thermometer designed to measure body temperature tells us about body health. The SAT, for example, was not designed to measure the effectiveness, let alone the characteristics, of schools. And yet we act as though schools are in good or bad shape depending on the direction of the curve of attainment on the test scores. We relax as it rises and express concern as it falls.

Many sincere persons are convinced that our schools should and could be better. But no sustained effort to make them so has been mounted. The back-to-basics movement has merely reinforced teachers in what they do most of the time anyway. Now there are signs that the decline in SAT scores is about to be reversed. If the period of decline resulted from conditions in schools such as those summarized above, it follows that the reversal will have resulted from correcting these conditions.

But surely we cannot take such a proposition seriously. We lacked a diagnosis when the scores were declining; we lack a diagnosis now. Test scores will continue to move up or down, without our knowing the reasons with a reasonable degree of confidence. To relax our concern over the quality of schools when test scores are rising is to sidestep the responsibility of examining conditions in our schools for purposes of determining strengths and weaknesses and taking constructive action.

There are many ways to do this. One way is to examine the schools' product, not on a narrow array of test items, but in relation to how well the schools appear to have served their clients educationally. After all, *education* is the business of schools, and we are not short on definitions of what education is and therefore of what schools should do.

Flanagan interviewed intensively a sample of 1,000 adults, aged 30, who were tested 15 years earlier in the districts where they attended school.[24] He concentrated on areas of development to which our schools ostensibly are committed—physical and material well-being, relations with others, community and civic participation, recreation, and personal development and fulfillment. The response to Flanagan's interviews leave one wondering about the seriousness with which we commit our schools to education and not merely to the mechanics of learning. There is little in the data to suggest that the high school curriculum contributed to job competence or satisfaction, later participation in civic and political activities, or life enjoyment. What these young adults remembered about schools were the learnings that creative teachers had managed to link up with their lives at the time they were adolescents. For most, school was either a meaningful experience at the time or never. We would be well advised, it appears, to look less to test scores in determining the quality of educating in our schools and more to what students are called upon to do.

Studies in addition to Flanagan's suggest that the most serious limitations of our schools may well be in areas where little public concern has been voiced and about which we have a false confidence. Raven reports on several Irish and British studies of educational goals thought to be commonly attained in schools. He found that teachers, students, and parents attach great importance to character development. "Nevertheless," he concludes, "all the evidence, both circumstantial and direct, suggests that these goals are not being well attained and that schools may be having . . . harmful effects in this area."[25]

When we turn to what some people consider to be central to the school's purpose—providing students with opportunities to solve intellectual problems and use higher cognitive abilities—further questions of effectiveness rise in our minds. Evidence is mounting to suggest that the school's limitations are much less severe in teaching the fundamentals of reading, writing, and figuring—the so-called basics—than in teaching more complex abilities. We live in an era of rapidly expanding opportunities to acquire information but of constricting opportunities to reflect, engage in sustained discourse with others, and clarify our beliefs about the times and circumstances in which we live. If our schools need improvements in the basics, they need—perhaps more—a fresh examination of their role in a society undergoing rapid change.

The first step in any program of examination and reconstruction is to determine what now exists. It is impossible to know with any confidence existing conditions in all of the elementary and secondary schools of the United States. But to have comprehensive information about even a representative sample would fill a void and, perhaps, be suggestive of an agenda. This was one of the major assumptions guiding my decision to launch A Study of Schooling. I wanted not a survey of a few characteristics of many schools, but a detailed account of activities and perceptions in some carefully selected elementary, junior, and senior high schools. A brief description of the Study follows. Subsequent chapters present and discuss the findings and their implications and present recommendations.

A STUDY OF SCHOOLING

A Study of Schooling was motivated in part by my belief that most efforts to improve schools founder on reefs of ignorance—ignorance of the ways schools function in general and ignorance of the inner workings of selected schools in particular. Few reformers of the 1960s regarded such knowledge as relevant to their intentions. Their mission was to bring new ideas and materials to the teachers who were their targets.[26] Seymour Sarason warned that schools have a distinctive culture that must be understood and involved if changes are to be more than cosmetic.[27] Lasting improvements effect changes in this culture. Principals and teachers who do not want what others seek to impose upon them often are extraordinarily adept at nullifying or defusing practices perceived to be in conflict with prevailing ways of doing things.[28] The result may be the appearance of change but no change.

Studying all of a school at once is virtually impossible. One inevitably looks at pieces and then seeks to put them together. The results are neither fully satisfying nor completely accurate. They are an approximation of reality—and then only one's own approximation. After exploring several alternative ways to seek insight into schools, my colleagues and I chose to compile "thick" descriptions of a few schools. Further, we decided that these descriptions would be a composite of perceptions—those of persons closely associated with each school as well as of trained, independent observers. Encouraged in this approach by the members of our Advisory Committee, we set out to compile the questions to which we wanted answers—about school functions, problems, and issues; about students' satisfactions, interests, and perceptions of teachers, classroom activities, and school climate; about teachers' values, satisfactions, teaching practices, and perceptions of principals, students, and one another; about some selected aspects of principals' views of the school, the teachers, and parental roles; about parents' satisfactions, expectations, involvement, and perceptions of problems facing their schools; about school and classroom organization; about the distribution of subjects in the curriculum, topics taught, and materials used; and on and on. We wanted students', teachers', parents', and principals' views of the same kind of things. We sought to compare the groups' perceptions of each other and to compare these with our own observations. Surely this overlapping, interconnecting array of data, once sorted out, would provide insights into and understanding of schools beyond anything available at the time.

There have been few efforts to study schools as total entities. There have been, rather, thousands of studies of various pieces, most of them seeking to determine the effects of some classroom practice on student achievement. Researchers criticize *schools* but tend to study students, teachers, or methods of teaching. At the time our venture began, it was greeted with some puzzlement and criticism. Researchers, young ones in particular, looked for small theories or hypotheses being investigated and, finding none, were critical. Some of the more polite skeptics suggested that the information already was available—but failed to produce the evidence when asked. A few kindly souls said that I already knew enough about schools and would serve humankind better by using what I knew to improve them. Some said that it would be impossible to make sense out of the large amount of data to be collected.

The climate of thought has changed since our work commenced. The publication of Rutter's excellent study of 12 secondary schools in London, England, has demonstrated the potential usefulness of studying the ethos of schools.[29] A leading educational researcher has pointed to the danger of ignoring potentially useful data when the search is geared too closely to affirming or denying a hypothesis.[30] And, at the time of writing this report, there is a rash of ongoing inquiries ostensibly designed to look at the institution of schooling as a whole, particularly at the secondary level.[31] Support is growing, apparently, for the proposition guiding A Study of Schooling— namely, that understanding schools is prerequisite to improving them.

My colleagues and I were fortunate in finding persons affiliated with more than a dozen philanthropic foundations and other funding agencies who shared this belief or otherwise saw merit in what we had set out to do. We were able to secure funding from two or three of these simultaneously for each successive task required to carry out what proved to be exceedingly difficult and time-consuming. First, we formulated our questions about schools. Second, we chose from an initial list of thousands (five hundred in the curriculum area alone) a much smaller number of the most important questions. Third, we transformed these general questions into more specific ones to be asked of each group on questionnaires and in interviews. Fourth, we modified existing techniques for systematically observing classroom practices, adapting them to our own purposes. We tried out and revised our procedures in nearby schools and classrooms. As we became more familiar with the range of responses to be expected, we built these into the questionnaires and observation forms for easy checking and, ultimately, scanning and tallying by computer.

Meanwhile, we were determining the nature and location of the schools to be studied, planning the logistics of collecting the data, and training a corps of data collectors. Figure 1-1 provides a brief description of the sample and some of our procedures. The selection of 13 communities in seven sections of the country produced a sample of 38 schools differing in several significant characteristics (one community combined the two levels of secondary education in one school). The fact that the elementary schools selected sent most of their students to the secondary schools studied provided us with a continuum of 12 years of schooling in each community.

We recognized from the beginning that gathering any significant amount of data in a sample representing all the different kinds of schools in the United States—a random sample—is impossible. Instead, we sought maximum diversity and representativeness in a sample of small size. Initially we concluded that 24 triples would offer the array desired. But costs in relation to available funds restricted us to 13 triples. Figure 1-1 reveals, however, a considerable degree of variability and representativeness in the schools chosen.

Perhaps this restriction to conform to available funds was a blessing— one not fully appreciated by us at the time. We sent more than 20 trained data collectors into each community, where they remained for almost a month, compiling a large body of data about each school. Just 38 schools produced data from many individuals—8,624 parents, 1,350 teachers, and 17,163 students. So far as I am able to determine, no other single study has made detailed observations of over 1,000 classrooms. We cannot generalize to all schools from this sample. But certainly, the thick descriptions compiled from several different perspectives raise many questions about schooling and about other schools with which you and I have some limited familiarity.

The schools we studied differ in location, size, characteristics of the student population, family incomes, and other ways. Nonetheless, as we shall see, they shared many similarities, particularly in modes of teaching and learning. Common elements emerged early in our analyses and built steadily into patterns. Consequently, it is reasonable to assume that these patterns extend beyond our sample into many more schools. It becomes not unreasonable, then, to assume that the problems and shortcomings emerging most consistently are to some degree characteristic of schools beyond our sample and suggest an agenda for school improvement.

However, even the most commonly identified problems and issues took on some unique aspects in the setting of each school studied. Though schools appear to be in many regards similar, they differ to some degree even in these regards. One of the major messages of this report is that improvement is essentially a school-by-school process, enlightened by the degree to which those associated with each school and trying to improve it have the data required for building a useful agenda. Many of the kinds of data we gathered are precisely what local school personnel require if their efforts are to be other than sporadic and aimless. Achievement test scores simply are insufficient. It is unrealistic to envision for each local school the array of data we gathered on each elementary, junior high, and senior high school in our sample. But it is difficult to envision a school's staff, students, and parents proceeding systematically to create new circumstances in their school without the availability of specific data on its present condition.

We gave each community a fictitious code name and repeated it for each school of the triple selected for study. Hence there is a community named Woodlake and the Woodlake Elementary, Junior High, and Senior High Schools. In most of the communities selected there are more schools than these three, however, especially at the elementary level. Detailed descriptions of the communities and their schools are not essential to understanding subsequent discussion, but most readers probably will find a little background information to be helpful. Consequently, I am including brief descriptions here, and demographic data are presented in Table 1-1.

The communities we selected are in urban, suburban, and rural settings. However, we should try to avoid conjuring up stereotypic images of these different classifications. Major cities such as Chicago, New York, Dallas, and Los Angeles contain within their boundaries a vast variety of communities. Within urban school districts differences in school facilities, student-teacher ratios, and support for special programs have drawn the ire and fire of civil rights groups.

Differences among urban communities are dramatically illustrated in just the four we selected—Manchester, Newport, Palisades, and Rosemont. They are located in relatively large cities ranging in population from 600,000 to well over 2,000,000 persons. Beyond that, similarities end. Manchester comes closest to the urban stereotype—a dominance of concrete and asphalt rather than grass, limited open space, rows of apartment buildings. Once a relatively affluent Jewish community, it is now almost all black. Palisades, on the other hand, more closely approximates the *suburban* stereotype than does any of the suburban communities we selected. Here are the expensive homes, manicured lawns, and predominantly white residents we so often associate with the suburbs.

Newport is not in the inner city; nonetheless, it is characterized by many apartment buildings and some single family dwellings, most small and often occupied by more than one family, and is a multiracial, multiethnic, highly transient community. Its population is shifting from predominantly

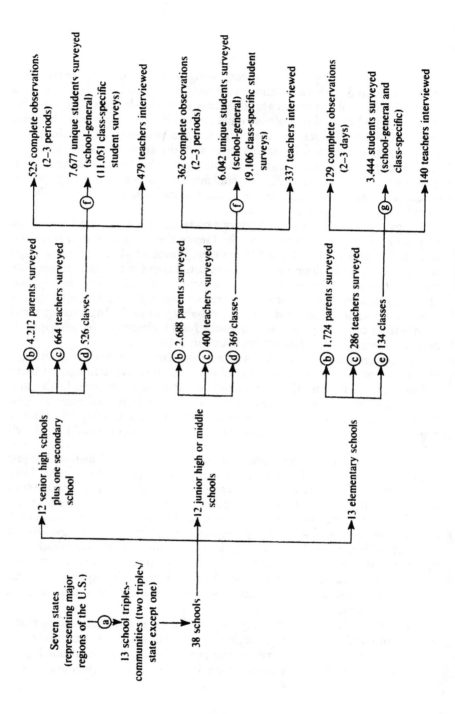

Seven states (representing major regions of the U.S.)

(a) → 13 school triples-communities (two triples/state except one)

→ 38 schools

→ 12 senior high schools plus one secondary school

(b) 4,212 parents surveyed
(c) 664 teachers surveyed
(d) 526 classes

→ 525 complete observations (2–3 periods)
(f) → 7,677 unique students surveyed (school-general) (11,051 class-specific student surveys)
→ 479 teachers interviewed

→ 12 junior high or middle schools

(b) 2,688 parents surveyed
(c) 400 teachers surveyed
(d) 369 classes

→ 362 complete observations (2–3 periods)
(f) → 6,042 unique students surveyed (school-general) (9,106 class-specific student surveys)
→ 337 teachers interviewed

→ 13 elementary schools

(b) 1,724 parents surveyed
(c) 286 teachers surveyed
(e) 134 classes

→ 129 complete observations (2–3 days)
(g) → 3,444 students surveyed (school-general and class-specific)
→ 140 teachers interviewed

20

Notes:

(a) Four stratification factors:

Ideal

- small/large student enrollment
- low/middle economic status
- rural/metropolitan location
- white/nonwhite/racial-ethnic mix

Obtained

- High school enrollment range: 60–2,700
- Median family income range: $5,000–$20,000
- Rural farming to inner city
- 99% white; 99% black; 99% Mexican-American; 50%–50% white-black; 50%–50% white/Mexican-American

(b) Surveys were mailed to every family at each school. These results represent an average 31% return rate.

Other community data sources from which survey data were obtained included:

- Central office/board of education
- School organizations
- Community organizations/agencies
- "Community others"

(c) Questionnaire packets were distributed to every teacher at each school. These results represent an average response rate of 86%.

Additional data collected from each teacher included:

- Curriculum materials
- Work-group sociometric data

Additional school data sources surveyed included:

- Principal (also interviewed)
- Assistant principal(s)
- Counselors
- Librarian(s)
- All other nonteaching professionals

(d) Secondary classes sampled according to eight-subject curriculum outline and these sampling considerations:

- high, average, and low-tracked classes
- nearly equal numbers of classes per period of the day
- representative distribution of teachers on sex and race/ethnicity

These results represent the following distribution of classes by subject area:

- English 17%
- Mathematics 16%
- Social studies 15%
- Science 12%
- The arts 12%
- Foreign language 4%
- Vocational/career education 17%
- Physical education 7%

(e) In most cases two classes at each grade level of an elementary school were sampled. These results represent nearly equal proportions of early (grades 1–3) and upper (grades 4–6) elementary classes.

(f) Secondary students sampled represented an average 62% of the total student enrollment. "Class-specific" refers to all survey questions asked of students pertaining to the specific class sampled. All other questions fall into the "school-general" category.

(g) Elementary students sampled represented an average 51% of the total student enrollment.

Figure 1-1. A Study of Schooling: Summary of Sampling, Data Sources, Procedures.

TABLE 1-1

Some Demographic Data on the Sample of Schools

School	Grade Span	Population Size			SES	Loc	Race/Ethnicity (%)					Sample Size			# Classes Sampled
		T	P	S			Wb	Bl	As	MxA	Other	T	P	S	
ATWATER															
Senior High	10-12	25	404	450	Mid	Sub	96	.5	2	.5	1	25	158	336	27
Junior High	7-9	24	408	496	Mid	Sub	94	1	2	1	2	23	157	342	27
Elementary	K-6	15	163	305	Mid	Sub	93	1	2	3	1	15	68	180	8
BRADFORD															
Senior High	10-12	63	1135	1350	Mid/Lo	Sub	90	8	0	0	2	48	382	741	48
Junior High	7-9	35	683	858	Mid/Lo	Sub	95	5	0	0	0	28	211	657	36
Elementary	K-6	21	366	613	Mid/Lo	Sub	99	0	0	0	1	20	114	351	12
CRESTVIEW															
Senior High	9-12	44	894	1091	Mid/Lo	Sub	99	1	0	0	0	44	330	576	48
Middle	6-8	32	633	725	Mid/Lo	Sub	99	1	0	0	0	32	257	430	27
Elementary	K-5	30	477	605	Mid/Lo	Sub	99	1	0	0	0	29	217	236	10
DENNISON															
Secondary	7-12	11	32	61	Mid	Rural	97	1	0	2	0	10	15	59	19
Elementary	K-6	4	28	48	Mid	Rural	97	1	0	2	0	4	10	38	3
EUCLID															
Senior High	9-12	24	219	262	Mid	Rural	100	0	0	0	0	23	81	246	40
Junior High	7-8	13	128	133	Mid	Rural	99	0	0	0	0	12	41	128	16
Elementary	K-6	21	208	315	Mid	Rural	100	0	0	0	0	21	71	261	12
FAIRFIELD															
Senior High	9-12	57	874	1137	Mid/Lo	Rural	53	4	1	42	0	44	304	696	46
Junior High	7-8	42	663	764	Mid/Lo	Rural	46	4	0	50	0	35	218	462	30
Elementary # 1	K-6	45	655	906	Mid/Lo	Rural	34	0	0	66	0	34	189	341	12

LAUREL															
Senior High	9-12	18	218	271	Lo	Rural	52	48	0	0	0	17	81	238	24
Middle	6-8	24	246	276	Lo	Rural	51	49	0	0	0	21	81	270	24
Elementary	K-5	24	356	513	Lo	Rural	51	49	0	0	0	23	101	264	12
MANCHESTER															
Senior High	9-12	114	2462	3006	Mid	Urban	0	99	0	0	0	66	482	937	48
Middle	6-8	62	1276	1547	Mid	Urban	0	99	0	0	0	32	301	790	35
Elementary	K-5	21	411	598	Mid	Urban	0	99	0	0	0	14	107	288	9
NEWPORT															
Senior High	10-12	85	2244	2508	Mid	Urban	47	9	17	18	9	78	358	841	46
Junior High	7-9	75	1497	1649	Mid	Urban	46	11	17	25	1	58	260	757	36
Elementary	K-6	28	534	701	Lo	Urban	31	10	20	38	1	26	124	319	12
PALISADES															
Senior High	9-12	68	1252	1402	Hi/Mid	Urban	50	50	0	0	0	59	461	768	48
Middle	6-8	49	774	825	Hi/Mid	Urban	50	45	1	4	0	41	305	492	36
Elementary	K-5	18	265	340	Hi/Mid	Urban	53	46	1	0	0	17	150	272	10
ROSEMONT															
Senior High	9-12	121	2008	2702	Lo	Urban	0	0	0	100	0	113	447	763	48
Middle	6-8	44	779	993	Lo	Urban	2	2	0	95	1	43	156	591	36
Elementary	K-5	30	349	521	Lo	Urban	0	0	0	100	0	30	75	216	10
VISTA															
Senior High	9-12	84	1882	2312	Mid	Sub	98	1	0	0	0	84	638	834	48
Junior High	7-8	49	1112	1188	Mid	Sub	98	1	1	1	0	48	416	662	36
Elementary	K-6	30	543	745	Mid	Sub	98	1	1	0	0	30	284	310	12
WOODLAKE															
Senior High	10-12	57	912	1202	Mid	Sub	80	5	10	3	2	53	475	642	36
Junior High	7-9	30	550	655	Mid	Sub	95	1	3	1	0	27	285	461	30
Elementary	K-6	24	393	581	Mid	Sub	92	1	5	1	1	23	214	342	12

white to predominantly Mexican-American; other minority groups, such as blacks, Native Americans, Japanese, Chinese, Filipinos, and Koreans, are significantly represented.

Rosemont is a community of apartments and very small, inexpensive homes. The population is almost entirely Mexican-American and is the most impoverished in our sample.

Of the four communities classified as suburban—Atwater, Bradford, Vista, and Crestview—Vista probably comes closest to our mental picture of the suburbs. But even Vista is not characterized exclusively by tree-lined streets, lawns, and well-kept homes of the middle-class and more affluent commuter. There are rural areas carrying on a little farming, and there are light manufacturing companies. Nonetheless, 90% of the dwellings are single family homes, with property values in the school attendance area ranging from $20,000 to $250,000 at the time of our survey. Although residents of the relatively large nearby city would view Vista as one of their suburbs, Vista has a considerable identity and even economic life of its own.

Bradford doesn't fit the conventional stereotype either. Although it is located close by one of the nation's largest cities, many of its residents go to work in nearby industrial areas outside the city. Bradford is essentially a blue-collar suburb, with a substantial number of apartments as well as modest homes. The fact that just a few interrelated industrial plants are the main employers of parents raises questions about the future of the schools during periods of recession.

Atwater is a suburb of a rather large city, a suburb possessing its own considerable sources of livelihood for the residents—storage warehouses and light industries, mostly in an industrial park. Many of its residents do work in the city, though, and indeed it is not easy for the visitor to determine where the city ends and its suburban neighbor begins.

Crestview also has some difficulties in self-identification. Parts of it have been annexed over the years by the city of which it is a suburb. The community is divided by an interstate highway; governmental functions are split between two townships; there are some open, rural areas. Most homes are comparatively inexpensive; there are few sidewalks or curbs; junked cars and trash are a common sight in yards.

If Crestview has rural touches, two of the other communities we chose—Woodlake and Fairfield—represent a real transition from a somewhat suburban to a predominantly rural ambience. However, Woodlake and Fairfield are not very much alike. The center of Woodlake resembles the commercial section of a suburb. One encounters, moving outward, homes on large lots and then small dairy, fruit, and vegetable farms. Larger towns are near; a city of over 500,000 people is not quite close enough for daily commuting. Fairfield also is characterized by small-scale farming. Although it is within daily commuting distance of a relatively large city, its ambience is more rural than suburban.

The large majority of residents in Woodlake are white. The largest minority group is Asian; the others are black and Mexican-American, for the most part. The fairly close balance of white and Mexican-American residents in Fairfield is shifting steadily toward the latter group.

Dennison, Euclid, and Laurel clearly are rural communities, but Laurel is significantly different from the other two. This small town serves an area of small farms, ranging in size from about 50 to 300 acres. Dennison and Euclid, on the other hand, are characterized by large farming and ranching operations, with some ranches in the latter exceeding 5,000 acres. The average size of farms and ranches for both Dennison and Euclid is about 1,200 acres.

We can see in these 13 communities prototypes of other communities in the United States. But even prototypic pairs, on closer examination, would be found to differ in various ways. And so it would be with schools. Certain generalizations can be made. For example, as one moves outward from urban to rural areas, one finds that schools tend to become smaller. But the trend is not consistent. Or as one moves from rural to urban communities, one finds an increase in minority populations. The generalization holds, but there are exceptions.

Table 1-1 summarizes some important data about the schools we studied in the 13 communities. The reader should note that we dropped the rural/suburban refinement in classifying the communities by location, choosing the discrete category designation thought to be most appropriate.

We see that the senior high schools in three of the four communities classified as urban—Newport, Rosemont, and Manchester—are the largest, ranging in size from 2,508 to 3,006 students. Palisades Senior High School, with 1,402 students, is the fifth largest. The urban junior highs also are relatively large—from 825 at Palisades to 1,649 at Newport. The range for the suburban group of junior and senior highs slightly overlaps the range for the urban group, suburban Vista having 2,312 students in its senior high and 1,188 in its junior high.

In line with conventional expectancy, the three rural districts supplied the very small secondary schools in our sample. The enrollment at Dennison was so low—61 students—that the junior and senior high levels were conducted as a single unit. Only suburban Atwater gave us a senior high school which, with 450 students, approached the small size of the senior highs of rural Laurel and Euclid and the senior high division at Dennison. It should be noted that Palisades Elementary, although urban, was among the small schools in our total sample, with 340 boys and girls.

Other data in Table 1-1 provide information about the race or ethnicity of the students enrolled and the socioeconomic level of the parents. Clearly, one could not predict with accuracy either of these characteristics simply by knowing a school's classification for location, although there is the usual trend toward less racial diversity in the suburban communities.

The parents at Palisades are the most affluent of our sample, even though the community is in a large city. The even distribution of white and black students was effected through busing in the black students. Obviously, some effort was made to secure a reasonable socioeconomic fit between the two groups. Not just the economic level but also the educational level of the parents was relatively high. At the other end of the scale with respect to income and education are the parents at Rosemont, also an urban community, populated almost entirely by Mexican-American families. The parents at Manchester, populated by black families, fell into the middle range of our sample for levels of both income and schooling. The Newport parents, the most diverse group racially and ethnically, were above average in schooling but below in income.

We deliberately avoided the most wealthy suburban school districts, given the size of our sample and the fact that we were able to obtain an example of a relatively wealthy suburban community in urban Palisades—and the added element of integration through busing. Among the four suburban districts chosen, Vista most closely fits the suburban stereotype—middle income parents, above average educational attainment in the parent group, and an almost exclusively white enrollment in the three schools.

Two of the rural communities—Dennison and Euclid—are very much like several of the suburban communities in the middle-range economic and educational level of parents. But parents at Laurel are poor and of relatively low educational attainment.

Data on financial support of the schools proved to be among our least trustworthy data. Indeed, we concluded that some of the figures obtained were virtually useless. The problem arises primarily out of the different ways school districts across the country distinguish between their sources of income and compute their expenditures.

Regarding per-pupil expenditures, there appeared not to be marked differences between the urban and suburban schools as groups. Support in Atwater consistently exceeded support in all the urban and suburban districts at all levels. To take one striking example, the difference between Atwater and Vista increased with successive levels of schooling so that by the senior high level, it seems that Atwater was spending twice as much as Vista.

Other communities also appeared to differ in the support given to levels of schooling or specific schools or both. The Newport community was relatively high in per pupil support, apparently, at both secondary levels but dropped below average for elementary schools. Even though Manchester was comparatively low at all three levels, teachers' salaries were among the highest, suggesting deprivation in other areas, such as instructional supplies.

Each additional statistic adds a little more to the uniqueness of each community and school. On the other hand, if we put together a considerable amount of demographic data, we begin to see communities and schools very much like others we've seen across this broad land. The elements of uniqueness escape us. What would most engage our attention is missing.

Visits would help. One would indeed see a strange, rather indefinable sameness, just as there is a sameness about hospitals—seating arrangements, materials being used, teachers' roles, students' roles, teaching methods, and so on. While these were not identical in the various schools we studied, they were not very different, either. But one would also see differences—for example, in the facilities of the urban senior high schools. All of the Palisades schools are rather handsome buildings, with attractive landscaping and ample playground space. The Manchester schools, on the other hand, are more like what we conjure up as typically urban—dull brick construction, concrete and asphalt running up to the schools' walls, some straggly shrubs, and limited playground space. The senior high at Rosemont has a rather stately, impressive entrance; hallways are wide and high-ceilinged. To a considerable degree the building contrasts with the surrounding small homes, duplexes, and apartment buildings, most in ill-repair. Newport Senior High is dull, drab, and rather depressing in appearance. At the time of our visit, it was exceedingly crowded.

Beyond facilities, other differences are visible to the eye. The students at Atwater Junior High School were as open and friendly as any I've ever encountered. The principal did a great deal of "business" during class breaks—congratulating a teacher on a recent award, joshing a student athlete about the basketball game lost the previous evening, checking on a student required to meet with him each day. The old, worn building seemed to take on warmth and vitality from its occupants.

The contrast with all three Fairfield schools was marked. It took several days to overcome the depression of spirits I experienced on visiting these schools. The demographics don't prepare us fully, either, for the businesslike atmosphere at Rosemont Senior High, or the generally pleasing ambience at Woodlake High, or the level-to-level differences seeming to be present at

Bradford. The senior high appeared to be in a state of near-collapse, but some interesting educational activities seemed to be under way in most of the primary classes.

We will become more familiar with some of these schools as we progress, and with the ways the schools of our sample differ most and least. And increasingly we will come to understand why uniform recommendations directed at schools generally so often fail to assist schools specifically.

SOME RECURRING THEMES

Earlier, I stated that it is virtually impossible to study and describe schools "all of a piece." We chose pieces of the whole appearing to characterize schools commonly, even though each may manifest itself differently from school to school. We referred to these as commonplaces of schooling—teaching practices, content or subject matter, instructional materials, physical environment, activities, human resources, evaluation, time, organization, communications, decision making, leadership, expectations, issues and problems, and controls or restraints. They combined to constitute something close to the whole of a school. Consequently, though some of these commonplaces may be more significant than others, none can be ignored in any attempt to describe and understand a school as a total entity.

We chose also to describe most commonplaces from the several major perspectives involved in our study—students', teachers', parents', observers', and, to a somewhat lesser degree, principals'. The number of commonplaces and perspectives, together with the almost unlimited potential for exploring relationships in the data, forced us to narrow as sharply as possible the array of questions to be asked of each respondent in regard to each commonplace. Yet it was necessary to gather sufficient information to provide the thick descriptions we believed to be necessary. And so even what we thought to be a rather parsimonious but sufficient array of questions, plus our own observations, produced a staggering volume of data.

The problems of organizing these data in a useful, meaningful way were complex. It appeared to us to be necessary but not sufficient to go through a preliminary sorting around both commonplaces and perspectives, e.g., students'. Consequently, we produced several very large data source books, each comprehensively summarizing all data relevant to a commonplace or group of respondents: for example, teacher data, student data, parent data, teaching practices, and decision making. Later, these proved useful in writing what follows.

This apparently unavoidable, time-consuming step proved to be instrumental to the later identification of a number of themes which tell us a great deal about schools and schooling, and which I develop in subsequent chapters. Each theme derives its qualities, for better or for worse, from the way several related commonplaces manifest themselves, as perceived by the several groups of respondents and observers. Fleshed out by the data, these themes collectively define and describe schooling, to the degree that the schools in our sample are representative. Using the themes as descriptors, it becomes possible both to describe a school and to array the schools according to how the data related to each theme differentiate one school from another. The themes thus help us see that schooling has a common set of characteristics and that school-to-school differences result from the sum total of how these characteristics manifest themselves in each school. On some characteristics, schools are very much alike; on others, they differ quite significantly.

The first theme is *school functions.* Schools appear not to be acutely self-conscious about what they are trying to do. But they inevitably perform functions—from baby-sitting to job preparation and intellectual development. We might hope that schools would emphasize their educational functions almost exclusively, but they do not.

A second theme is the school's *relevance* in the lives of its students. Students, presumably, are the school's primary clients. But they are not clients seeking out educational services in the way they seek health services. They go to school as part of growing up. There is no choice. It would be a surprise to find that students have clear, common purposes for being in school. It seems more reasonable to assume that school provides a compulsory setting in which boys and girls seek to satisfy their interests—find relevance—as best they can.

The problems of making school-based learning meaningful, to say nothing of compelling or exciting, appear and reappear in the succeeding narrative. One is forced to raise serious questions about the potency of schools and the conventions by which they function. For example, what are schools doing to recognize changes in the values of the young? We can make our schools more efficient. But making them relevant in the lives of boys and girls is one of the most demanding challenges we face.

A third theme is *how teachers teach*, and a fourth is *the circumstances surrounding teaching.* Teachers both condition and are conditioned by the circumstances of schools. Schools are, first, for students. But to ignore the fact that students are influenced by teachers, who in turn are influenced by their workplace, would be to lead us once again to simplistic diagnoses and inadequate proposals for school improvement. A fifth theme is the array of activities, materials, and tests constituting *the curriculum*. A sixth is *the distribution of resources for learning*. One of the most important of these is time. Children tend to learn what they are taught. The teaching requires the spending of time. Some schools are more businesslike than others in getting children into classrooms in the morning, out for recess and back, and through lunch. Some seem almost unaware that time is virtually the most precious learning resource they have at their disposal. School-to-school differences in using time create inequities in opportunity to learn.

Another aspect of this theme is the allocation of teachers to subjects—more to this one, fewer to that one. Such decisions reflect priorities—or, sometimes, thoughtlessness. Allocation determines, in large measure, the curricular framework within which the students of a secondary school have alternatives and make choices.

A seventh theme, *equity*, expands on the issues of equity involved in theme six. Some issues of equity regarding access to knowledge have little to do with the race or socioeconomic status of students. Others frequently do relate to socioeconomic status and race—particularly issues of differences in content and teaching practices encountered by students depending on their enrollment in high-, middle-, or low-track classes.

An eighth theme is what often is called *the hidden curriculum*—what I have chosen to call *the implicit curriculum*. Schools explicitly teach mathematics and have boys and girls learn to read, write, and spell, and so on. But they also teach a great deal implicitly through the ways they present the explicit curriculum—for example, emphasizing acquiring facts or solving problems—through the kinds of rules they impose, and even through the social and physical settings they provide for learning. Thus, they teach students to work alone competitively or to work cooperatively in groups, to be active or passive, to be content with facts or also seek insight, and on and on. In brief, schools implicitly teach values.

It is important to know what these values are and how consistently they are being reinforced in classrooms. Of course the question of what values schools should teach is one many of us would prefer to ignore. Meanwhile schools continue to teach values powerfully represented in the larger society. In the long run, schools teach both explicitly and implicitly what they are most insistently asked to teach.

A ninth theme is *satisfaction* as a criterion of school quality. Much attention is now given in business and industry to work satisfaction, the qualities that produce it, and the relationships between workers' satisfaction and productivity. Conditions for work and indeed the very structure of manufacturing and other industrial procedures have been overhauled as a concomitant of this interest. But relatively little attention has been given to comparable considerations in schooling. Yet the composite satisfaction of principal, teachers, students, and parents constitutes a significant indication of a school's quality, including achievement. Schools beset with problems of controlling student behavior, for example, are likely to fall below expectations based on socioeconomic status of families in the quality of education they provide and the results they produce.

A tenth theme is *the need for data*. The schools in our sample simply do not possess the information they need to set, with some confidence, an agenda for school improvement. When I talked with principals and guidance counselors, it became clear that very few of them could answer fundamental questions about the distribution of curricular emphases in the experience of students. They simply did not know the proportion of students in academic programs who simultaneously were enrolled in vocational education classes. Very few individuals in the group thought about curricula from the student's perspective. Consequently, they were largely ignorant about whether or not the curricula of individual students were well balanced.

Perhaps even more serious, we found little evidence to suggest any open meeting of the minds on the part of principals, teachers, students, and parents regarding school weaknesses, problems, and strengths. Yet our data usually revealed for each school some problems perceived by all of these groups to be serious. We discussed such findings with these groups in the three schools agreeing to participate in a major shakedown cruise for the entire data-collecting procedure. It came as some surprise to the teachers, for example, to learn that they, the students, and the parents selected many of the same problems as being most serious.

Two themes are so pervasive that they are more perspectives than threads making up the fabric of what follows. The first is the concept of *the school as the unit for improvement*. There is little point in concluding that our schools are in trouble and then focusing for improvement only on teachers, or principals, or the curriculum. All of these and more are involved. Consequently, efforts at improvement must encompass the school as a system of interacting parts, each affecting the others.

But there is more to this comprehensive approach than dealing with the school as a unit. Schools will improve slowly, if at all, if reforms are thrust upon them. Rather, the approach having most promise, in my judgment, is one that will seek to cultivate the capacity of schools to deal with their own problems, to become largely self-renewing. Schools will have great difficulty, however, in becoming self-renewing without support from their states and local districts and especially from their surrounding constituencies.

Which brings us to the second of these pervasive themes—in a word, *caring*. Our schools will get better and have continuing good health only to the degree that a significant proportion of our people, not just parents, care about them. Caring for our schools diminished markedly during the 1970s. There are some signs that a positive kind of concern is on the rise, though at present it falls short of a national or even a state-by-state movement. Offsetting these signs, however, people continue to run away from the public schools, and often are aided and abetted in this flight by shortsighted policies. Many non-parents see no reason to support a public system of education.

Even caring will not be enough, though, unless it is accompanied by a better understanding of what education is and what is appropriate for schools to do. In the future, the school's role in the processing of information will become less important. Increasingly, we have in our homes the means of instant access to information of infinite variety. Our schools need to use and teach the revolutionary new means of information processing and to go on teaching traditionally basic skills and facts. But if they do only these things, they soon will be obsolescent.

Schools must do the educating not consciously done elsewhere in society. This includes providing systematic encounters with all the major domains of knowledge, encounters designed to inform, enlighten, and stimulate thought. But schools are not likely to go beyond teaching facts and fundamental skills unless we ask them to. The agenda for reconstructing our schools grows out of the gap between the educating we expect of schools and what we perceive them to be doing. What follows is designed to illuminate this gap. The agenda that emerges will not be the same for everyone.

Chapter 2

We Want It All

At the White House Conference on Education of 1965, Vice President Hubert Humphrey said that our country would go down in history for having used its educational system to overcome problems of illiteracy, unemployment, crime and violence, urban decay, and even war among nations. However, just a few years later some citizens were asking if our schools were capable of teaching our young to read, write, and spell. The press picked up this theme vigorously, reflecting an impression that parents as well as other adults generally favored returning to a time of more limited expectations for schools. "Back to basics" became a popular slogan. Many school board members and school administrators responded as though this were a mandate from the people.

I was skeptical. For a nation that had given its schools a broad role and placed them at the heart of its well-being—perhaps overgenerously—to shift position as abruptly as the changing rhetoric suggested appeared unreasonable. Was not this rhetoric in part a reaction to overly grandiose expectations of the preceding decade? Such reactions have occurred in the past. But it does not appear to me that the school system in our society moves purposefully, swiftly, and distinctively in the direction of the prevailing rhetoric of criticism, whatever it is. Rather, it expands or contracts a little around the edges while continuing to play its traditional role—a sign that society doesn't want that role drastically changed.

Specifically, I was skeptical of two assumptions that were questioned rarely during the 1970s. The first was that parents were highly dissatisfied with the schools their children attended. It is one thing to be critical of schooling, especially when one reads or hears regularly that the schools are doing a poor job. It is quite another to think similarly about "my

33

child's school." Word of declining test scores nationwide is a piece of news ranking low in significance compared with whether one's own child enjoys school, is safe and attended to there, and appears to be doing reasonably well. Policymakers worry about statistics; parents worry about their children.

The second assumption I questioned was that parents wanted a more limited kind of schooling for their children. It seemed reasonable to assume that most parents want for their children the kind of education that equips them for work, citizenship, and a measure of personal well-being—which to me suggests a broad, general education grounded in the 3 Rs but involving much more.

The central theme of this chapter is what we do in fact want and expect of our schools. It is explored from both a historical and a contemporary perspective. The data gathered to enlighten this theme include state and school district directives, as well as the responses of more than 8,000 parents to questions we asked of them.

These data tend to support my belief that the trends of the 1970s, many of them continuing into the 1980s, do not signal an abrupt turning away from the comprehensive expectations for education that have characterized this country historically. But it would be a serious mistake to assume that it will be business as usual in the future for our system of public schooling. As I suggested in Chapter 1, the unravelling of certain major features of this system that has been proceeding for some time accelerated during the 1970s. One feature in decline is the coalition of legislators, educators, parents, and others that held the system together and expanded it.[1] Another is the configuration of home, school, and church that traditionally did the educating. If these components are not, in the future, what they were in the past, the school too will not be what it was in the past. The context of schooling is changing dramatically in other ways too. For example, recordings, radio, and television pervade every resting place, be it home or resort, and accompany us all from birth to death. Consequently, the electronic media and the schools now must be viewed side by side as major educating agencies—which again means that the place of schools in educating will change.

Our expectations for schools are both idealistic and grandiose, representing a synthesis of what many diverse segments of our population want. This is one of the problems of schools; there are so many expectations for them. Some of these are met through private schools, some through specialized academic or vocational public schools. But central to our traditions is the idea and ideal of a free public school, available to all, commonly educating—the common school. At the turn of the century an eight-grade elementary school (frequently called the grade school) was the typical common school. Then completion of a relatively common secondary school became the expectation of many parents for their children. Today, a twelve-grade school is generally expected to play a relatively distinct and distinguishable role in a configuration of institutions that educate. It does not exist, however, nor can it be understood, as an institution apart.

Accordingly, the effort to address the question of what our schools are expected to do must go beyond the data from A Study of Schooling. The Study is of schools only—a small number of schools and only nonspecialized public schools. Therefore the following discussion is not confined to our Study data; rather, my interpretations of these data are placed within a larger body of source materials and personal experiences regarding the educational scene in the United States. While the focus is on schooling, the context is a shifting ecology of educating institutions.

PARENTS VIEW THEIR CHILDREN'S SCHOOLS

The data we gathered tended to support my doubts that in the 1970s parents were highly dissatisfied with their children's schools and held narrow, more limited educational expectations for schools than had prevailed in the past. It is important to remember that these data were obtained during the second half of the decade, when the so-called back-to-basics movement was at its height. The decline in test scores was being widely publicized, and the public schools were experiencing widespread criticism in the daily press and popular weekly magazines.

We surveyed 8,624 parents—1,724 elementary, 2,688 junior high, and 4,212 at the senior high level. They varied considerably in age, income, race/ethnicity, and education. Regrettably, it proved exceedingly difficult to reach the adult clients of the schools studied. Only 31% of the total parent population of these schools responded, and we believe the sample to somewhat overrepresent the more educated and affluent. However, these probably are the parents likely to be most aware of polls and most publicly critical of the quality of education being provided. The response rate to the questionnaires varied widely from school to school, from a meager 16% at one to a more gratifying 57% at another.

We asked parents, as well as students and teachers, to grade their schools—A, B, C, D, or F (Fail)—and then we averaged the marks. None of our schools received an average D or F—not from students, teachers, or parents. About 10% of the parents clearly were dissatisfied; about 7% gave their school a mark of D, and another 3% gave a grade of F. But notice in Table 2-1 that average grades even as low as C were received

TABLE 2-1

Distribution of Schools Receiving Average Grades of A, B, or C from Students, Teachers, and Parents

	High Schools			Jr. High/Middle Schools			Elementary Schools		
	A	B	C	A	B	C	A	B	C
STUDENTS	0	5	8	0	7	5	1	12	0
TEACHERS	0	7	6	0	9	3	1	11	1
PARENTS	0	9	4	0	11	1	0	11	2
TOTAL	–	21	18	0	27	9	2	34	3

NOTE: No schools received an average grade below C. Because one junior high functioned as one school with a senior high, the number of junior highs graded as such was reduced from 13 to 12.

from the parent group by only 7 of the 38 schools. Of these, 4 were senior high schools.

Clearly, the predominantly B ratings of elementary and middle schools convey rather substantial satisfaction. Although B and C grades suggest a falling off in satisfaction at the high school level, the absence of average D and F grades tends to deflect the notion that schools are perceived as an unmitigated disaster. The data on high schools in particular suggest reservations and concern, but somewhat more among students and teachers than among parents. Interestingly, parents were more generous than either teachers or students in grading both the junior and senior high schools attended by their children. Overall, the data do not convey the deep parental dissatisfaction with their schools that supposedly has prevailed widely. Nor do they lead to the conclusion that parents have a perception of all being well with the schools their children attend.

There almost always are several levels of perception regarding schools, depending in large part on the nature of our experience with them. We are easily persuaded by polls on matters extending beyond our direct experience. The quality of schools and schooling is not very good, but the school down the street to which our own children go isn't bad—in fact, it's quite good. At least this kind of mixed vision is what is suggested by some Gallup Polls of the late 1970s and supported by the responses of the parents in our sample.

Now what of parents' expectations for schools? Our nation's overall goals for education can be informative here. At the beginning of A Study of Schooling, several colleagues and I examined a vast array of documents reporting the ongoing effort to define, over a period of more than three hundred years, the goals of education and schooling in this country.

Education and schooling usually are not differentiated in these documents, which in itself is significant. It commonly is assumed that the aims of education and the goals of schools coincide exactly. We concluded that four broad areas of goals for the schools have emerged. They are the following: (1) academic, embracing all intellectual skills and domains of knowledge; (2) vocational, geared to developing readiness for productive work and economic responsibility; (3) social and civic, related to preparing for socialization into a complex society; and (4) personal, emphasizing the development of individual responsibility, talent, and free expression. They are reiterated, somewhere, in the official documents of most states. These goals presumably frame the educational function of schools.

McIntire adapted these goal categories in a study of parents' educational expectations in a medium-sized school district. He found a high level of support for all of them.[2] In A Study of Schooling, we used these same categories in questioning parents about what they expected of their children's schools. On the questionnaire we spoke of social development as involving instruction which helps students learn to get along with other students and adults, prepares students for social and civic effectiveness, and develops their awareness and appreciation of our own and other cultures. Intellectual development involves instruction in basic skills in mathematics, reading, and written and verbal communication, and in critical thinking and problem-solving abilities. Personal development calls for instruction which builds self-confidence, creativity, ability to think independently, and self-discipline. Vocational development involves instruction which prepares students for the expectations of the workplace, develops skills necessary for getting a job, and fosters awareness of career alternatives. These statements imply a good deal more than what one conjures up mentally when the words "back to basics" are used. We asked respondents to rate each goal area on a scale ranging from "very unimportant" to "very important."

It is probably not surprising that parents, on the average, gave "very important" ratings to all four areas, with the vocational dropping toward the "somewhat important" rating for parents of elementary school children. Approximately 90% of the parents sampled at all three levels rated intellectual goals as "very important." Personal goals approached this percentage among elementary school parents and dropped only to 80% at junior and senior high school levels. Vocational goals were rated only slightly lower by high school parents and somewhat lower by junior high parents. Social goals were rated "very important" by 73% of the elementary school parents, with the percentage dropping only to 66% and 64% at junior and senior high levels, respectively.

We also asked teachers and secondary students in our sample of

TABLE 2-2

Relative Importance of Goals for Students, Teachers, and Parents

	High Schools	Jr. High/Middle Schools	Elementary Schools
STUDENTS	Vocational Intellectual Personal Social	Intellectual Vocational Personal Social	
TEACHERS	Intellectual Personal Social Vocational	Intellectual Personal Social Vocational	Intellectual Personal Social Vocational
PARENTS	Intellectual Personal Vocational Social	Intellectual Personal Social Vocational	Intellectual Personal Social Vocational

NOTE: Elementary school students were not asked for these ratings.

schools to rate the goal areas. Like parents, both of these other groups thought all four goal areas "very important," with the vocational sagging a bit toward the "somewhat important" category for elementary school teachers. The relative importance that all three groups attach to the several goal areas is seen in Table 2-2. Note especially the similarity between teachers' and parents' ratings.

One could argue that there was no hard choice here. There is virtue in all these goal areas, as in God, motherhood, and apple pie. We forced the issue a bit with a second question, asking each group (now including elementary students) to make a single most preferred choice among the four. In Table 2-3 the responses are summarized. Roughly half of the parents and nearly half of the teachers chose the intellectual category. But the fact that the other half distributed this preferential choice across the social, personal, and vocational goals implies that a substantial number of these parents and teachers would be unhappy to have such goals eliminated. Apparently even more students feel strongly about the importance of each of these goals. They spread their preferences more evenly across all four categories.

The message here, it seems to me, is that those closest to schools—parents, teachers, and students—see as important all four of those goal areas which have emerged over the centuries and which had become well established in the rhetoric of educational expectations for schools decades before the 1970s.

TABLE 2-3

Goal Preferences of Students, Teachers, and Parents (in percent)

	Social	Intellectual	Personal	Vocational	N
STUDENTS					
High Schools	15.9	27.3	25.6	31.1	6670
Jr. High/Middle Schools	13.4	38.0	18.3	30.3	4733
Elementary Schools	13.8	47.1	17.3	21.8	1567
TEACHERS					
High Schools	9.9	45.6	29.7	14.8	656
Jr. High/Middle Schools	13.9	46.7	29.3	10.1	396
Elementary Schools	14.0	48.9	33.5	3.5	278
PARENTS					
High Schools	8.7	46.5	19.3	25.5	4065
Jr. High/Middle Schools	9.5	51.1	21.1	18.2	2605
Elementary Schools	9.3	57.6	24.5	8.6	1681

Our data thus show no withering in goal commitments by the parent group we sampled, and indeed I do not know of serious studies that come up with a narrow list of parental expectations for schools. When it comes to education, it appears that most parents want their children to have it all. I believe, then, that many policymakers have been misinterpreting parents' expectations for schools and then overreacting to this misinterpretation.

A CHANGING CONFIGURATION OF EDUCATING INSTITUTIONS

It should not surprise us for parents to want comprehensive educations for their children. Indeed, it would be strange to discover the opposite. And it should not surprise us to learn that parents want a major part of the educating to be done in schools. For most parents today, life is very demanding. As I noted in Chapter 1, over half of the mothers with school-age children are now working. There is little time for recreation with one's children, let alone time to provide for their formal education. Schools today do not only educate. Together with television they also provide a baby-sitting service for parents who go off to work early and are not yet at home when their children return from school. Of course this was not always so. Indeed, the change in just a single generation has been dramatic. And until relatively recent times, things were profoundly different.

The early colonists transplanted to the New World, as best the circumstances permitted, the towns and villages they had known at home. They also transplanted, as best they could, "an educational configuration of household, church and school, each standing in time-honored relation to the others. . . . The configuration taught, in different combinations for different orders of the society, the values and substance of piety, civility, and learning."[3]

Of the three institutions, the school was the most marginal. Many of the immigrants had not gone to school at all. Those who had gone had attended a dame school for a year or two of instruction in writing and reading. A few had attended a grammar school where they studied more exotic things such as Latin and Greek. In the New World, schools—where they existed—provided merely an add-on to what was learned through household and church. The household mediated all learning acquired outside of it; the household modeled most of what was required for living beyond it. It turned to the church for teaching the larger meaning of life; it joined with the church in teaching piety. The shadows of both institutions fell over the schools. All three institutions buttressed each other in the rearing and educating of the young.

Increasingly, the press joined this trio in producing by the time of the Revolution a level of literacy among whites approaching that of the homeland. Although half of the child population attended no schools, reading was a significant part of the culture. There were books, almanacs, newspapers, the Bible, letters to be read and to be written. School was not the only place for learning to read. Older brothers and sisters, uncles, aunts, and parents nurtured all aspects of life. And this educating by the household was reinforced by other households in the community. Of course, there were many without this kind of nurturing. Some families were small and isolated and had little time for all that was to be done. Blacks had been rudely torn from households in Africa; the Native Americans were a people apart. As today, many generalizations about "the people" two hundred years ago simply did not apply to various groups in our culture.

Nevertheless, enough people learned to read to create a demand for things to read. The role of the press in the American educational scene has been underestimated, often ignored. It did much more than contribute to literacy. Printed materials opened up new vistas, presented alternatives, stimulated criticism, and helped communicate the idea of revolution. Certainly the press helped foment the American Revolution.

Following the Revolution, it was no longer appropriate to inculcate European ways. A new national character was in the making. It had to be taught even while it was being created—and transmitted to waves of immigrants. Parents were ill-equipped to do the teaching required. Schools assumed this responsibility as one of their functions.

The locus of work shifted from the household to factory and shop. The workplace became a shaper of values and outlook and, to a considerable degree, a place to discuss what one read in the press. The size of families declined, and families moved, separating relatives from children they had helped. There were fewer in the household to do the educating. And there were new perspectives to be acquired. The America emerging was not the homeland left behind.

As a result, though the traditional relationships among home, church, and school persisted, the relative educational influence of school and press grew rapidly. The institutional mix broadened as organized work expanded, commercial entities proliferated, government enlarged, custodial institutions grew, and specialized educational institutions came into being. The need for an American form of education to transmit these developments, articulated by eloquent spokesmen and extolled in the newspapers, together with unprecedented immigration into the second half of the nineteenth century, increasingly defined and enlarged the place of the school.

The shift in the balance between home and school as educators that took place in the nineteenth century accelerated in the twentieth. Increasingly the school took over, teaching smatterings of subject matter to which parents had not been privy and which they assumed their children needed to know. With business and industry wanting the vocational preparation that schools were providing and colleges more interested in the precollegiate preparation of their students, the school's mediating influence took on greater independence from the home. The emergence of an educational system, with its inevitable bureaucratization, and the professionalization of teachers and administrators differentiated and separated the educational roles of home and school. The advent of counselling in schools professionalized a client relationship different from the traditional joint nurturing relationship of home and school.

Nonetheless, the relationship between the two remained, in general, a productive, supportive one for decades into the present century. In the democratic society emerging, a home stressing ethnicity, family origins, and the significance of the individual within the household and a school emphasizing common learnings relative to a larger, dynamic world together came close to providing the desired educational balance.[4]

Yet we have never quite achieved the desired balance between the home teaching individuality and the school teaching commonality. Some would say that we have not come close. When the home was perceived not to be doing its nurturing, the school was asked to do more. When the school was asked to do more for more people, specifically since the 1950s, the range of values it inevitably embraced tended to broaden. And as a consequence, it was seen as less desirable by many of the kinds of people who had profited most from it in previous decades.

Paralleling these changes, the growth of schools as a daily gathering place for almost all youths helped create a powerful new educational force—the peer group. As the age of entering the work force went up, the length of attendance at school increased, and peer-group socializing took up the additional time that otherwise would have been spent at home with the family. The systematization of schooling created considerable segmenting by age and necessitated socialization into an age group, even as families moved about. A child in grade five in a school in Ohio entered a fifth-grade class on moving to Oregon. Peer-group mores became increasingly powerful. Teachers and even parents began to decline in significance as role models.

During the 1960s and 1970s, the electronic media moved in on this increasingly cohesive young group, catering to its interests, providing it a passing array of larger-than-life role models, creating its tastes, molding its habits of consumption, teaching it strategies to use with parents—educating while selling and entertaining. The teen-oriented television program *Making It* well exemplified how the medium can not only entertain but also introduce and reinforce attitudes toward home, school, and work. In several half-hour programs that I recall, all three were treated with essentially the same slightly patronizing, supercilious banter—wittily, irreverently, and clearly as of secondary importance to the basics in life for the targeted adolescent audience. Those basics, presented with verve to the beat of rock music, were the skills of risqué dialogue, moving in on one of the opposite sex, and dating—skills requisite to "making it" in the teenage culture, all modeled by beautiful young women and handsome young men. The message I received in several fast-moving half-hour segments was that these activities and the values behind them represented all that was important. This message was punctuated by that of the advertisers, joining the television network to mutual advantage. How could dull old work, school, and home compete? At best, presumably, they could provide money, a place of assured associations, and the rudiments of nutrition, all of which, probably in that order of importance, might be useful in making it.

Have the electronic media replaced home and school and started to "mediate" the life experience of the young? Has television become the common school? If so, what is left for the public school? Presumably, this should be what is not readily done by other institutions: fostering that learning which requires deliberate, systematic attention sustained over a period of years. Television does not effectively perform such educating.

Today, we function as individuals within a complex array of educating institutions and agencies. For this educational ecosystem to be healthy, it is essential for each educating organism to perform a needed function somewhat self-consciously, to be aware of the others, and in fact to portray the others empathetically. The television program *Making It* was a caricature of the worst in that medium. But it serves to remind us of what can happen when an institution increasingly becomes educative without also becoming conscious of its new role.

EVOLVING EDUCATIONAL EXPECTATIONS FOR SCHOOLS

Our school system grew phenomenally from soon after the middle of the nineteenth century to beyond the midpoint of the twentieth—in size, complexity, and even confidence. And as the school's role enlarged, the role of the other institutions in the traditional configuration declined and the school stood more and more alone. The beneficent, supporting shadow of home and church reached it less and less. The school's enlarged role resulted, however, not just from its assuming more of what homes and churches once did but also from society's increased educational expectations.

The first colonial schools were expected to take account of a child's need to read sufficiently well to comprehend religious concepts and the laws of the land. The teachings were to be conducted in an atmosphere of piety and respect for authority. Infringements were known about almost immediately in the home. Much of the teaching was tutorial; pupils often were taught individually in a group setting.

Three kinds of learnings proceeded in the classroom. There were the academics, steadily expanding. Simultaneously, there were moral learnings, including the work ethic, ratified by home and church and embedded in the school's custodial role. Then there was the social and personal learning to be derived from expectations for individual performance in the group settings of classrooms. All three remained part and parcel of schooling. The whole was pervaded by concepts of individual opportunity and responsibility. This relatively simple charge remained unchanged for two hundred years—into the second half of the nineteenth century.

Industrialization, accelerating immigration, and urbanization then changed these expectations rapidly. Parents were unable to teach the young many kinds of learning they appeared to require. Schools increasingly taught not just good work habits but also about the world of work;

they even began to prepare deliberately for specific vocations. They were called upon not just to reinforce the values and attitudes of home and community, but to teach the ideas and ideals of political democracy. Many of the concepts to be learned were quite abstract. The subjects of the curriculum expanded. New kinds of textbooks were required for their teaching. The amount of schooling gained by the young steadily surpassed that of their parents. Each generation became more schooled than the previous one.

One development peculiar to the twentieth century was the idea that education in schools should develop individuals for their own sake. Cremin succinctly paraphrases John Dewey's formulation of this intent "as a way of saying that the aim of education is not merely to make citizens, or workers, or fathers, or mothers, but ultimately to make human beings who will live life to the fullest."[5] For more than fifty years, goal statements for American education have testified to the importance of this kind of development of the individual. During the 1960s, in particular, various impressions of the concept appeared on the banners of those seeking free, open, or alternative schools. To the perhaps uniquely American ideas of unlimited geographic and economic frontiers for exploration and development was added the idea of unlimited individual frontiers.

The academic, vocational, and civic goals constituting the mandate to schools at the beginning of this century were to be achieved in the common school. The curriculum was common for all, except that the boys usually studied some form of manual training while the girls pursued courses that later became known as home economics. Only about one student in ten went on to secondary school, and a large proportion of these went on to college. It was assumed that these high school students required college-educated teachers. The state of California set a requirement of five years of higher education for secondary school teachers early in the century.

Well into the twentieth century, teachers in high schools had to concern themselves primarily with providing quality education for only a fraction of the students completing the usually eight-grade common school. But the Great Depression of the '30s removed job opportunities for youth. At the same time there was a growing belief that an eighth-grade education was insufficient to educate our increasingly heterogeneous population for participation in a democratic society. The legal age for leaving school moved up to 16 in most states. The diversity of the student population entering secondary schools began to increase. Pressure to provide educationally for this changing enrollment spurred the development of vocational education in many schools and the creation of trade and technical schools for students not planning for college-level academic studies.

The Supreme Court decision of 1954 ruled out race as a barrier to attending any school. The subsequent movement toward desegregated schools diversified school enrollments dramatically, even though change came slowly in suburban school districts. The issue initially was whether schools can be segregated and at the same time offer equal educational opportunity for all. The issue that had emerged for many people by the 1980s was whether schools can be integrated successfully and simultaneously provide quality education for all—particularly if this means diversifying the student population of local schools through busing.

The charge to public schools emerging from these complex, connected developments is formidable. First, they are to provide free elementary and secondary education in a "common" school embracing grades one through twelve or, in many states, kindergarten through grade twelve. Second, they are to utilize every possible means to assure optimum access to this expanded common school for an increasingly diverse student population. Third, each school is to both provide a reasonably comprehensive program of studies and assure a balance of academic, vocational, social, and personal instruction for each student. Fourth, each school is to provide such special instructional provisions as are needed to assure that individual differences, particularly those stemming from economic and racial or ethnic circumstances, will interfere minimally with access to such a program.[6] Equality and quality are the name of the game. These two concepts will frame dialogue, policy, and practice regarding schooling for years to come.

The charge to provide quality and equality simultaneously is formidable under the best of circumstances. Given present circumstances, we must address seriously the question of whether our system of schooling is up to it. It seems before one challenge can be met, another emerges. Currently, the traditional financial support of schools through local property taxes is crumbling and has been challenged in the courts. The message of the Supreme Court of 1954 has been obfuscated at state and local levels and by the Supreme Court itself. Rapidly changing demographics in most large cities are outrunning any possibility of desegregating schools, short of extensive busing and consolidation of urban and suburban school districts. As we shall see in subsequent chapters, there is not at any level of the system even minimal provision for renewing curricula and reconstructing schools to meet changing needs. With expanding career options for women, the pool of prospective female teachers is declining markedly. And there are millions of children and youths coming along who require unusual stimuli and support for their learning if they are to complete successfully a common school of 12 or 13 years.

Two prerequisites stand out as essential for schools to have even a

modicum of success. First, the central charge to them must be clearly understood at all levels of the system and by those persons schools serve. Second, a
new coalition comparable to the one that developed and sustained the present system of schooling must emerge. But this coalition must support more
than schools. It must embrace new configurations for education in the community that include not only home, school, and church but also business,
industry, television, our new means of information processing and all the rest
of the emerging new technology of communications, and those cultural
resources not yet drawn on for their educational potential. Education is too
important and too all encompassing to be left only to schools.

CLARIFYING AND ARTICULATING THE MANDATE

Unfortunately, the mandate to schools has not been made clear. The Constitution of the United States does not give the federal government responsibility for education and schooling. Further, there is no federal policy with
respect to the nature or quality of educational goals and programs. But federal agencies have entered actively into formulating policies and funding programs in harmony with their interpretation of equality of educational
opportunity. Consequently, even though responsibility and authority must be
assumed at state and local levels, state and local school systems have been
nudged—and shoved—this way and that because of federal laws, interests,
and funds. Indeed, many state departments of education are organized so as
to be effective conduits of these federal interventions in school policy and
practice.[7]
    It is difficult to determine just how much the federal interest in schooling
in recent years has detracted from the authority and especially the clarification
of responsibility for education on the part of states and school districts. At any
rate, the state and district documents we examined in A Study of Schooling
reflect much less than a clear mandate for schools. One would think that the
states would articulate very clearly where they now stand with respect to the
expectations for education and schooling that have emerged out of three hundred years of growth and change. They do not.
    More than three decades ago Ralph W. Tyler, one of our most eminent
educational statesmen, proposed that principals and teachers should have
available to them a set of a dozen or so educational goals to guide program
development and teaching in their schools.[8] These were not to be narrowly and prescriptively stated for separate subjects or grades. Rather,
they were to provide a common set of purposes for everyone to strive

toward. Elementary as well as secondary teachers, teachers of English as well as of social studies, science, and mathematics were to address themselves to how they might help students learn to think rationally, master fundamental processes of learning, develop positive attitudes toward work, and much more. Within this broad framework of common, general goals for education, they might then go on to clarify the particular contribution to be made by their own teaching of specific subjects.

Tyler recommended that such goals should suggest both the kind of behavior students were to develop and the domains of knowledge and human experience likely to be most relevant and vital in their learning. Further reduction and refinement of these goals was to be left to teachers, with whatever local help they could get. There was not to be further specification by states and school districts for fear of stultifying dialogue in the local school and usurping teachers' prerogatives.

We looked to state and district guidelines for the kinds of goals Tyler recommended. State superintendents of public instruction responded generously to our requests for documents in which expectations for schools might be found. We examined materials from all 50 states. Those from the seven states in which we studied schools were analyzed in greater depth, as were comparable documents from our 13 school districts. Because of the comprehensive coverage of states, we can formulate generalizations about this extensive body of material with some confidence. We must be much more constrained in generalizing from the sample of documents from the school districts.

The documents produced by states to guide education in local schools are not markedly different in what they contain and how they present their messages. Usually there is a philosophic preamble extolling the virtues of education. Almost always there is emphasis on the individual and the kinds of traits to be developed through education. The cultivation of cognitive abilities is paramount. States were quite consistent in stating their concern for mastery of basic skills and fundamental learning processes, often even using similar language in expressing their concern. Frequently missing were goals directed specifically to multicultural understanding and appreciation and to aesthetic development. These two goal areas, the first of which would include global understanding, must be thought of as emerging rather than established in states' articulated expectations. In comparing these documents with earlier ones, a major conclusion emerges: state guidelines have remained relatively consistent over the past fifty years in their commitment to the intellectual, social and civic, vocational, and personal development of students, with greatest emphasis on the first.

What is most disappointing in these documents, with some exceptions, is the rather disordered array of topics and form of presentation. There is something for everyone in the materials prepared by states. But because the documents range over such a variety of topics—goals, activities, instructional resources, suggestions for evaluation, and so on—one gets little sense of what is essential and what is secondary. It all reads as though teachers might ignore any or all of it. There is no clear mandate.

Should not all states make a clear commitment to schooling and back it with a statement of the support they intend to give? There is disagreement over the kinds of mandates that are most useful. In an earlier, informal inquiry into state mandates, I found a rather consistent reluctance on the part of state education officials to admit to any precise requirements for local districts or schools. The irony is that most states do intervene very directly through financial specifications, textbook adoptions, testing, specifying topics to be taught (such as drug abuse), and various aspects of instruction—elements which appear to be more controlling and yet perhaps less constructively guiding than a broad, legislated mandate would be. The nature and quantity of bills pertaining to schooling introduced into state legislatures—often several hundred in a year—boggle the mind. It has been common, for example, for the California Legislature to introduce in a single year over 500 bills related to public education and to pass a fifth of these. The California Education Code in effect in 1980 required 42 pages to set forth all the mandates related to bilingual education. It used only two pages to list the subjects to be taught in elementary and secondary classrooms. No doubt the volume and variety of state legislative activity has contributed to obfuscating the central educational charge not only to local school districts but to the states' own departments of education as well.

My major conclusion from perusing most state guides to education in schools is that this entire area is a conceptual swamp. We have assumed since ratifying the Constitution that the states share with local communities responsibility for providing, regulating, and guiding public schools. Nevertheless, there remains enormous ambiguity regarding the states' responsibility for leadership and execution. Are Machiavellian tendencies at work here? There are some advantages, from a politician's point of view, in keeping undefined those areas of policy which can be argued readily and alternatively from many persuasions. Schooling is one of these. The net result is, however, that the schools suffer from lack of a clearly articulated mandate and so are peculiarly susceptible to fads and fashions. These, in turn, become matters for legislative attention, which too often produces just more emergency splints, each holding in place a joint thought to be malfunctioning.

The district guides for local schools we examined were less philosophical and more directly oriented to the classroom than the state documents. Goals were more in number and more specific. Although goals paralleled state emphases, including the dominant commitment to cognition and subject matter, they appeared not to be derived from the state's commitment. Like state guides, district guides covered a smattering of many things— objectives, topics of instruction, suggested materials, hints for teaching, and on occasion, suggestions for time allocation. And like state guides, district directives were not organized, on the whole, in a comprehensive, orderly fashion. Even the goals often were a combination of behaviors desired in students, purposes for teachers, and admonitions to schools (e.g., "Improve articulation of programs between the elementary school, middle school, and high school").

When both states and local districts departed from *general* expectations in the form of total school programs and turned to curriculum and instruction in the subject fields, however, the nature of the documents changed. Three of our seven states, for example, produced subject-oriented guides intended to be helpful not just to local districts but to individual teachers. Indeed, some of these could be used, with very little modification or extra effort, as frameworks for entire courses. However, there were no trends in our data to suggest that teachers in the 18 schools we studied in these three states, more than teachers in the other 20 schools, perceived their curriculum guides as useful. Overall, teachers in our sample viewed state and local curriculum guides as of little or moderate usefulness in guiding their teaching.

The foregoing does not necessarily lead to the conclusion that there is nothing helpful that states and local districts can do to guide school programs and classroom instruction. But my observation is that the documents produced at both levels do not command attention. Commitments and expectations are there, if one digs for them, but lack precision, clarity, and a ring of authority. Neither state nor district officials come out loud and clear as to what our schools are for and how they intend to fulfill these commitments. It is easier or more appealing, presumably, to list expectations and requirements for teachers and students and hold both accountable.

The states must do better. Two of the theses running through this volume are that those working at all levels of the educational system must be accountable and that better schools will come about through multiple actions, no one of them sufficient in itself. "Accountable" is a good word. *Webster's Third* defines it as both "capable of being accounted for" and "subject to giving an account." In the second sense, state legislators and policymakers, including those at the district level, have been diligent in seeking to make others educationally accountable but have been restrained with respect to their own responsibility for articulating priorities based on careful studies of need and sound educational concepts.

If it is a message that educators and others are looking for, let that message be couched in the most compelling terms and have the highest professional appeal. The time has come, past come, for the 50 states to articulate as basic policy a commitment to a broad array of educational goals in the four areas that have emerged in this country over more than three hundred years.

These goals should be revised as needed and endorsed by each successive governor and legislature. Each local district should then reiterate the state's commitment and assume responsibility for assuring every child and youth a sequential, balanced program of academic, civic and social, vocational, and personal studies.

We have been told frequently in recent years that people want to go back to an earlier, simpler time in our history when the 3 Rs were the sole expectation for schools. If the preceding review of our educational history is reasonably correct, there was never such a time. I doubt that this time has now come.

GOALS FOR SCHOOLS

As much of the above suggests, what has been happening in recent years at both state and local district levels is a far cry from what Tyler had in mind. Comprehensive lists of goals are hard to find. Instead, one finds long lists of goals and objectives for the separate subject fields and, recently in many states and districts, lists of proficiencies students are to acquire for high school graduation or grade-to-grade promotion. And in my own visits to many schools, I find little evidence of goals consciously shared by the teachers and precious little dialogue about what their schools are for.

Some people would argue that there is not and cannot be agreement on a set of educational goals for schools. If not, how is it that we seem to know what specific proficiencies we want students to acquire and what tests to use in determining their competence? Clearly, there is inconsistency here. Others say that general goals are too vague and mean different things to different people. Of course; that is their virtue. They provide a common sense of direction but also some room for interpretation and adaptation to meet varying local circumstances.

In the spirit of Tyler's recommendation and the need for states to provide districts and schools with a guiding framework for curriculum planning and teaching, I offer below a set of goals derived from two inquiries conducted as part of A Study of Schooling. The first was the historical review of goals for schooling conducted at the very beginning of the Study. The second was the analysis of state documents just described, conducted toward the end of the Study. Although statements of goals were hard to find, often accompanying philosophical discussions or buried within recommendations for policy or practice, we were able to put together a list representing those most commonly appearing in the documents examined.

The list is presented here to guide school board members, parents, students, and teachers in the needed effort to achieve a common sense of direction for their schools and to build programs of teaching and learning related to these goals. They might very well serve as a beginning point in the dialogue about education and what schools are for that should be underway in this nation. There is no need to begin from scratch, as though we have no goals for schooling. Rather, we should be addressing ourselves to such questions as the significance and meaning of these goals, whether or not they are adequately comprehensive, their implications for educational policy and practice, and whether or not we intend to carry out what they imply for teaching and learning.

GOALS FOR SCHOOLING IN THE U.S.

A. ACADEMIC GOALS

1. Mastery of basic skills and fundamental processes
    1.1 Learn to read, write, and handle basic arithmetical operations.
    1.2 Learn to acquire ideas through reading and listening.
    1.3 Learn to communicate ideas through writing and speaking.
    1.4 Learn to utilize mathematical concepts.
    1.5 Develop the ability to utilize available sources of information.

In our technological civilization, an individual's ability to participate in the activities of society depends on mastery of these skills and processes and ability to utilize them in the varied functions of life. With few exceptions, those who are deficient in them will be severely limited in their ability to function effectively in our society.

2. Intellectual development
    2.1 Develop the ability to think rationally, including problem-solving skills, application of principles of logic, and skill in using different modes of inquiry.
    2.2 Develop the ability to use and evaluate knowledge, i.e., critical and independent thinking that enables one to make judgments and decisions in a wide variety of life roles—citizen, consumer, worker, etc.—as well as in intellectual activities.

    2.3 Accumulate a general fund of knowledge, including information and concepts in mathematics, literature, natural science, and social science.

    2.4 Develop positive attitudes toward intellectual activity, including curiosity and a desire for further learning.

    2.5 Develop an understanding of change in society.

As civilization has become increasingly complex, people have had to rely more heavily on their rational abilities. Also, today's society needs the full intellectual development of each member. This process includes not only the acquisition of a fund of basic knowledge but also the development of basic thinking skills.

B. VOCATIONAL GOALS

    3. Career education–vocational education:

      3.1 Learn how to select an occupation that will be personally satisfying and suitable to one's skills and interests.

      3.2 Learn to make decisions based on an awareness and knowledge of career options.

      3.3 Develop salable skills and specialized knowledge that will prepare one to become economically independent.

      3.4 Develop habits and attitudes, such as pride in good workmanship, that will make one a productive participant in economic life.

      3.5 Develop positive attitudes toward work, including acceptance of the necessity of making a living and an appreciation of the social value and dignity of work.

In our society, people spend a large amount of their time working. Therefore, an individual's personal satisfaction will be significantly related to satisfaction with his or her job. In order to make an intelligent career decision, one needs to know one's own aptitudes and interests as they relate to career possibilities. Next, one must be able to obtain whatever specialized training is necessary to pursue the vocation selected and to develop attitudes that will help one succeed in a field. This goal is important also for the continued growth and development of society.

C. SOCIAL, CIVIC, AND CULTURAL GOALS

    4. Interpersonal understandings

      4.1 Develop a knowledge of opposing value systems and their influence on the individual and society.

      4.2 Develop an understanding of how members of a family function under different family patterns as well as within one's own family.

      4.3 Develop skill in communicating effectively in groups.

4.4 Develop the ability to identify with and advance the goals and concerns of others.

4.5 Learn to form productive and satisfying relations with others based on respect, trust, cooperation, consideration, and caring.

4.6 Develop a concern for humanity and an understanding of international relations.

4.7 Develop an understanding and appreciation of cultures different from one's own.

In our complex, interdependent world, mental health is closely related to the larger social structure—to one's interpersonal relations. No one goes unaffected by the actions of other people. Whoever pursues a mindless, self-indulgent course offends the sensibilities, endangers the health, or even threatens the lives of others. Understanding oneself is not enough—one must transcend self to become aware of and understand other people and their institutions, other nations and their relations, other cultures and civilizations past and present. Schools should help children to understand, appreciate, and value persons belonging to social, cultural, and ethnic groups different from their own and thus to increase affiliation and decrease alienation.

5. Citizenship participation

5.1 Develop historical perspective.

5.2 Develop knowledge of the basic workings of the government.

5.3 Develop a willingness to participate in the political life of the nation and the community.

5.4 Develop a commitment to the values of liberty, government by consent of the governed, representational government, and one's responsibility for the welfare of all.

5.5 Develop an understanding of the interrelationships among complex organizations and agencies in a modern society, and learn to act in accordance with it.

5.6 Exercise the democratic right to dissent in accordance with personal conscience.

5.7 Develop economic and consumer skills necessary for making informed choices that enhance one's quality of life.

5.8 Develop an understanding of the basic interdependence of the biological and physical resources of the environment.

5.9 Develop the ability to act in light of this understanding of interdependence.

More than ever before, humankind is confronted with confusion regarding the nature of man, conflicting value systems, ambiguous ethical, moral, and spiritual beliefs, and questions about his own role in society. There is a major struggle over the issue of whether man is for government or government is for man. The question is not whether there should be some form of government, but what should be its roles, functions, and structures, and what are its controls? Young people now are becoming involved earlier in politics and national life, and minorities are demanding greater access to power in our country. A democracy can survive only by the participation of its members. Schools are expected to generate such participation.

6. Enculturation
   6.1 Develop insight into the values and characteristics, including language, of the civilization of which one is a member.
   6.2 Develop an awareness and understanding of one's cultural heritage and become familiar with the achievements of the past that have inspired and influenced humanity.
   6.3 Develop understanding of the manner in which traditions from the past are operative today and influence the direction and values of society.
   6.4 Understand and adopt the norms, values, and traditions of the groups of which one is a member.
   6.5 Learn how to apply the basic principles and concepts of the fine arts and humanities to the appreciation of the aesthetic contributions of other cultures.

A study of traditions that illuminate our relationship with the past can yield insight into our present society and its values. Moreover, one's sense of belonging to a society is strengthened through an understanding of one's place in its tradition, and its record of human aspiration may suggest direction for one's own life. All these perceptions will contribute to the development of a person's sense of identity.

7. Moral and ethical character
   7.1 Develop the judgment to evaluate events and phenomena as good or evil.
   7.2 Develop a commitment to truth and values.
   7.3 Learn to utilize values in making choices.
   7.4 Develop moral integrity.
   7.5 Develop an understanding of the necessity for moral conduct.

Society, religion, and philosophy provide guideposts for moral conduct. The individual is expected to control personal behavior according to one or several systems of values. Models for some of these values are implicit in other persons' behavior (parents, teachers, state leaders), and other values are manifested in the form of a moral code. Schools are expected to teach the young how to discern the values inherent in human behavior.

D. PERSONAL GOALS

8. Emotional and physical well-being
   8.1 Develop the willingness to receive emotional impressions and to expand one's affective sensitivity.
   8.2 Develop the competence and skills for continuous adjustment and emotional stability, including coping with social change.
   8.3 Develop a knowledge of one's own body and adopt health practices that support and sustain it, including avoiding the consumption of harmful or addictive substances.
   8.4 Learn to use leisure time effectively.
   8.5 Develop physical fitness and recreational skills.
   8.6 Develop the ability to engage in constructive self-criticism.

The emotional stability and the physical fitness of the student are perceived in state goals as necessary conditions for attaining the other objectives. But physical well-being, emotional sensitivity, and realistic acceptance of self and others also are ends in themselves.

9. Creativity and aesthetic expression
   9.1 Develop the ability to deal with problems in original ways.
   9.2 Develop the ability to be tolerant of new ideas.
   9.3 Develop the ability to be flexible and to consider different points of view.
   9.4 Develop the ability to experience and enjoy different forms of creative expression.
   9.5 Develop the ability to evaluate various forms of aesthetic expression.
   9.6 Develop the willingness and ability to communicate through creative work in an active way.
   9.7 Seek to contribute to cultural and social life through one's artistic, vocational, and avocational interests.

The ability to create new and meaningful things and the ability to appreciate the creations of other human beings help one toward personal self-realization and benefit human society. Schools have a role to play in cultivating such appreciation and creativity.

10. Self-realization
   10.1 Learn to search for meaning in one's activities, and develop a philosophy of life.
   10.2 Develop the self-confidence necessary for knowing and confronting one's self.
   10.3 Learn to assess realistically and live with one's limitations and strengths.
   10.4 Recognize that one's self-concept is developed in interaction with other people.
   10.5 Develop skill in making decisions with purpose.
   10.6 Learn to plan and organize the environment in order to realize one's goals.
   10.7 Develop willingness to accept responsibility for one's own decisions and their consequences.
   10.8 Develop skill in selecting some personal, life-long learning goals and the means to attain them.

The ideal of self-realization is based on the idea that there is more than one way of being a human being and that efforts to develop a better self contribute to the development of a better society. Schools which do not produce self-directed citizens have failed both society and the individual. Adults unable to regulate and guide their own conduct are a liability to society and themselves. As a society becomes more complex, more relative, more ambiguous, and less structured, demands upon the individual multiply. We have created a world in which there no longer is a common body of information that everyone must or can learn. The only hope for meeting the demands of the future is the development of people who are capable of assuming responsibility for their own needs. Schools should help every child to prepare for a world of rapid changes and unforeseeable demands in which continuing education throughout adult life should be a normal expectation.

These goals, or their approximations, appeared with sufficient frequency to suggest considerable national agreement, on a state-by-state basis. We are not without goals for schooling. But we are lacking an articulation of them and commitment to them.

CONCLUSIONS AND IMPLICATIONS

What parents, teachers, and students expect of schools is an important but insufficient criterion for determining what our schools should seek to do. To say that schools belong to their communities means little until we define community. It is the responsibility of the state, presumably, to raise expectations for schools beyond only those of local significance so that they encompass national and, indeed, global awareness and understanding.[9]

The picture emerging for me is one of substantial concurrence between what client groups expect of their schools and what official state and district documents say our schools are for but fail to articulate clearly. Not surprisingly, this concurrence is greater among the adults—parents and teachers— than the students. Presumably, state and local directives are written with adults, not children and youths, in mind.

What I find missing in the state and local pronouncements is a definition and clarification of what I call the education gap: "The distance between man's most noble visions of what he might become and present levels of functioning."[10] The clear and widely disseminated articulation of this gap would define educational needs and motivate large numbers of people to participate in change and reform. If this articulation fails to come from the state, from where might we expect to receive it?

My analysis suggests timidity on the part of the several states—a general failure to grasp the opportunity for leadership in a realm where the role of the federal government is ambiguous at best. Perhaps this results from an overdesire, for reasons of political expediency, to reflect the wishes of local constituencies. Whatever the reasons, the unfortunate consequence is the lack of a long-term agenda generated at the state level to guide educational effort at the district level. This lack, in turn, is conducive to galvanic and frequently insensitive responses to perceived but usually not carefully diagnosed problems.

I sense a degree of cynicism in the general absence of a definitive, forthright, idealistic commitment to education and schooling. There is on the part of many legislators with whom I have talked an understandable frustration about how to improve schools. This frustration is accompanied by considerable naivete regarding schooling and a belief that school people (particularly administrators) are inordinately resistant to new ideas—specifically the ideas of these legislators. Also, it is widely believed that teachers have an easy time of it, with a short work day and a long summer vacation. There follows a tendency to overlook the broad focus of reform and the awesome task of hammering out state policy, and to zero in on school and classroom—not to listen and learn, but to change things quickly. As Atkin puts it, government is in the classroom and in all probability will stay there.[11] But so long as those in state capitals concentrate almost exclusively on the accountability of administrators, teachers, and students, the state commitments we need will not be forthcoming. The message from those responsible for formulating state policy will continue to be punitive rather than inspirational. And those who legislate will continue to wonder why their "perfectly rational" solutions to obvious problems produce such bland and unsatisfying results.[12]

Many state officials will disagree with the foregoing. They will send me documents to disprove my generalization. Some of their protests will be well taken. Nonetheless, I am convinced that most, perhaps all, of the states are groping for rather than striding toward a definition of their authority and responsibility. When members of state boards of education tell me that they have no long-term agenda, that what happens from meeting to meeting depends on the items brought by members, I grow uneasy. When local superintendents desiring to effect change grow fearful of state restraints, my uneasiness increases. When textbook publishers tell me how difficult it is to get adoption of books and materials not clearly oriented to "the basics," I worry about what students are doing in the schools. And when I see how much time and energy are going into the development and use of proficiency tests for students—at the highest levels of policy making as well as at all other levels of the system—I wonder whether we have the right priorities.

The more I look at schools and our data from A Study of Schooling, the more convinced I am that we lack educational agendas for the several levels of the system. Further, we have not yet installed the mechanisms by which to get the data necessary to determine these agendas. And the needed data go far beyond the measures of student achievement on which we now largely depend for determining the quality of our schools.

Segments of these agendas emerge from the foregoing. As stated earlier, the first priority for each state is to articulate as basic policy a commitment to the four broad areas of educational goals that have steadily emerged in this nation.

A second priority for each state is to make clear that simply offering curricula in all four goal areas by each school is not sufficient. Each student must secure this balance in the course of his or her total precollegiate education. It becomes the responsibility of each school district, with the assistance of the state (e.g., through county offices or regional service centers), to develop a means of gathering data to continually assess each student's individual program and a means of guiding his or her curricular selections.

Third, states must use representative samples of these data to determine areas of overall imbalance and the kind of effort needed to correct this imbalance. For example, students with stated intentions of becoming physicians or engineers could be prematurely and excessively emphasizing science and mathematics. It might be necessary to enlist deans and professors of university schools of medicine and engineering in seeking to discourage this trend by altering their entrance requirements and selection processes.

Fourth, states should take the lead in emphasizing the limitations of schools' ability to fulfill society's educational functions, let alone do the other things schools are called upon to do. It should not surprise us that parents' concept of educational development for their children embraces all aspects of education. But it no longer is reasonable to assume that schools can or should do all or perhaps even most of the educating. It may be necessary to recognize that the school will continue to be a viable, appreciated institution only if we define its mission more precisely, including only those things educational which the rest of society cannot do well. Parents might accept a leaner role for the local school if they were aware of and had confidence in the educative possibilities of other institutions.

The state should be in the lead in planning and promoting alternative configurations of agencies and institutions for educational purposes. But it often constrains. For example, the formulas used for distributing resources often make it difficult for schools to enrich their programs by using the resources even of other parts of the system, e.g., for secondary schools to draw on the programs of nearby community colleges. But states need to go beyond the eliminating of restraints and deliberately experiment with a variety of collaborative educational delivery systems. They should vigorously and forthrightly endorse communitywide education and be alert in the search for ways to help local communities implement the concept.[13] This will not occur so long as states remain overwhelmingly and disproportionately school-based in their educational commitment.

The states need to gather and be sensitive to data pertaining to the total system of education. What is business now doing, and what might this sector do most effectively in the future? For what segments of the population is school attendance increasing and declining? What are nonattenders doing? What proportion of those registered in schools is not in daily attendance? What is the significance of these data? What is the impact of state policies and actions? Do they facilitate or inhibit local initiative and creativity? Do states gather the right kinds of data? Literally dozens of such questions having profound implications for the welfare of young people and our nation are begging for attention. But questions of this kind usually are not asked, in part because of our preoccupation with what schools are doing and our tendency to equate schooling and education. Offices adjacent to departments of education in state capitals frequently gather, for other purposes, large amounts of data relevant to education and schooling. But sharing information across departmental lines is not characteristic of bureaucracies—more because of unawareness and custom than unwillingness.

Preceding pages suggest the appropriate leadership role of states. The suggested agenda is intended to remind elected and appointed state officials of their leadership role at the very highest level of constitutional authority for education and schooling. They must not be timid in exercising this leadership. Only to develop regulations for holding educators accountable is to sidestep state responsibility.

Ironically, as states have gained power, especially because of their role in financing schools, the use of state prerogatives in seeking to get schools to do what legislators and other officials want them to do has not been markedly successful. In fact, it soon may be perceived as one of our major social failures. And with this increased power, states appear to have become less mindful of their role in setting a tone of challenge and stimulation. Instead, they often have been more punitive than supportive in the legislation enacted. Let the states send a strong message of guidance, challenge, and hope for education and accompany it with clearly articulated expectations for education in schools.

This is not the message that people closest to schools generally have been hearing in recent years. It is, I believe, a message they are ready to hear.

Chapter 3

Beyond Academics

Society in general and parents as a group, I believe, assume that the primary function of schools—whatever the other functions may be—is to teach academics, which they define, correctly if incompletely, as a few subjects and a set of communicating and thinking skills, starting with reading, writing, and arithmetic, that point toward goals of intellectual development. Although it would be a mistake to perceive intellectual goals as being served by instruction in academics only, I believe that these academics are what the parents and teachers in our sample, for instance, had in mind when thinking of intellectual as contrasted with social, vocational, and personal educational goals.

The very fact that the schools have been given much more to do than teach reading, writing, and arithmetic would make it reasonable to assume that parents in particular have more than passing interest in matters in addition to academics. But unfortunately the standard measures we use to determine the quality of schools get at academics almost exclusively—and a relatively narrow array of them at that. We try to use achievement test scores as a kind of thermometer indicative of good or bad school performance as scores rise or fall. We assume that public support is tied almost exclusively to readings from this thermometer. Likewise, interventions to improve schools are tied to the readings. If these are incomplete criteria of satisfaction, however, the diagnosis and subsequent remedies also will be incomplete.

The theme I pursue here is twofold. First, as we have already seen, teachers, students, and parents in the schools we studied want more than is implied by the words "intellectual development." They want some reasonably balanced attention to intellectual, social, vocational, and per-

61

sonal emphases in the school's program of studies. Second, even all of these would not be enough. The school is to be also, in the eyes of parents and students, a nurturing, caring place. The parents we encountered want their children to be seen as individuals—persons and learners—and to be safe. Their children want to be known as persons as well as students. Many teachers, too, would like there to be greater school attention to students' personal attributes such as those once implied by the word "deportment" on report cards, though, as we shall see more clearly later, they have a difficult time moving beyond the pedagogical baggage of academics to achieve such emphases.

I approach this theme with several questions. First, to what extent are the educational goals preferred perceived to be the goals emphasized in the schools of our sample? Related to this is the question of whether close congruence of preferences and perceived school emphases is reflected in satisfaction with the school, e.g., as expressed in the grade given to it. Next, what would be the net effect on school programs if the goals perceived to be emphasized were brought more in line with the goals preferred? Finally, what more precisely are the concerns that clients of the schools and those who work in them have in areas going beyond the educational functions of their schools?

Individuals surveyed in A Study of Schooling were drawn from selected subpublics of the larger public having vested interests in schools. Nonetheless the concerns and interests they expressed transcend academics sufficiently to raise in one's mind other, far-reaching questions about the mission and conduct of schools.

TOWARD ALTERNATIVE EDUCATIONAL EMPHASES

It will be recalled from Chapter 2 that nearly 50% of the teachers and approximately 50% of the parents—when asked to choose just one most preferred area of educational goals—selected intellectual goals. Preferences of the remainder were scattered across the other three goal areas. Students' preferences were more evenly spread among the four areas.

When asked to select the goal most emphasized at their own school, however, the percentage choosing intellectual was higher for all three sources of data—except parents at the high school level, where there was a slight drop. Data for goals perceived by all three groups to be most emphasized appear in Table 3-1.

Particularly interesting is the degree to which students and teachers perceived emphasis on intellectual goals to be dominant at their schools. Also, both teachers and parents saw the intellectual to loom especially large

TABLE 3-1

Perceptions of Goal Area Most Emphasized at Their Schools (in percent)

	Social	Intellectual	Personal	Vocational	N
STUDENTS					
High Schools	10.2	61.6	13.2	14.9	6784
Jr. High/Middle Schools	11.7	64.1	11.2	13.1	4733
Elementary Schools	11.1	61.4	11.9	15.5	1564
TEACHERS					
High Schools	18.0	52.2	6.8	23.0	651
Jr. High/Middle Schools	16.3	64.4	8.7	10.7	393
Elementary Schools	12.2	78.5	6.1	3.2	279
PARENTS					
High Schools	19.0	43.1	10.2	27.8	3858
Jr. High/Middle Schools	19.5	56.3	11.2	13.0	2994
Elementary Schools	13.6	68.9	11.4	6.0	625

at the elementary level. It would be difficult to conclude from these data that clients of the schools in our sample perceived academics to have been abandoned.

Figure 3-1 combines the data from two of our tables. Table 2-3 in Chapter 2 presented the goal preferences of students, teachers, and parents. Table 3-1, just discussed, presents data on the goal area perceived by these groups to be most emphasized at their schools. The bar graphs of Figure 3-1 reveal differences—sometimes small, sometimes quite large—between these preferences and perceived emphases for each group and for each goal area. The net effect of the difference is to suggest the direction of the shift that would occur if school emphases were to conform more closely to expressed preferences.

Some interesting observations emerge out of an examination of Figure 3-1. One effect of an effort by schools to eliminate the difference between preferred and perceived goals would be that personal goals would receive more attention at all three levels of schooling. Note especially how much additional attention would go to the personal goals if one were to respond to the differences between teachers' responses to the questions on goals. Second, intellectual goals would continue to be emphasized, but not so much. The net effect of following students' responses would be to reduce the dominance of what most students at all three levels perceived to be a substantial intellectual emphasis. The resulting changes would be least at

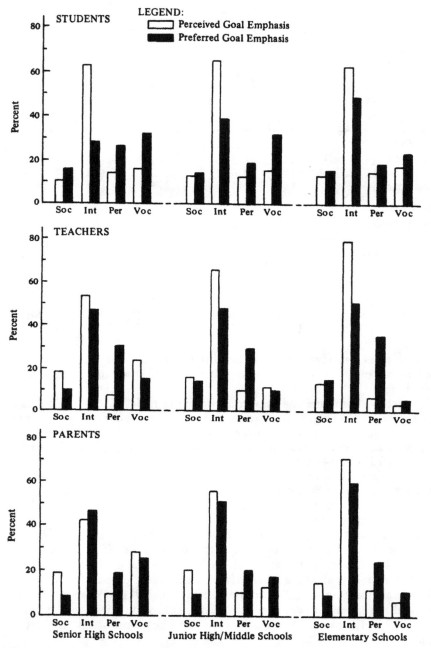

Figure 3-1. Comparison Between Perceived and Preferred Goal Emphasis (Social, Intellectual, Personal, and Vocational) for Students, Teachers, and Parents.

TABLE 3-2

Congruence Between Goals Preferred and Goals Perceived to Be Emphasized
(in percent)

	High Schools	*Middle Schools*	*Elementary Schools*
TEACHERS	35.35	45.92	52.90
PARENTS	41.15	47.50	59.28
STUDENTS	42.13	49.87	53.55

the elementary level. The net change in intellectual emphasis would be relatively small if schools acted upon parents' responses.

We were able to compare all individuals' goal preferences with their perceptions of the goals most emphasized at their school. In many instances, the goals most preferred and the goals perceived to be most emphasized were the same. The percentages of agreement are shown in Table 3-2. It will be seen that congruence between preferred and perceived goals was consistently higher at the elementary level. I conclude from this that in most instances it would be easier, politically, to arrive at goal agreements for elementary than for secondary schools.

Not surprisingly, congruence between preferred and perceived goals was highly related to individuals' satisfaction with the programs offered by their schools. Across all schools, parents, teachers, and students who perceived the goal area emphasized by their school to be the same as the one they preferred graded their schools significantly higher than those who did not. At the secondary level, those students who preferred the goals they saw emphasized expressed greater satisfaction with the education they felt their school provided them; parents who saw goal congruence were more satisfied with what their children were learning; and in all three groups those whose perceptions and preferences converged agreed more strongly that their school was providing learnings that would be useful in later life than did those who preferred a goal area other than the one they believed to be emphasized.

An implication of the foregoing is that each of the kinds of goals for schools that have emerged is supported by some substantial segment of this society, so that for schools to satisfy diverse populations they must provide broadly, not narrowly, in their programs. Suggested, too, is the importance of developing a climate wherein participants perceive that the goals they see as important are shared by the school and given emphasis in programs. But broad programs and agreement about schooling goals alone will not be enough to satisfy the clients of schools. School personnel must remember that the child in school may be seen primarily as one of a group but that parents' interests in the group are secondary to their concern for their own child's welfare. The grade parents gave their school was also positively associated with the perception that "my child receives a lot of individual attention" and satisfaction with the school's counseling service, and was negatively associated with such perceptions as "many teachers at this school don't care about students" and "average students don't get enough attention."

Data of the kind presented and discussed here help enlighten public policy regarding the setting of goals for schools, but they are of little use in seeking to understand and improve specific schools. Individual schools do not necessarily follow general trends suggested by averaged data. Some examples of schools selected from those we studied will help make this point.

Palisades Elementary is in a relatively affluent section of a large city. The district administrators who planned it perceived high community expectations. They chose a strong first principal with a deep commitment to understanding children, and worked closely with her in selecting the teachers. Palisades came to have the aura of a school concerned both with learning and with the personal needs of children. Later, when black children were bused in, the expectation of the central administrators was that they would receive at Palisades a good education and a positive reception.

Most parents, teachers, and children gave the school a high grade—its average grade was just a shade under A. Large percentages among all three groups viewed their school as thinking that intellectual, social, and personal goals were very important. Overall, they perceived the dominant emphasis to be intellectual, and, given their preferences, would keep it that way. Congruence between preferred and perceived emphasis was a whopping 82% for teachers, 74% for parents (highest for both groups among all 13 elementary schools) and 58% for students (third highest). Asked what one goal area they preferred, parents and teachers gave their choices almost exclusively to intellectual or personal, with intellectual leading by a wide margin. Students too chose intellectual most often, but there was a wider dispersion of preferences.

These parents expressed high satisfaction with the curriculum, as did the majority of those surveyed. The satisfaction level was lower for the arts and physical education than for reading and mathematics. I would guess that Palisades Elementary was affected less than many schools by the back-to-basics movement of the 1970s, except that the movement perhaps reinforced efforts to ensure appropriate instruction in mathematics and reading for the minority children bused in each day as well as for those living nearby. But the ethos of Palisades called for this, with or without agitation in the larger society. There appeared to be no significant differences in satisfaction levels between black and white parents surveyed.

In an interesting way, Palisades reflects a rather pervasive contemporary expectation for elementary schools. The school's job is an intellectual one. It should be concerned, however, about the personal development of children. With a solid academic program in place, increased attention should be given to the personal side—physical education for the body and the arts for creativity. These clients want it all too, but in an ordered sequence of priorities.

Parallel data on Fairfield High, which are very different, suggest the concerns that arise in the minds of teachers and parents when the intellectual appears to be underemphasized. Fairfield is a middle-to-low-income community lying just outside a major urban center and blending many suburban and rural characteristics. Its student population is white and Hispanic. In contrast to the situation at Palisades, the principal at Fairfield High experienced conflicts with both district administrators and a faction of teachers that limited the amount of influence and control he had in carrying out his job.

The high school was graded C, on the average, by parents, teachers, and students surveyed. All three groups shared an awareness of the school's pronounced vocational orientation. This orientation is relatively common to high schools serving this type of community. At Fairfield, however, 42% of the faculty, in contrast to an average of 22% for the other 12 senior highs, were classified as vocational education teachers!

Many of the teachers in this school would pull the orientation more toward the intellectual and the personal. Whereas 81% perceived vocational goals to be the ones most emphasized and only 12% the intellectual, when asked what should be, the response was nearly 26% intellectual, 26% vocational, and 40% personal (in contrast to 0% viewing the personal as most emphasized). Clearly, these teachers saw the school emphasis as being very much out of balance.

Congruence between goal areas preferred and perceived to be most emphasized was low for all three groups—the lowest of all schools for parents (29%), the second lowest for teachers (21%), and close to the lowest for students (39%). The net effect of responding to parental preference, then, would be to place more emphasis on the intellectual and less on the vocational. The responses of Mexican-American parents were in this direction but not as marked. Students, interestingly, perceived a predominantly intellectual emphasis and would give more attention to the other three goals, particularly the vocational. As we will see later, students in our secondary schools generally expressed greater liking for vocational than for any academic subjects. This preference was pronounced at Fairfield High.

If I were a board member, the superintendent, the principal, a teacher, a student, or a citizen/taxpayer in Fairfield, I would be most interested in these data. The predominance of C grades would be an initial warning. The lack of congruence between parents', teachers', and students' goal preferences on one hand, and their perceptions on the other, would be another. And I certainly would wonder about a school where so many students graded their school low, saw little congruence between goals they preferred and goals they perceived to be emphasized, and would like to see more emphasis on a function that already was perceived by many parents and teachers as receiving too much emphasis. Coming in as a new superintendent, I would find the data to be both valuable and disturbing—and would know that I had a tough job ahead of me. I would want to include students in any deliberations regarding new directions. Clearly, they would provide a useful perspective.

A hypothesis emerging from our larger body of data over all schools is that when they perceive intellectual goals to be dominant at their schools, parents, teachers, and students generally would place greater stress on other goals, except that high school parents would still slightly increase the intellectual emphasis. Our data show that at most schools (Fairfield is a notable exception) all three data sources do perceive their school to think that the intellectual is the most important educational function—above the social, personal, and vocational—and it appears there is a general readiness to shift attention to one or more of the other three areas. But, elaborating the hypothesis, *this seems to be the case only when one of them is not seen as dominating or coming to dominate over the intellectual.* Students would go farther than parents and teachers in giving the intellectual less attention than they perceived to be the case for their schools. Senior high school students appear to be a group apart. They view the intellectual goals to be most stressed; their preferences would eliminate this dominance.

Palisades Elementary nicely fits the hypothesis. Secure in the school's intellectual orientation, parents and teachers seemed ready to give personal goals more stress. And in fact a lot of redirection could occur before the dominant position of intellectual goals would be threatened. For instance, this school probably would rise to the challenge of becoming a demonstration center in the arts for all children, without losing its bearings.

Fairfield High comes under the qualifier attached to the hypothesis. At the time we studied the school, many teachers and a substantial number of parents viewed intellectual goals as receiving low emphasis—that is, when data on this area are compared with data relative to other goals and to the other high schools. The parents wanted to give more attention to the intellectual. Not surprisingly, the teachers, disproportionately vocational, were not prepared to go as far, but they too clearly desired a greater intellectual emphasis. All three groups wanted greater attention to the personal—a preference that calls for further exploration and additional data. Students fit the general pattern for their group and would redress their perception of intellectual goals being in the dominant position. A federal grant to enrich the vocational educational offerings is not what Fairfield High appears to need, and yet the superintendent told me another was pending. One can image similar schools across the country being the recipients of well-intentioned federal and state funds that reinforced apparent excesses and missed needs crying for attention.

On the receiving end, responsible use of funds provided requires data not now available to those to be held accountable for them—much, much more of the kinds of data provided so far in this discussion. These data would suggest the dialogue, diagnosis, and subsequent planning in which district administrators, parents, students, the school principal, and teachers might engage in seeking to assure attention to the academic, social, vocational, and personal education of the young.

BEYOND THE EDUCATIONAL FUNCTION

Just as a school can get into trouble for appearing to neglect the intellectual side of its educational function—the academics—it can get into difficulties for appearing to neglect the nurturing side of its custodial function. I am confident that parents have much more in mind than "discipline" when they begin to worry about school attention to the personal behavior of their children.

Unfortunately, when schools in our society appear to be slipping away from some norm with respect to either academics or control, the differences and subtleties in the perceptions of what is happening tend to be generalized into a cry for basics or discipline, as the case may be. Nobody in the schools is perceived to care about academic or personal standards anymore. Fortunately, parents' concerns with their own school transcend such generalizations and focus on specifics. These specifics include programmatic emphases and go beyond them to encompass their children's personal experiences with school and teachers. There do seem to be norms in these areas beyond which concerns are triggered. These norms move about; they are relative. But with most of them, there probably are zones they can move into that should convey danger signals to the alert educator.

Our data suggest a concern for the behavior and misbehavior of children and youths—on the part of young and old alike. And this concern appears to be pervasive rather than exclusively focused on the hours spent in school. Teachers' failure to control and discipline students does not emerge from the data as a major problem at most schools. As said earlier, one thing expected by parents is the safe care of their children and another is that they be seen as individuals. Paralleling parental concerns, students appear to expect attention to them as individuals—particularly as they struggle with the tasks and demands of school.

As I see it, this expected nurturing is, in part, residue from the once implicit assumption that the school should be during its hours of responsibility what good homes are expected to be the rest of the time. And perhaps the school, now more comprehensive than the church in enrolling the young, is expected or at least permitted to do more of what home and church once did together in the spiritual realm. At any rate, in the schools of our sample, from a low of 66% (in one of the high schools) to a high of 100% (in two elementary schools), parents we surveyed agreed rather strongly that "it would be all right with me to allow prayers at this school."

Polls have suggested an increasing realization on the part of some parents that they are not doing too well in nurturing the total development of their children, particularly in the adolescent years. This situation lends an urgency to the demand on schools that they do more. The schools' lack of attention to individuals (e.g., in large classes), as much as a perceived lack of attention to academics, fuels disaffection with traditional schools and continuing interest in alternative, parent-controlled schools.

We know that parents have become increasingly concerned about their children's safety in and on the way to school, just as teachers in many schools have become concerned with their own personal safety. We asked parents to express their level of agreement or disagreement with the statement: "My child is sometimes afraid of being beat up at school." Mild or strong agreement was expressed by 23%, 36%, and 24% of the parents surveyed at the three successive levels of schooling. Not surprisingly, there was a trend toward consistency among the three schools studied in a given community. At Euclid, for example, the percentages of parents stating mild to strong agreement with the statement were relatively low—13%, 12%, and 6% at the three successive levels of schooling. At Newport, the corresponding figures were high—41%, 53%, and 34%. At Fairfield, they were 35%, 42%, and 34%. The overall averages show greatest concern with the safety problem among parents of junior high students.

These data alone reveal the importance of probing more deeply into sources of parents' satisfaction or dissatisfaction with their school. If improvement is to occur, it is essential that there first be a careful appraisal to determine where to begin. Parents' overall ratings of their schools are not sufficient. Other data, also needing careful appraisal, show clearly that, with progression through school and the onset of puberty, students' interests change a great deal. In an earlier study of the first four years of schooling, my colleagues and I concluded that boys and girls in classrooms were involved in and engaged with learning activities to a degree that surprised us, since many of these activities appeared to us to be routine in nature.[1] Data from A Study of Schooling suggest that students in the junior and senior high school years are very much preoccupied with matters having little to do with the intellectual function of schools. What are the implications of this for efforts to improve schools?

What I endeavor to do on succeeding pages is to ferret out of all our different kinds of data the things pertaining to life in school which surround or accompany the school's performance of its educational mission and which may be of at least equal significance to parents, teachers, and students. Similarities and differences in the perceptions of these groups lead me to the conclusion that those associated with schools are not united in and consumed with a common, pervasive, educational mission. Indeed for many high school youths in particular, academics may be every bit as peripheral as the half-hour of *Making It* described in Chapter 2 portrayed the basic institutions of home, work, and school to be. And school as a place may be ill-suited to the mediating role it is expected by many of us to play in the lives of adolescents.

PERCEPTIONS OF SCHOOL PROBLEMS

We asked our teachers, parents, and students (except students at the elementary level) to rate the seriousness of a list of problems for their own schools. Their responses were coded on a three-point scale: 1 for "not a problem"; 2 for "minor problem"; and 3 for "major problem." Their rankings of more than very minor problems are presented in Tables 3-3, 3-4, and 3-5.

We found both similarities and differences among the groups in the responses. The number and intensity of problems perceived by both teachers and parents are least at the elementary level and less in the eyes of parents than teachers. Student misbehavior is high on the list for all groups and levels, and at the same time, teachers' lack of discipline is consistently less a concern. At both secondary levels, lack of student interest, lack of parent interest, and drug/alcohol use are all at relatively

TABLE 3-3

Rank Ordering of Problems with a Mean Score of 1.5 or More: High Schools

Mean Scores	Teachers	Parents	Students
2.3	Lack of student interest Lack of parent interest Student misbehavior	Drug/alcohol use Student misbehavior	
2.2	Drug/alcohol use		
2.1	Size of school/classes	Lack of parent interest	Student misbehavior Drug/alcohol use
2.0	Inadequate resources, e.g., personnel, buildings, equipment, and materials	Lack of student interest Teachers' failure to discipline	Organization
1.9	Student language problems Poor teachers/teaching	Poor teachers/teaching	Lack of student interest
1.8	Administration Organization	Lack of staff interest Size of school/classes Poor curriculum	Inadequate resources Poor teachers/teaching
1.7	Lack of staff interest Graduation standards Poor curriculum Rules and regulations interfere with education	Inadequate resources, e.g., personnel, buildings, equipment, and materials Rules and regulations interfere with education	Rules and regulations Poor curriculum Size of school/classes
1.6		Administration	Teachers' failure to discipline Administration
1.5		Prejudice/racial conflict	Prejudice/racial conflict

high levels of intensity. Lack of student and parent interest are problems of some significance at the elementary levels, as perceived by parents and teachers.

What we do not see ranked high in intensity by any group are problems of curriculum, administration, rules and regulations, graduation standards, and the like. Even the problem of poor teachers and teaching is seen, at worst, as a problem of mild intensity and is near the bottom of the list for elementary schools. From other questions we learned that over 80% of the parents surveyed were, on the whole, very satisfied with what their schools were providing in the various subject fields. Parental satisfaction with English, mathematics, social studies, and science declined from elementary to secondary levels of schooling. The reverse occurred

TABLE 3-4

Rank Ordering of Problems with a Mean Score of 1.5 or More: Junior
High/Middle Schools

Mean Scores	Teachers	Parents	Students
2.4	Student misbehavior		
2.3		Student misbehavior	Student misbehavior
2.2	Lack of student interest Lack of parent interest		
2.1	Size of school/classes	Drug/alcohol use	
2.0		Lack of parent interest	Lack of student interest
1.9	Drug/alcohol use	Lack of student interest Teachers' failure to discipline	Drug/alcohol use
1.8	Teachers' failure to discipline Students' language problems Inadequate resources, e.g., personnel, buildings, equipment, and materials	Poor teachers/teaching	Organization Inadequate resources, e.g., personnel, buildings, equipment, and materials
1.7		Size of school/class Lack of staff interest Rules and regulations Poor curriculum Inadequate resources, e.g., personnel, buildings, equipment, and materials	Rules and regulations Poor curriculum Prejudice/racial conflict Size of school/classes Poor teachers/teaching Teachers' failure to discipline
1.6	Poor teachers/teaching Graduation standards Rules and regulations Organization Lack of staff interest Poor curriculum		
1.5	Administration Staff relations	Administration Prejudice/racial conflict	Administration Busing for integration

for the arts, foreign languages, and vocational education. Poor curriculum
came out well down the list when parents, teachers, and students were asked
to choose their school's one biggest problem.

One aspect in particular of these data I find to be very thought provok-
ing. All of the groups rank "student misbehavior" high as a problem. Yet,
students place "teachers' failure to discipline" relatively low; indeed, in

TABLE 3-5

Rank Ordering of Problems with a Mean Score of 1.5 or More: Elementary Schools

Mean Scores	Teachers	Parents
2.1	Student misbehavior	
2.0	Size of school/classes	
	Lack of parent interest	
1.9		Student misbehavior
		Lack of parent interest
1.8	Lack of student interest	
1.7	Inadequate resources, e.g., personnel, buildings, equipment, and materials	Size of school/classes
	Student language	
1.6	Organization	Inadequate resources, e.g., personnel, buildings, equipment and materials
	Rules and regulations	Teachers' failure to discipline
	Teachers' discipline	Rules and regulations
		Lack of student interest
		Poor teachers/teaching
1.5	Staff relations	Lack of staff interest
	Administration	Poor curriculum
	Lack of staff interest	
	Poor curriculum	
	Poor teachers/teaching	

answering another question, the majority viewed teachers' discipline as "about right." It appears that all three groups tend to view the misbehavior of the young as pervasive, existing as a condition apart from efforts, including teachers', to control it. This hypothesis is strengthened by the data on students' concern for their own safety. The demand by segments of the public and many school board members that teachers exert stronger discipline appears, then, not to go to the roots of what must be viewed as a communitywide responsibility. The school alone cannot handle problems once shared and controlled by home, church, and school working hand-in-hand. If these earlier collaborations cannot be rebuilt, then perhaps we need new configurations of agencies and institutions sensitive to changing circumstances.

At both junior and senior high school levels, there is an interesting slant to the data once we look beyond student misbehavior and drugs/alcohol as problems on which there is rather close agreement among teachers, parents, and students. Teachers, noticeably more than the other two groups, pointed to problems such as class size and lack of student interest that impinge directly on their teaching. They identified less often such problems as poor teaching and lack of staff interest in relations between school and community that pertain closely to their own roles. This slant is accentuated when we look at their responses to the question, "What is this school's one biggest problem?" The most frequent choice was "lack of student interest." Our parents' top problems were student misbehavior and drugs and alcohol, reflecting deep concern about the behavior of their children. But other data point to parents' concern also about whether their children were nurtured as individuals in the school setting. Earlier we saw evidences of parents' concern over the safety of their children at school. Beyond safety, slightly more than half of junior and senior high parents disagreed with the statement, "My child receives a lot of individual attention from his/her teacher." Approximately the same number of parents agreed with the statement, "Average students don't get enough attention at this school."

Our data further suggest mounting concern on the part of parents over the attention given their children as these students advanced upward through the grades. Students, much like parents, reflected a greater concern than teachers over nonacademic problems. At schools where major problems were seen by students, misbehavior and drug and alcohol use were nearly always those identified. In seeking to improve our schools, we may discover that some gains in standardized achievement test scores will not satisfy the full array of interests that parents and students have in their schools, interests that reach to the whole of life and extend well beyond academics.

POWERFUL PEER GROUP PREOCCUPATIONS

When a study such as this one concludes that junior and senior high school youths are excessively preoccupied with physical appearance, popularity in the peer group, and games and athletics, the response sometimes is, "What's new about that?" Indeed, nothing. A quarter of a century ago C. Wayne Gordon documented the dominance of high school social life.[2] Other studies have confirmed and extended his findings.[3] The only surprise in our data, perhaps, is the apparent intensity of these nonacademic interests. Taken cumulatively, research findings regarding the youth culture lead one to wonder why we have taken so little practical account of them in schools.

Our findings in this area, placed side by side with other data on the youth culture, changes taking place in the larger society, and the general failure of schools to adapt to these changes, raise this query to a level of urgency. In 1961, James B. Conant, throughout his book comparing conditions in urban slums and suburbs, referred to the inequities, including those in schools, as "social dynamite."[4] Similar potential for explosion exists, I believe, in the present disjuncture between elements of the youth culture on one hand and the orientation of teachers and conduct of school on the other.

We appear to have reached a plateau and be headed downward in regard to the percentage of school-age youths enrolled in school.[5] Large numbers of young people who are enrolled roam the streets of our cities each day.[6] The average age of these dropped throughout the 1970s. Perhaps it is understandable that many teachers, prepared and oriented as they are, perceive the problems of their schools to be different from how their students perceive them. And perhaps if teachers did perceive quite differently than they do, the job of school keeping would become completely intolerable.

The data fueling my concerns are not cut from a single piece of cloth, but must be woven together to be of a piece. When this is done, they display incongruities arising over time, out of our general failure to rethink and redirect the uses of an institution. This pattern begins to emerge when some of our data from students are placed next to some perceptions of parents and teachers. The data on students pertain to perceptions of themselves and others, what is best about their school, and its most serious problems.

Students' personal views of how they were doing in school dropped off with upward progression through the grades. Whereas about 73% of those in our elementary school sample viewed themselves as "satisfied with how well I am doing in school," the percentage dropped to 66% at the junior high level and to only 57% at the senior high; on the other hand, students' self-concepts in relation to peers remained steady through the elementary years and then climbed somewhat during the secondary grades. Correspondingly, parents' generally high rating of the usefulness of their child's learnings at school declined from elementary to secondary schools. Likewise, the percentage of parents perceiving students not caring about learning increased with progression upward in level of schooling.

We asked junior and senior high school students to select from six classifications the students they perceived to be the most popular. Clearly, "smart students" is not the award-winning category in the popularity sweepstakes. Averaging by schools, we found it to be chosen by only 14% of junior high and 7% of senior high students. At the junior high level, popularity resided primarily with "good-looking students" (37%, averaged across schools) and "athletes" (23%). The combination of these two categories accounted for a whopping 79% of the choices at the senior high school level, averaged across schools. Athletics are a strikingly central part of both junior and senior high life. On the average, 51% of the students in junior and senior high school actively participated in sports teams, whether in or out of physical education classes, with this percentage going to nearly 80% for one junior high and 90% for one senior high.

Clearly, then, "school work" is not all of school for adolescents. Many junior and senior high school students may feel less than good about themselves academically and yet take great satisfaction from their athletic prowess and relations with peers. Large numbers may think it quite sufficient to be considered good-looking, popular, and one of the gang. Perhaps the educational aspect of school life simply declines in significance for large numbers of students as they feel less able to succeed in what the school sees as most important, and as they move into adolescence.

We asked junior and senior high school students to choose from among 12 possibilities in answering the question, "What is the *one* best thing about this school?" At both levels, "my friends" was the top choice, averaging 37% in the junior highs and 34% in the senior highs. "Sports activities" ranked second (15% and 12%, respectively), and "good student attitudes"—another question designed to tap into peer relations—placed third (10% and 12%). These percentages add up to an overwhelming 62% average in the junior highs and 58% at the senior level. And, at both levels, "nothing" (8% at both) outranked "classes I'm taking" (7% at both), and "teachers" (5% and 3%, respectively)!

Should these findings surprise us? After all, we are a very sports-oriented nation. For example, football, basketball, and baseball occupy a large part of television-viewing time. Athletes are among our top-paid performers. Few dancers, musicians, poets, or painters make a comparable living at their art. Teaching is one of the few vocations available to students who are good at English or history, and neither pays well nor frequently gets "glamour" treatment in popular magazines or on television.

The response to "good student attitudes"—meaning here friendly and cooperative students—compared to the response to "classes I'm taking," reveals the pervasiveness of social relationships in the workplace called school. School is a significant part of life into which one brings a full array of what matters; it is not simply preparation for something yet to come.

Instead of physical appearance, peer relations, and games and sports simply being part of the larger culture one carries into school, perhaps to be used there by teachers as motivating devices for learning, these interests appear to prevail. One wonders how much the academic side intrudes into the personal and social—at least for some students. It may be socially difficult in some schools to be smart unless one is regarded also as good-looking and athletic. And on the other hand, it may be too painful not to feel smart unless the academic side of school is seen as relatively unimportant.

In talks to parents and teachers Bruno Bettelheim has questioned the prospects of students taking school studies seriously once puberty begins. He recommends separation of the sexes for schooling purposes over the adolescent years. I am pleased to note that several studies of schools segregated along sex lines are being contemplated at this time. It would be interesting to see whether responses to the questions reported here are markedly different for youths segregated into single-sex schools.

Perhaps the interests appearing to dominate the lives of young people attending coeducational junior and senior high schools are so reinforced in their out-of-school lives that they would continue to dominate even in all-girl or all-boy schools. How, then, do we turn more attention to academic learning? Give special prizes and awards to top students? Provide more scholarly role models by hiring principals and teachers holding Ph.D. degrees? Might we want to go so far as to cut out interscholastic athletics? Few, if any, school boards currently are considering such possibilities.

We know that a significant percentage of young people ultimately proceed into college and that some of these find academic pursuits to be compelling. About 35% of those we surveyed said that they expected to go to a four-year college. But these expectations varied markedly from school to school—from 19% to 47% among the junior high schools and from 15% to 46% for the senior highs. My guess is that there is a certain contagion in these expectations. A student having doubts about going on probably would have these doubts more reinforced at one school than at another. Also, it appears that plans to attend or not to attend college can affect students' perceptions of how they are regarded within the school ambience. Many students agreed with the statement, "If you don't want to go to college, this school doesn't think you're very important." A student with this perception not planning to attend college might feel somewhat less than approved of in the school environment.

We see young teenagers entering into a period of considerable personal, social, and physical turbulence while constrained daily in a setting where the dominant expectations are academic or intellectual and require considerable passivity. No doubt, many are preoccupied with personal interests and problems in a secondary school often carrying from the past the prime role of preparing for college. In our sample of schools from less than half to less than a fifth of the student population had college attendance as a goal. Nonetheless, students know that planning to go to college and, no doubt, demonstrating the ability to do so are regarded as important in the school setting. Simultaneously, they are surrounded almost inescapably by a youth culture exhorting other values which, in turn, are mediated and reinforced by television, various commercial interests, and even major elements of the adult culture. And personal support for learning in the secondary school environment appears to be less than it was in the elementary school. Given all this, it is not surprising that the junior and senior high students we studied were not fired up over their teachers, the classes they were taking, or the curriculum. One must see an area of life as highly relevant to one's interests, goals, and satisfactions to be sufficiently aroused to identify with it.

The domains of dominant interest also, of course, include the areas of one's dominant problems. Earlier in this chapter we saw how students rated the seriousness of a list of school problems. Their two most frequently chosen responses to a second question regarding these problems underscored the emphases in their answers to the first. "The one biggest problem *at this school*" was perceived by a majority of junior high students to be either student misbehavior (with 40% choosing it) or drug/alcohol use (16%). Drug/alcohol use or student misbehavior was named most often as the one biggest problem by senior high students as well. Each accounted for 18% of their first choices at the senior high level.

Parents' perceptions of the school's one biggest problem closely paralleled students'. Drug/alcohol use (18% and 24%) and student misbehavior (17% and 12%) were the two top choices at junior and senior high levels, respectively. The problem of poor teachers and teaching was chosen more by parents than by students, but curriculum, as stated earlier, and administrative and organizational matters were not selected by many parents or students as the one biggest problem. Also, "teachers don't discipline students" was not a high first choice of parents (6% and 5% at junior and senior high levels, respectively), just as it was not with students (less than 3% at both levels). As groups, then, students and parents were not very far apart in their views of the school's problems.

The disjuncture between the youth culture and the school, to which I referred earlier, arises out of the juxtaposition of these data and data pertaining to teachers. Teachers, when forced to choose just one problem, did not respond as students did. Only approximately 3% of teachers at the junior high level and 4% at the senior high chose drugs/alcohol as the school's biggest problem. There was one exception: about 22% of the junior high teachers made "student misbehavior" their choice. As with their students, it was the teachers' top choice. This is not surprising. We have ample evidence that the restless exuberance of young teenagers is real and that it conditions the views and behaviors of their teachers. In general, however, most of the teachers in our sample perceived as most serious matters surrounding and affecting their teaching but appearing to be beyond their control—lack of student interest (emphatically the problem chosen as most serious by senior high teachers and a close second for the junior high group), school too large and classes overcrowded, lack of parent interest, administration, inadequate instructional resources. Most of the areas coming out low—under 5%—in the selections of the biggest problem were those relating to their own roles and performance as teachers. At both secondary levels—but more at the junior high—student misbehavior contributed to frustration in seeking to carry out their perceived teaching role.

Data here and surfacing from time to time in subsequent chapters suggest to me a picture of rather well-intentioned teachers going about their business somewhat detached from and not quite connecting with the "other lives" of their students. What their students saw as primary concerns in their daily lives, teachers viewed as dissonance in conducting school and classroom business but seemed not quite to connect with them as problems in the lives of their students. And our students, meanwhile, appeared not to be quite connecting with the learnings they presumably were there to pursue. Somewhere, I suspect, down in the elementary school, probably in the fifth and sixth grades, a subtle shift occurs. The curriculum—subjects, topics, textbooks, workbooks, and the rest—comes between teacher and student. Young humans come to be viewed only as students, valued primarily for their academic aptitude and industry rather than as individual persons preoccupied with the physical, social, and personal needs unique to their circumstances and stage in life. The school setting was not conceived to meet these needs, nor is it conducted with meeting these needs in mind. But students become variously adept at working them out here nonetheless.

To single out students as "lazy" or teachers as "indifferent" or administrators as "uncaring" is to make a simplistic analysis of a complex problem. There are no villains or groups of villains here. Of course some administrators are more insensitive than others, and there are substantial differences among teachers in the purpose, skill, and energy they put into a day's work. The same could be said for hospital administrators, social workers, and police officers. We would like to think that school principals and teachers are models of moral rectitude, love of children, and commitment to their calling (not just a job), but it is a long time since we took such criteria seriously in recruitment—if we ever did. This may be just one more myth about schooling that provides one more easy answer as to what is wrong with it.

We now have an educational system of great weight and complexity. Its needs and expectations, as well as those of adult and student workers and clients, and society's articulated and unarticulated goals are woven into the fabric of the local school. They are so interwoven that it is virtually impossible to sort out which are which. The realization of this complexity is a first step away from myths and simplistic notions of roads to improvement such as more discipline by teachers and proficiency tests for grade-to-grade promotion.

THE SCHOOL'S AMBIENCE

On preceding pages I have been presenting data on groups of individuals averaged across schools. The reader may be protesting that he or she knows schools quite unlike those implicitly described by these data. My intent has been to ferret out some of the reality with which all schools must deal and with which they variously deal well or poorly. The data on all 25 of our junior and senior high schools point sufficiently to a potentially volatile disjuncture between the youth culture and the daily conduct of these schools to suggest that no school can afford to ignore careful self-analysis in this critical area.

Schools will be found to differ in the seriousness of this disjuncture, as can be seen by examining two schools more closely. I shall do so not to contrast them, however, so much as to explore a thesis. This thesis, briefly stated, is that alike as schools may be in many ways, each school has an ambience (or culture) of its own and, further, that its ambience may suggest to the careful observer useful approaches to making it a better school.

There is not a great difference between Rosemont Junior High and Bradford Senior High regarding students' perceptions of the basis of popularity or the thing they like best about their school, but academic matters rate a somewhat higher place at Rosemont. Students at both schools identified drugs/alcohol and student misbehavior as the biggest problems; curricular and instructional problems are farther down the list. And yet there is a distinct difference in ambience between the two schools, the heart of which is that at Rosemont academics have not yet lost out and at Bradford they have. At Bradford, even though the students appear to put their social and personal lives ahead of anything academic, the schools' educational emphases have been so obscured that students also appear to feel cheated. While seeming to the casual observer to be infuriatingly the cause of academic disarray at this school, students are, rather, only part of the condition. Based on their responses to specific items, I suspect students themselves are resentful over their inability to score high enough on tests to go to college. Perhaps the student body itself—not a remote legislative bill—is the best source of motivation for a commitment to renewal.

At this point in my writing about secondary schools, I chanced to see on television a provocative little film made by some students at Van Nuys High School in California.* One of the students is shown conducting and reflecting out loud on interviews with fellow students regarding their career plans. She is curious as to why a group of minority students voluntarily travel by bus each day to Van Nuys from downtown Los Angeles. The answer she receives from these young people is that nobody cares about learning at the high school they normally would attend. Whatever their discomfort with the long trip and their normal misgivings about attending a remote school, they tell her, they see at Van Nuys some hope of being supported and reinforced in their desire to learn and go on to college. There is no hope for this at their local school, they say.

From this illustration of the point that school environments variously support a desire for academic learning we should not conclude, however, that hope lies only in predominantly white, relatively prosperous, suburban schools like Van Nuys High. As already suggested, Rosemont Junior High is not hopeless in this regard, and it is a very different school from Van Nuys High. The Rosemont community lies within the boundaries of a rather large city. The families of the three schools we studied there stand out as having the lowest incomes in our sample—49%, 63%, and 39% of high-, middle-, and elementary-school parents, respectively, reporting incomes of less than $5,000 annually. The student population was 95% or more Mexican-American at all three levels. Parents there had the least formal education of any group in our sample.

Students' academic self-concept scores at Rosemont Junior High were above the average for our group of schools. Interestingly, their views of themselves academically were higher than their self-concepts in other areas. Among the students perceived as most popular were "smart students," the category chosen by 38% of the students we surveyed, the largest percentage choosing this category in any of our schools. "Athletes" and "good-looking students" were the choices of 20% and 18%, respectively. Although these students were much like students in the other schools in their liking of sports activities—17% chose this category as "the one best thing they liked about school," as against 15% over all junior highs—they were at the bottom, compared with students at other

---

*Interestingly, this was one of a few high schools that were singled out by the news media in 1957 (following Sputnik) as examples of how American education had gone soft. Van Nuys was selected to show, derisively, boys cooking in a home economics class.

schools, in choosing "my friends." It will be recalled that this was the top category at the junior high level, with an average of 37% choosing it; 22% chose it at Rosemont. And Rosemont students were at the top of the list in choosing "the classes I'm taking" (11%) and "principal and other administrative personnel" (8%), and second from the top for "fair rules and regulations" (11%) and "teachers" (7%). Only 5% chose "nothing," the lowest percentage for any junior high school.

Of course, beyond the point that the orientation of students at Rosemont appears somewhat more academic than at some of the other schools, this comparative picture is relatively unimportant. For 11% and 7% of the students to choose "the classes I'm taking" and "teachers," respectively, as the one best thing will put no great joy in the heart of one who believes that classes and teachers are what school is all about. After all, "my friends" and "sports activities" together accounted for nearly 40% of the first choices. And "drug and alcohol use" was frequently chosen as the school's biggest problem.

Nonetheless, the intellectual and academic side of life appears to be finding a place in the total school experience of these young people. Other data, not all cited here, not only support my perception of this ambience but also suggest a substantial level of satisfaction with Rosemont Junior High School on the part of students, parents, and teachers. On the average, they gave it a grade of B. No other junior high school got as high marks from students; only one other was graded higher by parents. The congruence between the function individuals perceived to be most emphasized and the function most preferred was relatively high: 61% for teachers (highest for all schools), 50% for parents (fifth highest), and 58% for students (third highest). This agreement is a strong indicator of high satisfaction on the part of all three groups.

All three groups perceived intellectual goals to have a high place in the school's emphases. Teachers would keep them central; apparently they see schooling as a way up for low-income, low-education families. The parents and students value the academic orientation, too, but both groups also favor attention to vocational goals. For them, the importance of earning a living is beginning to loom large. For many students, who are almost entirely from a minority group not accustomed to advanced educational opportunity, education beyond high school probably appears to be unlikely.

To sum up, then, the physical, social, and personal drives of early adolescence are all here at Rosemont, ever present in and no doubt deeply affecting the learning process, but somehow the academic side has a place. One does not despair over Rosemont. With this school it seems reasonable to talk about the usual improvements—staff development programs for administrators and teachers, some curricular revisions, more and better teaching materials, and the like. Perhaps many of the most important educational tasks lie outside the school, in the community, where we find the roots of the kind of problems young people carry into their daily lives at school.

I feel quite differently about Bradford Senior High School. The community, which lies just outside of a large city, itself contains both a residential area and a rather heavily industrialized area where many of the parents work. The population of all three schools studied is as predominantly white as that at our Rosemont schools is Mexican-American. Compared with those at other schools in our sample, the parents at Bradford ranked relatively high in income, given their modest educational attainments. A fairly fortunate environment, a strikingly troubled high school!

Students at Bradford High were near the bottom of the comparison group of high schoolers in their responses to the statement, "I am satisfied with how well I am doing at school." Students perceived athletes (51% chose this category), good-looking students (31%), and gang members (10%) to be the most popular students, the three categories adding up to 92% of the first choices! "Friends" was the category most frequently chosen as the one best thing, and the 46% choosing this response constituted the second highest percentage doing so among our schools. And drug and alcohol use was a major concern of students. While students at Bradford High shared with those in the other schools the same basic interests, they did so to excess, to the virtual exclusion of everything academic.

Bradford High School ranked low on all the major indicators we used to determine the satisfaction level of teachers, parents, and students. All three groups graded the school C, on the average. A large number (in fact, the second highest for all of the schools studied, both elementary and secondary) perceived there to be many problems of high intensity. The lowest percentage of teachers (16%) and parents (29%), and the second lowest percentage of students (35%) perceived congruence between the educational function they preferred and the one they saw to be emphasized. Both teachers and parents would increase the intellectual and decrease the social emphases.

Even though students at Bradford, as at the other high schools, perceived the intellectual function to be most emphasized, they and their parents were concerned about the quality of education being provided. More than at any other school, both groups disagreed with the statement that "most of the teachers at this school are doing a good job" and agreed that "too many students are allowed to graduate without knowing very much." And more than at any other school, students disagreed with the statement that "this school gives students a good education" (parents were not asked this question). Among our schools, students at Bradford ranked highest in agreement that "many students at this school don't care about learning" and lowest in agreement that "we feel we have to get good grades all the time."

The data available to us suggest Bradford teachers' awareness of low academic standards and low status of intellectual concerns. They appeared concerned about the heavy dominance of social interests over academic matters. "Lack of student interest" was chosen by many teachers as the school's worst problem. Bradford is an exceptional school in that its teachers perceived standards for graduation and academic requirements, poor curriculum, administration, teachers' failure to discipline students, and even poor teaching to be problems of considerable intensity.

The impression I had on visiting Bradford was of a school just barely maintaining the level of control required for survival. I sensed that implicit trade-offs had occurred in which the students did not go quite to the brink in their behavior, and teachers pulled back from making academic demands. The active social process that went on openly among the students in the hallways and other nonclassroom settings continued not quite covertly in classrooms. Soon after my arrival, police broke up an altercation in the hallway which a vice principal told me involved both school and nonschool youths, spilling over from gang activity in the community. Later, I observed that students often took a long time to settle into their work following class-to-class shifts.

I was told that one vice principal was responsible exclusively for student affairs and that the other was in charge of curricular and instructional matters. I asked the latter about his satisfactions and frustrations and how he spent his time. He said that the potential for program development had attracted him away from a vice principalship elsewhere but that he found himself spending most of his time on student control. He admitted wryly that his physical characteristics—he was tall and athletic-looking—and popularity with young people, not his interest in the curriculum, probably were why he had been selected in the first place.

Putting together a total program is the responsibility of the local school—partly by default and partly because there appears to be no viable alternative. But when and how is this to be done? Teachers perceive themselves as called upon to teach and have time for little else. At Bradford, unlike many high schools, there is a person whose exclusive role is curriculum development, but other matters get in the way. The picture I got of the principal, from observation and hearsay, was of a man removed somewhat from the daily problems of students, by virtue of having two vice principals to deal with them, but nonetheless heavily involved with the paperwork and other administrative details associated with staff, students, and community. My appointment with him was delayed by a crisis related to the courts, which I gathered not to be at all unusual.

The daily behavior of large numbers of students at Bradford High was such that one might have concluded that they were the problems from which stemmed all other ills. But many students perceived their school as not providing them with a good education and seemed to see themselves as cheated, as victims of circumstances they would like to see changed. It might be more useful to view Bradford as a sick school, rather than as a delinquent or recalcitrant one. With such a view of a school in stress, we might tend not to demand more accountability from the teachers, but instead to seek ways of helping those in and close to the school set their own agenda for improvement. Obviously, a great deal of support and direct assistance would be required. In general, perhaps by seeing a problem school as an organism or ecosystem with its several parts in varying states of poor health, we would come closer than we do now to correctly diagnosing and remedying its ailments.

Bradford is not a community of crowded, virtually uninhabitable dwellings or of poverty, unemployment, and hard-core crime. The predominantly white parents are largely blue collar workers who enjoyed median incomes of approximately $20,000 per year at the time we collected the data (late 1970s). Although few had attended college, nearly 48% had graduated from high school. Eighty-nine percent classified themselves as moderate (55%) or conservative (34%) in political belief. These are parents we would expect to want a relatively traditional, basic education for their children. Whose fault is it that their children, many of whom apparently wanted something better themselves, were not getting it?

The state in which Bradford is located has been advanced in setting standards of competency and proficiency for both teachers and students. The district appointed a vice principal to give special attention to curriculum and instruction. The teachers were concerned about students' lack of interest in educational matters and their preoccupation with social, peer-group interests. Both parents and teachers viewed poor teaching as a rather serious problem. Clearly, the problems at Bradford are everybody's problem. They transcend the school to include the community. And they transcend the Bradford community to include state and nation.

Writing in *Newsweek* (August 18, 1980), a young black, Deairich Hunter, draws our attention forcefully to the most positive elements in the peer group and the possibilities for recruiting these elements in seeking to address the array of problems to be resolved. Here is the heart of young Hunter's important message:

I guess the best way to help the hard rocks is to help the ducks. If the hard rocks see the good guys making it, maybe they will change. If they see the ducks, the ones who try, succeed, it might bring them around. The ducks are really the only ones who might be able to change the situation.

The problem with most ducks is that after years of effort they develop a negative attitude, too. If they succeed, they know they've got it made. Each one can say he did it by himself and for himself. No one helped him and he owes nobody anything, so he says, "Let the hard rocks and the junkies stay where they are"—the old every-man-for-himself routine.

What the ducks must be made to realize is that it was this same attitude that made the hard rocks so hard. . . . The hard rocks want revenge because they don't have any hope of changing their situation. Their teachers don't offer it, their parents have lost theirs, and their grandparents died with a heartful of hope but nothing to show for it.

Maybe the only people left with hope are the only people who can make a difference—teens like me. We, the ducks, must learn to care. As a 15-year-old, I'm not sure I can handle all that. Just growing up seems hard enough.

Hunter wrote out of experience in a community of poverty and much greater disarray than prevailed at Bradford. The opportunity at Bradford is that the ducks probably are still in the majority. But there are hard rocks too, and unfortunately they only too often become role models for ducks who see themselves as not making it. With the peer group the prime mediator of life and a sense of being cheated educationally at school—a sense we get also in the responses of their parents—the ducks are ready to listen to messages unlikely to put them firmly on a productive road. A surge of unemployment for their parents—always a possibility in an area dominated by just a few interrelated industries, as Bradford is—could be a highly destructive force.

Clearly, Bradford High is not a place likely to be turned around by some tinkering with the curriculum, another vice principal, more instructional materials, and a more intensive staff development program—although such matters should not be ignored. Bradford needs comprehensive stocktaking and joint effort by administrators, teachers, students, and parents. They need to share the kinds of data we gathered, to become aware of the extent to which they see problems in common, and to eschew the naming of villains—if there is any collective enemy, they are all part of it. And governmental leadership, private support, police officers, churches, service agencies, and the like must play their active part as well.

Unfortunately, even this kind of collaboration too often becomes a bureaucratic monster, with different individuals and groups squabbling over turf in the name of "our children." In some communities, the do-good groups don't even bother anymore to invoke the welfare of children. They just get quickly into adult games.

The impression I get from some of our data is that the young people who are caught in the net of circumstances offer much promise for cutting through it. They are not too immature, too inexperienced, or too innocent for the tasks involved. Many of them have conceived babies, many drink alcohol and take drugs, some hold jobs, all will be eligible to vote soon. Our young people get caught up in the values, problems, and vices of adulthood at an early age. They are delayed unduly in assuming authority and responsibility commensurate with this early orientation to adult society. Why not call on them now to join with adults in tackling the problems of youth in and out of schools—the problems which, clearly, adults are failing to solve by themselves? I think our youth is ready to respond.

SOME CONCLUDING THOUGHTS

Although the educational expectations for schools are broad and comprehensive, they dare not neglect the academic and intellectual aspects of these expectations. Even students, who generally view the intellectual function to be uppermost in its emphasis, become concerned when they perceive their school to be sloppy and ineffectual in providing them with an education. Where those connected with a school perceive it to be at a given point in time, regarding its orientation to the several components of an educational function is likely to be a critical factor in the reception of any perceived reordering of priorities.

This observation introduces a perspective on change and improvement rarely dealt with in the literature. Proposed innovations are not necessarily threatening in themselves. But they may become threatening if they portend major displacement of what currently is deemed important—especially if what is deemed important already is perceived to be undervalued or in a state of erosion. Consequently, a proposed change taken in stride at one school may induce deep concern in another.

In addition, those who seek to change schools must avoid the assumption that adjusting the balance of attention to the several domains of the school's instructional program is all that need concern them. Our data suggest that the caring way in which the school conducts this educational function is a major factor in determining client satisfaction paralleling in importance perceived attention to intellectual matters in the instructional program. In the view of the parents we surveyed, at least, "Teach my child with tender loving care" might well be posted on the bulletin board side by side with "Knowledge sets the human spirit free."

At first there appears to be a puzzling contradiction between two sets of data on teachers regarding the personal side of educating their students. On one hand, more than any other group, they would markedly emphasize personal goals in the school program. On the other, they seem a step removed from the personal problems and interests of students. But we must remember that the personal educational domain and the personal nurturing of individuals struggling with problems of growing up are not the same thing, even though we might wish to relate them closely. The data suggest that teachers want to teach and that the role they have in mind is a far cry from nurturing students in the personal and social nonacademic aspects of their lives in school.

For teachers there is a reasonably clear job of teaching to be done, and there is nothing in our data to suggest that students have a basic disagreement with teachers on this central, educative task. Simultaneously, particularly at the junior and senior high school levels, students are preoccupied with many other aspects of their personal and social lives. Into these other aspects teachers in general seem not to intrude very far. Indeed, they appear either to be only mildly aware of the problems and preoccupations of students or to push them aside as not their primary concern. They may perceive the kind of involvement that would ensue as inappropriate or as potentially interfering with their central task.

There is a difference, however, between playing the role of surrogate parent in dealing with drug and alcohol problems, for example, and evidencing concern and support for the problems students encounter in their daily studies. If teachers' awareness, diagnosis, and remediation of individual students' difficulties go hand in hand with progress in learning—as other research suggests they do—then this kind of personal attention appears to be part and parcel of the instructional function. It is part of what is required for humanizing knowledge so that large numbers of young people of varied abilities may acquire it.

It is apparent from our data, however, that creating in schools, particularly senior high schools, compelling environments for learning is exceedingly difficult. Peer-group interests other than academic were near the surface in all schools; in a few they had virtually taken over. Some parents looked to the school for the discipline and guidance of their offspring they felt unable to provide. Without the household as supporting partner, the school is seriously handicapped in both its educative and its custodial functions.

Educators, accustomed to an ever-expanding educational system, often have difficulty, however, in even toying with the thought that at least part of this system may be failing to meet the needs of its clients—that the school may not be making the adjustments necessary if *all* young people are to gain access to knowledge and not merely attend classes. Uninterested students, not the institution, are the cause of malaise, they appear to be saying. Those who can and want to learn must be protected from those who don't. One answer is to divide these groups into separate tracks. Another is to give the nonacademically oriented students a heavy dose of vocational education, effectively separating them from the academically oriented. Some people would remove from school at an unspecified age those who appear unable or unwilling to take advantage of it.[7] Others would lower the legal leaving age to 14 and encourage the early departure of those deemed most troublesome or recalcitrant.[8]

There is a monstrous irony in all of these proposals. An educated citizenry, we have maintained, is requisite to a flourishing democracy. The rhetoric of Thomas Jefferson, Hubert Humphrey, and countless graduation speakers rings in our ears. And yet we frequently propose curtailing the general education of some of these future citizens because we consider them incapable of acquiring it. But perhaps the educational system is not yet adjusted to the tasks of providing the education our rhetoric continues to promise.

The above proposals focus on the student and not the institution in determining both the diagnosis and the remedy. This is to a degree understandable, given characteristics of the youth culture portrayed earlier. But we cannot afford to ignore the hypothesis that at least at the secondary level, the institution of schooling, as presently conceived and operated, is not capable of providing large numbers of our young people with the education they and this democracy require now and in the future.

Some of the large numbers of high school students who go on to four-year colleges concentrate on academic subjects; some go on to enter professional schools. Whatever the vicissitudes and lassitudes of the early years, school is and was "for them." In many instances, their continuance and performance in school could have been predicted, often when they were still in the primary grades.[9] Some scholars argue that most of the efforts to improve schools benefit such able students first, even when the changes were intended primarily for the benefit of those considered disadvantaged in learning. This is so, they say, because the traditional assumptions and principles guiding the conduct of schooling, to which some youngsters adapt better than others, almost always are intensified by the improvement efforts. Even when the target is those who are not adapting, students adapting well before the changes were introduced continue to adapt well and in effect build on their headstart.

Schools are not necessarily ideal places even for those students appearing to be most successful. My concerns are magnified, however, on turning to that larger group of students who do not grow up in academically oriented households, or who experience cumulative difficulties with school-based learning, or who are not turned on by academics, or who simply cannot or do not wish to defer employment. The academic program is much less "for them." There is evidence to suggest payoff for these students from intervention programs that comprehensively include a more careful sequencing of the curriculum, more frequent use of motivational devices, alternative approaches to learning, and that whole array of assumptions and techniques subsumed under the concept of mastery learning[10]—growth at least comparable to that experienced by more gifted learners experiencing less drastic interventions. However, such programs tend to be provided more often in the primary years, and the later falling off of nurturing support in learning relentlessly contributes to the school's inability to involve and hold students in academic pursuits. Participation in the youth culture may be no less for the more adaptive learners, but they are more able to succeed in the requirements for graduation while devoting energy to their personal and social lives.

In this whole social context, will the common school survive? In 2040 will adults born in 1980 find much common ground in discussing their school experiences? The realness of the question is underscored by the growing number of people desiring private schools for their children, not after paying taxes for public schools, but with vouchers provided out of the "private pursuit of the public purse."[11] Some seek such schools out of genuine concern for the curriculum, instruction, and size of classes and a belief that the existing educational system will not get better. Others seek such alternatives because they do not want their children associating with and being exposed to the values of an increasingly diverse student body. Others, having already enjoyed the benefits of free, public education, simply ignore or are unaware of the fact that the need for such remains great.

In the next two chapters I address the relation of the common school to this need from the perspective of access to knowledge for all students. Chapter 4 deals with what goes on in classrooms—with the means of making knowledge accessible. Chapter 5 deals primarily with the distribution of knowledge and teaching across the entire student population. Both chapters raise questions of equity in regard to access to knowledge.

I do in fact doubt that schooling, as presently conceived and conducted, is capable of providing large segments of young people with the education they and this democracy require, and I include among these young people a significant proportion of those now "making it." There are many things that can be done to improve all elements of schooling—a more compelling curriculum, professional education for teachers sufficient to separate them from ways they were taught, use of settings beyond the schoolhouse for some kinds of learning, communitywide attack on the most dangerous aspects of the youth culture, and so on. Done in concert, these could make a significant difference. But far-reaching restructuring of our schools and indeed our system of education probably is required for us to come even close to the educational ideals we so regularly espouse for this nation and all its people. The restructuring involves maximization of the educational resources of entire communities, with schools playing a much more precisely defined role than is now the case. I deal with both short- and long-term agendas in concluding chapters.

Chapter 4

Inside Classrooms

I stood in the open doorway of a classroom in one of the junior high schools we studied. It was one of a series of classes located side by side down a long hallway. The day was a warm one and the doors of three of the classrooms were open. Inside each, the teacher sat at a desk, watching the class or reading. The students sat at table-type desks arranged in rows. Most were writing, a few were stretching, and the remainder were looking contemplatively or blankly into space. In one of two other rooms with closed doors, the students were watching a film. It appeared to be on the cause and prevention of soil erosion. In the other, the teacher was putting an algebraic equation on the chalkboard and explaining its components to the class. In visits to several other academic classes that day, I witnessed no marked variations on these pedagogical procedures and student activities. Driving from the building, my companion commented, "I saw hardly any teaching all day." Was he right? Was there hardly any teaching—learning either? These questions are not easily answered.

Writers and speakers reinforce our own memories of classrooms like these with references to cells, each with thirty or so students, desks or tables in rows, a teacher at the front, and pupils looking toward the teacher. A snapshot of such a scene would freeze in time a teacher lecturing and questioning and students in various poses of listening and responding. A black-and-white print, rather than one in color, conveys the image.

We know that today classes sometimes deviate—we may find a hundred or more students in a carpeted open space, not necessarily rectangular, taking up the area of four conventional box-shaped classrooms; a conversation pit for group discussions and role playing; teachers and aides with clusters of students around tables or interest centers; bright colors; various pieces of instructional equipment in use. Back in the 1950s and 1960s there were books and articles extolling these living rooms for learning or damning them as palaces built at taxpayers' expense. One might readily have concluded then that the egg-crate school of memory and the teaching and learning associated with it were of the past.

Our findings suggest, however, that it would be premature to indulge in nostalgic contemplation of familiar things now replaced. The classrooms we observed were more like than unlike those in the old images so many of us share. Usually we saw desks or tables arranged in rows, oriented toward the teacher at the front of the room. Instructional amenities such as library corners, occasionally present in elementary classrooms, were rarely observed in secondary classes. The homelike chairs and rugs sometimes seen in primary classes rapidly became rare with upward progression through the grades.

Most adults recall from their own early experiences an elementary school day relatively unbroken by interruptions. The first block of time was given over, usually, to mathematics and language arts and continued from the opening bell to recess, a time interval of one and one-half to two hours. After a 15- to 20-minute recess, instruction in the basic academic subjects continued until a break for lunch. The afternoon block of time usually was given over to instruction in social studies, science (once or twice a week), and the arts and a recess-type break for physical education, often in the form of an organized sport. One teacher taught the whole. If a specialist taught at all, it usually was in music.

The basic pattern remains, but today's elementary school classroom does tend to be a more complicated place, especially in the cities. In our sample, at the lower elementary level (the first three grades) a full-time teacher, often assisted by a half-time aide, worked with an average of just over 27 children. Class size increased to an average of almost 29 children in the upper elementary years (grades four through six), and aides were much less frequently present. In many instances, the elementary school class did not stay together as a unit throughout the entire day. Small clusters of children left for periods of time to secure special instruction elsewhere in the building, especially in the lower grades and in urban schools. More often than most of us remember from our school days, there were specialized teachers in such subjects as arts (especially music), physical education, and remedial reading. When most of us went to school, one counted the number of classroom teachers in order to determine the size of the teaching staff. But in the schools we studied, there usually were additional professionals and aides playing an instructional role.

At the junior and senior high levels, the school day appeared to be very much as we remember it—broken into chunks of time, each chunk for a different subject, a different classroom. In our sample, these chunks averaged 55 minutes each at the junior high level and only a minute or two less at the senior high level.

What does go on—what teaching, what learning—in all these classrooms?

This chapter looks at that teaching directly and that learning indirectly, once again using data from A Study of Schooling to derive patterns and variations likely to enhance our understanding and enlighten approaches designed to produce improvement. The central focus is on teachers' pedagogical practices—grouping, individualizing, using time, making decisions, exercising control, etc.—and how they structure the classroom. It is difficult to get at the dynamics of what goes on in classrooms. And looking at what students do doesn't tell us all that they learn. But looking at classroom phenomena through the eyes of teachers, students, and observers tells us something about the relationships between teachers and students and among students.

Beyond description lie questions of interpretation and of valuing and judging. What shall we make of any patterns emerging? We lack in educational research the full body of knowledge needed for judging teaching. But we do have some useful knowledge about the kind of teaching most likely to produce student achievement and satisfaction in learning. Some of this is drawn upon in what follows. Also, we have some norms about what we believe is good for human beings in any setting. Some of these, too, are used in seeking to interpret the data.

TIME FOR LEARNING

Time Available

Perhaps because school occupied a large part of the daylight hours during childhood and adolescence, it looms large in our memories of growing up. Actually, however, most of us attended for less than half the days of the year. Today, average attendance across the nation is 180 out of 365 days. On these school days, children and youths attend from approximately 8:30 in the morning to 3:00 in the afternoon—slightly more than one-quarter of a 24-hour day. Again this is an average time. Practice varies somewhat.

From the parking area of one of the sites I visited, I could view at a glance where 12 consecutive years of schooling transpired. A six-year-old child entering the elementary school building on my right in 1980, if he or she remained in the community, would move over to the junior high school in front of me six years later and graduate from the high school on my left in 1992 at the age of 18. The junior high school principal who was my host for the day assured me that this did happen for a number of young people. They spent 180 days a year in these buildings and on this turf for 12 years. This is a brief time in human history but a long span of time in the life of a person. On the other hand, assuming a year of public or private kindergarten (about 18% of five-year-olds are not enrolled) and six hours of elementary schooling for 180 days of six successive years, a twelve-year-old will have spent about 7,020 hours in school, and this is only about 6.5% of total hours lived. By the age of fifteen, these figures are 10,260 hours in school and about 7.7% of hours lived. By the age of eighteen and graduation from high school, the percentage has climbed to only 8.5. Most of this time is spent in classrooms. Using data on watching television, I estimate that, for the average American child, the hours spent before a television set from birth to age eighteen range between 9% and 10% of total hours lived.

But long or short, the time children and youths spend in school appears to affect rather directly the amount of their learning as measured by tests. Increasing annual attendance from 175 to 185 days appears to enhance achievement.[1] This suggests that states should not reduce the length of the school year even for good purposes such as teachers' in-service education. Days for teachers' self-improvement should be added, not taken out of the instructional year. Instruction sustained year after year enhances achievement and this achievement is affected positively when studies in school are accompanied by related homework.[2] It seems apparent that simply the amount of time spent on a given subject is a powerful factor in learning. The total influence of school time appears to be greater for subjects such as mathematics, science, and literature, not usually taught out of school, than for subjects such as reading and language, the learning of which is heavily affected by the home environment.[3]

To the degree that teachers were reasonably accurate in reporting the amount of time devoted each week to the several subjects of the curriculum, it would appear that students varied markedly in their opportunity to learn simply because of the classrooms in which they were enrolled. There were wide elementary school-to-school differences in the figures on time distribution reported by teachers—from under 19 hours each week in one school to over 27 in another, and the secondary schools, too, varied in the number of minutes available for teaching and learning each day.

TABLE 4-1

Observed Percentages of FMI Frames Spent on Instruction, Routines,
Controlling Behavior, and Social Activity, Reported by Level of
Schooling (in percent, averaged across schools)

	Instruction	*Routines*	*Behavior Control*	*Social Activity*
Early elementary	73.22	18.99	5.52	2.27
Upper elementary	72.89	20.71	4.39	2.01
Junior high	77.42	18.02	2.88	1.68
Senior high	76.12	20.39	1.29	2.20

How Time Is Used

The availability of time, then, sets the basic framework for learning. After that,
how this time is used becomes a significant factor in students' accomplishment.
Many studies have shown the significance to achievement of time well spent.[4]

We sought to find out something about the extent to which teachers spent
their time on instruction, as compared with time spent on controlling students' behavior and managing classroom routines, and time for students'
socializing. We questioned students, we questioned teachers, and we observed
in classrooms, computing the time spent in each kind of activity during intervals of five minutes each, interspersed with other kinds of observation over
hours of class time, and then converting the total times into percentages of
total class time.

Teachers' estimates and our observations of time distribution come out
quite similarly at all levels of schools in our sample. Teachers reported spending about 70% of class time on instruction at both elementary and junior
high levels, about 73% at the senior high level. Our observational data produced slightly higher figures—73%, 77%, and 76%, respectively. These data
are broken down more precisely in Table 4-1 and Fig. 4-1 to show the cate-
gorization of time distribution in the five-minute intervals (FMI), averaged for
schools at each level and for type of activity.

The figure of about 70% of class time spent on instruction is similar to that
uncovered by other researchers. If a classroom should be comparatively low in
total hours of classroom time each day and low in time spent on instruction,
the net time on learning would be particularly low. Or the reverse combination could occur. Consequently, students could be experiencing quite different opportunities to learn.

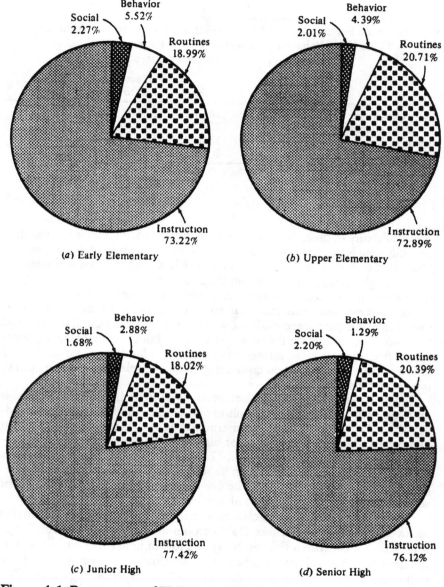

Figure 4-1. Percentages of FMI Frames Categorized According to Instruction, Behavior, Routines, and Social.

At the secondary school level, we were able to compare the several subjects for time spent on instruction, using school averages to compile percentages. For the most part, foreign languages come out at the top. Our conclusion from observations was that approximately 85% of class time in this field at the junior high level and 83% at the senior high level was spent on instruction. Our low was approximately 73%—for vocational education in the junior highs and English in the senior highs. In the responses of students and teachers, physical education tended to be at the bottom overall for time on instruction; foreign languages were at the top overall.

School-to-school differences for our sample were substantial. Using just our observational data, the range in percentages of time spent in instruction was from 63 to 79, 64 to 84, 69 to 87, and 68 to 84 at early elementary, upper elementary, junior high, and senior high levels, respectively. And, of course, these school averages include variation among classes within each of the schools. If time on instruction is as important in learning as many researchers think it is, there appear to be substantial differences in the opportunity to learn in the schools at each of these levels.

According to our data, Fairfield Elementary spent about 80% of class time on instruction at the early elementary level and about 84% in the upper elementary grades. Only 14% and 13%, respectively, were spent on routines. The comparative percentages for Laurel were 63 for instruction and 32 for routines in the three lower grades, and 64 and 29, respectively, in the three upper grades. It seems to me that these data alone provide the Laurel Elementary School faculty with a significant beginning point for improvement. Why is nearly a third of class time being directed to routine matters? What are these routines? Are they necessary? How might time directed to them be reduced and given over to instruction? These teachers need a staff development program directed first to classroom management. This should take precedence over any districtwide program for all teachers—unless the problem is shown, by gathering the necessary data, to be common to all schools.

Similarly, at the junior high level, Crestview spent, on the average, 69% of class time on instruction and 25% on routines, while Fairfield was spending 87% on instruction and only 9% on routines. Similar differences for the senior highs are apparent.

Of course we cannot equate time on instruction with quality of instruction. Although the Fairfield schools were first in observed amount of time spent on instruction at all but the senior high level, these schools do not appear to be among the most satisfactory in the eyes of students, teachers, or parents. Long before I saw the recorded data on the instruc-

TABLE 4-2

Students Who Selected Each Category as Taking the Most Class Time
(in percent)

	Early Elementary (N = 1775)	Upper Elementary (N = 1577)	Junior High (N = 8793)	Senior High (N=10,700)
Instruction	44	53	63	74
Behavior control	38	32	24	15
Routines	18	15	13	11

tional use of time, I had drawn some tentative conclusions from my independent observations at Fairfield. I had come away from both junior and senior high schools with an impression of sameness, emotional flatness, and lack of teacher enthusiasm in the classroom setting. Time to teach and learn only provides the initial opportunity. There is then great variation in how this time is used by teachers and students.

Some Student Perceptions

We endeavored to find out something about students' perceptions of the kind of classroom activity in which they saw themselves primarily involved. They were asked to choose among instruction, behavior control (which includes social activity), and routines as occupying the most time. The resulting data revealed the relative use of time in these three categories from the students' perspective. The percent of students choosing one or another of the categories is shown in Table 4-2 and Fig. 4-2.

It will be noted that the percentage choosing instruction increased markedly from only 45% in the early elementary grades to 73% in the senior high schools. There is nothing in the teachers' responses to our questions about time spent on each category and little in our observational data to parallel these marked differences in student perceptions. Approximately 37% of the children in the first three grades perceived behavior control to take the most time. The percentage had dropped to 15% by the senior high years. Why did the younger and older students view the ambience of their classrooms so differently?

Judging from our data, younger students see teachers not just as instructing, but as directing student behavior also. They are sensitive, I suspect, to teachers' questions as a means of eliciting required behavior. "What do you see in the picture, Harry?" is not just a stimulus to learning but also a cue that brings Harry back to the group from daydreaming or to

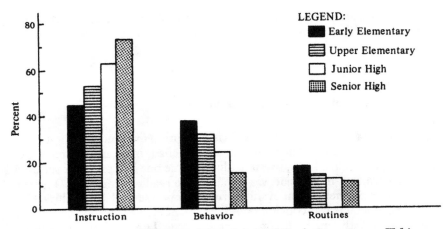

Figure 4-2. Percent of Students Who Selected Each Category as Taking the Most Class Time.

appropriate group norms if he has been poking Julie. Students may be rather reliable indicators of classroom dynamics not readily observed or sensed by visitors to classrooms. Any why not? They are at the heart of the process and undoubtedly have insight into what is going on. We have tended to overlook this rich source of intimate experience in seeking to know what goes on in classrooms.

CLASSROOM ACTIVITIES

Throughout the preceding discussion I have assumed, in line with recent research, that time alone is an important factor in learning. By finding more efficient ways to handle routines and by learning to manage the classroom with a minimum of time lost to social activity and controlling students' behavior, teachers can increase the amount of time spent on learning and, presumably, enhance achievement. It is reasonable to assume also, in the light of research, that the gains in achievement will be greatest if the students are actively involved and stay involved in learning when instructional time is increased.

It is relatively easy to study the involvement of a single student in learning activities and to speculate about what he is getting out of reading, listening, or watching. But studying a class of 25 or more individuals is exceedingly difficult, especially over the relatively long time periods required to determine the persistence of interest and involvement. Given this difficulty, it is not surprising to find substantial differences in the findings of researchers in this area. There are not, then, established norms by means of which we might judge a class to be high or low in student involvement.

The Complexity of Classroom Observation

Mrs. Wallace's was a first-grade class I visited during our study. Eight or nine children clustered around her, each on a small chair, in a carpeted corner of the room. Each held a book, presumably the same one in a textbook series. A girl with a red bow in her hair was standing and reading from hers. The rest of the children in the class sat in small groups around several small tables. One boy of two at a table was copying one-line sentences in a workbook, inserting each word directly under the one printed above. The other was coloring a plain piece of paper, putting green swirls of color above a brown lump (green leaves on a brown tree trunk?). At another table two girls were reading alternately to one another from pages covered with large print and pictures, the pages of a Dr. Seuss book. All of the children at the other tables were engaged in reading, silently, from simple, highly illustrated books, or drawing and coloring, or doing workbook exercises. In her corner, Mrs. Wallace was calling on a girl named Lisa to help the girl who was standing and reading to recognize the word "because."

This was a fairly conventional first-grade class. I've seen many like it. But even in such a familiar kind of class, recording as much as possible of the physical characteristics of the classroom setting, the materials being used, the activities in which the students are engaged, the teacher's use of time, and so on is a demanding task. All of these are there at once.

The sixth-grade class I visited later that day was more unusual and presented its special character to the observer quickly. During a brief greeting, Mr. Silvano explained that he was bringing to conclusion a five-week series of activities in science, each week having been organized around a scientific concept. For example, one of these was the concept of energy. He pointed to a table covered with batteries and wires and a set of mimeographed instructions. Groups of children were about to begin doing experiments at this table and four others in the room.

I then watched while the students, in clusters of five or six, moved about, performing five experiments in a rotated sequence, each illustrating one of the concepts they had studied. Each child cooperated in various degrees with the others. As each group left a table, Mr. Silvano replaced the expendable materials. At first there was confusion and noise. Then the groups grew relatively quiet as instructions were read and the experiments performed. Mr. Silvano said not a word but moved quickly from table to table as supplies were needed.

How does one record and classify this teaching and these teaching activities? For instance, was all of this time on instruction, or was the time spent reading the directions time devoted to routines?

That day I also visited the only senior high school in a district. It was blessed with superb facilities for vocational education which apparently were used by virtually all students. One part of these facilities was a large partially divided space replete with shops and equipment—from a darkroom for photography to forges for metal work and lathes for wood work.

The teachers were not easily found. They were busy demonstrating, correcting, guiding students, surrounded all the while by boys and girls, some asking questions, some busily engaged in making or shaping things. The students talked a lot, not always about the activity in which they were engaged, often helped one another, and most of the time appeared engaged in some task. Obviously they were enjoying themselves.

How does one record all this systematically? This was not a class in the usual sense. It was a combination of several classes, each offering an array of hands-on activities. Several teachers were involved, but each occupied his or her own "space." What they were doing was not exactly team teaching, and little of their teaching was of a conventional sort. They served as role models for students seeking to develop skills, interacting with students as older, more proficient peers rather than as authority figures. I found myself wanting to join in.

We sought to get insight into the life of classrooms both by recording what transpired over brief periods of time—the class in motion, so to speak—and by periodically describing the activity under way, the materials being used, and the like—as one would take a series of snapshots with a camera. And of course these observations could then be supplemented for interpretive purposes by the data gleaned from students and teachers through questionnaires and interviews. But how does one determine what percentage of time is being given over to instruction and what percentage to controlling behavior in the vocational education program just described? And how does one interpret other kinds of instructional settings? The more typical academic junior high classes I described at the beginning of this chapter would present the observer with less difficult problems of observation but would require interviews, for example, to tease out students' perceptions and thoughts.

If time on instruction is associated with students' achievement, then there is the danger that teachers will eschew all forms of pedagogy except frontal teaching. But some kinds of learning seem to require types of student involvement and collaboration not enhanced by teacher control and dominance, and prescriptions calling for just teacher-dominated forms of pedagogy can have negative effects on such learning.

It is easier to study the behavior of a single teacher than the behavior of an entire class of students. Consequently, researchers have endeavored to connect teacher behavior rather than student behavior to achievement. Until recently, their studies focused on the effect of some single variable such as a new method of teaching reading, usually over a rather short period of time. In general, they were unable to establish connections between these single interventions and either students' achievement or students' attitudes. No single variable in itself appears sufficiently powerful to influence student learning significantly.[5]

Rather, it appears that each of a number of approaches carries some weight, and orchestrated together, they can add up to a significant difference. One of these approaches involves arranging and rearranging instructional groups and methods to achieve changing purposes—for example, shifting from large group instruction involving lecturing to small groups necessitating student interaction. A second also has to do with variability—varying the focus of learning from textbooks, to films, to field trips, to library research in order to assure different avenues to the same learnings. A third approach, growing in recognized importance, stresses clarity of instructions and support for and feedback to the learner: expectations are clear; good performance is praised; errors or faulty approaches are pointed out just as quickly as possible; or a learner having unusual trouble with particular procedures being used is provided with an alternative method to the one used with the total group. High among the techniques of this approach is the use of diagnostic quizzes to make possible self-appraisal and corrective action, with the help of successful students, *before* an exam "that counts" is given.[6] Several excellent reviews of promising as well as ineffective pedagogical approaches are now available.[7] But more comprehensive, long-term studies of classroom phenomena designed to provide criteria for evaluating teaching are very much needed.

Factors thought to be negatively associated with learning tend to be the reverse of the above. To be avoided is the daily repetition of classroom activities that encourage passivity and rote behavior on the part of students—pedagogy that is not sensitively responsive to what is happening to individuals. Some students thrive no matter what the instructional approach, but also we know that students appearing to be less able can and do approach the learning levels of those successful students when instruction is dovetailed to their special needs.[8]

Some Activities We Observed

The data from our observations in more than 1,000 classrooms support the popular image of a teacher standing or sitting in front of a class imparting knowledge to a group of students. Explaining and lecturing constituted the most frequent teaching activities, according to teachers, students, and our observations. And the frequency of these activities increased steadily from the primary to the senior high school years. Teachers also spent a substantial amount of time observing students at work or monitoring their seat-work, especially at the junior high school level.

Our data show not only an increase in these activities but also a decline in teachers' interacting with groups of students within their classes from the primary to the secondary years. Several different kinds of data suggest that there is most interaction between teachers and individual students or small groups of students at the lower elementary level and a steady increase in teachers teaching the total class with upward progression through the high school.

As the "snapshot" data in Table 4-3 make clear, three categories of student activity marked by passivity—written work, listening, and preparing for assignments—dominate in the likelihood of their occurring at any given time at all three levels of schooling. The chances are better than 50-50 that if you were to walk into any of the classrooms of our sample, you would see one of these three activities under way rather than one of the other 10 listed in Table 4-3 and Fig. 4-3. All three activities are almost exclusively set and monitored by teachers. We saw a contrastingly low incidence of activities invoking active modes of learning. Except in the arts and vocational education, students were not very often called upon to build, draw, perform, role play, or make things. The incidence of activities requiring some kind of physical practice or performance did increase at the secondary levels—the result of the increased number of arts, vocational, and physical education classes in the curriculum.

During the past 15 years in particular, teachers have been exhorted to take account of and provide for student individuality in learning rates and styles. Our data suggest, however, that this is not something often or readily done. Students worked independently at all levels but primarily on identical tasks, rather than on a variety of activities designed to accommodate their differences. In general, there were more different kinds of instructional activities in elementary than in secondary classrooms; elementary school teachers varied the grouping configurations of their classrooms from time to time and occasionally even changed the content and their methods of teaching. Secondary teachers rarely individualized

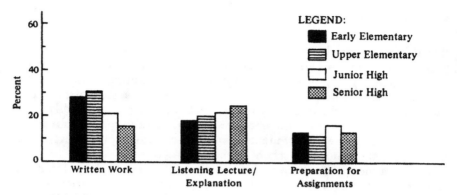

Figure 4-3. Snapshot Data: Rank Order of Activities (top three) by Probability of Students Having Been Observed Participating in Each (percentages).

classroom procedures. On the whole, teachers at all levels apparently did not know how to vary their instructional procedures, did not want to, or had some kind of difficulty doing so.

Critics of the schools have blamed declining test scores on widescale implementation of individualized learning and other "progressive" techniques during the 1960s and early 1970s. Whether or not the individualization of instruction enhances or impedes learning appears to be an academic question if the schools we studied are reasonably representative. In these schools traditional, not progressive, pedagogy dominated. It is interesting to note that the early elementary teachers varied classroom procedures more than the others, presumably to take account of student variability, and the early elementary grades are those that have held up best, nationwide, on tests of pupil achievement!

A disturbing surprise in our data is the limited amount of time students in our sample were observed writing and reading. In the eyes of some people the reason for having schools is to teach reading, writing, spelling, and mathematics. A substantial amount of student time in the early school years *is* spent in writing. But much of this, as we know from other studies, is answering questions in workbooks, filling in blank spaces in short narratives, and so on. The frequency of even this kind of writing at the secondary level was about two-thirds as much in junior high and half as much in senior high classes, as compared with elementary classes. Students' experience with writing decreased, then, as they moved from the upper elementary to the senior high school grades.

The state of reading in the classrooms we observed seemed quite dismal. Exclusive of the common practice of students taking turns reading

TABLE 4-3

Snapshot Data: Rank Order of Activities by Probability of Students Having
Been Observed Participating in Each at Any Particular Moment

Early Elementary Activity	%	Upper Elementary Activity	%
Written Work	28.3	Written Work	30.4
Listening to Explanations/ Lectures	18.2	Listening to Explanations/ Lectures	20.1
Preparation for Assignments	12.7	Preparation for Assignments	11.5
Practice/Performance-Physical	7.3	Discussion	7.7
Use of AV Equipment	6.8	Reading	5.5
Reading	6.0	Practice/Performance-Physical	5.3
Student Non-task Behavior- No Assignment	5.7	Use of AV Equipment	4.9
Discussion	5.3	Student Non-task Behavior- No Assignment	4.8
Practice/Performance-Verbal	5.2	Practice/Performance-Verbal	4.4
Taking Tests	2.2	Taking Tests	3.3
Watching Demonstrations	1.5	Watching Demonstrations	1.0
Being Disciplined	0.5	Simulation/Role Play	0.4
Simulation/Role Play	0.2	Being Disciplined	0.3

Junior High Activity	%	Senior High Activity	%
Listening to Explanations/ Lectures	21.9	Listening to Explanations/ Lectures	25.3
Written Work	20.7	Practice/Performance-Physical	17.5
Preparation for Assignments	15.9	Written Work	15.1
Practice/Performance-Physical	14.7	Preparation for Assignments	12.8
Taking Tests	5.5	Student Non-task Behavior- No Assignment	6.9
Discussion	4.2	Taking Tests	5.8
Practice/Performance-Verbal	4.2	Discussion	5.1
Use of AV Equipment	4.1	Practice/Performance-Verbal	4.5
Student Non-task Behavior- No Assignment	3.6	Use of AV Equipment	2.8
Reading	2.8	Reading	1.9
Watching Demonstrations	1.5	Watching Demonstrations	1.6
Simulation/Role Play	0.2	Simulation/Role Play	0.1
Being Disciplined	0.2	Being Disciplined	0.1

orally from a common text, reading occupied about 6% of class time at the elementary level and then dropped off to 3% and 2% for junior and senior highs, respectively. If our young people are not reading in school, where are they reading, and how much? We need studies not just of how children and youth spend their time in school and the time they spend in front of a television set, but of how they spend their remaining nonsleeping hours each day over weeks and months.[9]

THE AMBIENCE OF THE CLASSROOM

Four elements of classroom life in the schools of our sample come through loud and clear from our data. First, the vehicle for teaching and learning is the total group. Second, the teacher is the strategic, pivotal figure in this group. Third, the norms governing the group derive primarily from what is required to maintain the teacher's strategic role. Fourth, the emotional tone is neither harsh and punitive nor warm and joyful; it might be described most accurately as flat.

Patterns

No matter how we approach the classroom in an effort to describe and understand what goes on, the teacher comes through as coach, quarterback, referee, and even rule-maker. But there the analogy must stop because there is no team. There is, instead, a loosely knit group. Each student/player plays the same position, with varying degrees of skill. There is no inherent opportunity or reason to admire performances in other positions and how each contributes to effective team accomplishment. There is little or nothing about classroom life as it is conducted, so far as I am able to determine, that suggests the existence of or need for norms of group cohesion and cooperation for achievement of a shared purpose.

The most successful classrooms may be those in which teachers succeed in creating commonly shared goals and individuals cooperate in ensuring each person's success in achieving them. The ultimate criterion becomes group accomplishment of individual progress. But this would be countervailing to prevailing practice, at least as revealed by our data.

A great deal of what goes on in the classroom is like painting-by-numbers—filling in the colors called for by numbers on the page. This begins in the primary grades. The child-colors the house yellow, following instructions, and writes the word "yellow" beside the corresponding color. Later, with acquisition of greater reading and writing competence, he or she answers questions, in sentences, after having read several paragraphs. The teacher, through choice of assignments and materials, provides the ground on which figures are to be placed.

A similar thing occurs orally. Most of the time teachers tell or explain, providing students with both figure and ground. For about 15% of the time spent in such "frontal" teaching in the early elementary years and 9% in the high school grades we studied, they ask specific questions calling essentially for students to fill in the blanks: "What is the capital city of Canada?" "What are the principal exports of Japan?" Students rarely turn things around by asking the questions. Nor do teachers often give students a chance to romp with an open-ended question such as "What are your views on the quality of television?" The intellectual terrain is laid out by the teacher. The paths for walking through it are largely predetermined by the teacher.

For the most part, the teachers in our sample of schools controlled rather firmly the central role of deciding what, where, when, and how their students were to learn, and the more the decision was of the what and how, the less we found the students of our sample participating in making it. When students played a role, it was somewhat peripheral, such as deciding where they sat. At the elementary level, about 55% of the students reported not participating at all in choosing what they did in class. About two-thirds of our secondary students said that they did not help make such decisions.

Upper elementary school students, participating somewhat more on the average than secondary students in classroom decisions, expressed greater desire to do so. Students seemed to become more compliant and accepting of the teacher's role as they moved upward. They were being socialized into classroom expectations, especially that of accepting the authority of the teacher. The picture that emerges from the data is one of students increasingly conforming, not assuming an increasingly independent decision-making role in their own education.

On one hand, many teachers verbalize the importance of students increasingly becoming independent learners; on the other, most view themselves as needing to be in control of the decision-making process. The classroom is a constrained and constraining environment. The prospect of this setting slipping from their control is frightening for many teachers, not surprisingly. It is likely that they hold back from giving their students much "space" for fear they will take over, and no doubt students pick up the signals. As one high school student put it succinctly, "We're birds in a cage. The door is open, but there's a cat just outside." The vivid analogy does not portray the full complexity of the classroom, however. Teachers also are inside the cage and, to a degree, carry with them society's expectations for classroom behavior. Society expects teachers to be in charge of their classrooms.

And it appears, from our data at least, that they are. Teachers at all levels perceived that they had almost complete control over selecting teaching techniques and learning activities. Teachers at the junior and senior high school levels reported complete control over evaluating students; elementary teachers reported having a lot of control in this area. Teachers at all levels reported having a lot of control over setting goals and objectives; use of classroom space; scheduling time and instructional materials; selecting content, topics, and skills to be taught; and grouping students for instruction. The teachers in our sample appeared to be quite autonomous in all areas central to their teaching and therefore in creating the environment for learning within the constraints imposed by school schedules and classroom physical space. The constraints appeared to increase somewhat from elementary to secondary levels of schooling, with the result that teachers, and students as well, perceived their participation in and control over decisions to decline from lower to higher grades.

Looking through the eyes of the students we surveyed, teachers loomed large in the classroom. Our students perceived their teachers to be in charge of the classroom and, on the average, perceived themselves to be doing what the teacher told or expected them to do. At the elementary level, students quite consistently from school to school agreed that "I always do what my teacher tells me to do;" and "I do all the work my teacher gives me." At the secondary level, regardless of the particular school or class they were in, most students agreed that "I usually do my homework;" "I usually do the work assigned in this class;" and "I usually do everything my teacher tells me to do." They did not, on the average, perceive there to be a too strict set of class rules.

What is the source of this significance of teachers in students' perceptions of classroom life and their apparent willingness to conform? For the secondary students in our sample, at least, it doesn't appear to be simply good feeling. As reported in Chapter 3, they placed "teachers" and "classes" far down the list in selecting "the one best thing about this school" and placed "friends" at the top.

Peer group socializing with these friends and others did not in general seem to dominate classroom activity in the secondary schools we studied, however much it may have been in the minds of the students. But sometimes, as we saw with Bradford High earlier, it seemed on the threshold of doing so.

One begins to wonder if the predominant class pattern of individuals working largely independently in group settings serves an implicit function—that of blocking or at least holding at bay small group alliances which could become disruptive. Certain instructional practices may be used, in part, as policing devices—more so at the junior than the senior high level, probably because the turbulence of early adolescence challenges teachers to exercise more control. The organization and conduct of the classroom so that individuals work alone may not be conducive to productive team effort and the learning of collaborative values and skills, but at least it can prevent, to a considerable degree, the spillover of group allegiances and rivalries from outside the classroom and the emergence within of cliques and intergroup confrontations. Again, we see that the demands of managing a relatively large group of people in small space may become a formidable factor in determining and limiting pedagogy. It is difficult to know the degree to which these circumstances drain teachers and how consciously and contentedly they adapt to them. Is the ability to live rather comfortably with these restraints a necessary condition for long-term tenure in the public schools? What percentage of teachers who leave are those who find the limitations of classroom life to be too restraining and demanding?

Similarly, one wonders if the way classrooms are organized and run has something to do with the neutral emotional tone we observed in many of them. Whether we looked at how teachers related to students or how students related to teachers, the overwhelming impression was one of affective neutrality—a relationship neither abrasive nor joyous.

We observed little punitive behavior on the part of teachers, and though there may be reason to worry about the conforming demands of school and to wonder why there is not more enthusiasm and laughter, the teachers in our sample were not regarded, overall, by their students as brutes or ogres. Students at all levels generally perceived their teachers as being more positive than negative in their concern for them, although there were considerable class-to-class variations in the data. Secondary students did perceive some punitive behavior in their teachers, somewhat more authoritarian behavior, and still more signs of favoritism to certain students. But their negative rating of their teachers in these areas were not high, in our judgment. Similarly, students at all levels had rather positive feelings about their classmates.

In our data, whether or not teachers were perceived to be concerned about students appeared to be significantly related to student satisfaction with their classes. We found that students in classes where teachers were judged to be authoritarian were likely to feel less satisfied. No measure of students' relations with peers was as highly related to matters of student satisfaction in the classroom as were the measures of student-teacher relationship.

Earlier in this chapter I noted that learning appears to be enhanced when students understand what is expected of them, get recognition for their work, learn quickly about their errors, and receive guidance in improving their performance. These pedagogical practices are very much within the control of teachers, and it has been my experience that teachers recognize them as desirable pedagogy. But our data suggest a paucity of most of them. About 57% of the students in the early elementary grades answered "yes" when asked whether they understood what their teachers wanted them to do. Forty percent answered "sometimes."

Over half of the upper elementary students reported that many students did not know what they were supposed to do in class. Responding to questions about teachers' clarity in regard to directions, a majority of secondary students mildly agreed that they and their fellow students understood what their teachers were talking about. Clearly, however, a substantial minority of senior high school students (averaging 20% across classes at each school) were having trouble understanding teachers' directions and comments. Almost the same percentage at all levels perceived themselves as not being informed of their mistakes and corrected in their performance.

Both corrective teacher behavior and guidance in improving performance fell off somewhat from the early elementary to the senior high years, as inferred from our observational data. Also, we noted that teachers' praise of students' work dropped from about 2% of the observed time in the early elementary classes to about 1% in senior high classes. And just as we found little teacher positive reinforcement of students' performance, we found few negative responses on the part of teachers.

The pattern dominating in our data supports the conclusion that the classes in our sample, at all levels, tended not to be marked with exhuberance, joy, laughter, abrasiveness, praise and corrective support of individual student performance, punitive teacher behavior, or high interpersonal tension.

All of those characteristics we commonly regard as positive elements in classrooms were more to be observed at the early elementary level. A decline set in by the upper elementary grades and continued through the secondary years, with a sharp drop at the junior high school level.

As already suggested, there may be something self-protective for teachers in maintaining classroom control and a relatively flat emotional tone. We have no reason to assume that teachers, more than the rest of us, are persons who exude a high level of emotional identification with others. Teaching is what teachers expect to do every day. To reach out positively and supportively to 27 youngsters for five hours or so each day in an elementary school classroom is demanding and exhausting. To respond similarly to four to six successive classes of 25 or more students each at the secondary level may be impossible.

This last observation raises a nagging question about the conduct of schooling, particularly at junior and senior high school levels. If positive relations with teachers in classrooms are related to student satisfaction in school and corrective feedback is related to student achievement, then it becomes imperative to seek school conditions likely to maximize both. The never-ending movement of students and teachers from class to class appears not conducive to teachers and students getting to know one another, let alone to their establishing a stable, mutually supportive relationship. Indeed, it would appear to foster the casualness and neutrality in human relations we observed to characterize so many of the classrooms in our sample.

Nonetheless, having depicted a general picture of considerable passivity among students and emotional flatness in classrooms, I hasten to point out that students' views of life in their classrooms were not correspondingly negative. Rather, they tended to express liking for their subjects, view teachers as concerned about them, and view most teachers as liking or even being enthusiastic about their work. Large percentages expressed liking for the dominating classroom activity of listening to their teachers. Students apparently adjusted to the passivity of the classroom environment as they progressed upward through the school years. One wonders if many of those who left did not.

In our study of the first four years of schooling referred to earlier, my colleagues and I made the statement that students appeared more involved in their studies than the circumstances appeared to warrant.[10] We were expressing an adult perspective, and I am expressing an adult perspective here. Perhaps the young are basically both more accepting and sufficiently irrepressible to surmount what adult observers in classrooms perceive to be dull fare. Perhaps they perceive no attainable alternative to school or are not aware of markedly different possibilities for the conduct of the schools we have. Perhaps, by the early adolescent years at least, school is just a known set of circumstances conveniently providing for various peer associations and activities, and students keep the classroom experience relatively low in emotional drain in order to preserve energy for other things. At any rate, the adjustments that students—and teachers as well—make to the circumstances of schooling are not simply explained.

But one important thing is clear. Schools and classrooms cannot be understood or accurately and usefully described by the relatively simplistic input-output factory model so often used; they are better understood as little villages in which individuals interact on a part-time basis within a relatively constrained and confining environment. Many of the constraining elements are clearly visible even when the setting is vacated at the end of each day—those inherent in the confining space and arrangement of furniture. On entering each morning, there is a certain tacit acceptance of restraints and the relative passivity they require. In the elementary grades, at least, students spend a good deal of time just waiting for the teacher to hand out materials or to tell them what to do.[11] Perhaps this is why children so often are depicted as bursting forth from schools, unconstrained and unrestrained, in the later afternoon.

Variations and Deviations

On preceding pages, I have used phrases such as "on the average" or "generally" or "on the whole" both to suggest patterns and trends and to warn the reader against assuming unvarying consistency in our data. It is easy to forget that in some areas of our findings variability frequently is as characteristic as are patterns and persistent trends. We have seen that patterns changed from early elementary, to upper elementary, and then to junior and senior high schools. Also, there was variability from subject to subject and among classes.

Subject-to-subject variations. Where subject-to-subject differences showed up most distinctively and interestingly was between clusters of subjects taught at junior and senior high levels rather than, for example, between English and mathematics. Again and again we found the arts, physical education, and vocational education differing in various ways from the four subjects usually considered essential for college admission—English, mathematics, social studies, and science. The differences often were small or subtle, but they kept reappearing and steadily adding up. Likewise foreign language classes began to emerge, through successive pieces of data, as somewhat different from both the three less-academic subjects and those in the cluster of four academic subjects. We must remember, of course, that foreign languages represented a small part of the curriculum at both junior and senior high levels and were not taken at all by a large percentage of students. There were, as a consequence, fewer classes available to observe, and probably the students were not very representative of the total school population.

Teachers in the arts at both levels and in physical education in senior highs, more than teachers in any other fields, perceived themselves as having high control over decisions about nine different areas of their planning and teaching. They did not perceive themselves, apparently, as constrained by external requirements. The fact that junior high teachers of physical education perceived themselves as having somewhat less control in these areas may result from its being a subject required for all students at this level. Students perceived themselves as having the greatest or nearly the greatest decision-making role in these two subjects and in vocational education, thanks in part at least to teachers feeling free to delegate more of their own authority.

Regardless of subject, students reported that they liked to do activities that involved them actively or in which they worked with others. These included going on field trips, making films, building or drawing things, making collections, interviewing people, acting things out, and carrying out projects. These are the things which students reported doing least and which we observed infrequently. They were observed more frequently in the arts, vocational education, and physical education as a group of subjects than in English, mathematics, social studies, and science as a group.

I visited the schools we studied for purposes of gaining intuitive impressions about the areas we studied systematically and in depth. There was a great deal of telling, explaining, and questioning by teachers in all subjects, as well as a great deal of passive seatwork by students. But there was less of these in the arts, vocational education, and physical education classes I visited. There was a paucity of demonstrating, showing, and modeling on the part of teachers and of constructing things, acting things out, carrying out projects, and the like on the part of the students. But there was more of these in arts, physical education, and vocational education classes I visited. And the "hard" data gleaned from questionnaires and systematic classroom observations bear me out on all this. Still, it is fascinating that so much of what characterizes teaching in the academic subjects dominates those for which quite different pedagogy would seem to be more appropriate.

Again, I note a pattern, not a never-varying condition. It must be remembered that the generalizations from our data presented earlier in this chapter tend to fit teaching and learning in the arts, physical education, and vocational education as well as in the more academic subjects. My point is that the deviations that do emerge tend to reveal these three subjects as being a little less lecture- and textbook-oriented and involving a little more participation of students in decisions affecting their learning, greater student enthusiasm, less time on instruction, and a little more variation in pedagogical procedures. And in students' relative perceptions of their school subjects, these three came through as being more satisfying. Also of interest is that the more we perceived students to be involved in decision making in the arts, the less time teachers were spending controlling students' behavior. This was a finding uniquely associated with the arts.

It should not surprise us to learn that these three subjects consistently came out as the most liked in the eyes of the students sampled. Students in grades four through twelve were asked to indicate in a general, global way how much they liked each of several school subjects. Similarly they were asked to rate the importance and difficulty of these subjects. Table 4-4 and Fig. 4-4 portray the results in all three categories. We see the arts, vocational education, and physical education showing up consistently at the top for liking. (Vocational education was not included as a choice for upper elementary students because it is rarely taught at this level.) No academic subject was chosen above these at any level.

TABLE 4-4

Rank Order of Students' Attitudes Toward Subjects: By Level of Schooling

LIKING

UPPER ELEMENTARY			JUNIOR HIGH			SENIOR HIGH		
Subject	*% Like*	*N*	*Subject*	*% Like*	*N*	*Subject*	*% Like*	*N*
Arts	93.2	1621	Arts	85.9	5130	Arts	83.6	6903
Physical Ed.	86.9	1615	Voc./Career Ed.	81.0	4912	Voc./Career Ed.	80.8	6884
Math	81.5	1609	Physical Ed.	80.1	5177	Physical Ed.	79.8	6969
Reading/English	81.3	1622	Math	74.8	5160	English	72.1	7046
Science	80.9	1604	English	69.3	5231	Math	65.0	6966
Social Studies	65.6	1617	Social Studies	66.0	5184	Social Studies	65.0	6958
			Science	66.1	5068	Science	64.1	6908
			Foreign Lang.	62.0	4734	Foreign Lang.	52.8	6825

IMPORTANCE

UPPER ELEMENTARY

Subject	% Imp.	N
Math	93.9	1618
Reading/English	93.5	1617
Science	89.4	1593
Social Studies	88.9	1614
Physical Ed.	87.2	1621
Arts	80.2	1610

JUNIOR HIGH

Subject	% Imp.	N
Math	95.0	5154
English	91.5	5220
Voc./Career Ed.	85.1	4972
Social Studies	83.1	5146
Science	78.8	5045
Physical Ed.	75.3	5174
Foreign Lang.	73.5	4842
Arts	70.4	5103

SENIOR HIGH

Subject	% Imp.	N
Math	94.3	6988
English	93.6	7043
Voc./Career Ed.	85.9	6899
Science	79.2	6863
Social Studies	77.8	6961
Physical Ed.	67.4	6998
Arts	65.3	6929
Foreign Lang.	65.1	6784

DIFFICULTY*

UPPER ELEMENTARY

Subject	% Hard	% Easy	% Just Right	N
Social Studies	19.9	47.1	33.0	1602
Math	17.7	55.0	27.3	1610
Science	14.5	54.5	31.0	1594
Reading/English	10.7	46.3	43.0	1613
Physical Ed.	10.3	67.1	22.6	1609
Arts	3.4	78.6	18.0	1608

JUNIOR HIGH

Subject	% Hard	% Easy	% Just Right	N
Foreign Lang.	23.3	29.2	47.5	219
Social Studies	17.9	27.5	54.6	1420
Science	17.1	29.0	53.9	1056
Math	14.0	32.2	53.8	1670
English	12.5	31.6	55.9	1644
Voc./Career Ed.	8.2	42.0	49.8	1023
Arts	7.6	45.7	46.7	1176
Physical Ed.	5.0	45.8	49.2	754

SENIOR HIGH

Subject	% Hard	% Easy	% Just Right	N
Science	27.8	25.2	47.0	1313
Math	26.0	28.3	45.7	1587
Foreign Lang.	24.2	29.8	46.0	526
English	16.1	32.3	51.6	1793
Social Studies	15.9	35.2	48.9	1749
Arts	9.3	45.4	45.3	1474
Voc./Career Ed.	9.1	42.5	48.4	1726
Physical Ed.	7.8	54.0	38.2	768

*As perceived only by students who were currently enrolled in each subject.

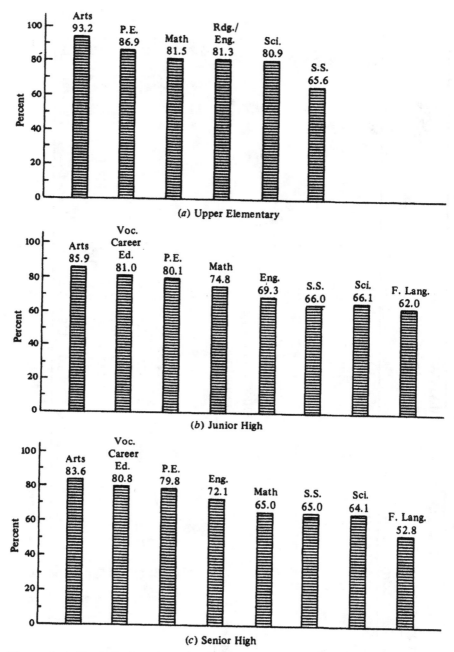

Figure 4-4. Rank Order of Students' Liking of School Subjects.

118

The high importance attributed to mathematics, English, and vocational education shown in Table 4-4 reflects society's expectations for these subjects and the allocation of resources to them in the schools we studied. Contrastingly, physical education, foreign languages, and the arts are not highly valued as school subjects in American society. A relatively low difficulty level was attributed to vocational education, the arts, and physical education by our students. One wonders if this results from the fact that these generally are electives. Grades achieved in them are not carefully scrutinized by college admissions officers.

The arts, physical education, and vocational education hold their collective place at the top when we look at students' responses to a different question shown on Table 4-5. We asked them to express their interest in the subjects they actually were enrolled in at the time we queried them. Among the academic subjects English dropped to the bottom and was replaced nearer the top by foreign languages at both junior and senior high levels. Although foreign language subjects are not generally attractive to students, only a small percentage of whom enroll in them, those enrolled expressed high interest in their courses. Usually, students so enrolled are college-bound. Rather consistently, the foreign language classes we observed tended to be businesslike, task-oriented, fast-paced, and satisfying to students. We noted that the time spent on instruction in these classes was greater than for any other subject. A substantial portion of this time was spent in practicing the languages—students interacting with teachers and other students in the particular language being learned. Here we see a certain similarity to the relatively high level of active student involvement characteristic of the arts, vocational education, and physical education. Also, foreign language classes were characterized, on the average, by a slightly higher level of corrective feedback than the other academic subjects. I believe it is fair to say that a similarity among all four subjects—foreign language and the three nonacademics—is that they provide models against which to check one's own performance rather quickly. There probably is more disagreement about correct models in English, for example, so that students have greater difficulty comparing their own writing with the models available to them. It was difficult, however, to find other similarities among the four subjects that tended to rank highest in student interest while enrolled.

Two classes compared. We went through several phases of analyzing data. We had promised principals and teachers in the schools we studied that we would provide them with some of the data we gathered in their schools and classrooms. Getting these back to them became a top priority. It turned out that we had examined and summarized most of the data

TABLE 4-5

Interest in Subjects Now Being Studied

UPPER ELEMENTARY			JUNIOR HIGH			SENIOR HIGH		
Subject	% Interesting	N	Subject	% Interesting	N	Subject	% Interesting	N
Arts	92.2	1611	Voc./Career Ed.	84.1	1022	Arts	86.8	1476
Physical Ed.	85.9	1620	Physical Ed.	83.6	752	Physical Ed.	85.1	769
Math	80.0	1612	Arts	77.6	1176	Voc./Career Ed.	83.4	1725
Science	79.6	1597	Foreign Lang.	74.7	217	Foreign Lang.	80.6	526
Reading/English	75.0	1622	Math	69.6	1666	Math	69.3	1587
Social Studies	66.0	1616	Social Studies	69.2	1416	Social Studies	69.0	1748
			Science	66.1	1060	Science	68.6	1315
			English	62.6	1645	English	68.5	1795

obtained from questionnaires and sent some of these data back to schools before the observational data were in a form suitable for analysis. Examination of the interview data, the most difficult to codify, came last.

As we examined the successive bodies of data, certain trends and variations on these trends began to emerge. Some teachers began to stand out as rather markedly different, not only in what we observed but also in students' perceptions of their experiences in their classrooms, in what we viewed as a positive direction. In what follows, I describe the classroom of one of these teachers and that of a second teacher who does not appear to be either very strong or very weak.

Both were in elementary schools. I chose teachers at this level because we observed these throughout successive days, whereas we observed junior and senior high school teachers for single class periods on different days. Observations of elementary school classrooms provided greater continuity, as well as descriptions of ongoing activities in an array of subjects. Also, the fact that there tended to be a greater variety of teaching procedures at the elementary than at the two higher levels suggested the possibility of finding considerable variety among teachers.

Our two classes—a fourth- and a fifth-grade—were among those studied at a suburban elementary school. Both were housed in traditional classrooms—single rooms with desks arranged in rows, no stuffed furniture, no carpets. Both classes were adequately stocked with books, magazines, maps, globes, and chalkboards, but no live plants or animals and no student-made decorations. Pretty ordinary places. Twenty-six fourth-graders—14 boys and 12 girls—constituted one class, and 30 fifth-graders—15 boys and 15 girls—made up the other. One student in each class was nonwhite. Each class had one teacher and no instructional aides.

The teachers of the two classes had similar goals for their students; they were concerned both with basic skills and the children's relationships with each other. Both teachers felt clearly in charge of their classes. Neither complained about too little time for instruction after class routines and student behavior problems were taken care of.

On first glance these classes seem very much alike, and they were. Nevertheless, on close examination one of them emerged as both more satisfying to students and more likely to enhance their learning. The other, while certainly not the least satisfactory in our sample, seemed in a number of ways not to match the first. The accumulation of small differences over a number of important variables appears to have made a considerable difference in educational experiences of students.

Three important indicators signal that the fifth-grade class was probably a more constructive learning environment than the fourth-grade class.

First, 81% of the class time was observed to be concerned with instruction, while only 17% was spent on classroom routines and a low 1.5% on controlling behavior. These percentages differed in a positive direction both from the average of classes at this school and from the average of all our upper elementary classes. The fourth-grade class was more typical, with 71% of the time spent on instruction, 25% on routines, and 3% on controlling behavior. Second, during the time of our observation, 90% of the students in the fifth-grade class were observed to be highly interested in the classroom activity at hand; in the fourth-grade class approximately 80% were so involved—not a small percentage but considerably lower. And third, 83% of the fifth-grade class compared with 73% of the fourth-graders responded that they usually felt good about what happened in class, again a small but important difference. And, in contrast, only 21% of the fifth-graders, compared to 42% of the fourth-grade class, said that students in their class didn't care about what went on.

Differences in the conduct of these two classes may provide clues as to why the fifth-grade class stands out as more positive. It was more interactive than the fourth, with higher percentages noted of both adult and student talk. Neither discussion nor even periods of student recitation were observed in the fourth-grade classroom. The dominant activities in this classroom were (1) the teacher lecturing or explaining to the total class, and (2) most of the students working independently on written assignments while the teacher explained or lectured to one student. These activities were also frequent in the fifth-grade class; however, substantial portions of time were spent also in reading and discussing or reciting. As noted earlier, a teacher's use of a variety of instructional activities appears to be linked with students' academic achievement.

The fifth-graders less often reported that they forgot things because they didn't practice and that students didn't know what they were supposed to be doing. More of them reported their teacher to be enthusiastic in teaching and that the work they did was at the right level of difficulty. These teachers were also viewed quite differently in their relationships with students. The fifth-grade teacher was seen as more concerned about students, and fewer students in her class reported that she exhibited favoritism. Although both fourth- and fifth-grade classes were observed to be essentially neutral in emotional tone, the fifth-grade class was higher in the percentage of teacher-student interactions of an overtly positive nature. In contrast, the fourth-grade class had a greater proportion of exchanges with negative teacher affect.

Undoubtedly related to these differences in teacher affect is a marked difference in the way students perceived class time to be spent. In the fifth-grade class 73% of the students reported that learning took up the most class time and only 10% thought getting students to behave was the dominant class activity. Of the fourth-graders, 46% thought that the most time was spent on learning, and 42% said that the most time was spent on behavior.

More of the fifth-graders reported they liked working in all types of groups and alone; more of them liked listening to their teacher and having discussions in all subject areas. Probably the most telling differences in attitudes, however, and learnings as well, are found in the open-ended responses to questions asking students to name the most important things learned in each subject. The fifth-grade responses reflect both the variety of instructional activity experienced and of concepts learned. They are, for the most part, specific in all subjects. In contrast, a common response among the fourth-graders in nearly all subjects was "nothing."

SUMMARY AND DISCUSSION

Although our data on the more than 1,000 classrooms we studied in depth varied on every characteristic examined—this variation was sometimes a little and sometimes a lot—we obviously found patterns of teaching and learning activity generally characterizing the classrooms of our 38 schools. And the repetitiveness of some of these raises in one's mind the possibility, if not the probability, that they would be found frequently in schools beyond our sample. They are summarized in the following descriptions of classroom life. (Not all of the data leading to the observations that follow are presented on preceding pages.)

First, the dominant pattern of classroom organization is a group to which the teacher most frequently relates as a whole. Much of what goes on is conditioned by the need to maintain orderly relationships among from 20 to 30 or more persons in relatively small space. Demands for such order are conveyed to students early, and their socialization into it is rather thoroughly achieved before the end of the early elementary grades.

Second, each student essentially works and achieves alone within a group setting. A class may be praised for its performance, but this recognition, more often than not, is for the sum or average of individual performances, not some shared, collaborative accomplishment.

Third, the teacher is the central figure in determining the activities, as well as the tone, of the classroom. The teacher is virtually autonomous with respect to classroom decisions—selecting materials, determining class organization, choosing instructional procedures, and so on.

Fourth, the domination of the teacher is obvious in the conduct of instruction. Most of the time the teacher is engaged in either frontal teaching, monitoring students' seat-work, or conducting quizzes. Relatively rarely are students actively engaged in learning directly from one another or in initiating processes of interaction with teachers. When students work in smaller groups, they usually are doing the same things side by side, and these things tend to be determined by the teacher.

Fifth, there is a paucity of praise and correction of students' performance, as well as of teacher guidance in how to do better next time. Teachers tend not to respond in overtly positive or negative ways to the work students do. And our impression is that classes generally tend not to be strongly positive or strongly negative places to be. Enthusiasm and joy and anger are kept under control.

Sixth, students generally engage in a rather narrow range of classroom activities—listening to teachers, writing answers to questions, and taking tests and quizzes. Strikingly similar "schooling activities" transcend teachers, grade levels, and subjects. Students receive relatively little exposure to audio-visual aids, field trips, or guest lecturers. Except in the arts, physical education, and vocational education, there is little hands-on activity. Acting out, role playing, dance, the manipulation of materials, and the like are rarely used as accompaniments or alternatives to textbooks and workbooks as media of instruction in academic classes.

Seventh, the patterns summarized above describe early elementary classes less well than they do classes in higher grades. They are quite commonly descriptive of upper elementary classes, and become more accurately descriptive with progression to junior and senior high schools. The variety of teaching techniques is greatest in the lower elementary grades and least in the secondary school years.

Eighth, large percentages of the students we surveyed appeared to be passively content with classroom life. In general, they felt positive about both peers and teachers. They expressed considerable liking for all subjects and classroom activities—even the repetitive listening to teachers' talk. The activities they liked most involve more physical movement and are activities in which they seldom engaged. The subjects they liked most involve more drawing, making, shaping, moving, and interacting. These were regarded as the easiest and the least important; they happen also to be electives at the upper grade levels, not required for college admission.

Ninth, even in the early elementary years there was strong evidence of students not having time to finish their lessons or not understanding what the teacher wanted them to do. A significant percentage saw themselves as not getting sufficient teacher help with mistakes and difficulties. A substantial portion of students in higher grades said essentially the same thing, even though some of those having the most serious problems presumably would have dropped out.

Philosophers and historians have addressed the school's responsibility for humanizing knowledge. They have in mind a process of organizing and presenting humankind's knowledge and intellectual tools in such fashion as to make them accessible to all. This is the central requirement of teaching. The pattern of circumstances just summarized for the classrooms of our sample of schools acts, I believe, against the fulfillment of the process.

The process of humanizing knowledge in schools so that all students gain access to it appears to have two central components. The first is made up of a teacher's personal attention—interest in both the learner and the subject matter which is to be conveyed to and internalized by students. The second is made up of pedagogical traits—all those techniques designed to keep the student overtly or covertly engaged in the learning. Both are educable. The first set is acquired developmentally, however, and is conditioned by both life experiences and by what the future teacher experiences in formal educational settings. Over time, certain attitudes toward others and even certain dispositions toward teaching develop and are carried into the teaching role. The second set can be acquired more quickly through guided clinical experience, just as artisans and professionals acquire whatever skills relate to the tasks to be performed.

The development and improvement of both sets of qualities and abilities become realistic goals for both preservice and inservice teacher education. We do not need to wait for profound changes in the social fabric of society or the organization of schooling in order to begin work on what appears to be a cornerstone in improving the quality of education in elementary and secondary schools.

The data of this and the preceding chapter suggest that both this nurturing behavior and these technical skills are recognized as important teacher attributes by both parents and students. Many teachers, too, see these behaviors and skills as conducive to student learning, and more than a few scholars advocate the importance of the theories of human development and learning these views reflect. Our data lead also to the conclusion, however, that the desired teacher and teaching traits were not nearly as characteristic of the classrooms we studied as we would like. Moreover, evidence of their presence and use declined steadily from the early elementary grades through the upper elementary, junior, and senior high school years. There was increasingly less use of teacher praise and support for learning, less corrective guidance, a narrowing range and variety of pedagogical techniques, and declining participation by students in determining the daily conduct of their education.

Paralleling the steady decline in these instructional procedures was a decline in amenities such as good instructional materials and attractive, comfortable classrooms. Also, the number of adults associating with the same group of students at any one time declined, and the length of the student-teacher relationship became much shorter as well as more fragmented. In the secondary schools no teacher could get to know many students well. Many students probably were not well known by any teacher.

We see in the above, then, both a decline from lower to upper grades in teachers' support of students as persons and learners and a junior and senior high school setting more conducive to casual than sustained student-teacher relationships. From Chapter 3 we recall declining academic self-concept scores among students after the early elementary grades. We recall also the dominance of peer group interest in friends, sports, and the like, beginning in the early adolescent years and remaining strong during subsequent years. Teachers and classes appeared to occupy positions of declining significance in the lives of the young after the upper elementary grades.

The picture that emerges is of classrooms becoming more routinized with respect to instructional practices by the later elementary school years, and older students increasingly voicing more interest in personal and vocational goals and less interest in the intellectual goals of schooling, with peer-group values becoming dominant. And, as stated in Chapter 3, we see a considerable disjuncture between teachers' orientation to students and their problems and what students (and, to considerable degree, their parents) perceived to be important about their school experiences and their fellow students.

My conclusion is that this combination of circumstances conspires to limit the school's role in the humanization of knowledge. At the very time strong support systems are required in order to keep students' involvement in school tasks at a high level of interest and intensity, these support systems are declining in power and variety.

Since the central focus of this chapter has been on what transpires in classrooms and since teachers are so central to classroom life, one might at this point engage in still another round of condemning teachers for indifference and ineptness. But I trust that the thoughtful reader is now becoming increasingly aware of the complexity of schooling and suspicious of simplistic solutions to problems.

Undoubtedly, marked upgrading in the pedagogical competence of many teachers in our sample is called for. Present practices designed to upgrade teachers are guided more by common sense than established knowledge—and the thing we know about common sense in this area and some others is that it is wrong about as often as it is right. And some students of the problem believe that there simply are not enough resources—especially competent persons—available for upgrading the large numbers of teachers who could profit from sustained improvement programs.[12] If this diagnosis is close to the mark, then the sudden availability of state and federal dollars for teaching teachers pedagogical skills will do little more than provide consultative fees to all those charlatans who will proclaim for themselves instant competence in whatever teachers are supposed to need.

Still, the discouraging generalized picture of classroom life painted on preceding pages can be altered. For decades, research on teaching ended up with a list of characteristics of good teachers that could not be differentiated from characteristics of good people. The implication was that good people should be selected as teachers and that little could be done to prepare them further; they would learn most of the necessary skills on the job. Apparently many did not. But techniques such as alternating teaching methods, using diagnostic tests, providing students with knowledge of their performance, and giving praise for good work can be taught and learned. Further, a teacher's shortcomings in these areas can be diagnosed and remedied. With a little knowledge about traits to be maximized and the availability of resources for videotaping lessons for purposes of self-examination, teachers can engage successfully in a considerable amount of self-improvement. The processes are neither threatening nor punitive when school staffs agree to take their teaching out of the closet and work together on improving it. They can be self-initiated, with support from the principal and some encouragement and resources from the district office.

Also encouraging is the clear evidence that students respond positively when the desired pedagogical techniques are employed. Even though the range in frequency of use of this pedagogy was relatively narrow in our sample of classrooms, greater student satisfaction with greater use clearly showed up. It is encouraging that what is associated with students' satisfaction frequently is found also to be associated with students' performance. And, finally, it is encouraging that many teachers believe these procedures to be desirable, whether or not they practice them. It appears, then, that we have a relatively specific and feasible agenda for improving one major component of schooling, pedagogical techniques, whether or not we are willing to spend time and resources in moving from diagnosis to remediation.

A second area for improvement is equally apparent and equally important. Individual school staffs need to become self-conscious about the efficient use of students' time in school, and individual teachers need to become more aware of how class time is utilized. Schoolwide surveys would help. And teachers might observe and record each other's use of time. I am convinced that all schools could pick up at least two hours each week of additional class time by aligning practice with policy in regard to beginning and ending times for the school day, recess, and lunch breaks. I am equally convinced that all or almost all teachers could add 10% more time to instruction and learning each week without creating undue pressures in the classroom through shortening "opening exercises" and "clean-up" activities. Both sets of gains would be derived by doing more quickly and efficiently these and other things now done casually or inefficiently. Engaging in total school and classroom improvement in time use could be an enjoyable collaborative challenge for principals, teachers, and students alike.

Deliberate, systematic attention to improved pedagogical procedures and better, more thorough and efficient use of time on the part of thousands of local schools over a period of from two to three years would cost little or nothing and probably would result in more improvement in student performance than could be effected in a similar period of time through the large-scale infusion of federal funds spread across a much wider array of supposed problem areas. And it most certainly would do more to secure goodwill for principals and teachers and gain community support for schools. Further, the activities involved in no way appear to contradict or to elicit the opposition of those organized segments of the education profession whose special interests frequently fragment and impede the improvement process. Needless to say, teachers would respond with varying degrees of enthusiasm.

Another direction for improvement involves the junior and senior high school years specifically. Fully within the control of principals and teachers is an examination of what might be done to invigorate teaching in the academic subjects. The data on our sample of classes are clear and convincing—teaching in the four basic subjects required for college admission is characterized, on the average, by a narrow range of repetitive instructional activities favoring passive student behavior. These activities are essentially those becoming dominant by the fifth and sixth grades of the elementary school. There are few surprises.

At no academic level is the need one of cramming more into the curriculum and into each lesson. Indeed, a sorting out of central principles from the clutter of specifics would be beneficial. A few concepts should be learned through a variety of approaches. For most students academic learning is too abstract. They need to see, touch, and smell what they read and write about. Time spent visiting a newspaper press, examining artifacts, or observing a craftsman provides reality and stimulus for later reading, explaining, and discussing. Drawing or building can be an alternative way of gaining insight. The effectiveness of such techniques has been known for centuries. Too often, it simply is easier to repeat a lecture or assign. textbook reading. But then there is no fresh stimulation. The accompanying lassitude of many students is to be expected.

If teachers can be persuaded to take the first step—namely, an assessment of their own classrooms designed to provide the kinds of data presented here—a beginning will have been made. Otherwise, the problem is shrugged off as existing somewhere else, perhaps, but not here. It is my hope that principals and teachers will read this chapter and say, "I wonder if the same situation exists in my school. Let's try to find out."

Most school staffs will see themselves as not able to make the necessary self-appraisals and then make constructive changes unless they can get help. Unfortunately, they often view the district office as judgmental and so prefer not to open up such a sensitive area. Some studies show the potential benefits of securing assistance from neutrals such as professors from a local university. Another useful approach is to establish collaborations with other schools, preferably in neighboring school districts, for purposes of giving mutual help.[13] It often is easier to secure assistance for a consortium than for individual schools.

I shall address processes of improvement in greater detail later. The essential point to be made here is that the upgrading of classroom life is best done on a school-by-school basis. Teachers assist each other.[14] Principals help create the setting and secure additional help from elsewhere. The action and rewards for in-service education and school improvement shift from where they have been traditionally—with the superintendent's office and districtwide activities—to the principal's office and the school as the key unit. Research increasingly supports such a process.[15]

For developing local agendas for improvement, data would not be averaged out as we have done in our search for patterns and hypotheses about critical problems of schooling. Nor do they need to be as comprehensive or detailed. But there should be school-by-school assessments to provide data that all persons associated with a school can use in setting priorities. Information shared in this way can be powerfully motivating for those who have a stake in Sigma Elementary or Beta High. The power for improving each school lies with the principal, teachers, students, and parents associated with it. The role of more remote authority and responsibility is to create supportive policy and provide the assistance needed to put this power to work.

Chapter 5

Access to Knowledge

Ours is a much-schooled society. The large percentage of children, youths, and young adults in the formal system of elementary, secondary, and higher education tells us only part of the story. In most parts of the country, courses in almost anything and everything are close at hand. And if one cannot or prefers not to enroll in a course, there are books, magazines, cassettes, and tapes on virtually anything one wants to learn.

With all this richness and diversity for learning so readily accessible, why all the fuss about assuring the availability of schools and the attendance of all children and youths in them at least to the age of 16?

We have sustained in this nation, not without disagreement, at least three propositions in support of a formal system of schooling to be attended by all for a prescribed period of years. The first is that there are essential traits of mind, skills of communication, and accretions of knowledge that can be acquired only through deliberate, systematic, and sustained cultivation. Since these are unlikely to be acquired casually, the requisite learnings should be selected and made available in schools. Second, in a democratic society each individual has the right to gain access to these learnings and therefore to schools. Third, a society espousing democratic tenets requires that a large percentage of its citizens possess the essential traits, skills, and knowledge and therefore that they attend schools. The last two of these propositions, in particular, have led to compulsory attendance up to the age of 16 in most states.

I shall not enter here into the arguments against compulsory schooling and for more informal and nonformal modes of educating.[1] Until recently, the foregoing propositions were rarely questioned (although fears regarding the too heavy hand of the state in education have been expressed for

130

centuries). In the United States these propositions produced the idea of a common school doing the following:

1. Providing a *free* education up to a given level which constituted the principal entry point to the labor force.
2. Providing *a common curriculum* for all children, regardless of background.
3. Partly by design and partly because of low population density, providing that children from diverse backgrounds attend the *same school*.
4. Providing equality within a given *locality*, since local taxes provide the source of support for schools.[2]

These elements have been challenged and subjected to new interpretations. The level of schooling thought to constitute preparation to enter the labor force has steadily increased. The right of children to attend the same school has been upheld by and challenged in the courts. The declining ratio of local to state financial support for schools has expanded the concept of "a given locality." And the increased diversity of students commonly attending has contributed to vast curricular diversity.

The case for equal educational opportunity has revolved almost exclusively around the question of access to a school to be commonly attended and around discrimination based on color, race, or creed, but other considerations are now likely to expand the dimensions of controversy. *Increasingly, the issue will be whether students, as a consequence of the schools they happen to attend and the classes to which they are assigned, have equality of access to knowledge.*

This chapter addresses this issue. It describes practices affecting students' access to knowledge in the schools of our sample. It explores assumptions presumably underlying the way these practices differentiated the educational opportunities and experiences of different groups of students. And it examines the issue of equity with respect particularly to poor and minority students' access to knowledge. We are concerned here, then, with both quality and equality in the educational opportunities schools provide.

VARIABILITY IN CURRICULAR EMPHASES

The initial determinants of students' curricular exposure are how elementary schools and teachers make use of time and how junior and senior high schools allocate teachers to the fields of knowledge. Data on the former provide a picture of how time is distributed among the curricular subjects and thus some insight into the nature of students' curricula.

Data on the second provide an approximation of curricular balance in schools and the curricula available to students. School-to-school differences tell us something about varying opportunities for gaining access to knowledge in different schools.

Elementary School Variability

Our data suggest that providing broad programs of study for children in elementary school need not be at the expense of the so-called basics—reading, language arts, and mathematics. This can be accomplished by assuring a minimum number of hours in the school week and using these hours efficiently for instructional purposes.

Teachers in the elementary schools we studied provided us with estimates of their allocations of time to the subjects of the curriculum over the course of a week. The totals of these estimates gave us an approximation of the time children attending these schools were in an instructional setting. Table 5-1 shows that the average for the 13 elementary schools was just under 22½ hours. The striking aspect of the data is the school-to-school range: from a low of just over 18½ hours to a high of 27½ hours. The amount of time at Dennison was 50% more than at Newport. Even if we allow for substantial error in teachers' estimates, it is reasonable to assume that school-to-school differences were substantial.

The first point to be made about these data is that there appear to be appreciable differences in the opportunities children have to gain access to knowledge in school simply because of where they happen to live. As we saw in Chapter 4, time in itself is a major factor in student achievement. Recalling the conclusion that about 70% of class time is spent on instruction, it appears that the time on classroom learning each day could be in the vicinity of only three hours—if the overall hours were low to begin with and the time spent on instruction was just average.

Table 5-1 reveals an average time allocation of 7.5 and 4.5 hours per week for the language arts and mathematics, respectively.* An average of 90 minutes daily on the former and 54 minutes each day on the latter—more than half the instructional time for these two subjects combined—appears quite satisfactory. But the range reveals school-to-school differences: from 6.4 hours per week at Atwater, Palisades, and Laurel to 8.8 at Bradford in language arts, and from 3.8 hours at Vista to 5.5 at Manchester in mathematics.

The average time spent on social studies and science together in these

---

*We believe the figure of 16% of total weekly hours for the arts (art, music, drama, and dance) as shown in Table 5-1 to be an excessive estimate, for reasons stated in Chapter 7.

TABLE 5-1

Elementary Teachers' Estimated Instructional Time in Subject Areas—Mean Hours Spent per Week and Percentage of Total Estimated Instructional Time

	Overall	English/ Language Arts	Math	Social Studies	Science	Art	Music	Drama	Dance	Foreign Languages	Physical Education	Total Academic
Vista	19.7	7.5 38%	3.8 19%	2.2 11%	2.1 11%	1.2 6%	1.2 6%	0.2 1%	0.3 1%	0.0 0%	1.2 6%	15.7 80%
Crestview	19.1	7.6 40%	4.5 23%	2.1 11%	1.3 7%	1.2 6%	1.0 5%	0.0 0%	0.2 1%	0.0 0%	1.2 6%	15.5 81%
Fairfield	24.7	7.9 32%	4.7 19%	2.5 10%	2.2 9%	2.0 8%	1.4 5%	0.3 1%	0.4 2%	0.2 1%	3.2 13%	17.5 71%
Rosemont	22.4	6.8 30%	4.4 20%	2.3 10%	1.6 7%	1.5 7%	1.2 5%	0.2 1%	0.4 2%	1.6 7%	2.6 11%	16.6 74%
Newport	18.6	8.4 45%	4.1 22%	1.8 10%	1.1 6%	1.1 6%	0.7 4%	0.0 0%	0.1 1%	0.0 0%	1.2 6%	15.5 83%
Woodlake	22.5	8.7 38%	4.5 20%	2.9 13%	2.1 9%	1.6 7%	1.1 5%	0.2 1%	0.1 0%	0.0 0%	1.3 6%	18.2 81%
Atwater	19.6	6.4 33%	4.0 20%	2.4 12%	1.6 8%	1.6 8%	1.3 7%	0.3 1%	0.4 2%	0.0 0%	1.5 8%	14.4 74%
Palisades	22.1	6.4 29%	4.5 20%	2.9 13%	2.4 11%	1.5 7%	1.2 6%	0.4 2%	0.4 2%	0.1 0%	2.4 11%	16.2 73%
Laurel	25.7	6.4 25%	4.4 17%	3.7 14%	3.0 12%	2.2 9%	1.3 5%	0.4 2%	1.2 5%	0.0 0%	3.0 12%	17.5 68%
Manchester	26.0	8.1 31%	5.5 21%	3.4 13%	3.0 12%	1.6 6%	1.5 6%	0.0 0%	0.4 2%	0.0 0%	2.6 10%	19.9 77%
Bradford	20.7	8.8 42%	5.4 26%	1.9 9%	1.6 8%	1.3 6%	0.7 4%	0.1 1%	0.1 0%	0.1 0%	0.7 4%	17.7 86%
Euclid	22.5	7.4 33%	4.4 19%	2.6 12%	2.3 10%	1.2 6%	2.7 12%	0.0 0%	0.2 1%	0.0 0%	1.6 7%	16.7 74%
Dennison	27.5	6.7 24%	4.3 16%	5.3 19%	5.3 19%	1.3 5%	2.0 7%	0.0 0%	0.5 2%	0.0 0%	2.0 7%	21.7 79%
Average number of hours / Average percent	22.4	7.5 34%	4.5 20%	2.8 12%	2.3 10%	1.5 7%	1.3 6%	0.2 1%	0.4 2%	0.2 1%	1.9 8%	17.2 77%

schools is 61 minutes per day. A half hour each day on each of these two subjects may be sufficient, but when we look at school-to-school variability, doubts enter our mind. Figure 5-1 compares 9 of our 13 elementary schools on overall time spent on instruction and time spent on social studies and science each week. The first set of three bars on the left show the averages for all 13 schools on each of these sets of data.

It becomes apparent that most of those schools providing less-than-average time for social studies and science also were below average in total time available for instruction. Conversely, those with average or above time spent on these two subjects were at or above average for total time on instruction. Laurel and Dennison were roughly an hour a week below average in language arts, but both were substantially above the average for time devoted to social studies and science.

It appears that elementary schools can eat their curricular cake and have it too. Why do we spend so much time debating (and more time and money implementing the outcomes of debate) over which school subjects are basic and must be taught when we can have all of the major ones without sacrificing anybody's definition of basics? The only logical answer is that we make policy and propose practice without sufficient data. When it comes to our schools, we too often make far-reaching decisions frivolously, on the basis of opinion and not information.

Let us look at how an instructional week might be balanced for the three upper elementary grades. First, let me assume that it would be relatively easy to become sufficiently efficient to have 23.5 hours available for instruction each week—just 13 minutes a day more than the average in our sample. Surely all schools could achieve such a goal. Let us allocate one and one-half hours each day to language arts and one hour to mathematics. It is difficult to conceive of children profiting proportionately from still more time. This leaves 11.0 hours for everything else. Let us give 2.5 hours each week to social studies, 2.5 to science, and 2.5 to some combination of health and physical education (or add some of this time to science if a science-health combination is preferred). We still have 3.5 hours each week for the arts.

But consider the curricular luxury if each school achieved an instructional week of 25 or more hours, as did Laurel, Manchester, and Dennison of our sample. There is now time to add to any of these subjects or to provide others. Additional time becomes available when good teachers use social studies, science, and health to provide rich opportunities for reading, writing, and discussing. Subjects then do double duty.

To those legislators, school board members, and others who often sound as though they would deprive children of access in school to social studies, science, health education, and the arts in order to assure atten-

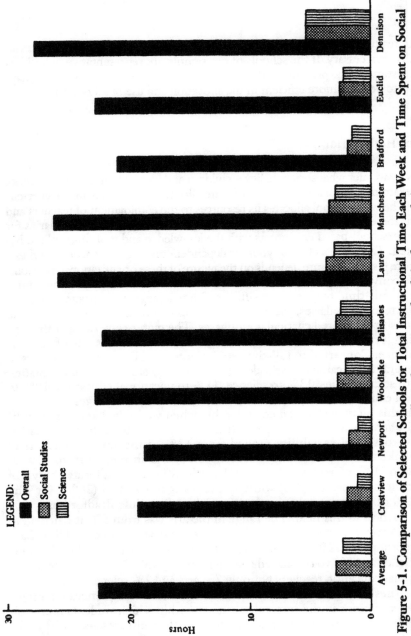

Figure 5-1. Comparison of Selected Schools for Total Instructional Time Each Week and Time Spent on Social Studies and Science. (Averages are for all 13 elementary schools in the sample.)

tion to reading, writing, spelling, and mathematics, let me simply say that the sacrifice is unnecessary. If the schools of our sample are representative, it will just be necessary for the principal and teachers of some elementary schools—perhaps most—to become more efficient in the allocation and use of school time.

Junior High Variability

One way to infer what society believes children and youths should learn in school is to examine the relative amounts of time allocated to subjects in the curriculum.[3] The way a school allocates its resources to the employment of teachers and assigns these teachers to a schedule of courses and classes sets the boundaries for students' school-based encounters with the knowledge and tools humankind has acquired. The more a child or youth is dependent on school for acquiring these, the more his or her future depends on the nature of these organizational decisions.

We converted the number of classes offered in each field into the equivalent of full-time teachers per subject. Since a large percentage of school costs is teachers' salaries, the resulting figures can be assumed to bear some relationship to desired curricular emphases. The picture emerging at the junior high level, when the data were averaged across schools, is one of curricular balance. Converted to full-time equivalents, the allocation of teachers to the several fields came out as follows: 22% to English, 17% to mathematics, 14% to social studies, 13% to science, 11% to vocational education, 10% to physical education, 11% to the arts, and 2% to foreign languages.

But this picture changed considerably when we looked at schools individually across subjects or compared them subject-to-subject. In mathematics, school-to-school variability ranged from 13% of the subject teachers at Woodlake to 22% at Palisades. Teachers of English ranged from 15% at Euclid to 31% at Crestview. One wonders why Manchester allocated only 4 of 54 teachers to science (7%) while Laurel assigned 3 of 15 (20%). Or why only 9% of Laurel's teachers were in social studies while Bradford had 18% of its teachers in this field. The range in the arts was from 5% at Fairfield to 21% at Atwater. In vocational education, the range was from only 4% at Laurel to a whopping 22% at Manchester. Atwater had 21% arts teachers but only 8% science and 8% vocational education teachers, while Manchester had 22% vocational education teachers but only 7% arts and 7% science teachers.

Are these differences and their unavoidable consequences—namely, marked variations in the curricular balance within which students meet college admissions requirements and make other choices—simply to be shrugged off as appropriately the use of local option with respect to the hiring of teachers? I doubt that, in the continuing controversy over local control of schooling, we have had in mind as probable, let alone desirable, the degree of curricular variability among schools that is implied by the data. And I am not at all convinced that this came about as a direct consequence of sustained dialogue in town meetings of the kind conducted and envisioned for the future when schooling was excluded from the Constitution as a federal responsibility.

I could be persuaded, rather, that these school-to-school variations in the employment and use of teachers are as much a result of omission as commission. They represent accretions of decisions made over the years: superintendent and board interpretations of hundreds of legislative bills, responses to local pressure groups, overreactions to current styles and fashions, immediate replacement of retiring teachers instead of responsive thinking about correcting imbalances, and the like. The imbalances reflect, more than anything else, a general lack of systematic decision making in this area and of the data likely to suggest the problems and enlighten the decisions.

The lives of school administrators, moreover, throughout the professional careers of many, have been crisis-prone and crisis-driven—desegregation, collective bargaining, declining enrollments, deficit budgets, rapid turnover in school board memberships, and so on. Curricular matters, however significant, are rarely of crisis proportions. For over a decade, they have taken second or third place to other things.

Senior High Variability

Overall, the senior highs of our sample represented a balancing of attention to mathematics (13% of the teachers), social studies (13%), and science (11%). English (18%), physical education (9%), and the arts (8%) dropped a little from their junior high level. Foreign languages rose to 4% of the teaching resources, from only 2% in the junior highs. The big change was the jump in vocational education from 11% to 24% of teachers.

School-to-school variability in the four basic academic subjects steadied somewhat, probably because an amount of each is specified for high school graduation and college entrance. Variability in the arts and physical education continued—from 3% at Fairfield to 12% at Palisades and Bradford for the arts, and from 6% at Vista and Rosemont to 14% at Newport for physical education. Schools varied markedly, apparently, in the importance attached to foreign languages. Ten percent of the subject teachers at Newport were in this field; there were no foreign language teachers at Laurel or Dennison.

But it is vocational education that catches our attention. Over 42% of the teachers at Fairfield were in this field—just slightly less than the total for English, mathematics, science, and social studies. The 41% total of vocational education teachers at Euclid is equal to the total of English, mathematics, science, social studies, and foreign language teachers. But at Newport, teachers in these five fields totaled 62% of the teaching staff, with only 13% in vocational education. Palisades, also with 13% of the teaching force in vocational education, totaled 66% for the five academic subjects. These two schools had 11% and 12%, respectively, of their teachers in the arts.

One of the fiscal necessities of schools is to schedule the teachers available rather regularly and evenly. At any given time, then, a substantially larger portion of the student body at Fairfield and Euclid would be enrolled in vocational education classes than at Newport and Palisades. Clearly Palisades, with 11 more teachers than Fairfield and a much smaller proportion in vocational education, is able to offer a much richer academic program. But let us compare the allocation of teachers at Rosemont, where the student population is 95% Hispanic, with the allocation at Fairfield High, where the students are 53% white, 42% Hispanic, 4% black, and 1% other. Total family income for Rosemont is lowest in our sample, and Fairfield is near the bottom. Rosemont allocated a larger proportion of teachers than Fairfield to every academic subject. The percentage (21) allocated to vocational education was half that of Fairfield.

Again one wonders how the marked curricular differences came about. I am unable to find in our data at either junior or senior high school levels reasonably consistent evidence that decisions to stress vocational education heavily in one school and something else in another were a rational, sensitive response to parental or community expectations. In general, parents appeared not to be intensively involved in setting goals or planning curricula for their schools. I am skeptical about claims that curricular variations are caused primarily by school boards and school administrators providing what local residents want most. Nowhere in the system is there either the necessary interaction or the relevant information. Nor are there available, usually, the time and resources for deliberate, sustained curriculum planning of the kind required to make fundamental changes in whatever now exists.

THE VOCATIONAL/ACADEMIC SPLIT

Several decades have passed since Harvard University published in 1945 its much-discussed report, *General Education in a Free Society*. At the outset the report set two goals for education: "help young persons fulfill the unique, particular functions in life which it is in them to fulfill, and fit them so far as it can for those common spheres which, as citizens and heirs of a joint culture, they will share with others."[4]

A substantial portion of the report was directed to how these goals should be pursued in high schools. Three units in English, three in science and mathematics, and two in the social studies would provide the barest minimum in "those common spheres" and would occupy about half of every student's curriculum. Beyond this core, each student's general education was to be rounded out by choice of an elective in each of these fields. General education was to be spread out over the entire span of the high school.

About a third of the total program still remained. "Here would be the chance for vocational and business courses, for work in the arts, for agriculture and home economics and a thousand other practical fields. As said many times, even these courses are not wholly vocational in intent, nor is the break complete between them and general education. On the contrary, they should carry forward the spirit of it into these realms and for these [non-college-bound] young people, exactly as does further mathematics or language for those who are going to college."[5]

Probably the most consistent theme of the report was "the binding experience of the common core" and the infusion of everything else with "the claims of a common culture, citizenship, and standard of human good."[6] There are not and must not be, said the Harvard Committee, authors of the report, two classes of citizens, separated by whether their diverse interests, gifts, and hopes depend on their heads or their hands.

Nearly fifteen years later James B. Conant, who had appointed the committee while President of Harvard, proposed a set of recommendations for the comprehensive secondary school.[7] A school to be attended by all youth, it was to reflect *both* the spirit and the substance of the Harvard Report: a common core of English, social studies, mathematics, and science; art and music for all (but with electives from which to choose); advanced work in the core subjects for the college-bound; and the opportunity for some electives beyond the common core in the general education subjects and vocational education. The specifics of Conant's recommendations became a checklist for school boards.

The Harvard and Conant reports were regarded by many at the time of their appearance as presenting rather liberal interpretations of the curricular provisions many educational leaders thought were required to meet the diversity of students coming into the secondary school, now to be attended by everyone, not just the college-bound. Today, their premises and proposals appear sadly anachronistic. The world and schools have changed.

They have changed so much that Mortimer Adler (who, with Robert M. Hutchins, viewed electives as an abomination) pessimistically stated in a 1978 interview that there was no longer the possibility of seriously discussing such issues as a common general education for all at the college, let alone the high school, level. Chaos in the curriculum was such, he said, that order could not be restored.[8]

I agree with his diagnosis but disagree with his prognosis. The struggle for equality of access to public schools is not over, but a new era in that struggle will turn more attention to what and how students learn in schools.

The public schools have assimilated to a considerable degree the diversity of population to be expected in a nation that set as a goal universal secondary education. The percentage of white fifth-graders going on to graduate from high school stabilized in 1974. The percentage of blacks in that cohort increased markedly during the 1970s. The percentage of students from Hispanic families entering high school increased dramatically, but achieving graduation for them remains a formidable problem.

But the central problem for today and tomorrow is no longer access to school. It is access to knowledge for all. The dual challenge is that of assuring both equity and quality in school programs. It is bound to take us back to the issues addressed by the Harvard and Conant reports—but in new dress.

Data from A Study of Schooling enlighten these issues and help to set the agenda. Two sets of conditions require attention. The first is an apparent division of secondary schools, particularly senior high schools, into essentially academic or vocational specialization. The second is a further division of the curriculum and accompanying pedagogy into courses presumed to be devoted to general education but in no way constituting a common core for all. I address the vocational/academic split first.

A Self-fulfilling Prophecy?

One of our most encouraging findings was the apparently high level of teachers' interactive involvement with their students in grades one through three. Of the 69 early elementary classes we observed, in only one, a second-grade class, was the pattern markedly different. Its teacher gave work assignments and then monitored the students at her desk most of the time—a pattern we observed much more frequently in higher grades.

In general, children in the first three grades liked all of their classroom activities. Over 65% responded positively to every activity, including taking tests. Their satisfaction and dissatisfaction related directly to their perceptions of their teachers. They viewed their teachers more positively if their teachers listened to them and helped them when they did their work wrong.

Although these children tended to like all of their subjects, the more academic subjects received somewhat fewer favorable votes than art or physical education. The academics were seen as hard by from 10% to 20% of the children. The students who liked school best, however, even at this early level, appeared to be more academically oriented; they were more likely to say that they liked reading and mathematics, taking tests, and completing work sheets. These students also appeared to be somewhat more verbal; they liked to talk about what they were learning. Many of those students who preferred painting and drawing were less likely to say that they liked taking tests or doing work sheets. They were also less likely to say that they liked school or schoolwork.

Let me draw some inferences from these and other data, against a backdrop of prevailing class organization in the primary grades. Organizing early elementary classes into instructional groups for reading and mathematics is about as common as a daily recess in schools. These grouping decisions are made during the first few weeks of the first grade. Teachers make them on the basis of their own judgment, sometimes with the assistance of test scores. Usually they set up three groups in each subject; two are more common in mathematics than in reading, and four are more common in reading than in mathematics. More regrouping occurs during the first few months of the first grade than thereafter. Indeed, shifts later are relatively rare.

One of the reasons for this stability in group membership is that the work of upper and lower groups becomes more sharply differentiated with each passing day. Since those comprising each group are taught as a group most of the time, it is difficult for any one child to move ahead and catch up with children in a more advanced group, especially in mathematics. It is not uncommon for a child in the most advanced group to have progressed five times as fast as a child in the least advanced group over the course of a year. Several children in the latter may be detained in the same grade for an additional year.

But according to research findings, repeating the grade generally does not improve students' subsequent performance.[9] Unless their learning problems are diagnosed and dealt with individually, these continue. By the fourth grade, children at the top and bottom differ in overall scholastic achievement, as measured by tests, by the equivalent of four full grades. In reading, this spread often is as much as six grades. These differences grow greater each year. They are not corrected by holding back for a year or two those doing poorly. This practice simply places an older nonachiever with younger classmates.

This research shows also that children performing in the bottom group, whether or not regularly promoted to the next grade, show up less well on indices of both personal and social adjustment. They are the students most likely to perceive themselves as not doing well in school or having high expectation of further failure, and most likely to want to quit.[10] They account significantly for the declining academic self-concept scores revealed in our data and reported in Chapter 3. Students' self-esteem in the academic area appears to be rather closely tied to their perception of which side of the separation they perceive themselves to be on. Schools convey to students certain values. Students sometimes come to perceive that "if you don't want to go to college, this school doesn't think you're very important."

With many others, I view schools as internalizing certain myths about human beings and their ability to learn which are well established in our society. Schools are not strongly countervailing institutions. And the circumstances of schooling make it harder rather than easier to follow alternative assumptions and beliefs.

One of these myths, a convenient one, is that there are essentially two kinds of people. Those of one group—perhaps our academically oriented group of early elementary students—learn to use their heads and should go on to work with their heads. Those of another—maybe those who preferred painting—learn to use their hands and should go on to work with their hands. School is where one cultivates the head. Consequently, "headedness" more than "handedness" is needed for and valued in school—especially in the "grammar" or "grade school." We recall from Chapters 2 and 3 that elementary school parents, more than high school parents, perceived intellectual goals to be most emphasized and preferred to retain this emphasis.

Teachers in elementary schools and of academic subjects are reinforced in many ways in the belief that their job is to develop minds and that this is best done through the academic subjects and an academic kind of teaching. Like other citizens, they tend not to see manual activity as both intimately connected with the mind and an alternative mode of learning. Arts and crafts tend to become supplemental, a relaxed, undemanding relief from the reading, writing, and arithmetic that really count, but of little value in themselves. Learning becomes a one-lane street, heavily dependent on symbols and the manipulation of symbols and not on things, the manipulation of things, and relating these things to symbols.

Those children who appear to relate most readily to the manual mode and least readily to linguistic and numerical symbols often are those judged as poor and slow learners. (This concept of poor and slow, in contrast to good and fast—and the relative irrevocability of these attributes—also is a well-established myth not countered in schools.) Their manual propensities are viewed more as evidences of a nonacademic bent than a fruitful, alternative avenue to be utilized in learning to read, write, spell, and compute. And our data show a decline in the modest use of alternative teaching approaches observed in the primary grades with advancement to the higher grades.

The higher grades bring with them a heavier instructional emphasis involving telling, questioning, taking quizzes and an avoidance of so-called learning by doing—except in the arts, physical education, and vocational education. What begins to emerge is a picture not of two kinds of instructional activities in each class appealing to alternative modes of learning, but of two curricular divisions in secondary schools. On one side are the more prestigious academic subjects, largely shunning manual activity as a mode of learning. On the other side are the nonacademics, generally characterized by the trappings of academic teaching but providing more opportunities to cultivate handedness and often featuring aesthetic qualities. My further interpretation is that the cultivation of manual skills frequently becomes an end in itself, not a means to some broader understandings of the kind, for example, that the committee writing the Harvard Report had in mind. Indeed, I see the very separation of headedness and handedness that the Harvard Report argued against and sought to avoid in general education at both secondary school and collegiate levels. This separation comes through clearly in the senior high schools we studied.

In preparation for the ensuing discussion, I immersed myself in the literature of vocational education, particularly the advocacy literature. The prime justification is that the good citizen must be prepared to become a producer of the goods and services which society requires.[11] The argument then breaks down into two component parts. The first pertains to the individual: liberal and vocational education are complementary in preparing one for effective living. The second pertains to society: vocational education provides for the nation's labor needs. The value of working with wood or metal as an alternative mode of inquiry and of work experience in developing the total person appears in the literature. But most often these virtues are quoted from philosophers (e.g., John Dewey) and educators other than specialists in vocational education.

Vocational education takes its place in the curriculum, according to most of its advocates, primarily to meet the vocational needs of 85% of the persons who enter and work in the nation's work force. It is, they say, a wise business investment for both the individual and the nation. Once established beside mathematics, science, social studies, and English, vocational education can be successfully held to be part of general education. Students are prepared not just with job skills but with an economic and social perspective on work. But the practical advantages of preparing for jobs also are very visible in the rhetoric of justification.

This rhetoric squares with the historical evolution of the purposes of schooling. Increasing industrialization and complexity of the workplace caused the home to become outmoded as vocational educator. It became the responsibility of society, through the public education system, to provide such instruction.[12] Social upheaval in the 1960s and 1970s and the accompanying efforts to provide schooling through the secondary years for increasingly diverse populations strengthened this argument. Universal schooling was interpreted to require more diversity of schooling. And more diversity—of jobs to be filled and of workers to be prepared for them—implied more vocational education.

There are evidences in our data, growing stronger in the senior highs, of students' and parents' awareness of careers and the role of school in them. For both groups the importance of vocational education increases. The curriculum in this field expands markedly from junior to senior high levels. There are courses which students preparing for college might elect to take in order to secure that array of academic, social, vocational, and personal instruction parents appear to desire. But a relatively large segment of the vocational education curriculum is made up of sequences of courses, to be taken in a given order, directed toward preparation for jobs. This kind of ordering parallels the progression in mathematics, science, and the other academic subjects. We begin to see two worlds of schooling, partly overlapping, one preparing for college and the other for jobs.

Further probing reveals these two worlds to be more separated than perusal of a school's curricular offerings might suggest. A student concentrating on academic subjects but wishing to enroll in vocational electives does not necessarily have a broad choice. He or she often discovers that a desired course is not available at the time wanted or that a prerequisite course must be taken first. Similarly, a student with a heavy vocational concentration encounters difficulties in lining up academic subjects. Some schools in our sample got around this problem by scheduling sections of academic courses specifically for vocational students. The net effect of this was, of course, to separate even further the two sides of the academic/vocational division.

Nearly all of the principals, counselors, and vocational education teachers in the high schools I visited spoke rather glowingly of the vocational education being offered. Almost invariably they spoke to the value of job preparation and placement for students who were not academically oriented and who had no chance of going to college. They were almost uniformly vague in responding when I asked about the percentage of academically oriented students enrolling at any given time in vocational classes. The important thing in their minds, clearly, was the significance of vocational education as a viable alternative to preparation for college and as a conduit to jobs. Ironically, research increasingly leads to the conclusion that vocational education in the schools is virtually irrelevant to job fate. [13]

I asked about the prospect of students switching over from a vocational to an academic concentration. It would be difficult to do this, I usually was told, after completion of the tenth grade and impossible at the end of the eleventh, without substantially increasing the length of time spent in high school. With two years yet to go, then, the two worlds of secondary education appeared quite far apart in those schools I visited.

There was no consistent pattern of vocational education dominating, as revealed by percentage of teachers in this field, in those schools with nearly all or a substantial percentage of minority students. But black and Mexican-American students frequently were disproportionately enrolled in certain specific types of job-preparatory vocational education classes in schools enrolling one or both of these minority groups as well as white students.

At Fairfield, for example, one of the mixed senior highs with a heavy vocational emphasis, a pattern of differential access to *vocational* learning was seen. We found first that the percentages of white and Mexican-American students taking vocational education classes were nearly identical to overall school percentages, which indicated that, contrary to what one might suspect at a mixed school, Mexican-American students were *not* being counseled into vocational courses per se in disproportionate numbers. Second, looking at the school's master class schedule, we found a wide variety of courses offered in the vocational area, including courses in agriculture, business, home economics and the trades. And third, from classroom data—descriptions of course content written by the teachers and the specifics of the format of classes, including length of class period and location—we found a tremendous variety among these vocational courses. Putting together these three chunks of information, the following pattern emerged relating student ethnicity, enrollment in vocational courses, and the concept of equal educational opportunity. Disproportionately large percentages of white students were found to be enrolled in vocational courses with more general content—home economics and Future Farmers of America agricultural classes—and in those oriented to-

ward business skills—bookkeeping, marketing, etc. In contrast, disproportionately large percentages of Mexican-American students were enrolled
in courses with content oriented toward specific preparation for low-level
occupations—cosmetology, auto repair, industrial and institutional cooking
and sewing, to name a few. Further, white students tended more to be enrolled
in classes of the usual school format, those of standard length and held in campus classroom. Mexican-American students tended more to be enrolled in
classes of extended length and in those held off campus, many in actual work
places.

The implications of these data are considerable. The kinds of differences
that emerged indicated that Mexican-American students more than whites
were being directed in their vocational training toward futures in lower-
class social and economic positions. Further, the format of many of the
courses taken by these students was likely to augment the effects of the content differences. These seemed not to be "regular" classes at the school. It
would not be surprising to find that students spending extended periods of
time off campus in vocational training would feel considerably distanced
from the on-campus program. Both their physical absence from school
and the development of peer associations at the work place could easily discourage students from continuing their education. Given the already serious dropout rate among Mexican-Americans—about 45% nationally—this
could be a most serious consequence. This pattern of differences was not
unique to Fairfield, but was found consistently in the vocational programs
in our secondary schools.

From other studies we know that students who are from economically
impoverished homes and frequently are black or Mexican-American are disproportionately enrolled in special, remedial classes in the early school years.
We know also that disproportionate numbers of poor children carry learning
deficits into the higher grades, where compensatory programs designed to
attack socioeconomic disadvantages tend to fall off. It should not surprise us,
then, to find disproportionate numbers in occupational training programs in
secondary schools, which are probably perceived by students and their parents
to offer greater promise of preparation for early entry to jobs. And although
these courses have academic requirements, they are viewed as easier than the
academic subjects. For some students, they offer virtually a fresh start in
what is at least partly an alternative mode of learning. Successive enrollment
in a vocational concentration also provides to poor students continuing association with peers of like interests, somewhat separated from the academic
environment long dominated by students with whom they may not have com-
peted successfully. School may become for some a more tolerable place

to be, with the opportunities it provides for association with friends, participation in sports, and preparation for and often some early participation in a job.

Without the availability of vocational education, the pressures on teachers to provide academic programs for diverse student populations undoubtedly would be greater. Simultaneously, I believe, there would be greater student dissatisfaction. Thus, advocates of vocational education gain fuel for their claim that it helps meet the needs of an increasingly diverse high school population in a society valuing universal secondary education and gainful employment.

But three questions nag at me. Is the division of secondary schools into students emphasizing vocational studies and others pursuing primarily academic programs a self-fulfilling prophecy reflecting a popular myth about learning that begins its relentless course in the primary grades? Is the ultimate fulfillment of this prophecy a further division of people into two classes of workers? Finally, is there equity among socioeconomic classes and whites, blacks, and Mexican-Americans in regard to the circumstances and the outcomes of the process? The answers put forward by some others who have studied schools are yes to the first two questions and no to the third.

My conclusions are similar. I believe that some assumptions implicit in the grouping practices of primary-level classes eventuate in the vocational/academic split found in most of the senior high schools we studied. Further, on the vocational side of this split there usually is more emphasis on job training than on general education. Job-training programs, in turn, disproportionately enroll children from poor families, many of whom also represent racial minorities. In preparing for specific jobs—often relatively low paying—these programs frequently do not provide knowledge and skills that readily transfer to other jobs. Consequently, many students do not have the vocational mobility needed in our kind of society. What appears at first to be a heartening consequence for students not prepared for college may have serious consequences both for the individual and for society.

I come to this analysis with a bias similar to that running through the pages of the Harvard Report: general education is the best preparation for effective individual functioning and responsible citizenship. I further believe that vocational education, including guided work experience, is an essential, not merely an elective, part of general education—and here I go beyond many of vocational education's strongest advocates. This means that vocational education is for all students, not just an alternative to academic studies for the less academically oriented. I want the college-bound students to include vocational studies too, just as I want to be sure that students not going to college secure a balanced program in academic subjects.

So long as vocational education is an elective of doubtful status and difficult accessibility for students preparing for college and not one of the five fingers of the hand described by the Harvard Report—mathematics and science, literature and language, society and social studies, the arts, the vocations—it will sit somewhat apart from the rest of the curriculum and have less than first-class status.[14] Justification for vocational education increasingly will depend on the school's success in job training, job placement, and upward job mobility for graduates—and not on vocational education's contribution to general education.

The issue is not whether our young people should be prepared for jobs. It is impossible to exclude for long questions of relevancy for work in any discussion of education. Presidents and deans of our most prestigious colleges and universities ruefully admit the heavy influence of a changing job market on the curriculum decisions of students. The issue, rather, is what kind of education contributes most to economic competence and satisfaction in work and life. And if this is a general rather than a narrowly specialized kind of education, how early in the lives of the young can we afford neglect of the former in favor of vocational training for targeted jobs?

Perhaps a marked swing toward the world of work would be entirely appropriate for many students at the age of 16, which most states set as the minimum permissible leaving age, if we could be reasonably sure of their previous exposure to and understanding of our "common spheres of culture." The attainment of such assurance would require, however, considerable school reorganization and curriculum development, and substantially more widespread use of those pedagogical practices now emerging as conducive to student satisfaction and learning. I believe these needed changes to be feasible and the goal of comprehensive general education for all up to the age of 16 to be attainable. But that we as a people are prepared to make the commitment and effect the improvements is not at all certain.

Most basic and difficult is whether we can change fundamentally over the period of a decade, let us say, the widely held belief that a significant part of the population is destined to have serious difficulties in school, and at best can be prepared only for jobs requiring relatively narrow programs of preparation. More formidable is the belief held by some—many of whom prefer not to dwell on it—that this is not only the way things are but the way things have to be if the least desirable and lowest paying job slots are to be filled. There are those who perceive these two beliefs to be so prevalent that our ideal of the common school cannot be realized. Short of a revolution in the surrounding society, they say, schools will remain an institution from which students gain uncommon benefits that reflect fairly accurately their privileged or disadvantaged socioeconomic status.[15]

A major issue arising out of the foregoing is whether the school has now come to that critical juncture in the twentieth century experienced by the household in the nineteenth. In the face of rapid industrialization, the family quickly became outmoded in preparing the young for jobs. In the current era of automation and rapid technological advancement, the school perhaps has passed its period of greatest effectiveness in providing job preparation, job placement, and subsequent vocational mobility for its students. There are those whose studies force us to seriously consider this possibility.[16]

I was forced to think about this issue as I walked through, and observed students in, the vocational education classes of the high schools we studied. The antiquated equipment in most of them would not have bothered me if its apparent function had been to assure all students an alternative mode of learning which we hope they will acquire through general education. The fact that the equipment did not parallel that of modern industry would have been of no significance. But it suddenly became of significance when principals, counselors, and vocational education teachers spoke eloquently about the preparation of the students using it for immediate successful entry into the job market. The incongruity often was startling.

By contrast, the program and the justification of that program by those with whom I talked at Woodlake High was refreshing. While some of the vocational education offerings there clearly were tied to the provision of skills for specific jobs, most were not. Further, most students, regardless of their career goals, were enrolled in vocational education courses, many of which sought to develop lifetime interests (e.g., photography) and not prepare for job entry. The principal and counselors at Woodlake were able to give me, independently, a reasonable approximation of the percentage of academically oriented students enrolled at any given time in such courses. Almost all took some of the courses in vocational education during their high school years.

On several indices of satisfaction Woodlake High ranked in the top three schools of our sample for both teachers and students. It was ranked somewhat lower by parents, who wanted a greater emphasis on intellectual goals but apparently not at the expense of the vocational program. Woodlake ranked fourth among our senior highs in regard to percentage of teachers devoted to vocational education (27%). But it was near the bottom in regard to teachers of mathematics and science (9% in each). Parents at Woodlake ranked fifth among our high school parent groups in average income, with a heavy concentration in the middle categories. They had high expectations for their school but were less than satisfied with some aspects of it, even while grading it quite high.

The possibility that secondary schools are not efficient and are no longer appropriate places for job training will be resisted on many fronts. It is all right for Woodlake to emphasize vocational education as part of general education, but what about schools in places of high unemployment and low income? And what about our labor needs? Many people believe that the end of public schooling is to satisfy the vocational requirements of American society. The extreme position is that "schools are factories, taking raw materials (students) and processing them through its operations (curriculums) to satisfy demands for products and services (jobs) in society."[17]

Accepting the need for society to have more typists, better automobile drivers, and a steady supply of health workers does not necessarily justify, however, the development of programs in stenographic skills, driver training, and practical nursing in the nation's secondary schools. There are other alternatives, some of which I explore in concluding chapters. We worry about increasing vocationalism in the so-called liberal arts college. Our data suggest that we should be far more worried about vocational preparation in the high schools—whether for immediate job placement or careers requiring college and university degrees.

THE ACADEMIC SPLIT

A parallel split, usually three-way, characterized the academic curriculum in the schools we studied. We found all 13 of our senior high schools to be tracked in three of the four basic subjects required for college admission: English/language arts, mathematics, social studies, and science. Ten of these were tracked in all four. Also, tracking was extensively used in the 12 junior highs we studied. And of course the grouping practices common to elementary schools, including those of our sample, are a form of tracking.

Tracking, on the surface, is an organizational arrangement by means of which students observed to be making varied progress in school are grouped so as to reduce the apparent range of achievement and performance in any one group. In elementary schools, such groupings ordinarily are within the same class, although it is not uncommon, particularly in large schools, for entire classes to be organized into slow, middle, and fast groups. Usually, there are further groupings within such classes for purposes of securing even narrower ranges of achievement within an instructional group. (Research shows, however, that the actual range in performance in any group is consistently greater than the organizational arrangement assumes and portrays.) In the secondary schools, tracking is almost invariably interclass; that is, entire classes are assumed to be low, middle, or high.

At the turn of the century, when just over 10% of America's youth attended high schools and approximately two-thirds of these were preparing for college, a relatively common curriculum devoid of tracking was provided. In a sense, what probably would be today's upper and perhaps middle tracks already were self-selected simply by attendance at secondary schools. Marked increase in high school attendance since then and, consequently, greater diversity in student populations changed all this. The growth in testing not only provided measures of achievement differences among students but also a seemingly scientific basis for sorting them. Tracking became widely practiced by educators as a device for endeavoring to reduce the range of differences in a class and therefore the difficulty and complexity of the teaching task. The practice has been reinforced from outside the school by those who believe that able students are held back by slower ones when all work together in the same class.

For many people, tracking appears to be such a rational, commonsense solution to a vexing problem that arguments against it often are ridiculed as soft, progressive, fuzzy-headed thinking. The concept has particular appeal for parents who believe their children to be above average in ability and therefore candidates for the more advanced classes. With advancing seniority, many teachers hope to be selected to teach the upper track students, who are believed to be more eager to learn and less unruly.

Ability grouping and tracking are more amenable to scientific study than are many things about schools. The research findings raise some serious questions about the educational benefits claimed for tracking and suggest some negative side effects. But these findings rarely are brought forward beyond the research literature to address tracking policies and practices. The more sensible or rational the conventional wisdom appears to be, the more difficult it is for research findings to penetrate. And when following the conventional wisdom promises to make a difficult practical problem more manageable, these findings have a difficult time gaining a hearing.

Ability grouping and tracking appear not to produce the expected gains in students' achievement.[18] As stated earlier, the achievement of students held back in a grade for an additional year is not usually enhanced. Indeed, it appears that such students achieve somewhat less well than do students of equivalent previous achievement who are promoted to the next grade. Students of average and especially low achievement tend to do less well when placed in middle or low than in mixed groups.[19]

Studies have shown there to be lower self-esteem, more school misconduct, higher drop-out rates, and higher delinquency among students in lower tracks.[20] Track placement affects whether or not students plan to go to college and the probability of their acceptance, over and beyond the effects of aptitude and grades.[21]

Finally, minority students and those from the lowest socioeconomic groups have been found in disproportionate numbers in classes at the lowest track levels, and children from upper socioeconomic levels have been found to be consistently overrepresented in higher tracks.[22] And the courts have ruled, in a number of cases brought to them, that classification of students on criteria that result in disproportionate racial groupings is discriminatory and therefore unconstitutional.

Tracking is classified in the educational literature under "school organization." Presumably, then, it generally is viewed as simply an organizational device for grouping together students appearing to be reasonably similar in ability and accomplishment. Consequently, researchers have tended not to examine the teaching practices associated with tracking; they have concentrated almost exclusively on effects of the practice. In keeping with the intent of A Study of Schooling, we probed into what was going on in the several track levels of the junior and high schools studied: curricular content, instructional practices, and social relationships and interactions.

In view of the importance generally attached to English/language arts and mathematics and the different nature of these subjects, we probed most deeply into them. What follows draws primarily from an analysis of tracking in these two fields. It should be noted, however, that tracking in social studies and science, the other two of the four basic subjects, is not markedly different.

I include here considerable detail about the kinds of data we examined. The findings from the classes studied revealed significant differences in curricular content, instructional procedures, and elements of the student-teacher relationship. They suggest the probability of marked inequities among students in regard to access to knowledge and pedagogical practices. Consequently, the implications of these findings may be the most significant and, perhaps, controversial of this entire report. They suggest an agenda for further extension of federal, state, and local interest in equality of educational opportunity. It appears desirable, therefore, to

TABLE 5-2

Classification of Classes in English/Language Arts and Mathematics Studied at
Junior and Senior High Levels

| | SENIOR HIGH CLASSES | | JUNIOR HIGH CLASSES | |
| | English/ | | English/ | |
Track Level	Language Arts	Mathematics	Language Arts	Mathematics
High	18	22	16	21
Middle	31	21	15	17
Low	12	18	18	16
Mixed	22	9	24	15
Total	83	70	73	69

provide the reader with considerable information about the data used in arriving at conclusions. This is an area of substantial research interest, except that
few studies have probed into the aspects reported here—and, so far as we were
able to determine, none of this type has examined so many classrooms.

Table 5-2 shows the distribution of all the English/language arts and mathematics classes we studied. The heterogeneous, or mixed, classes were those
in which no effort had been made to track or separate students by assessed
ability or achievement. The total enrollments of students were 3,452 for Eng-
lish/language arts and 2,304 for mathematics.

We were interested in finding out whether the content of the curriculum
differed from track to track, whether the instructional methods used were
different, and whether the social relationships and human interactions in
classes differed. We were interested also in exploring the differences between
tracked and mixed classes.

Our first question was whether the curriculum of classes at different
track levels varied in the instructional content made available to the students in them. We were able to identify in our body of data on topics
taught in junior and senior high schools two distinct types: college preparatory and life, or utilitarian, skills. High track classes at both levels
could be distinguished from the others by a significantly greater orientation toward college preparatory topics—in English, for example, the reading of standard works of literature, expository writing, grammar as
language analysis, preparation for Scholastic Aptitude Tests, and seman-
tics. These high track classes were less likely to be taught basic reading
skills, simple narrative writing, functional literacy skills (filling out forms,
etc.), language mechanics, and listening than were average or low track

classes. Average or middle classes were more like high than low track classes.

We pursued a series of such questions. I shall now summarize the findings.

High track classes spent a larger proportion of class time on instruction, and their teachers expected students to spend more time learning at home than was the case in the low tracks. High track classes devoted more time to relatively high level cognitive processes—making judgments, drawing inferences, effecting syntheses, using symbolism, and so on. Low track classes devoted a much larger share of instructional time to rote learning and the application of knowledge and skills. Again, the middle track classes were more like the upper than the lower track classes.

There were clear differences, also, in the kind of learning behavior sought. For example, almost half of the high school English teachers in our sample and a third of those in junior highs included in their lists of what they were trying to teach certain non-subject-related behaviors. In these lists, teachers described a more independent type of thinking—self-direction, creativity, critical thinking, pursuing individual assignments, and active involvement in the process of learning. Another group depicted a more conforming type of classroom behavior—working quietly, punctuality, cooperation, improving study habits, conforming to rules and expectations, and getting along with others. Teachers of high track English classes were more likely than others to seek in their students the more independent thinking behaviors. Teachers of low track classes much more frequently sought the more conforming types of classroom behavior. Teachers of middle track classes were more likely to seek some combination of the two, but again they were more like high than low track teachers in their expectations.

We used data from teachers, students, and observers to determine the variety of teaching practices and materials used in classrooms—different pedagogical approaches; use of textbooks, other books, work sheets, films, filmstrips, slides, television, teaching machines, etc. Students' perceptions were used to gain insight into the clarity of teachers' verbal instructions and expectations, as well as their enthusiasm and enjoyment of teaching. Likewise, we sought to find out whether teachers came across negatively or positively in their relations with students. Positive affect was noted whenever teachers used humor, supportive touching, or other overt expressions of enthusiasm and interest in students. Negative affect was recorded when the teacher was demeaning, sarcastic, punishing, or angry in interactions with students. Another dimension of teacher-student relationships explored was the kind of student behavior reinforced by teachers—whether conforming and passive or independent and autonomous. Finally, we explored a set of students' relationships with each other.

In almost every category we found consistent, significant differences among the classes of the three track levels. And these differences favored the upper tracks—that is, practices supported in the literature as most advantageous were perceived most frequently in the upper tracks and least frequently in the lower; and practices associated negatively with student satisfaction and achievement were perceived most and least frequently in the lower and upper tracks, respectively.

Specifically, effective instructional practices were found to be more characteristic of high than of low classes. Students in the lower tracks were the least likely to experience the types of instruction most highly associated with achievement. Only in the variety of material available for learning did low track students appear to have an advantage. There were distinct differences favoring upper tracks in regard to teachers' clarity, organization, and enthusiasm at both junior and senior high levels. Although teachers of middle track classes varied considerably, the general trend among them was toward practices found in high track classes.

Teachers in the upper track classes definitely expressed more clearly their expectations for students, and they were perceived by students to be more enthusiastic in their teaching. If these characteristics are associated with enhanced learning, as research increasingly suggests they are, then students in our upper classes appear to have been instructionally advantaged. Conversely, students in the lower tracks, requiring presumably even more of these attributes, were instructionally disadvantaged.

The environments in the classes at different track levels differed noticeably in the social relationships taking place in them. Students in high track classes saw their teachers as more concerned about them and less punitive toward them than did other students. Teachers in these classes spent less class time dealing with student behavior and discipline. Students in high track classes agreed the most strongly that other students were not unfriendly and that they did not feel left out of class activities. They reported the highest levels of peer esteem and the lowest levels of disruption and hostility among their classmates. Students in low track classes saw their teachers as more punitive and less concerned about them than did the other students. Teachers in these classes spent the most class time of any teachers on student behavior and discipline. Furthermore, students in low track classes agreed the most strongly that other students were unfriendly to them and that they felt left out of class activities. They also reported the lowest levels of peer esteem and highest levels of discord in their classes.

Not surprisingly, classes in the middle tracks fell consistently between the other two groups on these characteristics. On most, they were a little more like the high than the low track classes: curricular content, instructional practices, teacher-student relationships, and most aspects of student relationships with one another. Middle tracks were more like low tracks, however, in the student apathy and competitiveness we so often found in low track classes.

Our findings regarding untracked classes—that is, classes enrolling students of mixed ability and achievement—are significant. Part of the conventional wisdom in this area is that teachers of such classes will tend to direct their teaching to the lowest achievers, thus disadvantaging and slowing down the higher achievers. Our data challenge this assumption—most of the mixed classes resembled the high more than the low track classes in nearly all of the areas studied. Only in the curricular content of senior high math classes and instructional practices of junior high English classes were mixed classes somewhat more like low than high track classes.

The picture emerging from all of the foregoing is a relative isolation of the low track classes in our sample. This is revealed, first, in that the average, or middle, classes, although quite distinct from the high track classes, were considerably closer to them in the characteristics studied than they were to the low track classes. The picture of low track class separation is further supported by the greater similarity of mixed classes to high and average track classes than to low track classes. The assignment of students to the classes regarded as low in a school practicing tracking, according to our data, predicts for them diminished access to what increasingly are being recognized as the more satisfactory conditions for learning.

This last statement leads to another part of the pattern emerging from our data. Consistent with the findings of virtually every study that has considered the distribution of poor and minority students among track levels in schools, minority students were found in disproportionately large percentages in the low track classes of the multiracial schools in our sample. Conversely, disproportionately larger percentages of the white students in these schools were found in classes identified as high track. This dual pattern was most pronounced in schools where minority students were also economically poor.

Putting this part of the picture with the rest, we see disproportionate populations of minority students in classes perceived to be less satisfactory in several critical ways. Conversely, disproportionately large percentages of white students were enrolled in the classes perceived to be providing the more satisfactory teaching and learning conditions. There appear to be in our data, then, clear evidences of tracking's differentiating students in regard to their access to knowledge and, further, doing so disproportionately for minority students, especially poor minority students, as compared with white students.

The consistency of the use of tracking in the schools we studied provided an opportunity to look at tracks across schools. An interesting overall picture emerged. The substantial degrees of differences between tracks within a school that our data revealed tended to be repeated from school to school. In addition, it turned out that the students in the high tracks in schools A, B, C, and D were experiencing quite similar curricular content, instructional practices, and human relationships in their classes whether a school happened to be located in the northwest, southwest, southeast, or middlewest; and the same was true for the low tracks. Of course there were school-to-school variations, just as there were on almost everything we studied in these schools. But some profound similarities among schools make possible predictions regarding the behavior of the educational system.[23]

SUMMARY AND DISCUSSION

Looking across all 38 of the schools we studied and averaging the data, there is considerable surface credibility to the conclusion that the curricula were reasonably well balanced. This appears to have been so especially for the elementary and junior high schools. A modest improvement in the use of time and the allocation of the time gained to subjects other than language arts and mathematics would have improved the elementary school situation—without adding time to the length of the school day and week.

Overall, however, there was little attention to foreign languages at either the junior or the senior high level. And the emergence of vocational education as the field utilizing the largest percentage of teachers at the senior high level begins to create some concerns and reservations.

But it is the school-to-school variation at all levels that creates profound uneasiness, an uneasiness that grows greater in viewing precollegiate education from the early years of elementary school to the senior years of high school. It appears that children at Newport Elementary spent about 70% as much time on learning as the children at Laurel Elementary and distributed that time across subjects quite differently. And if the distribution of teachers can be taken as a significant criterion, the junior and senior high schools of our sample placed markedly different values on the importance of the several subjects. The school a child or youth happens to attend determines the curriculum available and likely to be taken— and there are, it appears, substantial differences in what is available.

Although these differences appear in some instances to reflect community and parental characteristics, it is difficult to square a school's emphases with its community context. We did not probe deeply into the specifics of community involvement in the development of school programs. Such data as we have suggest parent involvement in more peripheral matters. Long-term curriculum planning, enlightened by relevant data regarding current practice, is not characteristic of schools generally.

The game of chance associated with the school attended is only the beginning in a series of differentiations beginning in the early elementary grades and appearing to be highly predictive of students' academic and vocational futures. We now are very much aware, from many studies, that children come to school with varying degrees of readiness to learn. This readiness is significantly and differentially influenced by the economic and educational level of parents. Subsequent attainment is influenced by the advantages children carry into school from their homes.

Other studies as well as our own reveal in these early school years various kinds of intervention designed to compensate for the initial disadvantages brought into school by some children, particularly the poor. These interventions decline in number and variety with successive years of schooling. The major programmatic provision for individual differences is grouping, especially in language arts and arithmetic. Teachers usually are creative and sensitive in their use of euphemisms in identifying the groups—commonly high, middle, and low—so as to minimize negative associations with group membership.

There is some pupil movement from group to group, but membership in a low or high group tends to be quite stable throughout the first three years of school. Differences between the content studied and student achievement in the several groups grow greater with each successive year. There is some evidence in the literature to suggest that the upper groups experience a richer body of curricular content and that the lower groups experience more drill and rote learning.[24]

In most elementary schools grouping becomes less prevalent in grades four through six; total class instruction is the dominant pattern. Differences in academic attainment, now very pronounced, are evidenced in the gap between pupils who read fluently and those who stumble along when asked to read orally; in the quality of written work; in the work assigned by teachers; and in a host of other ways. It will be recalled from Chapter 3 that students' academic self-concepts declined steadily from the fourth grade on, according to our data. Other studies show that those students progressing slowly account for most of this decline.

The organization of classes for instruction changes markedly at the junior high level. Children accustomed to having one teacher or just a few each day now find themselves with five, or six, or seven daily in a succession of class periods. Most junior high schools are large enough to have several teachers in each subject and to be able to offer several sections of each subject at each of the three grade levels. In the schools we studied—and, presumably, the practice is not uncommon—students were assigned to these sections on the basis of present attainment levels. Other research shows that the level of the groups in which a child participated most regularly in the primary grades is highly predictive of track placement later: high, middle, or low.

The data presented in Chapter 4 revealed a steady decline in both the variety of teaching methods employed and the amount of teacher support, feedback, and corrective guidance provided with progression upward through the grades. A rather narrow repertoire of instructional procedures and limited attention to student support in the learning process, on the average, characterized the junior and senior high schools in our sample.

But within this picture of relative uniformity, there were marked contrasts between high and low track classes. Consistently, the differences in curricular content, pedagogy, and class climate favored the former. Consistently, the practices and atmosphere of the low track classes conveyed lower academic and, indeed, more modest expectations generally, as well as greater teacher reinforcement of behaving, following rules, and conforming. Consistently, students of low economic status and from minorities were disproportionately represented: high frequency of membership in low track classes; low membership in high track classes. Almost without exception, classes not tracked into levels but containing a heterogeneous mixture of students achieving at all levels were more like high than low track classes in regard to what students were studying, how teachers were teaching, and how teachers and students were interacting in the classroom.

From the first through the ninth grade, the 25 elementary and junior high schools in our sample provided what is best described as general education, with predominant attention to English/language arts and mathematics. Vocational education in the junior high, now paralleling social studies and science in teachers allocated to it, appears to have been conducted more in the spirit and substance of general education than of job preparation. Our data suggest that the elementary and junior high school today together constitute the contemporary common school. They suggest also, however, that it is only superficially common. Considerable uncommonness apparently results from the school one attends and the groups to which one is assigned.

It would be erroneous and quite misleading, however, to refer to the 13 senior highs in our sample as the common school. First, there were more uncommon than common classes in the curricula of students emphasizing college preparation in contrast to vocational education. Second, there usually was wide choice, dependent on school size, among courses satisfying graduation requirements and individual student goals. Third, there were substantial differences in the educational experiences, generally, of students in high, middle, and low tracks. Even if students enrolled in these schools were to pass a common examination for graduation, in no stretch of the imagination could their high school education be described as common or meaning essentially the same thing.

Finally, we found substantial similarity in content, instruction, and classroom atmosphere at each track level from school to school. Consequently, it appears that there could be less commonality in the school programs of all those students graduating from Vista High in a given year than among low (or high) track students graduating simultaneously from Vista and Newport.

Improving Schooling and Education

My general conclusion is that our 38 schools received children differentially ready for learning, educated them differentially in their classrooms, and graduated them differentially prepared for further education, employment, and, presumably, vocational and social mobility. The 17,163 students in our sample had quite different opportunities to gain access to knowledge during their years of schooling. At least some of these differences in opportunity to learn, it appears, were differentially associated with economic status and racial identification.

Our findings and conclusions reflect three arenas of inquiry and debate which have provided much of the context for school policy and practice in recent years. The first pertains to the power (and, indeed, the right) of schools to countervail the socioeconomic realities of the surrounding culture. The second pertains to the premises regarding human learning on which schooling is conducted and might be conducted. The third involves the practical possibilities of dealing with what appears to be a wide array of individual differences among those to be educated. I shall now turn to problems of improving schooling and education within the context of these themes.

The School and Cultural Reproduction

There appears to be little to debate in the observation that schools reflect the surrounding social and economic order. Likewise it seems obvious that the home, in spite of its steadily declining influence, advantages or disadvantages the child in enormously significant ways—especially the acquisition of language, attitudes toward others, social and economic values, physical stamina, health habits, and the like. The school, with its small percentage of time available, can seek realistically only to modify or shape slightly the areas of home dominance and to be of greater influence in just a few selected areas. Also it can seek, deliberately and consciously, to avoid reinforcing inequities inherent in the role of the home. This last is not easy because teachers themselves reflect their status in the culture. Consequently, if the school is to be anything other than a perpetuator of whatever exists in the society, states and local school districts must set—if they have a mind to—school policies that to some degree transcend and minimize the role of the classroom as reproducer of the culture.

"If they have a mind to" is a pregnant clause. Many of us are not of a mind to have our schools seek to countermand what is provided and nurtured differentially in homes. For some of us, even the faint prospect of schools seeking to do so is enough to turn us to private schools and the dismantling of the public school system. Equal access to public schools is a tolerable proposition until it leads to busing and the ultimate definition of equal educational opportunity as not just equal access but equal outcomes.[25] Alternatively, many of us believe a powerfully countervailing role for the school to be impossible and so turn attention to the reform of society, not schools. And some in this group think that the Workingman's Party of the 1820s had the right idea in proposing the early removal of infants from their homes as a feasible way to end the perpetuation of home-based inequities.[26]

This controversy has fueled turbulence and revolution and no doubt will continue to do so in parts of the world. Persons wishing to attack socioeconomic inequities directly will have little interest in what they see as a relatively puny role for the schools. Schools mirror inequities in the surrounding society and many people want to be sure that they continue to do so. Consequently, it is not easy to adjust inequities inside of schools. There is in the gap between our highly idealistic goals for schooling in our society and the differentiated opportunities condoned and supported in schools a monstrous hypocrisy.

Large numbers of spokespersons for colleges, universities, business, and industry claim that young people seeking higher education or employment are ill-prepared to engage in the reading, writing, thinking, and human relationships required. The claims have been made year after year for many years—since long before the present clamor over declining student achievement. And there has been plenty of supporting evidence, yesterday as well as today.

There is one fundamental difference between today and yesterday. At the turn of the century and for a few decades thereafter, the charges regarding poor preparation were directed to graduates of the eighth grade and elementary schools. Today they are directed to graduates of the twelfth grade and secondary schools—and of course are passed downward. At the beginning of the twentieth century, the ideal (and to considerable degree the reality) of the common school was to educate all children commonly until they were prepared for entry into the work force or continued formal education. This level typically was assumed to be reached on completion of an eight-grade elementary school. At this point, with no more vocational education than a little manual arts for the boys and simple home economics for the girls, a division occurred. The majority entered the work force; a minority entered the high school.

Today it is widely assumed that graduation from high school constitutes completion of the common school. By graduation time about 25% of the nearly 100% of elementary school graduates entering secondary schools already will have entered the work force or be unemployed and will not be on hand for graduation. Most of these will be ill-prepared in those areas in which employers depict high school graduates as deficient, whether or not they took vocational education or training during their school years and whether or not their school principals and counselors exhort the job placement virtues of these programs. Of the remaining 75% completing high school, less than half will go on to college immediately following graduation. The larger group will seek entry into the work force. Many of these will be considered by their employers as ill-prepared in the areas in which spokespersons for both colleges and the world of business and industry claim high school graduates to be deficient.

The workplace today is a more sophisticated place than it was even three or four decades ago. Persons lacking proficiency in language, computation, and independent thinking will gain access only to its fringes and will be severely constrained in job mobility and earnings. To the extent that the high school substitutes job preparation for opportunity to learn what the mainstream and not just the periphery of the workplace requires, it does a disservice. And in doing so, it reinforces rather than countervails society's inequities.

It can be argued that a very large proportion of jobs require no more than a tenth-grade education. Perhaps this is why we continue to perpetuate the incongruity of a minimum leaving age of 16 in most states but a graduating age of 18. We have in mind, presumably, ten years of general education rather than specific vocational training for the small percentage of those jobs for which schools might conceivably prepare. However, large numbers of the students in the schools we studied already were so deeply into vocational education courses that transfer to a predominantly academic curriculum was difficult or impossible.

What has occurred over several decades, it appears, is that the conventional expectations for common schooling, beyond which there will be a division between students continuing their education and those entering jobs, have expanded to encompass high school graduation. Presumably graduation means completion of a balanced, relatively common curriculum. In reality, however, only a fraction of those entering the tenth grade complete such a curriculum. I would place this fraction at a third over all schools. Assuming that this third is reasonably competent in the general requirements of the workplace, the clamor over ill-prepared students and workers pertains primarily to those in the other two-thirds.

To assure that a larger fraction will possess this competence—and, presumably, to "protect" the meaning of a high school education—many states are once again requiring graduation examinations. And there has been talk at the federal level of national examinations. The practice appears to be late, in conflict with other federal and state interventions in school, and punitive. We insist on our young being in school until the age of 16. We generate the convention of high school graduation being desirable. But to make employable the students who appear to lack scholastic aptitude and to assure workers for jobs not specifying a high school certificate of completion, we encourage—and indeed subsidize—job-oriented vocational curricula. The requirement of a general examination for graduation would appear to make it even more futile for most of these students to push on toward high school completion.

The resolution of the dilemmas and the ironies associated with them lies in curriculum reform, the sensitive diagnosis of students, and guidance in their selection of programs. One obvious solution is specification by regional accrediting agencies that not just the curriculum of each school but that of each student represent a balance of studies over the three years of the senior high school. If the minimum were 15% in English, 10% in each of mathematics, social studies, science, vocational education, the arts, and physical education, and 5% in foreign languages, a student still would have 20% of his or her time for following up special interests in any of these. The central problem in this recommendation is, of course, that the continued practice of tracking would assure anything but a common secondary school.

But perhaps a common secondary school up to the age of 18, within the present framework of schooling, is neither desirable nor attainable. A more radical alternative comes to mind. Why not general education for all through the age of 16 rather than 18? The curriculum to this point would be from 70% to 80% common for all. There would be no electives in this common curriculum, but students would be able to pursue areas of special interest (e.g., additional work in the arts) for the balance of time available.

This alternative implies much more than adjusting the length of the common school to the present legal age for leaving. It involves a reorganization of the present system of schooling into several units not corresponding to the present levels of elementary, junior, and senior high school. It also involves rethinking the years beyond. I develop such a plan in considerable detail in Chapter 10.

The School and Individual Differences in Learning

The initiative for doing more to keep the school from reproducing and perpetuating in its practices inequalities of the surrounding society must come primarily from without. Those forces that have kept the spotlight on equal access to schools will concentrate more in the future on policies designed to provide greater equity with respect to access to knowledge inside schools. Simultaneously, much can be done within schools to reduce those provisions and arrangements that conspire to thwart access to the most advantageous educational experiences.

The major professions seek continuously to provide their members with the knowledge and skills needed to transcend the conventional wisdom of the public they serve. Research and the transmission of the implications of findings to professionals are the ultimate weapons for fighting myths and quackery. Unfortunately, the floor of professional preparation with which teachers begin to practice is low, and as we shall see in Chapter 6, their links subsequently to opportunities for further professional growth tend to be weak. Consequently, teachers too often reflect in their practice the conventional wisdom about learners and learning prevailing in the surrounding culture.

Thus popular assumptions and myths regarding headedness and handedness, good and poor students, fast and slow learners, and the like are generally accepted and at the outset built into classroom organization. Instead of creating circumstances that minimize and compensate for initial disadvantages in learning, teachers unwittingly create conditions that increase the difficulty of eliminating disadvantage. The mixing of students performing well or poorly—and especially the creating of opportunities for the former to assist the latter—advantages those not performing well without disadvantaging the others. And yet in the key subjects of early schooling, language arts and mathematics, these students are grouped separately.

If teaching practices are to reflect in such ways the well-established notion that there are winners and losers in learning, as in everything else, teachers require only common sense and not much professional preparation. A vicious cycle is created and so there is little support either for preparing teachers professionally or for paying them as professionals.

Grouping children by ability or achievement reflects what many people believe to be desirable or necessary, appears to provide for present individual differences, and helps teachers accommodate to a difficult pedagogical problem. Also, it is a procedure experienced by teachers when they were students that is passed along from teacher to teacher with little or no questioning. This form of classroom organization can be justified, many teachers believe, as a way to satisfy the popular plea to individualize instruction and learning. In practice, however, teachers tend to believe, as stated earlier, that the grouping practice itself has largely taken care of pupil variability. Consequently, providing further for individual differences through instructional modifications is not necessary. Ironically, then, a device practiced in the name of individual differences actually may contribute to thwarting attention to students' individual learning problems. Steadily, it appears, the decline in the most desirable pedagogical techniques with upward progression through the grades revealed in the schools we studied is greater for the low groups.

Tracking in the junior and senior high school years compounds the process. There is a growing separation between the kinds of content studied in high and low tracks, and also a separation of vocationally oriented and academically oriented students.

This relentless process is justified by resorting, on one hand, to the myth of inevitable and irrevocable human variability and, on the other, to the popular rhetoric of providing for individual differences in learning. A self-fulfilling prophecy appearing to "prove" the prevailing assumptions is created. Practices justified as providing for human individuality appear, rather, to result in giving up on many individuals.

A deeper, more comprehensive professional preparation involving attitudes, knowledge, and pedagogy will be required of teachers if this situation is to be turned around. But schools can begin now with the more optimistic pedagogical assumption that nearly all children can learn, given appropriate support, corrective feedback, and time. School principals can do much to set the expectation that it is teachers' responsibility to have each child succeed. Retaining a large percentage of poor students in a grade for an additional year is less proof of standards than of instructional ineffectiveness. The good teacher is not the one who fails a third of the class but the one who brings an overwhelming percentage of children to mastery of the material. The district superintendent and central office staff, in turn, can assist by both reinforcing these messages of hope and responsibility and bringing to local schools teaching resources, support for staff development, and the encouraging insights now emerging from research.

Some advocates of mastery learning believe that differences in individual learning rates can be eliminated. Provocative though this idea obviously is, it has, I believe, less practical significance for the next decade or so than the inherent concept of nearly all students being able to learn mathematics, science, social studies, and the rest *if appropriate learning conditions are established.* In the light of this proposition, we have scarcely begun the task of providing universal education through the secondary school—that great experiment for which this country has been widely praised.

There will continue to be, I believe, even under highly favorable teaching conditions for all, substantial differences in intellectual orientation, knowledge, and work habits among high school graduates. In part this will be because school is not the only place one learns. But let us assume the somewhat more modest and increasingly justifiable claim of exponents of mastery learning, that virtually all students can be brought along a full grade per year by techniques involving peer assistance, diagnostic testing, corrective feedback, and the like.[27] And let us assume that completion of ten such years assures the mastery of a balanced curriculum—in effect the completion of a common school. Presumably, some students would have chosen more advanced courses in the basic subjects from the 20% or so optimal schedule recommended earlier.

There is no doubt in my mind that we would have in this 16-year-old cohort a better educated youth group than now completes our secondary schools. Some of these would be well qualified to go directly to college—the well-qualified percentage would equal that of today's high school graduates. Many more would reach a comparable level if provided the opportunity to continue their academic studies, perhaps in a community college, while engaged in vocational education and work during subsequent years. I discuss in Chapter 10 some of the possible options for youth following graduation from secondary school by the age of 16.

I do not exclude the possibility of pursuing these options within the framework of a secondary school enrolling youth to the age of 18. This alternative no doubt would be more readily acceptable because it involves less change. But this is reason enough to reject it. Unfortunately, the easiest alternatives to effect are those that don't change anything.

Chapter 6

Teachers and
the Circumstances
of Teaching

It is accurate, I think, to characterize the economic, social and political context of schooling as having been more negative than positive during the 1970s. School personnel perceived themselves to be working in an atmosphere of criticism, declining confidence and support, and little appreciation. Further, the studies of Coleman,[1] Jencks,[2] and scholars abroad[3] were widely interpreted to mean that teachers, at best, contribute modestly to the intellectual motivation and academic attainment of their students. Their contribution, some researchers concluded, ranks a poor second—far behind that of the home. This is not an inspiring proposition for educators.

Simultaneously, however, more encouraging evidence regarding the role of the teacher in the classroom was accumulating. I have referred to some of the studies presenting this evidence in preceding chapters. This work suggests that able teachers, under favorable circumstances, do make an important difference in students' learning, especially in those areas not likely to be attended to in the family. These studies are in fact consistent with the popular notion that teachers constitute the one single element of schooling most influencing students' learning.

Some people even go so far as to say, "Everything depends on the teacher." It seems reasonable to expect the teacher to be a key factor in the schooling process; and indeed our data showed that students' perceptions of their teachers' interest in them as persons were related to their satisfaction in the classroom. Yet we know that teachers, who are able to demonstrate certain effective teaching practices when called upon to do so, do not necessarily use these practices hour after hour in the classroom, and that they are restrained and inhibited by circumstances under which they teach—such as too many students in a confined and relatively inflexible space, too many hours each day with classes, administrative controls and restraints, interruptions, and students whose minds are on matters other than the subject matter before them.[4] These are things teachers often identify as limiting their effectiveness.

So while studies of teachers and teaching and popular belief support the importance of teachers in the school learning of children and youths, the notion that "everything depends on the teacher" is simplistic and exaggerated. An array of factors make up the quality of school life; teacher behavior is one of them, and the others are many and various. They include a school's sense of mission, the principal, policies and directives of the central office, parental interest and collaboration, traditions, the stability of the faculty and student population, and so on.[5]

If teachers are potentially powerfully influential in the education of children and youth in school but the circumstances of teaching inhibit their functioning, then we need to modify these circumstances so as to maximize teachers' potential. The directions of school improvement become reasonably clear: diagnose and seek to remedy the impeding conditions; improve teachers' knowledge and skills. This chapter seeks to glean from our data some insights into the teachers and the circumstances of their teaching in the schools of our sample that might suggest ways of accomplishing these things.

The sample of teachers described here resulted from our initial selection of schools. They are the teachers we happened to find there. We surveyed 1,350 of them—286, 400, and 664 at the three successive levels. Of these, we interviewed 956—140 elementary, 337 junior high, and 479 senior high teachers.

TEACHING: THE JOB AND THE ROLE

It is frequently charged that teachers have an easy time of it—a short day and long vacation periods. This can be a careless charge. For instance, the vacations teachers receive in a nine-month year, September through May, are equivalent to what many workers enjoy in a twelve-month year. June, July, and August usually are nonworking months. But they are inaccurately described as a vacation. Some teachers are employed in the educational system during those months, and many more are employed out of it. They prefer paid work to unpaid leisure.

The length of the working day and week is a more complex matter. It proved difficult to put together a composite picture of the working week for the teachers in our sample. What emerged from our data was a combination of the inflexible schedule normally associated with blue collar jobs and a little of the flexibility associated with a profession, especially at the secondary level. Daily teaching constituted the largest, relatively inflexible portion. Beyond this, there were planning lessons, correcting papers and examinations, reporting student attendance, going to meetings, reporting to and conferring with parents, and providing various kinds of data for school records. There were variations in working time among our teachers paralleling variations that are reported nationally. In adding up the hours, one arrives quickly at a minimum work week of 37½ hours for the teachers in our sample—comparable to the work week of many blue collar workers and secretaries. But for those appearing to be most dedicated it is easy to see how this figure climbs to 50 or even more hours each week.

Many schools districts specify, sometimes in a negotiated agreement, that teachers be in the building for a specified time each day, frequently from 8 A.M. to 4 P.M. Districts and schools vary in regard to the time allocated to teaching and other activities during these hours. Union contracts often prohibit any requirements taking time over and above these specified hours. But the work week varies in length and kind beyond such specifications. Teachers of the first and sometimes the second and third grades tend to have a shorter teaching day, with children usually arriving at 8:30 or 9:00 A.M. and departing at 2:30 or 3:00 P.M. But the nature of their work with children is such that they spend substantial chunks of time each day preparing materials and arranging the room for the next day's demands. Elementary school teachers—upper and lower—generally do not have periods set aside for planning during the day. It appears that they take an average of ten hours a week preparing for instruction. With the addition of time also for instructional duties, the work week adds up to 40 or more hours. In a survey conducted by the National Education Association in 1967, teachers reported an average work week of approximately 47 hours, figures somewhat higher than ours. Elementary school teachers reported about two hours less time per week than did secondary teachers.[6] These figures approximate our own sufficiently to suggest only modest change over succeeding years.

High school teachers more frequently have a planning period during the day. But 40% of our sample reported spending 2 to 3 hours per week per class directed toward preparation and another third reported spending 4 to 6 hours this way. If each taught five different classes, we get a picture of 10 to 15 and sometimes more hours a week spent on preparation. For some teachers, one preparation might serve for several classes, but again, hours for the other activities listed must be added. Our data at both elementary and secondary levels suggest a minimum of 37½ hours of work per week, a modal range of 40 to 45, and a high of just over 50. Clearly, teachers who seek to plan very carefully, to create alternative kinds of classroom activities, or to assign and read essays regularly cannot do what they expect of themselves within a normal work week.

National statistics tell us that large numbers of teachers moonlight, especially those raising children. Given even the minimum demands of teaching, it is difficult to see how they can do this without neglecting their jobs and families and depleting their energy. If we add to these circumstances the general assumption that the professional preparation of many teachers is incomplete and must be supplemented while on the job, we begin to have grave reservations regarding the prospects of improving schools and teaching without resorting to very unconventional strategies. The task of simultaneously upgrading two million teachers and the circumstances under which they teach takes on formidable proportions.

One rather unique characteristic of teaching may have more of an impact on job satisfaction than we realize. The lunch break is a significant part of the work day for most workers. Stand at noon in the lobby of any large office building. The exuberant chatter of hundreds of workers bursting forth from opening elevators is deafening. They are off to shop or to lunch with friends and fellow workers, perhaps with a carafe of wine to enhance the flow of conversation. Contrast this scene with lunchtime in the average school. In the elementary school in particular, teachers are required or urged to eat with their children. Often this is done in a room that doubles as a gymnasium and smells accordingly. Where there is a special room for teachers, it often is small and unattractive. Whether or not there is a separate room, students are ever-present and require some attention.

Cafeteria staffs usually do an admirable job of serving large numbers of people reasonably nutritious, inexpensive food under demanding circumstances. Principals, teachers, and students occasionally have joined to create a lunchroom environment with amenities such as small tables, tablecloths, and a vase of flowers on each. Even under the best of circumstances, however, lunchtime at school falls far short of providing the freedom, relaxed ambience, and refreshment of lunchtime for most workers outside of schools—and so falls short of providing for teachers the opportunities to establish personal relationships with each other.

We must remember, too, that apart from their lunch hours teachers are walled off from one another for most of the day. Teaching may be a more lonely and socially circumscribing vocation than we realize. What effects this may have on teachers' behavior, self-renewal, and relations with students are difficult to estimate.

Why Teachers Teach and Why They Would Leave

It seems reasonable to assume that men and women go into teaching for much the same reasons other people go into a vocation or profession. They may like the idea of teaching or follow in parents' footsteps or be persuaded by friends. All these were among the reasons given by teachers in our sample. But a large portion (57%) of the prime reasons for entering teaching chosen by these teachers clustered around the nature of teaching itself: the desire to teach in general or to teach a subject in particular (22%); the idea of teaching as a good and worthy profession (18%); and a desire to be of service to others (17%).

There are times when individuals and groups become eloquent in depicting teachers as being full of love for children and dedicated above all else to serving them. This is not the picture I get from our data; nor do I derive the opposite. Rather, teachers are made of clay like the rest of us and have not uncommon aspirations to engage in satisfying work. Liking the children was not, for most in our group, the major reason for entering teaching. This was chosen by about 15% of the elementary school and 11% of the secondary school teachers. This does not mean that the others do not like children. It means only that liking for children was not, for the large majority, their primary reason for choosing to teach. Not surprisingly, money wasn't either.

Love for children is an elusive concept to which a degree of mysticism readily is attached. It is nice to think that all teachers love all children, but it is more realistic to believe that we cannot count on this attribute and know little about its development. Rather, we should expect teachers to seek to understand children's learning problems and to provide constructive guidance. These attributes, clearly, are educable. And the conditions under which teachers seek to do these things are modifiable.

It comes as no surprise that the teachers in our group who entered teaching because of the professional values inherent in it, an interest in or desire to teach a subject, or liking for children said most frequently that their expectations had been fulfilled and that they would be likely to select teaching again. Those who chose teaching because they were influenced by others or for economic reasons were the least likely to report fulfillment of career expectations.

Overall, 74% of the teachers reported that their career expectations had been fulfilled, and 69% said they would again select education as a career. Comparing the three levels of schooling, we find that elementary school teachers expressed the most career fulfillment (80%) and greatest likelihood of going into education for a second time (77%). Junior high teachers were lowest in both categories (67% and 64%, respectively).

The 1967 report of the National Education Association referred to earlier again reported somewhat higher figures.[7] (It is difficult to compare these data because the questions asked in the NEA study of five school districts were slightly different from ours.) The NEA report and other studies reveal that married women would be the group most likely to enter teaching again; men teaching at the secondary level would be least likely. Studies also show that the energies and interests of women teachers flow back and forth between claims of the family and claims of the work in rhythmic stages of the life cycle. Their interest in teaching at any given time appears not to be closely tied to incentives provided by school systems.[8]

I assume that good schools depend in part on a reasonably stable, professionally satisfied teaching staff. Information about why their teachers left or would leave is important knowledge for school districts to have. Teachers quit, it appears, for the same kinds of reasons other people move from one line of work to another. The teachers in our sample chose such reasons for leaving as being frustrated in what they wanted to do or disappointed in their own performance.

Interpersonal conflicts—with fellow teachers and the administration—and poor resources were chosen relatively infrequently at all levels as reasons for leaving teaching. Even problems with students ranked low. It was personal frustration and dissatisfaction in the teaching situation that appeared to bother most teachers. If one goes into teaching with expectations of being able to teach and be of service and then is frustrated in realizing these expectations, dissatisfaction sets in and quitting becomes an alternative. There is nothing unusual about this.

It is interesting that though money was not a major reason teachers gave for entering teaching, it ranked second as a reason for leaving. We might speculate that, anticipating rewards intrinsic to the work, teachers begin with a willingness to forego high salaries. However, when confronted with the frustration of these expectations, the fact that they sometimes are paid less than the bus drivers who bring their students to school may become a considerable source of dissatisfaction as well.

There is now an extensive body of research into both the conditions of the workplace and the frustrations of unskilled, skilled, and professional workers, and the conclusions from the studies have been widely used in programs of improvement, often negotiated and built into contracts.[9] By contrast, there have been surprisingly few comparable studies of schools. Talk of securing and maintaining a stable corps of understanding teachers is empty rhetoric unless serious efforts are made to study and remedy the conditions likely to drive out those already recruited. The relatively low monetary return for teaching makes it even more urgent to enhance the appeal of teaching as satisfying human work by improving work conditions.

In summary, the large majority of our sample, at all levels, tended to be idealistic and altruistic in their views of why they chose to teach. Also, the percentages expressing fulfillment of career expectations and a desire to enter teaching a second time appear to me to be quite high, though lower than they were in the mid-sixties. There was a noticeable decline at the junior high school level with respect to both answers. There was a clear, positive, relationship between expressions of career fulfillment and selection of the more professional and idealistic reasons for entering teaching. All in all, it seems to me that our data should make us somewhat optimistic about appealing to teachers to join with others in planning and conducting efforts to improve our schools, especially if such efforts are accompanied by efforts to eliminate whatever most interferes with satisfaction in teaching. For just one example, additional weeks of summer employment focused on school improvement, with appropriate salary adjustments, would provide an incentive.

Teachers' Beliefs about Teaching

The back-to-basics movement of the 1970s was fueled in part by the charge that the schools had been taken over by a generation of teachers stressing progressive beliefs and practices. That is, instead of exercising firm control in the classroom and concentrating on fundamental skills and subject matter, teachers had become overly permissive in regard to both student behavior and academic performance. The consequences, it was charged, were poor discipline and poor student achievement.

Our data were collected in the late 1970s. They reveal in our sample of teachers neither strong and consistent agreement on the virtues of progressive classroom practices nor strongly shared, consistent values. Indeed individual teachers were not internally consistent in their educational beliefs. Overall, these teachers endorsed traditional beliefs a little more strongly than they did progressive beliefs. If our sample is reasonably representative, it is difficult to believe that the classrooms of the 1960s and 1970s were populated by people markedly different from those teaching earlier or later. It is exceedingly doubtful that teachers as a group are tossed this way or that by fluctuations in philosophical belief so that school practice for a time becomes overwhelmingly traditional or progressive. The rhetoric about what *should* be undoubtedly shifts more rapidly and strongly than either the beliefs or practices of teachers. Constructive attention to our schools would be vastly enhanced if more of us could resist the tendency to blame the ills of schooling on rampant progressivism or any other "ism."

Data on our teachers' beliefs about their work do provide, however, some useful insights into teachers and teaching. They were asked to express the extent of their agreement or disagreement with 21 statements of belief about student-teacher relations, teacher control, what should be learned, student participation in planning, and so on. The six response options ranged from "strongly agree" to "strongly disagree." We chose about evenly items commonly associated with progressive and traditional views. We classified as traditional, for example, belief in strong teacher discipline and control and in the teacher's dominant role in teaching. We classified as progressive a positive view of students' independent thought and belief in student participation in planning classroom activities, to cite two more examples.

There was very little consensus. At all three levels of schooling these teachers—like other teachers, according to other studies—endorsed traditional and progressive beliefs simultaneously.[10] More than half strongly agreed that good teacher-student relations are enhanced when the teacher is clearly in charge of classroom activities, maintains classroom order and control, and assures that students are kept busy. But there was simultaneous rather high agreement that learning is enhanced when teachers praise generously the accomplishment of individual students, that the best learning atmosphere is created when the teacher takes an active interest in the learning problems of students, and that student participation in planning is desirable. These latter are things frequently endorsed as desirable in teacher preparation programs and in workshops and classes taken while on the job. Junior high teachers endorsed traditional beliefs more strongly than did their counterparts in elementary or high schools, but only mild or moderate agreement with the 21 statements was the dominant pattern at all levels.

In these and other data we begin to see a picture of what many teachers in our sample apparently believed in and wanted to do as teachers. They agreed, generally, on the importance of basic skills and subject matter and of increasing students' store of information about the various fields of knowledge. At the same time, they perceived the necessity for teachers to be in control of classroom circumstances. Presumably, if student behavior gets out of hand, teachers cannot fulfill their central function of teaching. My interpretation is that teachers, aware of the rather crowded box in which they and their students live each day, see the need to be in control, to prevent unruly students from dominating, as a necessary condition for student learning—even though they might prefer simply to act on their beliefs about good pedagogy. A class out of control and a teacher's giving praise generously for student accomplishment are incompatible. A class out of control is not a class engaged in academic learning.

Teachers' Perceptions of Problems

As reported in Chapter 3, when asked to select what they perceived to be their school's one biggest problem, teachers tended to select problems affecting their teaching but appearing to be beyond their control—lack of student interest, school too large and classes overcrowded, lack of parent interest, administration, inadequate resources, and, at the junior high school level in particular, students' misbehavior. These are matters that get in the way, frustrating teachers' daily efforts to perform their central function. Students and parents, on the other hand, were more inclined to select students' personal problems (e.g., use of drugs and alcohol) and much less inclined to select problems directly related to the environment for learning and teaching. When asked not to choose just one problem but to rate on a three-point scale the seriousness of problems in a list, secondary teachers elevated drugs and alcohol to approximately the intensity level perceived by students and parents. But, in general, they continued to rate as most serious problems of student behavior, lack of student interest, and lack of parent interest which they perceived to impinge upon or frustrate their teaching role.

The two different kinds of problems—both affecting students' learning experiences—suggest differing responsibility and strategies for school improvement. The matters teachers identify as frustrating their pedagogical role are essentially school- and school-district-based. That is, they are matters which the board, the superintendent, the principal and, indeed, the teachers collectively can do something about. They provide an agenda for improving the circumstances under which teachers work, elements of which teachers see as frustrating their desire and efforts to teach. The drug and alcohol problem, although it may manifest itself in schools because schools are a daily gathering place for youth, is not just a school problem. Nor are the behavioral problems of the young. They are society's and each community's problems.

Once again, what comes through clearly, though, is the need for school-by-school agendas based on hard data. Schools vary enormously in both the problems perceived by those most closely associated with them and the intensity or seriousness associated with these problems. One might well regard as self-serving a list identified only by teachers. But when teachers, parents, and students perceive there to be a substantial number of serious problems and agree on the nature of several of these, a useful agenda emerges.

It seems reasonable to assume that a school with many problems of great intensity would be a quite different place than a school with fewer problems of less intensity. It would appear to follow that at schools of the first type there would be less energy on the part of teachers and students for the teaching-learning process. Problems such as "size of school," "inadequate resources," "lack of parent interest," "administration," and "rules and regulations" (federal, state, and local policies), perceived by teachers to be beyond their control, probably would cause day-to-day frustration in their working environment. Other problems, such as drugs and alcohol use among students, appearing to be even further beyond their control, might be expected simply to add to a sense of frustration and impotence.

The skeptic asks, "So what? Schools are not for teachers but for students." In order to test the assumption that the press of many problems perceived to be intense does interfere with the teaching-learning process, we correlated the students' perceptions of the quality of their education—as measured by agreement or disagreement with the statement, "This school gives students a good education"—with the composite problem scores for teachers and students. We found a strong relationship. It supports the hypothesis that intense problems experienced in the school and classroom environment by students and teachers negatively influence the quality of education provided, as perceived by students.

Teachers' Satisfaction

Studies of a variety of workplaces suggest that remedying conditions tending to frustrate and irritate the workers increases both their satisfaction and productivity—up to a point. It is reasonable to assume that this is equally the case for teachers. However, although there are studies on teacher satisfaction, it has proved difficult to establish a pattern of relationships between environmental problems and satisfaction and, in turn, between teachers' satisfaction and a criterion of productivity such as student achievement. More common are studies showing that supportive conditions such as sensitive leadership by the principal, availability of help, and involvement in schoolwide decisions, tend to be associated with greater enthusiasm, professionalism, and career fulfillment on the part of teachers.[11] And as we have seen, there is some evidence in our data that positively oriented teachers tend to have a positive rather than a negative influence on the classroom learning environment.

But it should not be necessary to establish these relationships scientifically in order to accept the proposition that teachers, like other humans, are entitled to a satisfying workplace. Then if we were able to ferret out the elements of what makes their workplace satisfying to teachers, we would have specific entry points for improving it. Using this knowledge to change the workplace no doubt would enhance our ability to establish the nature of any existing patterns of relationship between school conditions and students' satisfaction with the education provided and perhaps even their achievement. We would be in a good position then to differentiate the influence on students of assorted conditions of the workplace from teachers' personal characteristics, which are less amenable to analysis and direct intervention. Even if student achievement improved only modestly or not at all, teachers at least would benefit from improvements in the circumstances under which they teach.

In our extensive body of information on schools were many data from which we might deduce bases for schools' appearing more or less satisfying to the teachers in them. These data were derived from 120 questions asked of teachers about their school and work. The questions clustered into several categories: there were questions about the climate of the environment as determined by teachers' autonomy in carrying out their work, the quality of staff decision-making processes, friendships with other teachers and parents, personal safety, and so on; about facilities and resources available for all students; about the availability of resources related to teachers' work and comfort; about teachers' personal satisfaction with their career choice; about teachers' perceived problems with students; and about teachers' perceptions of parents and parents' role in the school. And of course there were the letter grades by which teachers graded their school and the congruency between goals teachers perceived to be emphasized and goals they would prefer.

I shall not enter here into the complex processes by means of which positive and negative responses of teachers were determined, tallied, and compiled for schools. The net result was a separation into two sets, those schools perceived by teachers as "more satisfying" and those perceived as "less satisfying" than the other schools in our sample. When all of the data were added up, six high schools emerged as clearly "less satisfying" and three as distinctly "more satisfying" in the eyes of teachers. It will be recalled from Chapter 3 that for each school we compiled a composite problem score that was a combined measure of variety and intensity of problems perceived by teachers, parents, and students, respectively. Of the six "less satisfying" high schools, three received the highest average score for number and intensity of problems from teachers, students, and parents. These were Newport, Bradford, and Manchester. The six were also the first six in rank order for problems as perceived by both teachers and parents; five were the top five for problems as perceived by students. The three schools coming out as "more satisfying" for teachers—Dennison, Euclid, and Woodlake Highs—also were the three schools perceived by teachers and students and three of the four schools perceived by parents to have the fewest and the least intense problems.

The pattern was similar for the junior highs. Fairfield, Laurel, Newport, and Bradford emerged as the less satisfying group of schools for teachers. They were perceived by teachers, parents, and students to be high in problems. Atwater, Vista, and Euclid constituted the more satisfying group for teachers. They were perceived by all three groups as low in problems.

The pattern was less pronounced at the elementary level, primarily because there was less consistency between teacher and parent views on school problems. Elementary students were not asked to rate school problems. But even here, Fairfield, Crestview, and Manchester, three of the four less satisfying schools emerging from the data derived from teachers, were the three schools ranked highest for problems by teachers, and Fairfield was ranked highest by parents. The most satisfying elementary schools, such as Dennison and Vista, were perceived to be low in problems by both teachers and parents and more satisfying by teachers.

The emerging hypothesis is that schools staffed by teachers who are less than satisfied are likely to be schools perceived by teachers, parents, and students as having a greater array of serious problems. Conversely, schools in which teachers are more satisfied with their careers and teaching circumstances are relatively unlikely to be perceived by teachers, parents, and students as having serious problems. Happily, these are likely also to be the schools most frequently perceived by students as giving them a good education.

These observations do not lead to the conclusion that "everything depends on the teacher." Quite the contrary. They lead to the proposition that "everything," presumably the quality of education provided by a school, depends on the interaction between teachers—more or less competent, more or less satisfied—and the circumstances of schooling. But this too is an oversimplification. The words "circumstances of schooling," as well as "competent" and "satisfied," encompass a very large array of variables. As these and the relationships among them become better understood, our ability to improve schools will improve.

There has been growing support in recent years for the view that the importance of the principal to school quality and improvement is great.

Indeed, as with teachers, some people have gone so far as to claim that "everything depends on the principal." We found in the schools we studied a relationship between teacher satisfaction and strong leadership by the principal. There were striking differences in perceptions of their own professional power and autonomy between principals of schools perceived by teachers to be "more" and "less satisfying." Principals of schools that teachers found "more satisfying" felt themselves to be significantly more in control of their jobs and use of time and to have more influence over decisions regarding their own schools than did principals of schools perceived by teachers as "less satisfying." Without exception, the principals of the "more satisfying" schools saw the amount of influence they had as congruent with the amount of influence they thought principals *should* have.

Yet again, as with teachers, it is simplistic to attribute "everything" to the quality of the principal's leadership. Our data in fact show that the degree of staff cohesiveness and the nature of the problem-solving and decision-making climates at schools were factors also highly related to teachers' satisfaction. The principal's role plays a part but it would be a mistake to identify it as the sole or even major factor determining either school climate or teacher satisfaction.

Fewer teachers at the "more satisfying" schools than at "less satisfying" schools saw either "administration" or "staff relations" as a problem. Correspondingly, all the principals of "less satisfying" schools saw "poor teaching or teachers" as a problem at their schools, in contrast to only half of the principals of "more satisfying" schools, most of whom, moreover, saw it as only a minor problem. Fifty-seven percent of principals at "less satisfying" schools, compared with 20% at "more satisfying" schools, saw "staff relations" as a problem at their schools.

Some of the literature on the subject suggests that a good principal, as far as teachers are concerned, is himself or herself a strong, autonomous person who treats the teaching staff as professionally independent.[12] Without doubt, teachers will experience greater work satisfaction and higher morale when they are viewed by their principal as the professionals they perceive themselves to be. Correspondingly, we found that principals of the schools perceived by teachers to be "more satisfying" were more likely to perceive their teaching staff as competent professionals than were the principals of the "less satisfying" schools.

Of course, apart from their own qualities, circumstances expedite or detract from the ability of both teachers and principals to perform at high levels and have satisfying work, and some of these circumstances are on the fringes of or outside of their span of control. We found, for example, that the "less satisfying" schools for teachers tended to be larger, to expend less per pupil, and to have higher student-teacher ratios than the "more satisfying" schools. Interestingly, salaries did not differentiate the "more satisfying" schools in our sample from the "less satisfying," attesting to the commitment teachers frequently make to their profession. But also their reasons for leaving attest to the importance of paying attention to those areas of their concern that lie beyond what principals and teachers can do alone.

Disturbingly, 10 of the 14 "less satisfying" schools in our sample served primarily black, Mexican-American, or racially mixed student populations. Of the 10 "more satisfying" schools selected from all levels, only two served such populations; the other eight enrolled predominantly white students. We must note that some of these "more satisfying" schools were small and that the relationship between small schools and teacher satisfaction just mentioned was substantial. Nonetheless, the data suggest teachers encounter some added difficulties affecting their satisfaction in schools serving nearly all minority or mixed student populations.

We must give attention, then, to the workplace. The circumstances of teaching must provide optimum opportunity for teaching and learning to proceed. When teachers find themselves restrained and inhibited by problems of the workplace that appear to them not to be within their control, it is reasonable to expect frustration and dissatisfaction to set in. Undoubtedly, teacher effectiveness, in turn, is constrained and the very problems frustrating teachers are exacerbated. Students' perceptions of the quality of the education being provided decline. It is reasonable to assume that the actual quality of this education declines also.

A Puzzling School

One school in particular presents a puzzle with respect to teachers' perceptions. This is Rosemont High School. In Chapter 3 I described Rosemont Junior High School as a place with most of the usual problems of schooling which appeared, nonetheless, to be coping quite well and maintaining a rather well-balanced academic ambience. All three of the Rosemont schools we studied received an average grade of B from teachers, students, and parents except Rosemont High School, which received an average grade of C only from its teachers. Generally, students were more severe in grading their schools than were teachers, but here we find the teachers giving their school a lower mark than did either students or parents. And Rosemont was one of the six high schools emerging in our "less satisfying" group in the eyes of teachers. Why?

Let me add some additional data. When our three composite problem scores were added together for each school, the total for Rosemont High was very close to the median for all high schools. However, looking at these scores separately, it is clear that teachers, more than students or their parents, perceived Rosemont as a place of problems. When we look at the nature of the problems perceived by teachers, students' language, lack of parent interest, and lack of student interest headed the list. Parents agreed, in large part, placing lack of parent and student interest immediately behind students' misbehavior and drugs/alcohol. Teachers identified lack of teachers' discipline of students and poor teaching as rather serious problems too, but farther down the list, after drugs/alcohol, student misbehavior, and organization of the school and equal to school size (2,702 students). We see, then, the bulk of their perceived problems to be outside of themselves, embedded in students (language, lack of interest, drugs/alcohol, misbehavior), parents (again lack of interest), and the school (size and organization). These things apparently frustrated their efforts to teach. The parents, too, perceived some of these problems to be serious but also perceived the school, apparently, as doing a rather good academic job, worthy of a B grade.

In Chapter 3 I cited some statistics pertaining to the Rosemont community—within a rather large city, the lowest family income in our sample, the least formal education among parents, a school population that was 95% Mexican-American. The teaching staff of the high school was 63.3% white, 27.5% Mexican-American, 8.3% black, and 0.9% other. Given the family backgrounds of these students and the high percentage of non-Hispanic teachers, it is easy to see why students' language emerged as a problem. Also, we know that parents of low income and limited education tend not to become as closely involved as other parents in school affairs, especially when many of them do not speak English. Further, these parents were highly satisfied with the school's curriculum—the highest average satisfaction scores among all parent groups, using a composite score based on eight subject fields.

We see in Rosemont High, given all of these circumstances, a demanding challenge for teachers and ample reason for their frustration—frustration appearing to be much greater, on the average, than that of parents and students. But I think that still another, related matter must be taken into account. Rosemont distributed its teaching resources in relatively balanced fashion with respect to academic and vocational education and solidly across the four basic subjects—English (22%), mathematics (13%), science (15%), and social studies (13%). With 21% of its teachers in vocational education, Rosemont ranked just below the average allocation for our sample of schools. At the time we visited it, Rosemont High, like Rosemont Junior High, described in Chapter 3, was striving to maintain intellectual goals and an academic ambience.

We know that Mexican-American children are disproportionately represented in special and remedial education classes by from four to five times their proportion in the school population. We know that the percentage dropping out during the high school years is excessively large. There is no reason to believe that the predominantly Mexican-American school population in the Rosemont schools enjoyed abnormal readiness for learning. Nor is there any evidence in our data to suggest unusually creative and extensive pedagogical efforts to compensate for a slow start by these children or a lack of home resources for learning.

The apparent desire of Rosemont school personnel at all levels for academic opportunities for these children, shared to a considerable degree by parents, managed to sustain the academic ambience well into and to some extent even through the junior high years. But then this ambience appears to have begun to come apart. The senior high parents, although expressing satisfaction with the curriculum and the school program in general, would opt for increased vocational emphases, a desire shared by their adolescent children.

Following the central thesis developed so far in this chapter—that teachers enter teaching to teach students and their subjects and become frustrated when circumstances interfere—the apparent lack of satisfaction among Rosemont High School teachers becomes increasingly understandable. We can push forward on the assumption that this country needs and its citizens can acquire the kind of general education recommended in Chapter 5. But the circumstances to be overcome in assuring this for all are formidable, requiring the best we can devise and provide in teaching resources, settings for learning, administrative and community support, and enlightened policies.

I noted earlier the dominance in our sample of "less satisfying" schools, as perceived by teachers, of predominantly minority or of racially and ethnically mixed student populations. Schools of predominantly white student populations were disproportionately represented in the schools emerging as "more satisfying." A reality of recent years is that our schools—particularly high schools—have been absorbing increasingly diverse student populations. This trend will continue. Principals and teachers have been strained in seeking to cope with problems they probably were not well equipped to handle.

It is likely, however, that the greatest strains are now of the past. Educators are learning more about these circumstances and how to deal with them. Special preparation is now a part of many teacher education programs. Whereas desegregation and integration have been the central goals, providing quality education for all students is now paramount. Let us hope that equity and quality can be achieved simultaneously. This is a challenge, of course, that cannot be met successfully by teachers alone.

TEACHERS: COMPETENCE, AUTONOMY, AND INFLUENCE

Adequacy of Preparation

After examining an extensive body of data on how the teachers we studied perceived themselves, I find myself using words such as "competent," "autonomous," and "influential" regarding classroom decisions. Junior and senior high school teachers, in particular, viewed themselves as well prepared to teach their subjects. Not surprisingly, elementary school teachers, who teach all or most subjects, showed variation in their perceptions of being prepared. Teachers at all levels generally saw themselves as being the decision-makers in the instructional area and of being influenced in what and how they taught primarily by their own backgrounds of preparation and experience.

Table 6-1 presents data on teachers' perceptions of inadequate preparation. Of the four basic subject areas commonly considered to be central in the curriculum, our elementary level teachers perceived themselves to be rather poorly prepared to teach only one—science. Nearly a quarter of the group said that they were not adequately prepared in this field. Less than 5% checked themselves as inadequately prepared in English/language arts, mathematics, or social studies, the lowest percentage for this group of subjects being in mathematics.

In preceding chapters, I have raised questions, however, about the preservation in elementary school of teaching and grouping practices not well designed to sustain all students in learning. To the degree that teachers' self-perceptions of their preparation square with an estimate of what teachers need to know about a subject, a hypothetical conclusion is that shortcomings lie more in pedagogy than in academic background. However, only some aspects of pedagogy are relatively universal; others reside in characteristics of the subject to be taught. It may be, then, that a gap exists in teacher preparation programs. This is a gap to be closed by more attention to the composite implications for teaching of how students learn and how subjects are structured. This relationship between the nature of learning and the nature of specific subject-matter domains was of great interest among curriculum reformers in the late 1950s and throughout much of the 1960s. It did not find a solid place in teacher education programs, however. And the lively interest reflected in large-scale curriculum development projects during those years has faded away. Further, this interest in the pedagogy of subject matter expressed itself more at the secondary than the elementary level in any case.

It should not surprise us that nearly 30% of the elementary school teachers perceived themselves as not adequately prepared in the arts and

TABLE 6-1

Percentage of Teachers Who Feel Not Adequately Prepared (NAP) in Subject(s)
They Are Currently Teaching

Subject	SENIOR HIGH SCHOOLS		JUNIOR HIGH/ MIDDLE SCHOOLS		ELEMENTARY SCHOOLS	
	N teaching	NAP, %	N teaching	NAP, %	N teaching	NAP, %
English	159	5.9	126	3.2	234	4.7
Math	101	4.0	93	4.3	201	2.0
Soc. st.	111	0.0	66	4.5	175	4.6
Science	91	6.6	55	7.3	150	23.3
Arts	88	1.1	59	0.0	148	29.1
For. lang.	36	5.6	11	0.0	8	12.5
Ind. arts	39	0.0	17	0.0	3	0.0
Bus. ed.	48	2.1	10	0.0	1	0.0
Home ec.	29	0.0	15	0.0	3	33.3
P. E.	72	1.4	39	2.6	59	18.6
Spec. ed.	24	12.5	32	6.2	22	4.5
Gen. ed.	23	8.7	20	5.0	103	1.0
Total*	814		543		1107	
Overall % NAP		3.57		3.50		10.48

*At the elementary level, where one teacher teaches several subjects, this N represents the number of responses. This occurred also at the two secondary levels but much less frequently.

that nearly 20% described themselves similarly in relation to physical education. When specialists are employed, they are most likely to be in these fields (in addition to the remedial teaching frequently classified as special education). And when regular teachers teach these subjects, they are likely to do so rather casually and informally, sometimes allocating them to a somewhat recreational status.

There appears to be some irony regarding the special interest groups that have grown up over the years around both the arts and physical education. Leaders in these fields usually lobby for staffing the elementary schools with specialists, frequently using the argument that regular classroom teachers are ill-prepared to teach in them. There is some truth to this argument, our data suggest. But if one were serious about increasing the status and teaching of these subjects in elementary schools, perhaps the specialist route would be precisely the wrong approach. Neither the importance of these fields nor a constituency for them is established among those who do the regular "bread and butter" teaching. They remain peripheral. By contrast, reading, mathematics, and other academic subjects become central and basic, and preparation for them becomes standard in programs of teacher education.

Why specialists in the arts and physical education, if not in English, mathematics, and social studies? Perhaps we should assure that each elementary school be staffed with an array of teachers each of whom teaches all or most subjects but each of whom also is prepared with such depth in one subject as to be able to serve as a consultant to the rest of the teaching staff.

At the junior and senior high school levels we were dealing with a sample made up primarily of teachers specially prepared in the subject. In Table 6-1 we see that not a single teacher of the arts, foreign languages, industrial arts, business education, or home economics in the middle schools perceived himself or herself as not adequately prepared. These, with the addition of physical education, happen also to be the subjects students studying them said were most interesting. Before we note what appears to be a neat relationship between these two sets of data, we must observe it to be less at the senior high level. No teacher of the social studies felt inadequately prepared in the subject, one not highly rated for liking or interest by students. On the other hand, all our industrial arts and home economics teachers felt themselves adequately prepared; the percentages in the arts, business education, and physical education viewing themselves as ill-prepared were very low, and senior high students rated these subjects highly. In general, then, the teachers of the subjects for which students expressed greatest liking and interest tended also to be the ones taught by teachers who viewed themselves as adequately prepared. However, the percentages of teachers in middle or senior high schools perceiving themselves to be not adequately prepared in their subjects were small overall—less than 4%. More preparation in their teaching fields does not appear to have been a need generally felt by the secondary teachers we studied.

The responses at all levels regarding special education warrant attention. The percentage of teachers expressing inadequate preparation increased quite markedly from the elementary to the senior high school level—from 4.5% to 12.5%. Overall, significant segments of our data suggest growing difficulty in meeting students' learning problems and needs with upward progression through the levels of schooling. The self-perceptions of special education teachers appear to me to be a kind of barometer reflecting the increased pressure and difficulty of dealing with learning problems among older students. These teachers apparently felt increasingly less adequate to cope with them. These data underscore others that suggest the need for sustaining strong support systems throughout the length and breadth of schooling if all or nearly all students are to be reasonably successful in school-based learning.

Teaching across several subjects simultaneously is common practice in elementary schools and, it appears, creates few subject-matter problems for teachers. But integrated curricula, such as core programs, always have presented high school teachers with difficulties, as our data on general education suggest. The jump from junior to senior high in regard to teachers' expressed inadequacy in foreign languages probably results from spreading a few teachers thinly across advanced courses. There has been for some time a shortage of science, mathematics, and foreign language teachers—a problem creating recruitment difficulties and, no doubt, the employment of some individuals who are and feel less than well prepared. Subject-matter preparation appears to be a selective, not general, problem in teacher education and recruitment.

Finally, the teachers in our sample responded very positively to the statement, "Most of the teachers at this school are doing a good job." This was true from level to level and school to school, with greater variability among schools than among levels. The general picture, then, is of teachers viewing themselves as well prepared in their subjects (with some exceptions at the elementary school level) and their colleagues as performing well. One wonders if these teachers would respond with alacrity to proposals for school improvement focused primarily on the need to upgrade teachers' qualifications and current effectiveness. My conclusion is that they would not.

Isolation

We compiled a substantial amount of data pertaining to teachers' links to sources of influence in their teaching and to one another. The teachers we studied appeared, in general, to function quite autonomously. But their autonomy seemed to be exercised in a context more of isolation than of rich professional dialogue about a plethora of challenging educational alternatives. The classroom cells in which teachers spend much of their time appear to me to be symbolic and predictive of their relative isolation from one another and from sources of ideas beyond their own background of experience.

Over 75%, regardless of subject area taught or level of schooling, indicated that they were greatly influenced in what they taught by two sources—their own background, interests, and experiences; and students' interests and experiences. They were moderately influenced, they reported, by textbooks and other commercially prepared materials, state and district curriculum guides of the kind described in Chapter 2, and other teachers. They were only slightly or not at all influenced by district consultants, parent advisory councils, state examinations designed to measure competency in courses not necessarily taken, or teacher unions. Although outside resource people generally were available, they drew upon them only a little and said that they were of limited value. The farther away the resources persons—for example, based in federal or state rather than district offices—the less they were valued and used. In general, elementary teachers drew upon a wider range of resources for their teaching than did secondary teachers.

The teachers in our sample had some association with others in college courses, in-service classes and workshops, and meetings of educational organizations, but rather brief and casual kinds of associations. They rather rarely joined with peers in collaborative endeavors such as district committees or projects. Nor did they visit other schools or receive visitors from them very often. There was little in our data to suggest active, ongoing exchanges of ideas and practices across schools, between groups of teachers, or between individuals even in the same schools. Teachers rarely worked together on schoolwide problems.

The elementary teachers in our sample attended a greater variety of programs designed for their personal and professional improvement than did our secondary teachers. The elementary teachers tended to attend sessions on topics cutting across subjects—human relations, teaching methods, child growth and development, etc. Those attended by high school teachers tended to be subject-specific. The in-service activities engaged in by secondary school teachers were more often college- or university-based than was the case for elementary teachers. The professional improvement activities and behaviors of the two groups of teachers appeared sufficiently different as to suggest the need for differing strategies designed to help them with their varied needs and problems.

One significant impression coming through from our data in this area is fragmentation. From time to time, programs of staff development provided by a district suggested adoption of a current fashion such as teaching according to behavioral objectives. But there generally appeared not to be districtwide emphases representing both a common commitment and relatively comprehensive participation by all teachers. No single program appeared to capture the simultaneous attention of all or most teachers. Rather, teachers participated in small numbers in a rather broad range of staff development activities, suggesting no clear setting of priorities or in-depth attack on chronic problems.

Inside schools, teacher-to-teacher links for mutual assistance in teaching or collaborative school improvement were weak or nonexistent, especially in the senior high schools. Most teachers taught alone in a classroom. A large majority said that they never observed instruction in other classrooms. Those who did said they observed only once or twice a year. But approximately three quarters of our sample at all levels of schooling indicated that they would like to observe other teachers at work. In general, teachers themselves perceived their awareness of one another, communication, and mutual assistance not to be strong. Although generally supportive of their colleagues, they had only moderate knowledge, they reported, about how their colleagues actually behaved with students, their educational beliefs, and their competence. Not surprisingly, knowledge of and communication with fellow teachers was greater in small schools. Finally, teachers perceived that they and their colleagues were not deeply involved in resolving schoolwide problems—a finding that agrees with our findings on their in-service education activities.

Some research suggests that the school as a unit has been relatively weak in effecting improvement.[13] Rather, the state, through the legislature, and teachers in their classrooms dominate the decision-making process. Strong awareness of the importance and potential power of the individual school as the key unit for educational improvement is a very recent phenomenon—and appears not yet to have affected practice significantly in the schools we studied.

The very nature and conduct of the schooling enterprise appear to operate against the concept of principals, teachers, parents, and perhaps students working together on schoolwide problems. If the schools of our sample are representative, there are not infrastructures designed to encourage or support either communication among teachers in improving their teaching or collaboration in attacking schoolwide problems. And so teachers, like their students, to a large extent carry on side by side similar but essentially separated activities.

It will require more than exhortation to change this situation. Improvement of those circumstances that transcend individual classrooms no doubt will require the allocation of time and rewards for nonteaching activities, a differing perception of responsibility on the part of teachers, and job preparation extending beyond pedagogy and classroom management. To date, this proposition has been largely ignored by those seeking to improve schools through intervention from without.

Autonomy

The classroom is indeed the teacher's domain, and here, according to our data, teachers perceive themselves to be quite autonomous. Our teachers saw themselves to be in control of what they taught and how. Beyond their own preparation and experience, as well as students' interests, all other influences were seen as relatively insignificant.

To the question, "How much control do you have overall in how you carry out your own job?" the most frequent response was "a lot." This was the second choice available from a list of five ranging from "complete" to "none." There were some consistencies across all three schools in a few triples, suggesting the possible impact of district policies, the superintendent, or a union. Teachers at all three levels in Atwater and Dennison—schools mostly coming out well on teacher satisfaction—reported comparatively high levels of control. Teachers at all three levels in Manchester and Fairfield—schools generally doing not so well on indices of teacher satisfaction—reported low levels of control over their decisions. Fairfield teachers were perceived by us to be under rather tight control by the superintendent and a board which had not yet granted any teachers the security of tenure.

We asked teachers if they wanted more or less control over their jobs or whether they had about the right amount. Not surprisingly, only a handful of teachers thought they had more than they wanted. Overall, a large proportion, 76%, reported that they had the right amount; 23% said that they had less then they wanted. In general, these responses were consistent across levels, with senior high teachers slightly exceeding elementary and junior high teachers in reporting too little (25%).

School-to-school differences were marked. The range in percentages of teachers reporting that they had the right amount of control was from 50% to 90% for elementary schools, 62% to 100% for junior highs, and 48% to 100% for senior highs. Again a sign of possible outside impact on all schools in a triple: Manchester, with the most highly organized teachers' union, had the lowest percentages in all three instances.

When we bored in close to the tasks of teaching, a generally high level of perceived control held up. Approximately two-thirds of the teachers at all levels perceived that they had "complete" control in their selection of teaching techniques and students' learning activities. Two-thirds of the junior and senior high teachers also reported "complete" control over evaluating students, but fewer elementary school teachers did so. While a majority of teachers at all levels reported "complete" or "a lot" of control over other areas of their planning and teaching, the proportion of teachers reporting these levels of control decreased progressively with each of the following: setting goals and objectives, selecting content and skills to be taught, use of classroom space, grouping students for instruction, choosing instructional materials, and scheduling the use of time.

But teachers saw themselves generally as having less consistent control in areas beyond their classrooms. We probed further into their percep-

TABLE 6-2

Teachers' Perceptions of Their Influence over School Policy Issues

Rank	Cluster Titles	Mean Scores	Interpretations
1	Curriculum, instruction, and pupil behavior	2.45	Substantial influence, approaching a lot
2	Communication with parents	2.20	
3	Extracurricular and community related issues and activities	1.79	
4	Dress codes	1.69	Some influence
5	Teachers' assignment to grades or classes taught	1.52	
6	Scheduling and conducting staff meetings	1.50	Midway between some and no influence
7	Fiscal management	1.42	
8	Teaching assistants	1.38	None, or very little influence
9	Professional personnel	1.13	

tions by asking them to indicate how much influence they perceived themselves as having over 33 policy issues covering a rather broad and varied range of school life. For each policy issue, they checked one of three responses: "a lot of influence," "some influence," or "no influence," which were coded 3, 2, and 1, respectively.

Table 6-2 shows the varied pattern of teachers' perceived influence when the 33 items were grouped into nine clusters. Predictably, they felt most influential regarding issues of curriculum, instruction, pupil behavior, and communication with parents. They felt least influential concerning fiscal management and the selection and evaluation of colleagues. There was relatively little variation in the overall pattern across schools at the same level, and it held up for teachers at the three levels of schooling. Generally, however, elementary teachers felt somewhat more influential than middle school teachers, who in turn felt somewhat more powerful than their high school counterparts.

Table 6-2 suggests a marked decline in teachers' sense of powerfulness as the focus moves from the classroom to the school as a whole. It also suggests, and further analysis confirmed, that our teachers felt more potent concerning policies that govern students than policies directed at the teachers themselves. Teachers apparently perceive themselves as powerless regarding fiscal management and personnel decisions but quite potent in regard to the curriculum, instruction, pupil behavior, and parent communication.

It is interesting to note that school principals perceived the teachers as more powerful and involved in the decision-making process than the teachers perceived themselves to be. This was true for all but one school. In some schools the difference—computed by subtracting the teachers' average score over all 33 items from the principals'—was considerable. Thus the desire of teachers to have more influence could come as a surprise to some principals, when, as is the case frequently, the two groups find themselves to be on opposite sides in collective-bargaining negotiations. Participation in fiscal management and the selection and evaluation of peers would appear to be areas particularly ripe for negotiation in the collective-bargaining process.

DISCUSSION

Transcending the Circumstances of Teaching and Learning

Pedagogy is not like painting, an art that begins and builds from an uncluttered canvas. The place we call school imposes a variety of restraints. One set of restraints arises out of the intermingling of students' expectations and interests with those of their teachers. Research beyond that reported here portrays teachers as believing that it takes a teacher to stimulate intellectual curiosity and interest in school.[14] Our data show that they value highly the academic function of schools and perceive themselves as critical to its performance. Secondary school students, in particular, value the intellectual side much less, according to our data. Securing the grades necessary to a high school graduation certificate appears to be more important than the actual content of schooling and the classes taken. For many, vocational training for purposes of getting a job is of prime importance—an immediately practical goal far more compelling than any desire to learn what teachers of academic subjects have to offer. In addition, the nonacademic side of school—peers, games, sports, and the like—appeared to be the dominant interest of large numbers of secondary students.

Lacking a commonly internalized goal of needing and wanting to learn what teachers have to offer, students beyond the primary years are not likely to create voluntarily the orderly, receptive circumstances in which teachers, in turn, see themselves as most effective and satisfied. This may at least partly explain why control of the classroom situation looms so large for teachers beyond the early grades as a necessary condition and one for which they must take major responsibility. Establishing control, especially at the secondary level, becomes a mechanism both for personal survival and for maintaining the minimal conditions under which teaching and learning can proceed. The forward-looking pedagogical techniques they may value, if not fully operationalized by teachers, are subjugated to their perceived need to exercise control. The pedagogy to which they increasingly turn in the higher grades involves the time-honored survival techniques they probably learned from experienced teachers during the student teaching part of their preparation programs.

Other studies reveal a marked discrepancy between the values dominant in teacher education courses and those more frequently found among practicing teachers.[15] The former correspond quite closely to the more progressive beliefs about teaching and learning revealed extensively among the teachers in our sample. The latter tend to be those values pertaining to control and order that also show up side by side with the other set of values in many of the teachers we studied. Faced ultimately with taking charge of their own classrooms, it appears that large numbers of secondary teachers resort to practices designed to keep students passive and under control just at the time when adolescents should be taking more charge of their own education. The more "professional" values acquired are not forgotten, it appears. They are held in what often turns out to be a permanent state of abeyance.

Recently we have been hearing about teaching methods that are "proven" and "really work." The literature on what pedagogical practices work for what purposes and with what students is becoming quite substantial. Often overlooked in efforts to put the new methods into practice, however, are the nuances of this relatively recent research; for example, although negative or abrasive teacher responses to students' performance appear to be almost uniformly nonproductive in learning, the evidence on praise is less consistent. Thus, it appears that even teachers who have been exposed to new practices presumably related very positively to student achievement do not necessarily use them effectively in their classrooms.

The irony in all this is that too few of the kinds of engagements we want young people to have with knowledge occur in the classroom setting. Students do not often get involved in projects where they and their classmates set and achieve goals that are important to them. Consequently, the norms for their behavior are not self-imposed, arising out of the need to pursue activities productively and collaboratively. The norms are imposed by the teacher who, in turn, appears to be responding to perceived restraints of having large numbers of students in a small space. As a further irony, some research suggests that students' "time on task" diminishes as the teacher moves away from frontal techniques involving lecturing or questioning the entire class. The implication is that teaching involving teacher dominance is the preferred procedure. But as a consequence, one fears, the potential meaningfulness of personal encounters with learning lies just outside of the schooling experience for many, indeed perhaps most, students.

We must be careful not to view this apparent disjuncture between students' lives and full engagement with what schools have to offer as arising solely out of the circumstances of the classroom. Hess and his associates have documented the early and continuing role of the home in setting children's expectations for school.[16] Parents from low socioeconomic groups caution their children against getting hurt or into trouble, encouraging them to be passive and to adopt a low profile. Middle-class parents encourage their children to get out of school everything they can that will advantage them later. These differences tend to accentuate with increasing age and grade level of the children. Neither set of expectations is compatible with the view that the school presents opportunities for personal growth and fulfillment. Increasingly, students come to internalize the instrumental role of school. What is learned and its value apart from the instrumentality of marks and grades become secondary.

In all of this, we see ample grounds for teachers to be frustrated if their major expectations are to fire their students with enthusiasm for history or biology. School principals can help to set the tone of students' orientation to school and improve the classroom conditions under which teachers teach. Teachers' professional skill in transcending the circumstances inhibiting students' learning is of great importance, needless to say. But the problem of student motivation for academic learning extends far beyond schools and classrooms. Our young people must receive from the surrounding environment more powerful reasons, incentives, and role models for academic learning and intellectual development than now prevail. Particularly important, it appears, is the need for home and school to be close, for the mutual purpose of all children and youth learning more about their world and their relationship to it. We still fall far short of viewing students as the real clients of schools and of doing what we can to make schooling fulfill the function of individual development and responsibility.

Professionalism: Rhetoric and Reality

In general the practicing teacher—to the degree we can generalize from our findings—functions in a context where the beliefs and expectations are those of a profession but where the realities tend to constrain, likening actual practice more to a trade. It undoubtedly is too late to turn back the clock with respect to embellishing teaching with the trappings of a profession. But a question arises as to whether the circumstances of teaching can be made conducive to developing in all teachers the behavior a profession entails. By its very nature a profession involves both considerable autonomy in decision making and knowledge and skills developed before entry and then honed in practice. The teachers in our sample, on the whole, went into teaching because of these inherent professional values. However, they encountered in schools many realities not conducive to professional growth.

Is it realistic to expect teachers to teach enthusiastically hour after hour, day after day, sensitively diagnosing and remedying learning difficulties? During each of these hours, according to Jackson, teachers make 200 or more decisions.[17] During each day of the week, many secondary teachers meet hour after hour with successive classes of as many as 35 students each. As one teacher said to me recently, "It is the sheer emotional drain of interacting with 173 students each day that wears me down."

Even if the best in pedagogy is practiced for a few years, the demands on teachers are such that some will turn to routines that make the least physical and emotional demands. And from where are they to get the additional time and energy required to address the curricular problems identified in Chapter 5? Some teachers prepare themselves, probably deliberately, to leave the classroom. Teaching is perhaps the only "profession" where the preparation recognized as most advanced (the doctorate) almost invariably removes the individual from the central role of teaching in an elementary or secondary school—and to a higher salary.

One solution, which probably would not be popular among noneducators, has the virtue of appearing to solve four critical problems over time. This would be to reduce the instructional time of teachers to approximately 15 hours per week (as in Japan)—the top teaching load at colleges and universities—while simultaneously initiating school-based programs of curricular and instructional improvement shared by the entire staff. First, teachers presumably could teach, as one might hope, for three hours each day. Second, the curricular deficiencies discussed in Chapter 5 could be addressed, simultaneously providing for teachers an intellectual challenge now largely missing (and providing linkages to subject-matter specialists and behavioral scientists in universities). Third, professional staff development could be built into the work week, as it is at the college and university level. Fourth, the need to provide for children and youths beyond what schools can do best would provide an urgency regarding the use of nonformal and informal educational resources of the entire community.

It may be that an effective school day requires a shortened, more intensive, experience with academics (3 or at most 4 hours) for students now accustomed to a rather leisurely school day of 5 or 6 hours. The rest of a busier day would be devoted to a less academic program of vocational education and the development of personal talents under the supervision of adults who themselves engage in these activities, thus providing "do it" rather than "tell it" role models. Teachers, as we now think of them, would spend an additional four hours in the tasks of developing more viable curricula and in preparing markedly improved lessons.

Recognizing the immediate objection of increased costs of schooling, I have asked teachers whether they could work out such a distribution of their time and still arrange for a comprehensive program of studies for student bodies comparable in size to those of the schools in which they now teach. They are convinced that they could during a week of 20 hours directed to teaching classes; they are not quite so confident about so doing during a 15-hour teaching week. But those with whom I talked would like to try. Teachers apparently see in this proposal possibilities for both teaching with greater enthusiasm and being more creative in devising alternative learning situations for students.

Obviously, such a plan moves to a higher level of feasibility with increased volunteerism among lay citizens. Volunteers for educating children and youths, both in and out of schools, also would provide role models beyond those most acclaimed in the media. It is reasonable to assume that some of these could be provided as part of a school's regular educational program by bringing in artists, political and business leaders, scientists, doctors, lawyers, and the like—or by taking groups of students to them. Students, in particular, think that this would be a good thing to do, but little of it is done. Such options for both supporting the educational process in schools and strengthening community involvement in educating the young become feasible only when we allow our minds to escape from the fetters of conventional thinking about our schools. The costs need not be higher, but such options do call for a redistribution of resources, more volunteerism, and imaginative collaboration among educative and potentially educative agencies in communities.

Teaching as a Career

Our study of schools did not look into either the characteristics of persons who enter teaching as a career or the larger social and economic context in which teaching occurs, but some excellent studies are available. Particularly significant are those of Lortie, cited earlier, and Waller.[18] When one puts together our data on the in-school circumstances of teaching and the data from other studies on both these circumstances and the larger context, one cannot be sanguine about attracting into and holding in teaching a continuing stream of dedicated, well-prepared professionals. I have spoken on previous pages to the social constraints in the school environment, such as schools' conventional lunchtime practices. Although the isolation of teachers in the community, referred to frequently in novels and historical treatises, is not nearly what it once was, many young women teachers still report feelings of "being watched," especially in small communities.

Both Waller and Lortie have noted the "flatness" of teachers' salary scales. Usually, the ending salary is only about twice the beginning salary at the time of retirement. Our data showed that although only 2% to 4% of our elementary and secondary teachers selected teaching for economic reasons, the percentages who would leave for such reasons ranged from 18% to 25%. The slow growth in salary levels, among the slowest of all occupations, is a major factor in causing economic reasons to loom as a factor in deciding to leave teaching. The opportunities to remain in the education profession and enjoy higher salaries are few and usually involve moving from teaching to supervision or administration. Add frustration that comes from a host of factors that inhibit what many entered teaching to do and one wonders why so many men and women continue to serve in quiet dedication. In fact, in recent years the opportunities and encouragement for women to enter fields beyond the traditional ones of teaching, nursing, and secretarial work have increased markedly, and proportionately fewer women are entering teaching than was the case just a few years ago. And we have relied in this country, as in many others, on a substantial corps of women to staff our schools, particularly at the elementary level.

Those women—and men—who do enter teaching today work in circumstances that include some gain in their autonomy in the community accompanied by some loss in prestige and status; an increase in the heterogeneity of students to be educated, especially at the secondary level; increased utilization of schools to solve critical social problems such as desegregation; a marked growth in governance of the schools through legislation and the courts; continuation of relatively low personal economic return; limited opportunities for career changes within the field of education; and continuation of school and classroom conditions that drain physical and emotional energy and tend to promote routine rather than sustained creative teaching. Merely holding teachers accountable for improved student learning without addressing these circumstances is not likely to improve the quality of their professional lives and the schools in which they teach.

Chapter 7

What Schools and Classrooms Teach

In this chapter I endeavor to sort out what the schools and classrooms of our sample appeared to be teaching. I discuss both the explicit and the implicit curriculum. The latter frequently is referred to in the literature as "the hidden curriculum," but this is a misnomer. If at all hidden, it usually is only slightly obscured.

By explicit curriculum I mean the curriculum conveyed through the curriculum guides prepared for teachers, the array of courses offered by schools, the topics listed for these courses, the tests given, the teaching materials used, teachers' statements of what they are trying to teach their students or have them learn, and the like. The so-called extracurriculum of games, sports, clubs, school newspapers, student governance, and so on, is also considered here to be part of the explicit curriculum.

By implicit curriculum I mean all those teachings that are conveyed by the ways the explicit curriculum is presented—emphasis on acquiring facts or solving problems, stress on individual performance or collaborative activities, the kinds of rules to be followed, the variety of learning styles encouraged, and so on. The implicit curriculum includes also the messages transmitted by both the physical setting for learning and the kinds of social and interpersonal relationships tending to characterize the instructional environment.

Schools teach some subjects and topics because they have taught them traditionally. Some topics convey high status and are supposed to have been encountered by students going on to college. Schools teach ways of thinking and behaving because teachers were taught them and see no reason to change. Teachers teach some things because they think society expects them to and other things because the circumstances of schooling suggest the need for them. And as we have seen, some of these things are taught differentially to different groups of students. However, my concern in what follows is only a little with why schools teach what they teach. My purpose, rather, *is to describe and, to the degree possible, infer from our data what the schools in our sample taught most and least commonly.* Others might infer differently. Throughout, *I endeavor to keep before the reader the question of whether or not what these schools appear to be teaching is what they should teach.* Persons with differing expectations for schools will derive different answers to this question. I attempt to answer it from my own beliefs regarding what schools are for and therefore should teach.

SUBJECTS IN SCHOOL CURRICULA

Table 7-1 summarizes the data on allocation of instructional time to subjects provided by a sample of early and upper elementary teachers. Clearly, they reported by far the largest number of hours devoted each week to the language arts and mathematics—well over 90 minutes each day to the former and just under an hour each day to the latter in the three primary grades; just under 90 minutes to language arts and over an hour a day to mathematics in the three upper elementary grades. This appears to be a very substantial commitment to what most people define as basic and what was given top priority in most of the state educational documents used in compiling the list of goals for schooling presented in Chapter 2.

We see how the other subjects are relegated to lesser status. This becomes a problem when the teachers of schools such as Newport and Crestview elementary schools make use, for whatever reasons, of less than 20 hours of instructional time each week. Such teachers tended to retain their attention to language arts and mathematics, but social studies and science were seriously short-changed.

We are skeptical about the teachers' reports of time devoted to the arts at both levels. We were endeavoring to determine the relative attention paid to the visual arts, music, drama, and dance. But by asking the teachers to provide the amount of time devoted to each, we probably got an excessive total. At any rate, our data on time given over to the arts in elementary schools produce a higher figure than commonly is reported by other researchers. Goals implying the arts were the lowest in frequency of mention in the state documents; they tend to be relatively low in time devoted to them in elementary school classes.

TABLE 7-1*

Elementary Teachers' Reports of Allocated Hours of Instruction
per Week Averaged by Subject

	EARLY ELEMENTARY		UPPER ELEMENTARY	
	Average Hours	*Number of Teachers*	*Average Hours*	*Number of Teachers*
English/language arts	8.46	65	7.41	59
Mathematics	4.65	65	5.12	58
Social studies	2.09	66	3.83	59
Science	1.65	66	2.93	58
Art	1.50	66	1.29	58
Music	1.08	66	1.35	57
Drama	0.10	61	0.07	55
Dance	0.29	62	0.17	54
P. E.	1.49	65	2.26	58

*The careful reader will note some discrepancies between Table 5-1 (Chapter 5) and Table 7-1. They result from the difference between comparing school-to-school averages with the average results obtained from a sample of teachers representing all schools.

Table 7-2 presents percentages of the instructional program in subject areas in secondary schools. It is difficult to make comparisons with our elementary schools because the data gathered at the two levels differ in kind; the junior and senior high data were computed by translating the total course offerings into teacher equivalencies. Nonetheless, it appears that the stress on mathematics in the upper elementary years continues at about the same level into the junior high grades. There is a drop in attention to English, however, and vocational education emerges as a subject to which approximately 11% of the teaching force is assigned. The role of

TABLE 7-2

Total Instructional Program in Subject Areas at Junior and Senior High School Levels (in percent)

Senior High		Junior High	
Voc. ed.	24	English	22
English	18	Math	17
Math	13	Soc. st.	14
Soc. st.	13	Science	13
Science	11	Voc. ed.	11
P. E.	09	Arts	11
Arts	08	P. E.	10
For. lang.	04	For. lang.	02

vocational education intensifies in the senior high school grades. There is a further drop in English and in addition a drop in mathematics, which occurs presumably because many students no longer enroll in math courses once they complete the minimum requirements for graduation.

On the average, the elementary schools of our sample devoted, according to the teachers surveyed, approximately 54% of the weekly instructional time to reading, language arts, and mathematics. As shown in Table 7-2, the junior and senior highs, on the average, allocated 39% and 31%, respectively, of courses and teachers to English and mathematics. Looking at academic subjects in general, on the average for the schools in our sample, a dominant portion of the instructional program or of teachers available was devoted at all levels to the four subjects considered most commonly to be the central academic subjects and those most important for admission to college—English, mathematics, social studies, and science. Together, they took up 76% of the total estimated hours of class time each week at the elementary level, and 66% and 55% of the teaching force at junior and senior high school levels, respectively. For both groupings a strong position is maintained, but there is a decline in emphasis. Overall, vocational education emerges as a subject nearly paralleling social studies and science in emphasis at the junior high level and exceeding each of the other subjects, on the average, at the senior high level. This appears to be generally congruent with societal expectations as expressed in the state documents, to mirror the interests of many of the parents in our sample, and particularly to reflect the preferences of large numbers of students. For some schools, however, the ratio of vocational courses and teachers to academic courses and teachers appears to me to be excessively high. And when this ratio is what I consider to be beyond a reasonable balance, I note a growing discrepancy between what teachers and parents observe to be the programmatic emphasis of their school and what they would prefer that emphasis to be. The occasional exception to this generalization appears to be characterized by unique circumstances. Dennison High, for example, is a very small rural school with highly satisfied parents. About equal percentages perceive the major emphasis to be vocational as perceive it to be academic. But the net effect of following parental preferences would be to substantially increase attention to vocational education. This appears not unusual, given the expectation that most of the students will be working, ultimately, in some part of the agricultural milieu in which the school resides.

Tables 7-3 and 7-4 confirm a point made in Chapter 5: junior and senior high schools in our sample varied markedly in their allocation of courses and teachers to the subject fields, especially when one looks beyond the academic fields. The overall averages shown in Table 7-2 are misleading.

TABLE 7-3

Percentages of Full-time Teacher Equivalencies (FTEs) in Subject Areas: Junior High/Middle Schools*

	Total N of Teachers	N of Subject Teachers	English		Math		Soc. Stud.		Science		The Arts		For. Lang.		Voc. Educa.		P.E.		Total Academic	
			N	%	N	%	N	%	N	%	N	%	N	%	N	%	N	%	N	%
Vista	49	47.3	10.0	21	8.0	17	7.0	15	8.3	18	5.0	11	0.0	0	6.0	13	3.0	6	33.3	70
Crestview	32	30.3	9.3	31	5.0	16	4.0	13	4.0	13	4.0	13	0.0	0	2.0	7	2.0	7	22.3	74
Fairfield	42	39.2	9.8	25	6.0	15	5.0	13	5.0	13	1.8	5	0.6	2	6.0	15	5.0	13	26.4	67
Rosemont	44	41.8	10.0	24	8.0	19	6.0	14	6.8	16	3.0	7	1.0	2	3.0	7	4.0	10	31.8	76
Newport	75	59.6	11.0	18	10.4	17	8.6	14	5.0	8	8.0	13	0.8	1	8.0	13	7.8	13	35.8	60
Woodlake	30	30.7	8.0	26	4.0	13	4.0	13	3.0	10	4.0	13	0.7	2	2.0	7	5.0	16	19.7	64
Atwater	24	24.0	4.0	17	4.0	17	4.0	17	2.0	8	5.0	21	0.0	0	2.0	8	3.0	13	14.0	58
Palisades	49	44.6	12.0	27	10.0	22	6.0	13	3.0	7	3.8	9	0.8	2	3.0	7	6.0	13	31.8	71
Laurel	24	15.0	4.0	27	3.0	20	1.4	9	3.0	20	2.0	13	0.0	0	0.6	4	1.0	7	11.4	76
Manchester	62	54.2	9.6	18	9.6	18	7.0	13	4.0	7	4.0	7	2.0	4	12.0	22	6.0	11	32.2	59
Bradford	35	32.4	7.0	22	5.6	17	5.8	18	5.0	15	3.0	9	0.0	0	4.0	12	2.0	6	23.4	72
Euclid	13	6.5	1.0	15	1.0	15	0.8	13	1.0	15	0.8	13	0.3	5	0.8	13	0.7	10	4.2	64
AVERAGE	35.5		8.0	22	6.2	17	5.0	14	4.2	13	3.7	11	0.5	2	4.1	11	3.8	10	23.9	68

*Percentages based on total FTEs in subject areas only—other teaching (e.g., special ed.) was excluded.

TABLE 7-4

Percentages of Full-time Teacher Equivalencies (FTEs) in Subject Areas: Senior High Schools*

	Total N of Teachers	N of Subject Teachers	English N	English %	Math N	Math %	Soc. Stud. N	Soc. Stud. %	Science N	Science %	The Arts N	The Arts %	For. Lang. N	For. Lang. %	Voc. Educa. N	Voc. Educa. %	P.E. N	P.E. %	Total Academic N	Total Academic %
Vista	84	80.0	16.0	20	10.0	13	9.0	11	10.0	13	9.0	11	3.0	4	18.0	23	5.0	6	48.0	60
Crestview	44	44.0	9.0	20	6.0	14	6.0	14	4.0	9	4.3	10	1.2	3	10.6	24	3.0	7	26.2	59
Fairfield	57	53.2	9.2	17	5.0	9	4.8	9	5.0	9	1.6	3	1.0	2	22.6	42	4.0	8	25.0	47
Rosemont	121	118.6	26.2	22	16.0	13	15.6	13	17.6	15	6.0	5	5.0	4	25.0	21	7.2	6	80.4	68
Newport	85	70.2	13.7	20	8.0	11	7.7	11	7.0	10	7.7	11	6.7	10	9.2	13	10.0	14	43.2	62
Woodlake	57	54.8	11.8	22	5.0	9	7.0	13	5.0	9	4.0	7	2.0	4	15.0	27	5.0	9	30.8	56
Atwater	25	23.6	5.0	21	2.2	9	4.0	17	2.0	8	2.0	8	1.0	4	5.0	21	2.4	10	14.2	60
Palisades	68	63.8	10.0	16	9.4	15	10.0	16	8.0	13	7.4	12	5.0	8	8.0	13	6.0	9	42.4	66
Laurel	18	20.0	3.0	15	4.0	20	3.0	15	3.0	15	2.0	10	0.0	0	3.0	15	2.0	10	13.0	65
Manchester	114	111.0	25.0	23	15.0	14	17.0	15	14.0	13	4.0	4	6.0	5	21.0	19	9.0	8	77.0	69
Bradford	63	50.0	8.0	16	8.0	16	6.0	12	6.0	12	6.0	12	3.0	6	7.0	14	6.0	12	31.0	62
Euclid	24	14.5	2.0	14	1.3	9	1.0	7	1.3	9	1.5	10	0.3	2	6.0	41	1.0	7	6.0	41
Dennison	11	8.5	1.0	12	1.0	12	1.0	12	1.0	12	0.5	6	0.0	0	3.0	35	1.0	12	4.0	47
AVERAGE		54.8	10.8	18	7.0	13	7.1	13	6.5	11	4.3	8	2.6	4	11.8	24	4.7	9	33.9	59

* Percentages based on total FTEs in subject areas only—other teaching (e.g., special ed.) was excluded.

They suggest a curricular balance much greater than that revealed when one looks at the distributions school by school.

As observed in Chapter 5, the most striking variation across schools in resource allocation to subjects is in vocational education, especially at the senior high level. When schools seek to meet both the expectations of higher education, on one hand, and of an assumed job market, on the other, considerations of what constitutes good education for the dual aim of developing individual potential and responsible citizens are relegated to secondary importance. The problem of putting together balanced programs of instruction, using only full-time teachers, can become complicated.

I will use Dennison and Euclid High Schools to illustrate the problem, which is severest in small schools. The former enrolls only 61 pupils at both junior and senior high levels and is staffed by 11 teachers, of whom only eight and a half teach school subjects. Of these, three teach vocational subjects. Euclid enrolls 262 pupils and employs 24 teachers, of whom 14½ teach school subjects. Of these, six teach vocational education. At both schools (where parents in substantial numbers perceive academics to parallel or exceed vocational education in the curriculum) parents would increase an already heavy emphasis on the vocational side of the school's program. But unless teachers are added, this cannot be done without having serious repercussions for the academic side. Dennison, with its three vocational education teachers, assigns only one teacher to each of the four academic areas, none to foreign languages, and a half-time teacher to the arts. Euclid, with its six vocational education teachers, has two teachers of English but has only fractionally more resources than Dennison in other academic fields.

The availability of only one or one and a fraction teachers each for English, mathematics, science, and social studies (to say nothing of no teacher or a third of a teacher for foreign languages at Euclid) has serious consequences for what is offered in these subjects. Either integrated programs of study must be prepared—something no level of schooling does well—or a smattering of several subjects in the field (for some of which the teacher will be ill-prepared) must be offered, or the teacher must select a single discipline as the only offering in the subject area. But 35% of the available teaching force, as at Dennison, or 41%, as at Euclid, provide the vocational education staff at these schools with a kind of curricular luxury not enjoyed by other teachers. Is this the way we want it for our secondary schools—even though the parents at both schools appear to be endorsing this arrangement and asking for even more of it? We frequently say that schools belong to the community, but how far beyond the local school and its service area should our concept of community extend? What is the responsibility of schools to their clients? What should schools do when meeting the apparent wishes of parents constrains the areas of knowledge schools bring to their students?

Some of the restraints schools face in responding to both special interests and a broad mandate for general education arise from within the educational system. The system does not take readily to the idea of part-time or noncertified personnel. Consequently, innovative schemes designed, for example, to put together one full-time, certified vocational education or social studies teacher and several part-time, noncertified persons with some specialized area of competence have not flourished.

(And, of course, such schemes are least useful in rural areas such as those served by Dennison and Euclid High Schools, where part-time specialists are in short supply.) Nonetheless, one cannot resist pondering the possibilities of arrangements which would bring together new and creative configurations of potentially educative resources available outside as well as inside schools. Somehow, we must get over our mental hang-ups regarding the places, people, and time available for educating our young people.

COURSES, TOPICS, TESTS, AND MATERIALS

In addition to using interviews, questionnaires, and observations to get insight into curricula, we sought to secure as much information as could be obtained from school records and materials packages prepared by teachers at our request. We examined the master schedules of course offerings, teachers' lists of topics and skills taught and to be taught, textbooks used, tests and quizzes, data gathered in interviews with teachers, and so on. The information sought was not uniformly available; there were great variations in the comprehensiveness of what teachers provided; some provided virtually nothing. But the number of documents provided and the quantity of information derived from them are vast.

In what follows, I endeavor to stay as close as possible to what I defined earlier as the explicit curriculum—centrally, courses, topics, tests, and materials. However, it is not possible to make a clear separation between the explicit and the implicit. They interweave in interesting ways, sometimes making it very difficult to sort out the intended from the unintended.

English/Language Arts

English/language arts formed the backbone of the curriculum in the classes we studied, especially at the elementary level. The various subjects and activities falling under this rubric—reading, composition, handwriting, speaking, listening, spelling, grammar (especially studying the parts of speech), letter writing, literature, using the dictionary—occupied more time at the elementary level and more teachers at the secondary level (combining both junior and senior high schools) than any other subject.

The dominant emphasis throughout was on teaching basic language use skills and mastering mechanics—capitalization, punctuation, paragraphs, syllabication, synonyms, homonyms, antonyms, parts of speech, etc. These were repeated in successive grades of the elementary years, were reviewed in the junior high years, and reappeared in the low track classes of the senior high schools. Scattered among these basics were activities suggesting more self-expression and creative thought—story writing, acting out a scene from a play or theme from a novel, reading poems, book reports, story telling, interviews, and the like. In lists of what they taught, teachers at the junior and senior high levels included biography, fiction, nonfiction, poetry, folk tales, short stories, creative writing, keeping a journal, writing original poetry and short stories. But at some schools teachers reported very few of these things.

Reading instruction in the junior and senior highs appeared to be a matter of remediation involving the mechanics of word recognition, phonics, and vocabulary development. In English, there was still a substantial emphasis on the basics of grammar and composition—punctuation, capitalization, sentence structure, paragraph organization, word analysis, parts of speech. In line with the findings of our analysis of tracking reported in Chapter 5, lower track classes tended to emphasize the mechanics of English usage, whereas high track classes were likely to stress the intellectual skills of analysis, evaluation, and judgment, especially through literature. The low track classes were unlikely to encounter the high status knowledge dealt with in the upper tracks and normally considered essential for college admission.

The most commonly offered courses in English at the high school level were those combining mechanics with some literature, courses only in literature, and courses in grammar and composition—in that order. These formed the core of the required English in our high schools. Beyond this core were electives in journalism, speech, and creative writing.

Teachers in all schools and at all grade levels used a wide array of commercially prepared materials in their teaching of the language arts subjects, especially such mechanical aids as ditto masters for the preparation of students' worksheets. The abundance of textbooks in use in elementary grades paralleled in their titles our teachers' listings of basic skills they were seeking to develop—*New Phonics, Reading Skills, Patterns of Language, Basic Spelling Workbook, Creative Growth with*

Handwriting, Writing Oral Language, Sounds of Language, Progress in English, Spelling and Writing Patterns, etc. For the most part, these are standard, graded series published by the major companies in the field—Ginn; Scott, Foresman; Laidlaw; Follett; American Book; Harcourt, Brace, Jovanovich; Lippincott; and others. Whatever the series, the topics covered are very similar.

Textbooks and workbooks appeared with great frequency at the junior and senior high levels, repeating and extending the materials used to teach language usage skills of the elementary grades. Junior high teachers listed some literature commonly studied in their classes. Works considered to be of relatively low reading difficulty but high interest included *Durango Street, The Outsiders, The Pigman, The Almost Year, Death Be Not Proud.* Classics and nearperennials included *The Adventures of Ulysses, Flowers for Algernon, The Birds, To Kill a Mockingbird, A Habit for the Voyage, A Guest in the House, The Perfect Time for the Perfect Crime, Lilies of the Field, Kon-Tiki.* Also on the teachers' lists were anthologies of poetry, short stories, and selections from other forms of literature. We got the impression that students encountered major American and European authors primarily through these anthologies of short pieces rather than through entire works such as novels which could demand extensive time and effort outside of the classroom.

The overlap in texts used at the senior high school level was not great. There was some repetition across schools by track levels. The smaller schools had a smaller range in number and variety of courses offered, and this cut down on the frequency of repetition in textbooks used. As at the junior high level, however, there was substantial repetition in the array of topics listed for instruction.

Senior high literature teachers included in their lists of materials many of the authors and books long associated with secondary school curricula—for example, Shakespeare, Dickens, Ibsen, Poe, Longfellow, Whitman, and *Romeo and Juliet, A Tale of Two Cities, Huckleberry Finn, Moby Dick, Julius Caesar, Gulliver's Travels, Les Miserables, Catcher in the Rye, The Cherry Orchard.* The teachers also provided us with a long list of anthologies of short stories, poems, and other selections, especially from American and Western literature. Encounters with literature were far fewer for students in low than in high tracks.

Notable in the materials gathered from teachers was an emphasis on expository writing to the neglect of creative, fictional writing. There was an absence of references to studying the historical development of the meaning of words and language. Also missing at the secondary school level was an emphasis on developing listening skills—although we note from other data that students at all levels were called upon to listen a great deal of the time.

Remember the Friday morning spelling test? It's still there. Most of the elementary teachers in our sample listed it. As indicated in Chapter 4, tests increased in frequency of use with progression upward through the levels of schooling. Standardized tests often were used at both junior and senior high levels for placing students in classes. Teacher-made tests at these levels appeared to be designed and used, not for diagnosis, but for assessing and marking students' achievement as well as for controlling students' behavior. At all levels, these tests called almost exclusively for short answers and recall of information. Workbooks and worksheets, often a part of daily instruction, were used cumulatively by many teachers to mark pupil progress and achievement. These frequently were duplicated from commercial materials. The directions given on worksheets often were "copy the sentence" or "circle each verb" or "combine two sentences into one" or "add correct punctuation." If teachers gave tests involving writing paragraphs or essays, they seldom so indicated.

We saw, then, in the English/language arts program a kind of repetitive reinforcement of basic skills of language usage throughout the twelve grades—a heavy emphasis on mechanics in the topics covered by teachers, textbooks stressing these topics, and workbooks, worksheets, and quizzes emphasizing short answers and the recall of specific information. Occasionally, something markedly different caught one's eye—the second grade teacher who listed drawing conclusions, recognizing inferences, using the context to derive meaning as topics for student learning; several teachers at one elementary school who emphasized expression and communication over the mechanics of language; a secondary teacher who related the study of world literature to current international problems. Although junior and senior high school English classes broke the general pattern to some degree, the tests and quizzes remained remarkably similar in format.

One wonders about the readiness of students in the lowest tracks of the junior and senior high schools who were still confronted again and again with these now familiar patterns. What was new to arouse their interest?

Mathematics

Just as basic reading and writing skills dominated the elementary language arts curriculum, the mathematics curriculum in the elementary schools we studied was almost entirely basic skills. Teachers included these skills in their list of topics of instruction: numeration, addition, subtraction, multiplication, division, fractions, decimals, percentages, money, telling time, and rudiments of geometry (shapes and measurement). It appears that the same skills were taught in successive years, with slight increases in the level of difficulty. What does not come through clearly is whether the teachers had in mind the use of successive topics as a means to developing skills in some cumulative fashion. The common bonds relating each topic to the preceding ones were rarely revealed.

The middle school classes usually were designated Mathematics 6, 7, 8, and 9. The dominant theme was a review of basic operations—addition, subtraction, multiplication, and division, with further attention to fractions, decimals, and percentages. Some teachers reported giving attention to money management and other skills usually taught in consumer mathematics courses. A few schools offered introductory algebra in the eighth grade, but more commonly algebra was not offered until the ninth. Junior high students in high track classes encountered algebra, but low tracks continued to emphasize utilitarian skills. As with the elementary school, teachers' listings of what was taught were almost exclusively made up of topics, not the concepts or skills to be acquired from the study of topics.

School to school, our high school teachers reported a nearly identical range of mathematics courses, from remedial ones emphasizing basic skills to courses in algebra and geometry, with some schools offering calculus, trigonometry, and computer programming. Again, teachers mostly listed topics, not skills, in reporting what they taught and the topics listed were very similar from school to school. They began with the fractions, decimals, and percentages listed for junior high schools and moved up into topics from geometry, calculus, and trigonometry. The tracking patterns revealed substantial curricular differences from track level to track level within schools.

Overall, the impression that emerged from the analysis of English and language arts was one of great curricular similarity from school to school. This impression comes through even more strongly for mathematics. A fifth-grader leaving Tenth Street School in Portland, Maine, it appears, would encounter essentially the same mathematics program on moving to Tenth Street School in Portland, Oregon. This would be true also for a student transferring to another junior or senior high school, if that student were placed at his or her previous track level—which probably would be the case.

Like most teachers in our sample, teachers of mathematics chose their own backgrounds and students' interests and experiences as highly influential sources of what they taught. But mathematics teachers, somewhat more than other teachers (except foreign language teachers), generally reported that the textbooks recommended by states and districts were of relatively high influence. Our data on instructional materials strongly support the generalization that the mathematics curriculum was dominated by textbooks in the classrooms we studied.

The textbook series used reflects repetition of work on basic skills, with slight grade-to-grade increases in level of difficulty. Whether school programs determined textbook content or the reverse occurred is difficult to decide. The two reinforce each other. The production of a textbook series is a costly business not likely to be undertaken unless a rather close fit with what exists is virtually assured. Consequently, the products of different companies end up being very much alike. When large-scale reform appears to be taking place—as was the case with the so-called new math during the 1960s—the publishing companies tend to follow, not lead.

Textbooks used at the seventh- and eighth-grade levels reviewed at a somewhat higher level of difficulty the basic operations taught in the elementary schools. Commonly, algebra texts were introduced in the ninth grade, but students in high track classes often encountered algebra by the eighth grade. Texts used at the senior high level were differentiated according to track level. Those for high tracks introduced algebraic, geometric, and trigometric concepts and calculus; they were almost devoid of basic skills. Several schools used textbooks and workbooks on computer programming. Texts used in the low tracks included "survival" topics—writing checks, balancing a checking account, making deposits, preparing income tax forms, borrowing, insurance, household finance, etc.

Even more than in English/language arts, the use of workbooks and worksheets was interwoven with, and not always distinguishable from, testing. Teachers frequently used the results of students' work on worksheets as a basis for marking their performance. More formal tests and quizzes were characterized by worksheet-type exercises—filling in the result of a computation, choosing the correct response, using a formula to solve a problem, completing a sentence, and so on. There was little school-to-school variation in the types of short answer responses called for in these tests. More complex types of questions appeared in the advanced secondary school courses taken by students in the higher tracks—setting up equations, factoring, working out geometric proofs, calculating logarithms, and formulating hypotheses or conclusions from data.

The impression I get from the topics, materials, and tests of the curriculum is of mathematics as a body of fixed facts and skills to be acquired, not as a tool for developing a particular kind of intellectual power in the student. One might expect to see by the upper elementary years activities designed to use basic skills previously acquired; instead, these skills reappear as ends in themselves. Interestingly, mathematics teachers somewhat more than teachers in the other academic subjects perceived themselves as seeking in their students processes related more to learning how to learn than to merely acquiring mechanics. Many wanted their students to be logical thinkers, to learn how to attack problems, and to think for themselves. Why, then, did so few mathematics teachers in our sample appear to get much beyond a relatively rote kind of teaching and textbook dependency not likely to develop powers of critical reasoning?

Social Studies

Our data suggest a firm place in the curriculum for English/language arts and mathematics, and considerable agreement on a common body of topics and skills to be taught. There appears to be much less certainty on the part of the schools, particularly at the elementary level, about either the importance of the social studies subjects or what should be taught in them. Secondary students, for their part, considered the social studies to be less important than English/language arts, mathematics, and vocational education, about as important as science, and more important than foreign languages, the arts, and physical education. Junior and senior high students viewed the social studies to be among the least useful subjects in relation to their present and future needs.

The curriculum at the elementary level was amorphous, particularly in the lower grades. Many first- and second-grade classes put together the themes of understanding self and others with discussion of the family and the community. There were more field trips—to community resources and facilities—than occurred later. The intent, apparently, was to begin close at hand, with oneself, and expand one's understanding of the immediate environment. By the third grade, children frequently were studying community needs such as health care and problems such as conservation of water. Some classes made forays into other cultures (Eskimo and Maori) or learned about the dependence of their community on other communities for certain foods, raw materials, and manufactured goods. The fourth grade often involved study of the early colonization and exploration of America, with accompanying use of maps and globes. By the fifth and sixth grades, the themes of history, geography, and civics made a strong appearance, mostly in the context of the growth and development of the United States but frequently with some attention to other countries.

Asked to identify what they were endeavoring to teach, the teachers surveyed listed map skills quite consistently. Commonly, too, they listed such things as acquiring the ability to work in groups, skill in oral expression, facility in library use, understanding similarities among cultures, and an array of the more complex intellectual processes—forming hypotheses, making comparisons, understanding sequences, formulating generalizations and conclusions, and using imagination.

The varied, amorphous character of the elementary school social studies program gave way to much greater school-to-school uniformity at the junior high level—United States history, world history, world geography, and commonly, a course in the history of the state in which the school studied was located. There appeared to be high agreement that United States history should be taught in the eighth grade. Teachers noted the expectation that their students would acquire map skills, the ability to take notes, proficiency in the use of dictionaries and encyclopedias, and the skills of oral and written expression. As did elementary school teachers, junior high teachers listed an array of complex thinking skills—understanding relationships, drawing inferences and conclusions, understanding cause and effect, etc.

According to our sample, "the basics" of social studies at the senior high level are American history and government. These appeared in some form at all schools. Beyond these courses, all schools but one offered electives. These included economics, sociology, law, anthropology, psychology, world history, the history of the state, world cultures, human relations, current events, and the history and/or geography of a variety of other countries. There was quite common agreement on what to teach about American history and government, but the schools offered a rather wide range of courses and topics in some of the electives. The skills most commonly sought, according to the teachers, were in map reading, library use, test taking, and writing and thinking.

The variety of topics and skills taught in the elementary schools was reflected in the wide range of textbooks and materials used in classrooms. Surprisingly, in spite of the relative uniformity of the junior high school curriculum, only two or three textbook titles were repeated across even a few schools. Likewise, the senior high classes were characterized by wide variety in the books found in use. Yet there was a certain sameness too—in the textbooks on history and government, for example, a kind of remoteness or detachment from real people living in a time and a place.[1] All secondary schools supplemented whatever textbooks were used with newspapers, magazines, and filmstrips.

We can assume that the tests teachers give reflect what they believe to be important and in turn convey to students the kinds of things they are expected to learn. Following this assumption, it appears that teachers in the early primary grades of our sample tended not to view social studies as an important subject significant in the evaluation of their students. Either they gave no tests or they depended on appraising students' understanding through oral questioning. Written testing began in the three upper grades of the elementary school and increased in frequency in junior and senior high schools.

Social studies, as a field of learning, appears to be particularly conducive to the development of reasoning—deriving concepts from related events, testing in a new setting hypotheses derived from another set of circumstances, exploring causal relationships, drawing conclusions from an array of data, and so on. Teachers at all levels listed these and more as intended learnings. Their tests reflected quite different priorities. The tests we examined rarely required other than the recall and feedback of memorized information—multiple choice, true or false, matching like things, and filling in the missing words or phrases. Some essay-type questions were used in the upper elementary grades and reappeared in the secondary schools, but these were not the dominant pattern.

All of the children and youths enrolled in the schools we studied encountered the history, geography, and government of the United States. For most, initial encounters in the upper elementary grades were renewed in both junior and senior high schools. A more exhaustive study than ours (and preferably a longitudinal one) will be required to determine the amount of repetition experienced in these several encounters. My impression is that students beyond the elementary school would perceive themselves to have been here before—a perception likely to be intensified by the familiar form of the materials and, as we shall see, the methods of instruction.

One puzzling question is why upper elementary school students liked the social studies less than any other subject. Our data show they perceived it to be one of the most difficult subjects. Was this the reason? At the secondary level, social studies came a little behind English and mathematics in liking and on a par with science. The topics commonly included in the social sciences appear as though they would be of great human interest. But something strange seems to have happened to them on the way to the classroom. The topics of study become removed from their intrinsically human character, reduced to the dates and places readers will recall memorizing for tests. This is precisely the implication of a study conducted at the junior high level many years ago. Students were asked to rate their interest in a list of topics selected from several subjects, including the social studies. Topics from the social studies were rated high, but social studies as a subject was rated relatively low in interest among the several curricular fields.[2]

One thing we cannot be sure of from our data is that all students in the schools studied engaged in some reasonably comprehensive analysis either of Native American culture or of some other Western or Eastern culture. Clearly, some did. But the comparative study of cultures does not emerge as a basic in the curricula we examined. Nor did we find much inclusion of global or international content. Over half of all the students in our sample believed that foreign countries and their ideas are dangerous to American government. The emphasis on this nation and the relative lack of understanding of the rest of the globe showed up as well in answers to other questions we asked these students. Our findings are in line with those of another study in which it was found that the United States was the only country (among eight) where there was substantially less interest among fourteen-year-olds in discussion of foreign affairs with friends and parents than in the discussion of national affairs.[3]

Many of the teachers in our sample appeared not to have sorted out the curricular and instructional ingredients of a social studies program designed to assure understanding and appreciation of the United States as a nation among nations and its relationship to the social, political, and economic systems of other countries. No doubt, their dilemma merely reflects ambiguity in the surrounding society regarding our nation's role in a world of growing interdependence—the world in which our young people live and will live as adults.[4]

I conclude by noting the preponderance of classroom activity involving listening, reading textbooks, completing workbooks and worksheets, and taking quizzes—in contrast to a paucity of activities requiring problem solving, the achievement of group goals, students' planning and executing a project, and the like. The abilities involved appear very similar to those developed in the language arts. Indeed, in many ways, instruction and learning in the social studies look more like instruction and learning in the language arts (without the emphasis on mechanics) than in the social sciences. It appears that we cannot assume the cultivation of goals most appropriate to the social sciences even when social studies courses appear in the curriculum.

Science

The allocation of time and resources to the natural sciences in the schools we studied was less than, but close to, the allocation to the social studies. The low amount of time in the elementary schools and relatively low percentage of teachers in the secondary schools suggest some lack of certainty about the importance of science as a field of precollegiate study.

Like the elementary curriculum in the social studies, the science curriculum in the elementary schools was amorphous. At the same time, it was repetitive. Also, an interesting shift in orientation made itself apparent, often, at the fourth-grade level. Teachers in the first three grades frequently appeared to place the child's personal orientation to the natural world above the child's mere possession of information about science. By contrast, many teachers in the upper three elementary grades appeared simply to be teaching the children about some of the topics and methods of science.

Topics taught in the first three grades included animals, plants, seasons, light, color, heat, sound, magnets, pulleys, and the use of microscopes. Many of these appeared again in upper elementary classes along with the solar system, weather and climate, oceanography, simple ecological systems, electricity, the refinement of plants and animals into their different forms, and health-education topics such as nutrition and drugs/alcohol. This subject-matter was designated simply first-grade science, second-grade science, and so on.

Courses offered at the junior high level were labeled Life Science 7, Earth Science 8, Physical Science 8, General Science 9, etc. Topics taught in the elementary schools reappeared among junior high topics—plants, animals, the earth's atmosphere, the solar system, magnetism, light and energy, pollution, oceanography, space. The concepts implied grew more complex—taxonomies, communities and population, human body systems, plant and animal reproduction, genetics, geological time, food chains, basic chemistry. Again some programs included topics common to health education programs, such as venereal disease and sex education.

Small high schools limited the science curriculum to just a few basic courses—Physical Science, Biology, and Chemistry. Large high schools offered these and many more. For example, Manchester listed a baker's dozen—Physical Science, General Science, Earth Science, Horticulture, General Biology I, General Biology II, Lab Biology I, Lab Biology II, Physiology, General Chemistry, Chemistry I, Chemistry II, and Physics.

It usually was possible to sort out from course titles the courses for the college-bound and those for the non-college-bound. Rosemont was very clear in this differentiation: courses were listed Applied Physical Science or Academic Physical Science, Applied Biology or Academic Biology. While only 21% of the curriculum was in vocational education courses, slightly below the average for our high schools, the Rosemont High student body was clearly divided into those with an academic and those with a vocational emphasis. One took academic or applied science courses in accordance with which side of this division one was on.

Teachers' stated expectations for students' learning were much closer to the goal expectations we tend to have for science education than were their teaching practices. Elementary school teachers stated that they wanted students to be able to compare and contrast phenomena, explore the interrelationships among living things, interpret environmental changes, make inferences from data, formulate hypotheses, observe and classify, develop habits of inquiry, and so on. These abilities were repeated by junior high teachers, but they also referred to more specific habits and skills such as learning scientific terms, reading charts and diagrams, constructing models, applying mathematics skills to science, and dissecting.

The words *study habits* (or *skills*), *organizing information, scientific method,* and *critical thinking* appeared over and over at both junior and senior high levels in what teachers told us. The lists of what they intended their students to learn provided by senior high school teachers were highly repetitive of those provided by junior high teachers, but they were also noticeably more comprehensive. These senior high teachers tended more often to list the subbehaviors involved in critical thinking as well as the parent term: At both secondary levels, there was ample evidence to suggest the proposition that these teachers saw as desirable the involvement of their students in scientific processes and ways of thinking. However, our observations of classrooms lead me to the conclusion that the gap between the expectations and the teaching practices of most junior and senior high science teachers in the sample was formidable. Once again teachers were not able, apparently, to square their performance with their theory.

If teachers' responses to our questions were reasonably complete and accurate, one must conclude that the supply and variety of instructional materials available in the elementary classrooms were exceedingly limited. The section of the questionnaire requesting information from teachers regarding materials beyond textbooks was in some instances completely blank. A few teachers—a small percentage of the whole—sent us self-made materials of relatively high quality. But textbooks dominated. Since textbooks appear to be by far the major vehicle for teaching science, clearly proficiency in reading becomes a requisite for comprehending science information and concepts.

Frequently, senior high teachers reported the uses of kits which provided not only the objectives, unit plans, and activities but also the tests for evaluating the attainment of objectives. Teachers in both junior and senior high schools using such kits claimed that these enabled them to individualize instruction, but the materials sampled in our study suggest that the only differentiation for students was some variation in time allowed for completion. Every student was expected to complete the same readings, worksheets, experiments, and tests—and to come to essentially the same conclusions.

A few generalizations about our data, in addition to those already made: First, the science curriculum appeared to link at various levels with health on one hand and mathematics on the other, the former more frequently at the elementary level, the latter more frequently at the secondary level. For example, nearly half of the senior high teachers responding to our request for information listed metrics as either a topic or a set of skills taught. Second, mention of learning about the lives of great scientists or science as a career was missing at all levels. Third, it was difficult to hook up the topics listed with the teachers' frequent mentions of scientific and critical thinking. That is, I could not readily see how the intellectual behavior mentioned was to be developed via the topics listed. In fairness to the teachers, the demands of the reporting task did not lead them naturally to relate these two sets of responses. Nonetheless, this suspicion of a gap is heightened by the data on observed teaching practices and the data on testing. Once more, the tests used emphasized heavily the recall of specific information rather than exercise of higher intellectual functions. The total body of data available leads me to the hypothesis that neither science nor social studies, as taught and studied in our sample of schools, emphasized adequately those intellectual abilities normally associated with both fields.

Foreign Languages

Foreign languages occupied a very small proportion of the secondary curriculum—4% of the allocation of teachers in the senior highs and a mere 2% in the junior high schools. One small senior high school offered none; another offered as much Spanish as one teacher could handle. Five of the 12 junior highs offered no foreign language instruction.

The language most consistently taught at both levels was Spanish; it was followed by French and German. Four of the 13 senior highs offered Latin; two relatively large high schools (with markedly different student bodies, incidentally) offered all of these and Russian. At both levels, with one exception, Spanish was the language when only one was taught; Spanish and French or Spanish and German was the combination when only two were taught. One junior high offered Latin only—the only school at this level offering the subject. Needless to say, the chance for a rich offering of four or five languages was directly related to the size of the school.

Grammar was taught at the junior high level, but overwhelmingly the curricular emphasis there was vocabulary development. Beyond this, the teachers reported the goals of proper pronunciation and the ability to carry on simple conversations. Becoming familiar with the culture of the countries represented by the languages was mentioned only occasionally.

In the senior high schools, according to the teachers, vocabulary development was not a prime goal but, rather, something to take place concurrently with a primary emphasis on listening, speaking, reading, and writing. "Conversational fluency" loomed large as a topic, and the development of cultural awareness and appreciation now took on substantial importance. It appears that grammar was taught directly, as in the junior highs, but also was taught as a concomitant of writing. An impression coming through at the senior high level in particular is of students' "doing" the language—that is, of their role as participants in language usage.

Junior high schools appeared to be somewhat more textbook-oriented. All of the senior high schools also used textbook series but made greater use of tapes and language laboratories in which they listened to the language, recorded their own use of it, and listened again. The ubiquitous worksheet and workbook, so common in the teaching of academic subjects, appeared frequently in language courses at both levels.

Tests at both levels stressed recall of specific information—for example, memorized grammatical rules in the junior highs and word and phrase recognition in both groups of schools. At the senior high level, there was considerable stress on technical mastery as demonstrated in short-answer tests and in taking dictation in the foreign language or translating from one language to another. Tests rarely called for writing original paragraphs or short essays.

The overall impression of the foreign language program is that of a relatively fast-paced, orderly process, controlled in part by the subject's own internal discipline. At this relatively beginning level of instruction, there is little room for students' creativity. One does not, for example, think up alternative English vocabulary for French nouns. Time spent on instruction was highest and time spent on controlling behavior was lowest among the subject fields. Students enrolled in foreign language classes ranked the subject high for liking as compared with the other four central academic subject areas.

Teachers of foreign languages, more than teachers of other subjects, perceived themselves to be very much in control of all instructional decisions—what they taught and how—and were very satisfied with their level of control. It appears that they did not share this decision-making authority with their students. The curricular and instructional message communicated by teachers appeared to be, "Here is the program and I am in charge." Practices in a given language were remarkably alike from class to class and school to school. Once in the program, students became active participants in the doing that language learning requires.

It must be remembered that foreign languages are required for graduation in a minority of high schools and for admission to a minority of colleges. But they frequently are desired by students who want to be prepared to seek admission to any college or university. Consequently, enrollment in foreign language classes tends to be self-selected. Undoubtedly this means a more highly motivated and more academically able student group than is found in subjects required for all or in subjects-of-last-resort for students experiencing learning difficulties.

The Arts

Clearly, the visual arts and music dominated the arts curriculum of the elementary schools we studied. Children were taught the rudiments of using crayons, watercolor paints, and clay. They modeled the clay. They used the crayons and watercolors to draw and paint pictures of things around them and stories read. They colored—oh, how they colored!—shapes, animals, and scenes depicted in workbooks; they painted simple still lifes; occasionally they created their own pictorial images.

Music included sight reading, singing a variety of songs, many of them songs that have survived successions of school-goers, and appreciation, including music from other lands. Patriotic songs were learned and sung repeatedly. Most schools offered some kind of children's performance during the year in which music was the dominant theme.

Beyond these commonly found programs in music and the visual arts, there were scattered evidences of dance, pantomine, puppetry, performing plays, acting out, embroidery, hooking rugs, and, in one school, filmmaking. Also, beyond the usual activities in the two customary subjects some children made collages, learned about the different musical instruments and sometimes learned to play one or more, studied different careers in music, and learned about famous composers. Most classes paid heed to the advent of seasons and holidays in their activities.

Junior highs typically offered the visual arts as Art 7, 8, 9 and music as either Music or Vocal Music 7, 8, and 9. Other offerings included crafts, band, chorus, graphic arts, designcraft, orchestra, drama, cinema, girls' chorus, boys' chorus, concert band, cadet band, glee club, guitar, and more. The topics listed by teachers were almost invariably tied to the technical aspects of the art form—techniques of using different media in the visual arts, "proper playing habits," rhythm, melody, harmony, line, texture, pattern. The junior highs also stressed learning the "performance and rehearsal disciplines" of music.

To an array of relatively common courses in music, visual art, and general art appreciation, the senior high schools added a wide array of arts and crafts and especially specialized music courses. Chorus and band courses were relatively common across schools. Courses in jazz music, ceramics, photography, sculpture, and consumer music were all offered somewhere but not commonly.

Teachers at all levels stated goals intrinsic to the arts but also listed goals that transcend them—power to see beyond the surface of things, a positive attitude toward experimentation, pride in workmanship, appreciation of human dignity and values. However, my impression of the arts, as of other subjects, is that these transcendent goals took secondary position—a remote secondary position—to emphasis on the use of tools and on performance. Students in junior and senior high music classes spent an inordinate amount of class time on rehearsals for performance at the upcoming football game or some other event.

At the elementary level, the visual arts, drama, dance, and physical education were the only subjects not oriented to textbooks. Apparently, these were not used, if the teachers reporting to us were accurate and complete in their provision of information. Visual arts teachers used the arts tools, paints, and paper as their primary materials of instruction. We must not assume, however, that arts classes were dominated by student activity; teachers still talked a lot even in these classes, and teachers of music did use textbooks, particularly the series of Silver Burdett.

Teachers in the junior and senior high visual arts classes used books for teachers extensively in planning their classes, but did not use textbooks for students in the usual way. An array of books on the arts and textbooks for students were used in these classes but not as whole-class resources. There was little school-to-school overlap, apparently, in the use of these courses for teaching and learning. Again the Silver Burdett series dominated in music classes.

At elementary and secondary levels, paper-and-pencil tests were used less in the arts than in other subjects, with the exception of physical education. More often, evaluation was based on participation, performance, or a finished product. Conventional tests were used more often in music than in the other art forms. Tests at all levels usually were teachermade. Tests and quizzes increased in frequency with increase in grade level.

Consistently at all levels, students rated the arts as more interesting and enjoyable than the academic subject fields and also as relatively unimportant and easy. Although they did not participate a great deal in selecting learning materials and activities, students did this more in the arts than in the academic subjects. Both principals and teachers in our sample viewed the arts as providing students with unique opportunities for personal development and aesthetic experiences, and the arts programs of these schools, more than other programs, did seem to capture the personal interests of students.

But I have two major reservations regarding the conduct of the arts programs in the schools studied, reservations which I fear might well be extended to schools more broadly. First, I am disappointed with the degree to which arts classes appear to be dominated by the ambience of

English, mathematics, and other academic subjects. Arts classes, too, appear to be governed by characteristics which are best described as "school"—following the rules, finding the one right answer, practicing the lower cognitive processes. Admittedly, most arts classes in our sample are less well described by language conveying conformity than most classes in the academic subjects. Nonetheless, they did not convey the picture of individual expression and artistic creativity toward which one is led by the rhetoric of forward-looking practice in the field.[5] A funny thing happens to the arts, too, on their way to the classroom.

Second, there was a noticeable absence of emphasis on the arts as cultural expression and artifact. The need for expression lies just back of the human need for food, water, and socialization. Yet the impression I get of the arts programs in the schools studied is that they go little beyond coloring, polishing, and playing—and much of this goes on in classes such as social studies as a kind of auxiliary activity rather than as art in its own right. What does not come through in our data is much if any indication that the arts were being perceived as central to personal satisfaction in a world rich in art forms, processes, and products. To grow up without the opportunity to develop such sophistication in arts appreciation is to grow up deprived.

Vocational and Career Education

I have been using the words "vocational education" as a form of shorthand to embrace both vocational and career education. This abbreviation will not endear me to specialists who endeavor to make clear definitional distinctions between the two.

The meaning of career education appears to be quite clear and consistent whether one examines definitions or practice. It is education designed to introduce students to the world of work, the array of careers available, what these careers involve, and the preparation likely to be needed for them. Such education appears not to have a well-defined place in elementary schools. Topics about various kinds of work and the people who do it—firemen, policemen, postal workers, astronauts, scientists, doctors, writers, and so on—appear in the elementary social studies, science, and health curricula. A few schools offer career education units of study not specifically integrated with other subjects, usually in the higher grades. At the secondary level, courses such as career planning leave little doubt about their intent and fit the definition.

Vocational education outstrips career education in secondary schools and is much more difficult to pin down. Leaders in the field, such as Barlow, stress the importance of vocational education as part of general education, very much in the tradition of the writers of the report *General Education in a Free Society*, who argued eloquently for vocational education for all—that fifth finger on the hand of general education.[6] But what this means becomes obscured in the writing of some advocates and even more confused in practice. Much of this writing deals with the importance of vocational education for that majority of students who do not go on to college. Frequently, the point is made that this education should prepare not only for general understanding of the workplace but also for specific work. Our data suggest that preparing for specific work dominates in practice.

The junior highs in our sample offered courses appearing to be oriented to at least three possible purposes of vocational education: providing life skills, providing a hands-on approach in subjects justified as providing general education through media other than books, and developing beginning skills in a possible occupation. Courses with such titles as Homemaking, Home Economics, Home Arts, Domestic Arts, and Consumerism fit into the first category. Courses such as Metal, Wood, Crafts, and Plastics occupy the second. Courses appearing to be more job preparatory included Office Practice and Building Maintenance. Courses such as Typing, Drafting, and General Mechanical Repairs provide life skills but also are preparatory for jobs requiring such competencies. Overall, the junior high curricula appeared to emphasize either things likely to be useful in general living or learning through alternative media requiring a hands-on approach.

A distinct shift toward the teaching of occupational skills occurred at the senior high level. Courses in homemaking and home economics reappeared. But there was a profusion of courses appearing to be far more preparation for jobs than preparation for the enrichment of daily living—Cosmetology, Upholstery, Auto Body Repair, Building Construction, Vocational Printing, Intensive Office Education, Meal Management, and sequences of courses in typing, shorthand, and bookkeeping. It is clear that preparation for careers involving the use of typing, shorthand, and bookkeeping was an accepted function of many of the senior high schools in our sample. Somewhat less evident were courses providing experiences in a variety of jobs serving the needs of the community for food, power, communications, and the like. Not surprisingly, courses in farming economics and management showed up in schools located in rural areas.

In summary, the so-called vocational education curriculum in the secondary schools of our sample embraced six groups of courses: career education, home economics, distributive education (marketing and economics), industrial arts, business education (particularly secretarial skills) and agriculture. The number of courses offered ranged from over 20 at Euclid and at Fairfield Senior High, with over 40% of their teaching force assigned to them, to only two or three in each of three fields—typing, industrial arts, and home economics—at Laurel, with 15% of teachers assigned. Most of the large high schools offered great variety and diversity of subjects generally taught by teachers specialized in them. They often offered sequences of two or more courses directed at specific occupations.

Textbook series in virtually all of these domains of vocational education were in general use in both junior and senior highs. These included workbook-type exercises for students to perform. There appeared to be somewhat more use of commercial packages and kits in this subject area than in the others, particularly at the senior high level.

Testing practices were similar to those used by teachers in other fields, heavily emphasizing checking from among choices and short answer responses. Products and ability to perform commonly were used as evidences of attainment. The widespread additional use of pencil-and-paper tests in a field lending itself so well to evaluation by performance comes as a surprise.

Vocational education courses, compared with courses in academic subjects, tended to be characterized by greater involvement of students in what they were to do or study, more hands-on activity and movement, and somewhat less time spent on instruction. Teachers more frequently tended to model the process or performance required and to give direct assistance to students. The standard teaching techniques of lecturing, questioning, and monitoring students dominated, but not so excessively as in the academic classes.

Physical Education

Our data show a steady rise in time and teachers allocated to physical education from the lower elementary grades through the junior high and then a slight decline in the senior high schools. Emphasis on athletics more than makes up for this junior-to-senior high slippage. That is, there is increasing attention in the later years to that part of the school program devoted to students who demonstrate athletic ability.

There was great variation in the kinds of programs offered in our elementary schools. In some, anything that might be called a program was virtually nonexistent. Physical education appeared to be a teacher-monitored recess, with the students engaged most of the time in group sports, their specific nature changing with the seasons. Some schools clearly made a concerted effort to teach the rules and rudimentary skills of soccer, volleyball, kickball, baseball, and the like, interspersing such outside "dry day" activity with "wet day" emphasis on health, safety, review of the rules of games, and nutrition, frequently with the help of films. A few schools had programs emphasizing the education part of physical education—space and body awareness, rhythmic movement, animal mimetics, how to practice different body movements without interfering with others, and how to use different body parts consciously.

All the junior highs in our sample required physical education classes at all grade levels for all students not specifically excused for illness. Students attended classes averaging 50 minutes each either daily or on alternate days. Some health education was taught in connection with physical education classes. Occasionally there was a special course for students with handicaps or posture problems.

Topics listed by junior high teachers give us an idea of the scope of these physical education classes: aerobic conditioning, archery, badminton, baseball, basketball, bowling, conditioning and corrective exercise, dance, dodgeball, fitness, football, folk dance, gymnastics, handball, hockey, kickball, ping pong, pool, raquetball, shuffleboard, skating, soccer, softball, speedball, tennis, track and field, trampoline, tumbling, touch football, volleyball, wrestling, yoga. But a few teachers asked to list what they taught omitted topics completely in favor of the outcomes or qualities sought: self-discipline, concentration, agility, strength, coordination, quickness, endurance, leadership, cooperation, sportsmanship, responsibility, respect, confidence, fun for all.

Although the above describes topics common also to the senior high curricula, two shifts were apparent in senior high. First, there was a relatively common core of gymnasium-based activities frequently described as warm-up exercises, often approaching the level of gymnastics in the skills of controlled movement they involved. Second, an emphasis on competitive team sports, an emphasis already present in the junior highs, that became markedly greater in the senior high schools—as opposed to sports likely to be played individually throughout life. The number of offerings in individual sports increased, in fact, at the senior high level, but to a considerable degree, students perceived these too to be competitive. Also, participation in team games such as football, baseball, basketball, and soccer far exceeded the relatively sparse availability of and participation in individual sports such as swimming and wrestling.

We found in physical education a subject not dominated or even moderately characterized by tests, workbooks, and worksheets. Teachers used books as their own source of ideas and information. At all levels, evaluation was based almost exclusively on performance. Occasional paper-and-pencil tests required short answers to questions of terminology, rules, and certain procedural matters, such as use of equipment. Although health education took a secondary place to physical education when the two were combined, formal written tests were used frequently to evaluate health knowledge. Most teachers, it appears, will resort to paper-and-pencil tests whenever the possibility of employing them emerges. It is interesting that there was very little diagnosis of physical skills as a basis for further refinement. There was, however, some actual performance testing of physical skills.

One classroom characteristic not escaped in physical education is listening to the teacher. More than in academic classes, students actively performed exercises, practiced skills, and played games, but teachers still managed to talk a lot. As in the arts and vocational education, students participated more frequently in making decisions about their learning than was the case in the academic subjects, and they ranked physical education high for liking but relatively low for importance and difficulty.

The most visible characteristic of physical education programs in the schools we studied was the emphasis at all levels on learning and playing competitive team sports. These make varying demands for close cooperation, depend heavily on each individual's performance, and invariably involve strong competition between groups in a single class, between classes, or between schools. Education in the acquisition of skills in sports not requiring the availability of a group took a poor second place to the emphasis on group sports. A dominant theme even in the individual sports was competition. Students in particular perceived the competitive ambience to be considerable. There is in the literature on the role of physical education in schools considerable stress on the development of skills likely to be useful in lifelong recreational activities such as individual sports. The gap between this ideal and the practices we observed and analyzed appears to be substantial.

Beyond the School Subjects

It is customary for secondary school students, in particular, to participate in some activities offered outside of the regular subject fields—sport teams, special interest clubs, student government, groups organized around the performing arts, honor societies, a variety of community service activities, and so on. We probed a little into students' participation in these, but this so-called extracurriculum was not a major focus of inquiry.

Once again the high involvement of youth in sports and games surfaced. At all but two junior highs and four senior highs, a greater percentage of boys and girls participated in sports teams than in any other activity. The average number of participants dropped a little from junior to senior high schools. This could be partly a consequence of more senior high students being employed and of the increase in interscholastic sports involving fewer students more intensively. And certainly the increase in spectatorship contributes to the drop.

There was heavy involvement, too, in special interest clubs. Indeed, in a few of the schools at both levels the amount of participation vied with participation in sports teams. On the average, the percentage of students engaged in this kind of activity was higher in senior than in junior high schools.

Another area of frequent student participation was music, drama, and dance. The percentage of students involved was greater at the junior than at the senior high level.

Nearly a third of the student body at both levels reported participation in some sort of service activity pertaining either to the school or the community. We found that approximately one student in seven was involved in student government, which we treated separately from the service category. Participation in honor societies presumably was not an open choice. Our finding that about 19% of the students at both levels, on the average, were members suggests that such groups are still alive and well.

School-to-school variation in all of these categories was very wide—as wide as in any of the school characteristics we studied. The variations related in some degree to the vagaries of school resources and policies. We were unable to relate them to such factors as student ethnicity or school transportation patterns. Not surprisingly, a higher percentage of students participated in the smaller schools. It takes a larger percentage of students to manage student governance, for example, in a small school than in a large one. In this our data support what others have found in relation to school size and the opportunity for students to be active in the variety of activities offered.[7] It simply is more difficult for large schools, which frequently occupy relatively small areas, to offer extracurricular activities proportionate to the size of the student body—even though, of course, the array of activities usually is broader.

What we need to know more about is *who* participates. We know from other sources that schools tend to reflect the larger society in that some individuals are involved in almost everything while others are at the periphery. In general, those students in our sample who reported participation in extracurricular activities had higher self-concept scores than those who did not. One suspects that students doing reasonably well in their classroom studies more frequently participated in what the schools were offering beyond academics and felt better, usually, about the entire range of their school experiences.

Diversity and alternatives in school programs are justified on the grounds that there will be opportunities for everyone. But students who are confident in themselves, like some adults in the larger society, tend to benefit first and most from what is available. Schools need (1) data likely to pinpoint those students who appear least able to help themselves, and (2) ongoing practices designed to assist these individuals in becoming confident and resourceful. Schools reflect only too faithfully the differential success patterns surrounding them. This reflection of life does not justify a role of cultural reproduction for the school. The school is, after all, an educational institution, charged with responsibility for developing individual aspirations and abilities. But perhaps we are more comfortable with a school that maintains rather than threatens the status quo.

THE IMPLICIT CURRICULUM

Learning from the Ways of the Classroom

Our trained observers gathered data in complete observations of 129 elementary, 362 junior high, and 525 senior high classes. They described the architectural arrangement of the classroom, seating and grouping patterns, furnishings, and materials and equipment. During each day of observation they provided an overview of the space and materials available and of the decision-making and other interactive processes in evidence. Throughout the day in the elementary schools or through class periods in the secondary schools, they recorded what each adult and student was doing, the size of student groups, and the nature of the activities in progress. During successive five-minute intervals they focused on interactions from which we were able to deduce *who* (teacher or student) was doing *what* (questioning, lecturing, correcting, responding, etc.) to *whom* (teacher or student) and *how* (e.g., verbally or nonverbally, with positive emotion, with guidance, etc.) and in what *context* (instructing, controlling behavior, social interaction, or classroom routines). These are almost exclusively matters of process. They describe an ambience or climate of the classroom from which, we must assume, students are acquiring values, attitudes, and ways of thinking or behaving.

The data reveal the physical environment of most of the classrooms to be highly similar, devoid of amenities likely to provide comfort, unattractive or at least aesthetically bland, and cramped for space (just a few square feet per person). They lacked, commonly, decoration in the form of wall hangings, prints of good paintings, contrasting colors on walls, doors, and cupboards, and the like. Classes in the early elementary grades generally were rich in displays of children's art products, as well as posters, plants, and other decorative features designed to recognize children's work and create a pleasing environment. Sometimes the result was a visual jumble of accretions—more going up on the walls each day and nothing coming down. But the net effect was far more interesting than that produced by senior high classrooms, where such things rarely adorned the rooms. The picture is of increasing drabness as one moves upward through the grades.

One would hope that the lunchrooms might provide a pleasing aesthetic contrast. This proved rarely to be the case. Indeed, they tended to be even more drab, almost invariably lacking the students' art products sometimes seen in classrooms. Only occasionally were there signs of any effort to create an attractive setting for eating. The stream of children in some schools scraping food from their plates into large bins only added to the generally unpleasant scene. And yet we know that some schools do better, with pictures on the walls, bright tablecloths, and even flowers on the tables.[8]

The business community increasingly has recognized the importance of brightly painted or softly muted walls, music in nicely furnished resting places, and a host of other embellishments. Some business offices feature murals, mobiles, and watercolor or oil paintings. Why should the workplace of teachers, children, and youth be so sterile, and why do those in this workplace do so little about its aesthetic qualities?

And centrally, what are students learning from all of this? There is no evidence to suggest that they learn more mathematics or science in more aesthetically pleasing schools. But it seems reasonable to assume that school and classroom, as physical entities, educate in subtle ways—that they add to, detract from, or are neutral in the daily facilitating of civility, lively aesthetic tastes, and satisfying personal life styles. I can only conclude from our data that the schools we visited—like most of the schools I have visited over the past three decades—generally provided physical environments ranging from neutral to negative in their probable impact on the humans inhabiting them.

An often-repeated purpose of educational institutions is to teach human beings to use the tools of our civilization. We were less than encouraged by what was provided to fulfill this purpose in the schools we studied. How did almost all of them manage to shield themselves so effectively from the technological revolution now well under way? The common absence of modern technological devices for learning in the classrooms we observed seems to convey the implicit, erroneous message that these have nothing to do with the educative process. The patriarch of the tools of schooling is the pencil, the matriarch is the pen, and the rest of the family is an assortment of crayons and plastic measuring sticks. I found a few calculators in an elementary school—in a special mathematics center, inside a cupboard, and used on special occasions with a few children. Calculators were in use in some high school mathematics classes, but I found no microcomputers in use at any level. In schools where students are involved with some form of computer, the machine too often is being used to program the learner, but in Seymour Papert's vision:

> The child programs the computer and, in doing so, both acquires a sense of mastery over a piece of the most modern and powerful technology and establishes an intimate contact with some of the deepest ideas from science, from mathematics, and from the art of intellectual model building.[9]

Children at Lamplighter, a private school in a suburb of Dallas, Texas, begin this quest when only three or four years old.

For Seymour Papert and others abreast of this technology, the relationship between child and computer in today's classroom is akin to the relationship between child and pencil in yesterday's. Except that it scarcely exists. Our world is being transformed by the extraordinary capability of this most versatile of man-made tools. But for most of us, including our children whose world will be transformed even more as they become adults, this ongoing revolution, with its accompanying transformation of the economy, communications, and even social relationships, is largely a secret. The almost complete failure of the schools in our sample and of schools generally to open up this secret directly reflects the ignorance and lack of foresight of the surrounding society. There are, fortunately, some contemporary signs of change.

We found in the explicit curriculum a few references to understanding the computer and some occasional introductions to its use. These were as likely to be in mathematics, social studies, or science classes as in vocational education courses. How can vocational educators possibly justify their use of goal statements such as "understanding the workplace" and not assure computer literacy in high school students? How can we, as a people, continue to be almost completely unconcerned about this inexcusable omission of one of the most important inventions of all time, the basis of a social revolution capable of molding the destiny of every human being? Perhaps, as with radio and television, computers will be peripheral to the school experience. If so, schools could well become peripheral to human experience.

Computers, of course, are merely an enhancement of that most significant of all tools, the human mind, and the vast body of data we gathered through observing successive five-minute periods of interaction and interspersing these with "snapshots" of classroom activity leads me to somewhat similar hypotheses regarding what schools do about mind development and about computers. The fact that between 5% and 10% of the classes observed were places of reasonably intense student involvement with learning gives us a glimpse of the possible. But the lack of this in a very large percentage tells us something of the task of improvement to be confronted.

Students in the classes we observed made scarcely any decisions about their learning, even though many perceived themselves as doing so. Nearly 100% of the elementary classes were almost entirely teacher dominated with respect to seating, grouping, content, materials, use of space, time utilization, and learning activities. A similar situation prevailed in 90% of the junior high and 80% of the senior high classes, and the increase in student decision making was in only one or two areas, usually somewhat removed from the learning activity itself, and more in the arts, physical education, and vocational education than in the academic subjects. Perhaps students simply expect this and so see themselves as taking part even when their participation in decisions is limited.

We observed that, on the average, about 75% of class time was spent on instruction and that nearly 70% of this was "talk"—usually teacher to students. Teachers out-talked the entire class of students by a ratio of about three to one. If teachers in the talking mode and students in the listening mode is what we want, rest assured that we have it. These findings are so consistent in the schools of our sample that I have difficulty assuming that things are much different in schools elsewhere.

Clearly, the bulk of this teacher talk was instructing in the sense of telling. Barely 5% of this instructional time was designed to create students' anticipation of needing to respond. Not even 1% required some kind of open response involving reasoning or perhaps an opinion from students. Usually, when a student was called on to respond, it was to give an informational answer to the teacher's question.

Conversely, teachers were not responding to students, in large part because students were not initiating anything. Or when a teacher sought and got a student's response, the teacher rarely responded in turn directly to that response with supportive language, corrective feedback, or some other meaningful acknowledgment. Teachers' responses, if any, were more likely to be nonpersonal, such as "all right"—a kind of automatic transition device in a presentation directed to the whole class. Indeed, the bulk of the lecturing dominating at all levels was to whole classes. Teacher-to-small-group interaction rarely occurred at any level. When students did become involved actively in the dominant lecturing mode, it was almost always to respond to the teacher, not to initiate an exchange.

As I have said before, this relationship between teachers and classes of students was almost completely devoid of outward evidences of affect. Shared laughter, overt enthusiasm, or angry outbursts were rarely observed. Less than 3% of classroom time was devoted to praise, abrasive comments, expressions of joy or humor, or somewhat unbridled outbursts such as "wow" or "great."

No matter what the observational perspective, the same picture emerges. The two activities, involving the most students, were being lectured to and working on written assignments (and we have seen that much of this work was in the form of responding to directives in workbooks or on worksheets). When we add to the time spent in these learning modes the time spent on the routines of preparing for or following up instruction, the extraordinary degree of student passivity stands out. The amount of time spent in any other kind of activity (e.g., role playing, small group planning and problem solving, constructing models) was miniscule—and does not add up to a great deal even when the totals for all such deviations are computed. Students were working alone most of the time, whether individually or in groups. That is, the student listened as one member of a class being lectured, or the student worked individually on a seat assignment. Usually, in the course of a day, students in elementary classrooms encountered up to five different kinds of activities or groupings but with advancement through the grades to secondary schools, they commonly encountered only lecturing and seat assignments.

The foregoing is generally descriptive of what our several kinds of observations told us and is applicable to most classes at all levels; there were more hands-on activities and physical movement in the lower elementary grades and, of course, in the arts, physical education, and vocational education. In effect, then, the modal classroom configurations which we observed looked like this: the teacher explaining or lecturing to the total class or a single student, occasionally asking questions requiring factual answers; the teacher, when not lecturing, observing or monitoring students working individually at their desks; students listening or appearing to listen to the teacher and occasionally responding to the teacher's questions; students working individually at their desks on reading or writing assignments; and all with little emotion, from interpersonal warmth to expressions of hostility.

In seeking to describe all of this sameness, my colleague Kenneth Sirotnik recounts a scene in Andy Warhol's film *The Haircut*. For what seems to be an interminably long period of time, the camera focuses on a man's face and head and on the tools of a barber at work. At long last, there is a twitch. The audience cheers in nearly hysterical relief. Sirotnik then describes an imaginary Warhol film of the modal classroom just described:

> We would watch the secondary classroom unfold, fifty-five minutes during which a hint of affect would be cause for celebration—positive affect would be nice, but even negative

would suffice, as a welcome change from the flat affective neutrality pervading the screen. If it were a physical education class, we would break out in applause were the teacher actually to spend time helping a student (or group of students) perfect their baseball swing instead of monitoring whatever physical activities were in progress. If it were a science class, we would cheer wildly were the teacher actually to demonstrate the effects of air pressure and vacuums instead of only explaining them or monitoring the total class as students worked independently on their written assignments.[10]

We do not see in our descriptions, then, much opportunity for students to become engaged with knowledge so as to employ their full range of intellectual abilities. And one wonders about the meaningfulness of whatever is acquired by students who sit listening or performing relatively repetitive exercises, year after year. Part of the brain, known as Magoun's brain, is stimulated by novelty. It appears to me that students spending twelve years in the schools we studied would be unlikely to experience much novelty. Does part of the brain just sleep, then?

Follow-up studies of Project Talent interviewed 30-year-olds about their recollections of schools.[11] What they remembered and found useful were those experiences in which they became interested and deeply involved. We know from studies done years ago that the facts students are able to recall in classroom examinations are up to 80% forgotten just two years later. The 30 schools in the eight-year study of the late 1930s and early 1940s endeavored to find alternative ways to secure student interest and involvement in the subject matter.[12] Even the examinations used called not just for the recollection of information but for reasoning with or beyond data provided in the test. These tests reflected and reinforced the importance of the reasoning abilities teachers were attempting to stimulate in their classes. Preparation of a series of volumes on general education and how to foster it accompanied the innovative activities under way in the schools.[13]

This important work of several decades ago, as well as much of what has since been in the forefront of educational thought, stresses the importance of teachers' finding ways to make subject matter relevant to students, to involve students in setting their own goals, to vary the ways of learning, to use approaches that employ all of the senses, and to be sure that there are opportunities for relating the knowledge to experiences or actually using it. These things are not easy, and teachers learn some of the rhetoric but rarely practice the techniques in teacher education programs or later. A current misunderstanding about the improvement of pedagogy is that teachers simply need to learn to do better what they are doing now. It is important, of course, for teachers to be superb at lecturing and skillful in questioning students. But providing inducements for improving only in these limited aspects of teaching is to reinforce the repetition of what already is grossly in excess.

Some Student Perceptions

Someone else might interpret differently our data on specific student perceptions of their classroom experiences. My general conclusion is that the students we studied for the most part held relatively benign views of these experiences—more positive than negative but far from either enthusiastic or full of dislike. But virtually all of the indices fell off toward the negative side with upward progression through the grades.

Whereas over 80% of the upper elementary students said they liked the arts very much, just 51% of the senior high students gave this response.* Social studies dropped from a low 35% to just 25%. Mathematics, which was very much liked by 56% of the upper elementary students, was very much liked by only 27% of those in the senior high school. Only English and mathematics retained throughout the secondary levels a high percentage of students rating them very important, and the latter slipped from 82% in the upper elementary grades to 68% in the senior high schools. Science enjoyed a rating of very important by 62% of upper elementary boys and girls but dropped to 37% among senior high students.

Secondary students appeared to have faith that most of the subjects they were studying would be more useful later than they viewed them to be now. Only English, mathematics, and vocational education were seen by more than 30% of junior high students as very useful now. Only vocational education climbed above the 30% figure at the senior high level, with 43% of the students viewing this subject as very useful now. Only the arts failed to secure a vote of 30% or more from the junior high students for "very useful later." Among high school students, on the other hand, only mathematics (40%) and vocational education (57%) were expected to be very useful later by more than a third of the students.

One would like to believe that students in schools find their learning experiences to be very interesting most of the time. The only subjects getting ratings of "very interesting" from more than a third of junior and senior high students taking them were the arts, vocational education, physical education, and foreign languages. It is depressing to see English coming out so poorly (about 23%), especially given the relatively high ratings for importance given to this subject field.

*These are more refined classifications of data than appear in Chapter 4. Whereas the latter employed "liking" as a general category, these data are subjected to an analysis including degrees or levels of liking.

The more we got into specific classroom practices, the more the "like very much" percentage dropped off. It was especially distressing to see that the kinds of classroom practices found most often were well liked by relatively small percentages of students. In grouping practices, for example, not more than a third of the students in any of the subject areas at the junior highs said they liked working alone or as a total class "very much"—the two ways they almost always work. This was the case as well at the senior highs, except for the arts and physical education, where slightly greater percentages said they liked these grouping patterns. Much the same was true for the most commonly found instructional materials and activities. At neither secondary level did more than a third of the students in any subject say they liked worksheets or textbooks very much. While greater percentages of math students—35% and 39% at the junior and senior highs, respectively—than students in other subjects reported that they liked listening to their teacher very much, these percentages are still quite small. Further, no more than 26% of the students at either secondary level in any subject said they liked writing answers to questions very much. And these activities were the most frequent ones.

How would I react as an adult to these ways of the classroom? I would become restless. I would groan audibly over still another seatwork assignment. My mind would wander off soon after the beginning of a lecture. It would be necessary for me to put my mind in some kind of "hold" position. This is what students do. Films of relatively good frontal teaching (lecturing and questioning the total class) clearly reveal how quickly many students turn their minds elsewhere or simply doze.

Students may not simply get up and leave. For many, there is no viable perceived alternative anyway. School is where their friends are. To resist or rebel would be to shake up the controlled ambience and go against the grain of the trade-offs necessary for peaceful coexistence in a small space. One learns passivity. Students in schools are socialized into it virtually from the beginning.

As in the Warhol-like film, little deviations from the norm become important—a heavy sigh halfway through a test, Pete's swaggering walk to the pencil sharpener, a bird on the windowledge, an unusually inane announcement on the public address system. Even the teacher laughs. Everyone feels good for a moment. And the seatwork goes better for a while.

What do students perceive themselves to be learning? We asked those in our sample to write down the most important thing learned in the school subjects—six subjects at the upper elementary level and eight in the junior and senior highs. Scanning their responses provokes few surprises, given the kind of classroom life consistently revealed in our other data.

"Nothing" was not a frequent response, nor was it rare. At the secondary level, in particular, some students attempted to explain why they made no choices of the most important thing learned: "To be honest, I haven't learned much but I would like to, but all we do, or rather all she does, is talk and I get bored with the same routines every day." Another high school student in a different subject wrote, "We are trying to learn how to debate, but he never has told us how, he has just told us about his great class last year." A student in a ninth-grade mathematics class answered as follows: "Nothing we haven't learned before, and he's always writing referrals." These sorts of responses tended to group for certain classes, but statements ranging from "nothing" to "a great deal" were sometimes given by different students in the same class, at all levels.

Most commonly, students listed a given fact or topic—"about nouns" or "fractions" or "what a hero is" or "I learned new words" (a senior high school student's response). Sometimes, students simply chose a division of the subject such as grammar or logarithms. Commonly, too, but with much less frequency, students identified a skill—"how to write term papers," "learned to march" (naval sciences), "how to debate," "how to work problems faster." These kinds of responses were given relatively frequently for English/language arts and mathematics. The topics or skills listed for these two subjects by students in the fifth grade frequently were repeated by students in the sixth, seventh, eighth, and ninth. More than students in other subjects, students in these two subjects mentioned something about tests—usually learning to take them.

Noticeably absent were responses implying the realization of having acquired some intellectual power or done something creative. Indeed, when the response "learning to create my own things" appeared in the list of all answers given by an entire class, the words seemed to stand out in color. Similarly, there was little about human relationships in the form of statements either about satisfaction in working with others or about learning the ways of other people. One might have expected the latter in a course entitled "Our Modern World," but it was dates, places, political entities, and names of leaders of the French Revolution that students reported.

A somewhat different emphasis pervaded the arts, physical education, vocational education, and several courses outside of the mainstream such as journalism and sociology. There was a noticeable shift away from the identification of subjects and topics toward the acquisition of some kind of ability or competence, although the former still prevailed: "The thing that was most important was mixing color" was the respone of a junior high student in Art 7. A student in General Mechanical Repair 8 wrote, "I learned to weld and cut with the torch and I helped weld a trailer." Almost every student in a physical education class enrolling boys from grades seven and eight said, in some form, "playing basketball, football, and baseball." A senior high class in journalism stood out for both the frequency of well-written, correctly spelled statements and the degree of emphasis on learnings transcending the subject matter. Examples included, "Learned how to write decently and convincingly" and "how to communicate more clearly with others." Although the members of a senior high class in sociology included some negative comments, it appears that this was one of the few courses in the schools we studied that got rather deeply into cultural differences and the structure of society: "The most important thing I have learned in sociology is that our culture is not the only one in the world"; and "Learned about the habits and values of other people in society."

There was a marked difference between students' responses in one advanced academic class and a general course—Calculus (grade twelve) as contrasted with Algebra B (grade ten). Most of those students in the latter simply referred to the subject: "Little more about math"; or "How to do math"; or "How to do Algebra better." The calculus class clearly enrolled the college-bound, who wrote such things as the following: "All that I have learned in this class will pertain to my life later on, and is extremely important"; "Since each new concept is built on the old ones, everything I learn is important"; and "Many times in this class I get wrong answers, but in this class you learn to learn from your mistakes." No student spoke of being bored and not one wrote "nothing."

Alas, the flat and vague responses of the Algebra B students were more typical of our sample. There was, in general, a lack of intensity—and particularly pleasure, enthusiasm, or sheer fun—in what students said about their classes. For many, it appeared, even being asked to respond to a question about the most important thing they had learned in a class came as a surprise. They often answered this question very much as they might answer a question about their country's major cities—as if the subject was something just beyond their domains of real interest and involvement.

SUMMARY AND DISCUSSION

The allocation of time and teaching resources in the elementary and secondary schools in our sample reflected those goals most commonly articulated and most likely to appear first in educational documents furnished by the states for our study. On the other hand, there is a lack of parallelism between what many other goal statements convey and what we observed in schools and classrooms. This can be sensed by rereading the list of goals for schooling presented in Chapter 2, a list largely based on the states' goal statements, in the light of this chapter so far. I shall try to illuminate the discrepancy further in the ensuing discussion.

Our data, whatever the source, reveal not only the curricular dominance of English/language arts and mathematics but also the consistent and repetitive attention to basic facts and skills. Developing "the ability to read, write, and handle basic arithmetical operations," as the states' educational documents put it, pervades instruction from the first through the ninth grades and the lower tracks of courses beyond. What the schools in our sample did not appear to be doing in these subjects was developing all those qualities commonly listed under "intellectual development": the ability to think rationally, the ability to use, evaluate, and accumulate knowledge, a desire for further learning. Only *rarely* did we find evidence to suggest instruction likely to go much beyond mere possession of information to a level of understanding its implications and either applying it or exploring its possible applications. Nor did we see activities likely to arouse students' curiosity or to involve them in seeking solutions to some problem not already laid bare by teacher or textbook.

And it appears that this preoccupation with the lower intellectual processes pervades social studies and science as well. An analysis of topics studied and materials used gives not an impression of students studying human adaptations and explorations but of facts to be learned. One finds little of activities likely to promote an understanding of the basic interdependence of the biological and physical resources of the environment, or of the manner in which heritages and traditions of the past are operative today and influence the directions and values of society. Yet it is to goals such as these that such subjects supposedly are to be committed.

There appears not to be in relation to social studies and science the kind of social pressure for the basics brought to bear for English/language arts and mathematics. Indeed, quite a few adults deride the tendency of schools to teach relatively inert facts in social studies and science while largely ignoring deeper insights and higher order intellectual skills. Why, then, does the teaching of these subjects not rise above a pedestrian level? One plausible explanation is that the norms tend to be set by the teaching of English/language arts and mathematics. These are the most dominant subjects; students regard them as of high importance and, relatively, of considerable use later in life. The teaching of them probably helps to set the norms from which most teachers hesitate to stray.

Another explanation lies in what I have been calling the circumstances of schooling. Effective teaching in social studies and science calls for visits to governmental bodies in session, fields and ponds, industrial laboratories, and the like. Teaching such subjects well calls for departing from textbooks and workbooks in seeking to use multiple resources—films, an array of source books, perhaps construction materials, and small conference rooms. Field trips, deviant ways of teaching, small rooms, and the like call for different schedules and arrangements not conventionally and, therefore, not usually available in schools. Publishing companies attempting to cater to the cutting edge of instructional practice usually lose money. It is more profitable to market textbooks, in spite of the competition. Teachers may start out "fighting the system," but it is much easier, ultimately, to settle down into conventional ways of teaching. And one tends to look more "normal" by doing so. The cards are stacked against innovation.

Two major deficiencies stand out in all aspects of the curricula we studied, from state and district guides to the most important learnings perceived by students. The first is a failure to differentiate and see the relationships between facts and the more important concepts facts help us to understand. The second, closely related to the first, is a general failure to view subjects and subject matter as turf on which to experience the struggles and satisfactions of personal development.

Some evidence to suggest teachers' differentiation of facts and concepts is found in their statements of what they wanted students to learn. But the mixing together of topics (magnets) and concepts (energy) in single lists reveals that the use of the former to develop understanding of the latter was not at all clear in the minds of these teachers. There was scarcely any evidence of this process being operationalized in the classroom. The emphasis on facts and the recall of facts in quizzes demonstrates not just the difficulty of teaching and testing for more fundamental understanding but the probability, supported by our data, that most teachers simply do not know how to teach for higher levels of thinking—e.g., applying and evaluating scientific principles. This should not surprise us. Their own teachers, for the most part, probably did not know how to do this either.

Regarding the second point, lower elementary teachers frequently appeared to teach, at least part of the time, with some awareness that the topics they introduced were instrumental to personal development. But the subject as both end and means began to dominate in the upper elementary grades. We know from other inquiries that school staffs tend not to engage in dialogue about larger goals than those pertaining to acquiring the knowledge and skills embedded in school subjects.[14] Consequently, it is not often in the nature of a school for everything that goes on there to be viewed and treated as though contributing to traits of mind and character. Rather, one teaches or "takes" algebra, and the goal of learning algebra is reinforced by tests and marks in algebra.

There is a place on the report card for marking citizenship too, but this is something one possesses to some degree. It is not something to which the activities of school are deliberately directed. Teachers are oriented to teaching particular things—the particular things they were taught in school.[15] Relating these particular things to some larger purpose is not something they think about very much or have been prepared to do. And the professional literature on such matters available to teachers is long on philosophy and short on pedagogical operations. Conversely, the literature on the teaching of school subjects is long on operations and devoid of theoretical justification. Once again, teachers are reinforced in teaching the facts and skills of the school subjects as though this was primarily what school-based education is all about. And, in practice, it is. This is true even though most teachers stated that the needs and interests of students were major determinants of what they taught. Many of the curriculum reform movements of the 1960s, particularly in mathematics and the natural sciences, attempted to change this orientation, but the new approaches were not readily accepted by either parents or teachers.[16]

Although instruction in the arts, physical education, and vocational education emphasized performance, there still was a surprising amount of student listening. It is difficult to justify the amount of teacher lecturing in many of the arts classes we observed. Only occasionally is there need for a teacher to lecture to a class in painting. Essential points are better made, even if frequently repeated to individuals, in the context of a student's ongoing performance. And far too much of the performance we observed was teacher- rather than student-determined. The arts are expected to provide opportunities for creative problem solving and disciplined performance. One fears that teachers in the arts behave all too frequently like teachers in academic subjects because of the prevailing view—among other teachers, not just lay citizens—that the arts are soft and on the edge of importance. Arts teachers should boldly demonstrate the potentiality for doing through the arts what cannot be done readily through the other fields.

Vocational goals for schools appear in the documents of all states. They emphasize the development of career awareness and attitudes and habits that will lead one to participating effectively in economic life. Where these goals address the importance of salable skills, they do so in the context of economic independence. Although these intentions made their appearance in the evidences of curricula we examined, they did not dominate. Indeed, they were quite secondary to purposes of training.

Initially, instruction in the manual arts was introduced into the curriculum largely to provide for the simultaneous development of hand and head. The medium for the activity—paper, wood, metal, or soil—called for skill in the use of hands while presenting a problem for the mind. The purpose was not to prepare carpenter, tinsmith, and gardener, although one might become some of all three, but to provide alternative avenues for intellectual development and the honing of some useful skills. Before the expansion of vocational education, most secondary schools offered and conducted in this spirit manual arts classes for boys and household arts classes for girls. Some still do, with greater mixing of the sexes. And not long ago one could find a few elementary school classes, usually in the social studies, where children busily hammered and sawed, constructing the pioneer villages described in their textbooks and translating abstract concepts into concrete experiences.

My visits to classrooms and the data gathered in A Study of Schooling suggest that the intellectual roots feeding such practices have withered. Some lower elementary teachers did use projects involving construction and the like, but these appeared to be instrumental to the utilization of basic skills and not in the spirit of a fresh intellectual challenge involving manual activity. Almost all of the secondary school principals, counselors, and vocational education teachers with whom I attempted to discuss the issues of hand-oriented problem solving as part of general education for all students were politely puzzled by my comments and queries. Except for a very few, they were unable to provide me with data either about the percentage of students involved in non-job-oriented vocational education or about teachers using activities involving manual skills to promote intellectual development. They were far more comfortable discussing the successful job placement of students majoring in vocational subjects. Secondary teachers of academic subjects, meanwhile, shunned hands-on activities, relying almost exclusively on lectures and written assignments.

The goals set forth for schools are particularly idealistic in the social, civic, cultural, and personal domains. It is here that we find the most altruistic expectations for understanding differing value systems; developing productive and satisfying relations with others based on respect, trust, cooperation, and caring; developing a concern for humanity; developing the ability to apply the basic principles and concepts of the fine arts and humanities to the appreciation of aesthetic contributions of other cultures; and developing an understanding of the necessity for moral conduct. And it is here that we find statements about developing the ability to use leisure time effectively, to criticize oneself constructively, to deal with problems in original ways, and to experience and enjoy different forms of creative expression. I conclude that the schools in our sample were contributing minimally to the attainment of such goals. With respect to some, they were rather neutral. With respect to others, they contributed negatively. And as is the case with other goals, they contributed differentially to individual students and groups of students.

Only a few of the schools were architecturally pleasing—and then usually more by contrast with the ugliness of others than by virtue of their own merits. One set of three—elementary, middle, senior high—on a flat site was so drab, dirty, and unadorned with landscaping or color that I could only wonder about the impact on students who had to spend twelve consecutive years of their lives there. Even the teachers sitting in their unattractive lounge appeared drab, as though chosen for their compatibility with the site. The superintendent spoke of importing the design from California but failed to explain why grass and trees in the courtyards had been allowed to die. In another part of the country a triple occupied three sites, each close to the others. One came to the red brick buildings through a fringe of trees. Did this aesthetic setting, the handsome buildings, and the terraced, landscaped, spacious grounds have any impact on those in attendance? They appeared higher spirited than those at the other triple, but perhaps my own sense of pleasure distorted my perceptions.

But while I believe that schools provide unique opportunities to create pleasing places to live and work, I am less distressed by their aesthetic deficiencies than by the apparent absence of participation by parents, teachers, and students in their improvement. Here is an opportunity for young and old to share civic responsibility and develop aesthetic awareness simultaneously. Such activity could be buttressed in classrooms through engagement in "City Building," a pedagogical approach developed by Doreen Nelson through which students study the adaptations of humans to their environment, learning about architectural design and ecosystems while expanding their skills in reading, writing, and speaking.[17] Some teachers achieve similar lifelike integration of academic, vocational, social, and personal education through *The Mini Society Approach to Instruction in Economics and Other Social Sciences,* by Marilyn Kourilsky.[18] This kind of instruction takes civics, economics, and aesthetics out of the textbook and puts it into students' lives. But it is in short supply.

With individual activity in a group setting its hallmark, the total class group is largely a condition necessitated economically, not a vehicle for teaching the requirements of cooperative endeavor. Students rarely set group goals, the attainment of which depends on a division of labor and the successful orchestration of the pieces. There is very little in our data to suggest the possibility of developing "productive and satisfying relations with others based on respect, trust, cooperation, and caring" in the schools we studied. There is little to convey the legitimacy of students helping each other with their individual assignments. Rather, our data suggest that to seek help is to run the risk of "cheating," and to give help is to give away some of whatever competitive edge one enjoys. The most charitable view one could have of this is that schools do not deliberately seek to promote anitsocial behavior. On the other hand, they appear to do little to promote the prosocial behavior many of our goals for schools espouse.

In the personal domain, a goal speaks to the school's role in preparing for the wise and creative use of leisure time. The schools I attended provided for my participation in soccer, basketball, football, and volleyball. These required minimal provision of equipment—a ball, a bat, a net. Neither schools nor households could afford the costs of the protective uniforms now required for competitive sports, or the skis, racquets, and other equipment required for individual sports. Once having left school, I lost the groups of five, nine, or eleven required for the pursuit of these recreational activities. I was not prepared in the skills required for participation in golf, tennis, skiing, badminton, and the like. Our data suggest that schools have not changed much in their neglect of the physical abilities relevant to the sports most played by adults.

Presumably, children and youths learn something of teamwork in the group sports dominating physical education classes and the extracurricular side of school. But as noted in the analysis of the physical education programs, activities were pervaded by stress on competition. My argument is not against competition. It is against the near-absence of anything designed to deliberately cultivate the values and skills of constructive social interaction and group accomplishment which we extoll as a characteristic of our people but neglect in the breach.

The gap between the rhetoric of individual flexibility, originality, and creativity in our educational goals and the cultivation of these in our schools reveals a great hypocrisy. From the beginning, students experience school and classroom environments that condition them in precisely opposite behaviors—seeking "right" answers, conforming, and reproducing the known. These behaviors are reinforced daily by the physical restraints of the group and classroom, by the kinds of questions teachers ask, by the nature of the seatwork exercises assigned, and by the format of tests and quizzes. They are further reinforced by the nature of the rewards—particularly the subtleties of implicitly accepting "right" answers and behaviors while ignoring or otherwise rejecting "wrong" or deviant ones. Only in the "less important" subjects and the advanced sections or academic courses are there evidences of some significant cultivation and reinforcement of more creative or intellectually independent behaviors.

It is difficult to be sanguine about the moral and ethical learnings accompanying many of the experiences of schooling. My perception is that the emphasis on individual performance and achievement would be more conducive to cheating than to the development of moral integrity. I have difficulty seeing how much of what goes on in classrooms would contribute to understanding and appreciating the contributions of others. I see little in the curriculum, explicit or implicit, likely to promote keen awareness of humanity. Given this curriculum, the findings from our own and other studies regarding relatively limited understanding of other cultures and some suspicion toward them among our own young people do not surprise me. Particularly lacking in our data is anything to suggest the deliberate involvement of students in making moral judgments and in understanding the difference between these and decisions based on scientific facts.

One need not speculate abstractly on the cultivation of goals of self-realization in schools. In general, students doing well feel good about themselves and those performing poorly do not. I wonder about the values in feelings of success derived primarily from personal performance compared with the performances of others. There are not in our data findings to suggest that schools encourage seeking to outdo one's own previous performance. And I wonder, conversely, about failure that leads individuals to feel that they are not good at all. What are schools doing to develop the ability to "assess realistically and live with one's limitations and strengths"? A small percentage of students receive a large percentage of the failing grades, year after year. It is difficult to perceive this as useful failure. Schools would be markedly different if their ongoing function was to assure successful performance. We would not put up for long with a physician who sent our child home with an F for health but no assistance in becoming healthy.

Finally, I wonder about the impact of the flat, neutral emotional ambience of most of the classes we studied. Boredom is a disease of epidemic proportions. Many of their escapes from boredom leave people unsatisfied, unfulfilled, and fretful. For millions, television is a sedative; for others, drugs and alcohol provide a temporary escape. Overall, the senior high school students in our sample chose drugs and alcohol, above all others, as their school's worst problem. Is boredom in schools the beginning of the problems boredom tends to generate?

Why are our schools not places of joy? What better place to cultivate the free self? In Stephen Bailey's words:

> Surely, the educational system has no higher function than to help people to have creative engagements with the world of the free self. For if the world of the free self is appropriately cultivated, its felicitous admixture of playfulness, concentration, and socializing can affect, infect and help to liberate the worlds of work and coping. The free self then becomes not a mere segment of existence but a quality of existence.[19]

Bailey's words remind us of this strangely unique characteristic of classroom life—the not quite successful but extraordinarily persistent pretense that human existence can be segmented, that part of it can be left outside the classroom door. The whole comes together again in the hallways, on the playground, and off the school site. But to bring the whole person into the classroom and to attempt to deal with him or her there, in large numbers, is to threaten the very existence of this partial ecosystem, which is neither abrasive nor uncomfortable. Deviant behavior, such as excessive fear and unbridled laughter, might destroy the balance.

One can see how the circumstances of schooling inhibit movement, small group work, and even overt expressions of joy, anger, and other feelings. It is far more difficult to understand the relative paucity of vicarious experiences designed to connect students in some more passionate and compassionate way with the wholeness of human existence and especially with such existential qualities as hope, courage, and love of humankind. These qualities are portrayed particularly through the humanities and especially through literature—myths and fairy tales, novels, drama, and poetry. The early years of schooling appear to me to be shockingly devoid of fairy tales, with their extraordinary ability to symbolize through dragons, heroes, and caring for another the challenges, problems, and opportunities life presents. There are dragons yet to slay—poverty, disease, senseless violence, and prejudice, to name only a few. The tragedies and triumphs of human striving are portrayed in all the forms of literature. There is no assurance from our data, however, that students were delving into them, especially if enrolled in the lower tracks of the English courses. For the most part, they were repetitively preoccupied with the mechanics of usage. Reading beyond textbooks and workbooks appeared not to be a dominant activity. Indeed it appeared, rather, that many students could graduate from twelve years of schooling with only a superficial minimal exposure to significant literary works.

For years, schools and teachers have been criticized for their neglect of the fundamentals. But if our sample is at all representative, it appears that teachers are very preoccupied with trying to teach children and youths precisely what we blame them for not teaching. Then, when we put what they are doing under a microscope and compare it with our most idealistic statements regarding what schools are for, we don't like what we see.

Which way do we want it? Do we want schools and teachers to respond to the messages they hear, the messages telling them to work particularly on children's ability to read, write, and handle arithmetical operations? If so, we should not anticipate much change in what schools do now. English/language arts and mathematics will continue to dominate the curriculum. The other subjects, with the exception of vocational education in the high schools, will continue to have an uncertain, uneven place in the curriculum. The methods of lecturing, questioning, monitoring seatwork, and testing, together with the present materials of instruction, will continue to prevail. About 15% of those in attendance will do very well, another 15% to 25% will do reasonably well, and minority students will slowly increase their membership in these groups. From 15% to 25% will not complete high school, and minority students will continue to be overrepresented in this group. Standardized achievement test scores probably will rise enough to be acceptable, and since a larger percentage of students coming into the major universities will write and spell somewhat better, the pressure to improve schools will diminish a little for a few years.

But the quality of educating in schools will not have improved. Indeed, quite conceivably it could be worse—more boring, less fun, more repetitious, still fewer encounters with significant intellectual problems, even more siphoning of nonacademic students into vocational training, and fewer experiences with the arts. Nonetheless, the nation's teachers will have responded to what they hear. This is what they have heard all along, except in occasional periods of serious effort at reform such as in the decade beginning about 1957 and ending about 1967.

Or do we seriously believe in and want for our schools at least some of what is implied in all those good statements coming after the one about reading, writing, and figuring? If so, a phoenix will rise before us, and it will indeed be an unfamiliar bird—and perhaps an unlikely one too. Because now we will be confronted with the need to involve students in a variety of ways of thinking, to introduce students to concepts and not just facts, to provide situations that provoke and evoke curiosity, to develop in students concern for one's own performance in work and the satisfaction of meeting one's own standards, to cultivate appreciation of others through cooperative endeavors, and to be concerned about the traits of mind and character fostered in schools. No longer will it be sufficient to teach some facts of geography, a little algebra, or the mechanics of language. The school subjects will become means for learnings that transcend them.

Does the foregoing provide a little flavor, a glimpse, of what we want? I am not at all sure that it does. The educational activities implied reflect what states proclaim the schools to be for and what most of the parents in our sample appeared to want. But we have not fully considered the implications of the grand phrases. How many creative thinkers do businesses need? What kind of nation is one awash with autonomous individuals? How many artists and museums can we afford? We are a nation predominantly oriented to the instrumental values of education. If more schooling does not assure a better job, what good is it?

Still, we keep on repeating our idealistic expectations for schools. We must have some belief in their relevance and worth. Either we must decide our expectations are unrealistic and settle for schools just a little better than what we now have or put our money where our mouths are. So far, we have designed and supported schools capable of doing only the simplest parts of the whole. We can do better.

Realism tells us that the road to significant change is long and cluttered. We have failed, rather consistently, to recognize the nature and magnitude of the tasks involved. Part of our failure is in not recognizing that schools alone cannot teach what our young people require in a world most of us scarcely comprehend. Part of our failure stems from a great irony: those who still live in the past confidently set the norms for educating those who will live in the future. The time is past come for us to look more carefully into what we have wrought and the alternatives we might seriously endeavor to create.

Chapter 8

The Same But Different

It has been said that a school is a school is a school and if you've seen one, you've seen them all. To the extent that the schools we studied are representative of many more schools, there is truth in this observation. But only partial truth.

Statements inferring sameness are close to the mark, it appears, when they are about those things we tend to regard as most uniquely and peculiarly the ways of schooling—the mechanics of teaching, the kinds of activities in which students are engaged in classrooms, the modes of learning encouraged, instructional materials, tests and quizzes, grouping practices, and classroom arrangements. These are the things to which an observer's attention is drawn. These were the things most commonly included in our observations of classrooms.

We already have seen the extraordinary sameness of instructional practices in the more than 1,000 classrooms observed. Arraying these data by schools did not change the basic picture. We found some exemplary classes, but these were scattered about from level to level and school to school. These classes tended to be different in degree rather than kind. That is, the teachers tended to do somewhat more or less of what characterized the classes generally.

We have seen, too, that the schools we studied differed. But the many illustrations of difference I have used were mostly in areas other than observed pedagogical practices. With some exceptions—for example, the

246

distribution of teachers to subjects and a very few extraordinary classes—these differences were in the perceptions of those persons with a stake in the schools. It appears that the didactics of the classroom can be—and indeed are—very much the same from school to school and yet often are presented within a context of considerable school-to-school difference in the eyes of principals, teachers, students, and parents. Schools are more different, it seems, in the somewhat elusive qualities making up their ambience—the ways students and teachers relate to one another, the school's orientation to academic concerns, the degree to which students are caught up in peer-group interests other than academic, the way principals and teachers regard one another, the degree of autonomy possessed by principals and teachers in conducting their work, the nature of the relationship between the school and its parent clientele, and so on. These kinds of differences are unlikely to be experienced by visitors and observers who have no real stake in the conduct of the school. But they are strongly experienced by those who do.

We also have seen that our schools were differentially satisfying to those in and around them. Indicators include the grades they gave to their schools, the perceived congruence between goals preferred for the school and goals perceived to be most emphasized, and substantial differences between schools in teachers', students', and parents' perceptions of problems and the seriousness of these problems. There are also scattered evidences in the data to suggest that parents' satisfaction was derived in part from their perception of classroom practices. But since they seemed overall to know little about what went on in the classroom, their satisfaction or lack of it may have been part of their general perception of their school. Our data lead to the conclusion that the level of satisfaction experienced and expressed by those closely connected with schools tells us little or nothing about *how* teachers teach. But high or low levels of satisfaction may be quite powerful indicators of the quality of the relationship between teachers and students in classrooms.

Inside the classrooms we observed, teachers lectured and questioned, students listened, textbooks were the most common medium for teaching and learning—there was much pedagogical conformity. But there were subtle differences, too. These differences are of the kind differentiating the fourth- and fifth-grade classes of the same school described in Chapter 4. The fifth-grade teacher spent less time controlling students, was perceived to be fair, showed somewhat more concern for students, and arranged tasks that students found not to be hard or too easy. Also, students in this teacher's class had somewhat higher regard for one another, were relatively less competitive, and were a little more likely to regard their classmates as interested rather than apathetic about their classroom learning experiences. Many little things add up to a classroom climate perceived by students to be more or less satisfying.

It appears, indeed, that the environment of the classroom conveys important meanings to the student. I am struck by the fact that just a little show of teacher concern, the absence of teacher favoritism, the presence of peer esteem, an appropriate level of task difficulty, and other indices related to the personal well-being of individual students added up to more positive views of the class experience. Good teaching builds bridges to individuals. It is much more than the honing of mechanics.

Surrounding the classroom is a school ethos which also is perceived by students to be more or less satisfying. Peer-group interests in games, sports, and one another dominate almost uniformly. These aspects of school life appeared to be almost out of hand at Fairfield, for example, to the virtual neglect of academic matters. Many students said that this school was not providing them with a good education. At Dennison, on the other hand, there were evidences that a more studious atmosphere was managing to transcend the still powerful peer culture. Students were more satisfied with the education being provided. Earlier I described some of these school-to-school differences. As with differences in classroom climate, they appear to be more subtle than immediately apparent.

The satisfaction level of other persons in and close to schools as well is related, apparently, to such characteristics of school and classroom climate. An array of these characteristics come together in more or less positive ways corresponding to the satisfaction or dissatisfaction of all those connected with the school. There are significant differences in climate between a school viewed by teachers, students, and parents as relatively high on indicators of satisfaction (e.g., a grade of B+) and one rated much lower (e.g., a grade of C−).

From several indicators of school satisfaction, I found myself able to predict the presence of other characteristics differentiating the schools. My predictions were far from perfect, but some interesting patterns emerged. For example, schools at all levels tending to rank high or low on a composite of satisfaction indicators predictably tended to rank correspondingly high or low, or more exactly favorably or unfavorably, on perceptions of curriculum relevancy, violence and fear, and several other school issues.

It was surprising the degree to which the more satisfying schools that were rated positively on characteristics of school climate also were schools in which students viewed their classroom climate positively. The three senior high schools rated highest by teachers, students, and parents on indicators of satisfaction also were the three senior highs in which students had the most positive views of their classroom climate. All four of the elementary schools ranking lowest on satisfaction indicators also were the four schools of this group in which students had the most negative views of their institution.

Expanding on an earlier point regarding our findings, there was no parallel relationship between these indicators of satisfaction with the school as a whole and the actual practices of the classroom. Nor was there a close relationship between students' perceptions of classroom climate and these practices. In other words, the sameness of instructional practice reported earlier virtually transcended all classrooms and all schools. The teachers appeared to behave very much alike with respect to the mechanics of their teaching. But apparently, other elements in their behavior, the circumstances of teaching, and the conduct of the school differentially influenced the satisfaction level of those most closely involved with each school. Whatever these elements are, they appear to cluster by schools and not just in a few extraordinary classrooms.

This conclusion—which will be a shocking one for some readers—should not be taken to suggest the further conclusion that teaching methods, materials, and the like are unimportant. I spoke passionately to their importance in the preceding chapter. They may well be the characteristics of schooling holding the greatest potential for the creation of truly effective schools. We will not find this out, however, simply by refining the bland, repetitive procedures of lecturing, questioning, monitoring, and quizzing now characterizing classrooms. And this is what in-service education of teachers, or so-called staff development, seeks almost exclusively to do. Mere refinement of conventional practice is not sufficient. We will only begin to get evidence of the potential power of pedagogy when we dare to risk and support markedly deviant classroom procedures.

In this connection, one disappointing implication of the data is that the schools enjoying the most favorable perceptions appear not to have taken advantage of this asset in creating such classroom procedures. For them, too, certain conventional ways of conducting the schooling enterprise are the preferred norm. The principals and teachers in these schools, who in general perceived themselves to have a great deal of power and influence, did not take advantage of these attributes to redesign teaching and learning. Conversely, the teachers with more negative views of their workplace were no more likely to demonstrate markedly inferior pedagogy. Both groups, it appears, were conditioned and restrained by the power of existing regularities. They did not attempt to explore other possibilities.

In the pages that follow, I describe ways in which the schools in our sample differed and seek to sort out some of the traits associated with the more and less satisfying schools of our sample. Then I conclude the chapter by discussing, in the light of all the differences and similarities, the problems of improvement and, in fact, of fundamentally exploring other possibilities.

COMPARISONS OF SCHOOL PROFILES

My colleagues and I arranged dozens of major variables, each comprising many smaller variables, into categories describing aspects of life and practice in the schools and classrooms of our sample. Using these categories, it was possible to compile a profile of each school, a profile that then could be compared and contrasted with the profiles of all other schools at the same level.

Before proceeding to these comparisons, however, it seems important to reaffirm the primary goal of the study—that of suggesting hypotheses about schooling that emerge from an exploration of comprehensive data about a small but very representative set of schools. The analyses in this chapter reflect this goal. I will be drawing inferences based upon only the 13 high schools, 13 elementary schools, and 12 middle schools in our sample—a rather "thin" sample if our goal had been to confirm research hypotheses with tests of statistical significance. But the data-based description we have of each school is extraordinarily "thick"; that is, each school has been profiled on an extensive array of contextual information collected over the course of a month of intensive observation. As a result, we have come to know each of the 38 schools rather intimately. And because of this knowledge we are comfortable in drawing heuristic inferences from the data about them.

The first comparison of schools was on a set of variables indicating teachers', students', and parents' level of satisfaction with their school—their grading of it, the congruence between each individual's perceived and preferred goal emphasis, their perception of the number and intensity of school problems, and satisfaction with both the curriculum as a whole and each of the subject fields comprising it (parents only). The finding from this comparison was that all three of the schools in six triples consistently placed in the top half for relative satisfaction and all three schools of five triples placed in the bottom half. The six triples were Dennison, Euclid, Woodlake, Atwater, Palisades, and Vista. The five were Bradford, Fairfield, Manchester, Newport, and Laurel. The schools in the Euclid triple consistently placed in one of the top two positions on the satisfaction indices. The Fairfield schools consistently placed in one of the bottom two positions. Rosemont placed in the top half only at the junior high level, but high in this top half for this one school. The Crestview schools bounced about a little below the top and above the bottom half.

The schools in the top half for satisfaction tended to share some demographic characteristics—most were relatively small, the student population was predominantly white (except for Palisades), parental education and family income were above average for the group of schools, and most were rural or suburban. All three Vista schools, suburban in location, were relatively large, and although parental education and income there were on the high side for our sample, the per-pupil expenditures for schooling were low. The three Palisades schools were urban; the enrollment was made up almost equally of black and white students; the elementary school was small, and the two high schools were of average size. But parents in all three schools enjoyed relatively high education and income.

The five triples consistently in the bottom half for satisfaction were quite varied in their demographic characteristics. The Laurel schools were relatively small and rural, with an almost equal balance of white and black students. Parental education and income were low. The Newport schools were urban, large, and very diverse in student population. Parent income and education varied considerably. And although the Manchester schools were large, urban, and almost entirely black, the parents enjoyed above average education and incomes for our sample. Fairfield had a rural location, the two secondary schools were roughly average in size among the sample, the elementary school was comparatively large, the student population was slightly more Mexican-American than white and included a small percentage of blacks, and parent education and income were below average for our sample. The Bradford schools were suburban, close to average in size, and predominantly white in student population, and their parent clients were above average in income but below in education.

We see here some support for the stereotype of the most satisfying schools in this country—that they are small, rural or suburban, predominantly white in population, and supported by parents who are above average in education and income. But this is not necessarily so, it appears. The parallel stereotype—that the least satisfying schools are large, urban, predominantly minority in student population, and serve poor families of a low educational level—stands up less well. The characteristic "large" appears to be consistently descriptive of the less satisfying schools and consistently not descriptive of the more satisfying schools.[1] This is a characteristic that is modifiable. Perhaps it is time that we did something about it.

The deviations from the stereotypes are of particular interest. Rosemont fits the demographic data conventionally associated with inadequate schools. Its three schools were urban, with high enrollment at the secondary level, were virtually entirely Mexican-American in student population, and had a very low level of income and educational attainment on the part of parents. But Rosemont did not rank in the bottom five for satisfaction at any level. The Bradford schools appear to have most of the demographics associated with more favorable conditions but are providing little in satisfaction. And more penetrating analyses of some of the more satisfying schools reveal shortcomings quite out of keeping with their natural assets. Small size, rural or suburban location, and high parental education and income seem to favor but certainly do not assure the development of outstanding schools. It proved not possible for us to associate consistently the cultural and climatic differences among schools with easily documented givens. We were unable to explain away important differences this simply. Rutter, in his studies of secondary schools in central London, enjoyed a relatively controlled situation with respect to demographic features. And yet he found distinctive differences in the climate and ethos of these schools.[2] Factors other than size, resources, and socioeconomic level of the student body were powerfully at work.

After having arrayed the schools according to relative satisfaction, we compared them on a number of other characteristics. The first set of these we labeled "school-related issues." They comprised curriculum relevance, academic ambience, and violence and fear as perceived by teachers, students, and parents; quality of education provided (students only); and students' academic apathy or lack of interest, and accessibility of counselors (these last two for secondary students only).

When the schools had been arranged according to the most and least favorable perceptions on these characteristics, it became obvious that the ranking paralleled very closely the ranking of schools for general satisfaction. Indeed, at the senior high school level, the rankings of schools for the two sets of characteristics were almost identical. In brief, the ordering of schools on the general criterion of satisfaction virtually predicted their ordering on the above more specific issues and problems, particularly for the senior high schools.

After proceeding in this way across nearly a dozen such broad sets of school and classroom characteristics, I conclude the following: the rank order of a given school among schools at the same level on the criteria of satisfaction proved to be a rather good predictor of the relative ranking of that school on nearly all of the other sets. And across the sets of characteristics, these associations appear to be somewhat more consistent at the senior high than at the junior high and elementary levels, and particularly consistent for schools at the "most satisfying" and "least satisfying" ends of the satisfaction scale. This latter consistency became clearer when the schools at each level were separated into quartiles for each set of characteristics, three to the quartile. (Four of the 13 schools at the elementary and senior high levels constituted the fourth, or bottom, quartile.)

Although there was also a trend toward all three schools in a *triple* maintaining their similar positions on the several sets of characteristics, it was a weak one. The trend was somewhat stronger for the less satisfactory schools and particularly for three such triples—Manchester, Fairfield, and Bradford.

At the senior high level, the three schools ranking in the first quartile for satisfaction retained their relative positions with the other schools for five other sets of characteristics. These schools are Dennison, Euclid, and Woodlake. The profiles for these three schools based on the six sets of characteristics, in comparison with the other ten schools at this level, look something like this. Teachers, parents, and students expressed relatively high-level satisfaction with their schools. The issues of irrelevant curriculum, academic apathy, violence and fear, inaccessibility of counselors, weak academic ambience, and general poor quality of the education offered were of relatively low concern. Students viewed both school and classroom climate positively. Teachers had a positive view of their workplace—the principal's leadership, the quality of the problem-solving process, staff cohesiveness, their power and influence over schoolwide decisions, and their control over their planning and teaching decisions. Also, they viewed themselves as spending more class time on instruction and relatively less on routines and controlling behavior.

This comparatively positive picture can be extended for Dennison and Euclid High Schools. The relationship between parents and teachers at these secondary schools was quite close, and parents viewed themselves as participating and informed.

At the other end of the rankings for overall satisfaction with the school, the three least satisfying high schools clustered together on other characteristics with about equal consistency. These schools are Manchester, Fairfield, and Bradford. Their profiles differ quite markedly from those of the three senior high schools perceived by teachers, students, and parents to be most satisfactory. The problems of curriculum relevance, weak academic ambience, students' apathy, violence and fear, inaccessibility of counselors, and poor quality of the education offered loomed relatively large. Students in all three of the least satisfying high schools were markedly more negative in their views of both school and classroom climate. Teachers were more negative in their perceptions of their own classroom practices. And, consistently, parents in these three high schools reported having little contact with teachers and little knowledge of their schools.

The differences between the most and least satisfying junior high schools were in the same direction on virtually all sets of characteristics but were much less marked. Whereas the three most and the three least satisfying schools tended to hold their relative positions on as many as a half-dozen sets, at least one school in each group (and often two) changed positions on each set. Among our junior high schools, then, it apparently is more difficult to differentiate the characteristics of more and less satisfying schools.

Why is this so? The most promising hypothesis coming to my mind is that the onset of puberty, occurring for most girls and nearly all boys during the middle school years, becomes the dominant force in their lives for several years to come. Whether or not they perceive themselves to be good looking and popular overrides most other considerations both in and out of school. Recall the dominance of "my friends" as the one best thing about school and "good-looking students" as the most popular in the answers high school students gave to our questions. Satisfaction in school has to do with peer-group relations and personal perceptions of social relationships which no doubt make heavier demands in the first few years following puberty than later. Would segregation into all-girl or all-boy middle schools change the ambience of schooling at this level?

Junior high teachers, somewhat more than teachers at the other two levels, expressed the need for control over the classroom and frustration over the problem of "reaching" their clients. Also, the percentage of junior high students choosing their teachers as the one best thing about their school was slightly lower than at the senior high level. These and other bits of data support the hypotheses: students of junior high age are struggling intensively with some new problems of peer-group status and personal identity; the academics they encounter are only peripherally related to these concerns; their satisfaction stems from their perceived success in peer-group relationships and not from characteristics of schools as such. It would have been necessary for us to delve more deeply into the peer culture at each school in order to get greater insight into students' sources of satisfaction. Correspondingly, teachers' satisfaction at this level may be influenced by characteristics of students' personal and social lives at school. At any rate, the clusters of characteristics we examined did not relate as closely to satisfaction indices as was the case at elementary and senior high levels.

The concept of the junior high school came into existence in large part to provide for this age group. It was to be a distinctive school, departing creatively from the norms of schooling. Nothing in our data suggests this departure. Instead, we see teachers struggling just a little harder to maintain the regularities of schooling as we see them to be.

The elementary schools in our sample fell between the senior and junior high schools in regard to the consistency with which various other characteristics were associated with schools perceived to be most and least satisfying. It is interesting to note that students in the four elementary schools perceived by teachers, students, and parents to be least satisfying consistently perceived their classroom climate the most negatively. Indeed, the five most satisfying and the seven least satisfying elementary schools retained their relative positions with respect to students' perceptions of their classroom climate.

Also, it appears that a positive affective tone of the classrooms—the absence of dissonance between teachers and students and among students—is a vital element of climate in satisfying elementary schools. On no other characteristic did the most and least satisfying elementary schools in our sample repeat their relative rankings so consistently.

At all three levels of schooling there were marked differences in the ways principals and teachers viewed their workplace and their jobs—differences that must be included among the factors differentiating the more and the less satisfying schools. Principals of the more satisfying schools saw the amount of influence they had as congruent with the amount they thought principals *should* have; were less inclined to see poor teaching, poor teachers, and staff relations as problems; and generally disagreed with the statement, "Average students don't get enough attention at this school." Principals of the less satisfying schools tended to react oppositely on all these indices and were highly consistent in viewing poor teaching, poor teachers, and staff relations as problems.

Just as the principals of the more satisfying and less satisfying schools differed in their perceptions of teachers, teachers' views of their prinicipals differed significantly at the two sets of schools. Fewer teachers at the more satisfying schools saw the administration or staff relations to be a problem. Repeatedly, teachers at the more satisfying schools commented that their principal supported teachers to the fullest, went to bat for teachers, or gave excellent back up. Only one teacher of a less satisfying school spoke of his principal as "very supportive of me." When teachers in this group of schools referred to receiving support from a principal, they usually were referring to one who had left the school. In general, it appears, "good" principals are associated with more satisfying schools. A good principal, from the viewpoint of the teachers in this study, is himself or herself relatively autonomous as a person and leader, treats staff members as colleagues and professionals, and is consistent in dealing with teachers and students.

This profiling and clustering of schools on major characteristics proved fruitful not only for the patterns that emerged but also for revealing sharp and presumably significant variations within the groups of more and less satisfying schools. For example, although all three Woodlake schools ranked relatively high on our criteria of satisfaction, all three came out rather poorly with respect to parents' perceptions of contact with teachers and knowledge about the school, appearing on this set of characteristics to be more like the less satisfying group of schools. I conclude that matters of school-community relations head the list of priority areas to pinpoint for improvement at Woodlake. The superintendent might well take the lead.

Overall, Woodlake elementary school fared less well comparatively in its group than did the junior and senior high schools. Our data revealed severe tension between the teachers and the principal. (The principal was removed at the end of the school year during which we gathered data.) This negative factor was not sufficient, apparently, to drag down overall satisfaction to the level of the least satisfying schools. Other positive characteristics sustained it. Nonetheless, our data showed a festering situation that undoubtedly would have worsened, to the general detriment of the school. A fascinating follow-up would be to study the school's course of development after appointment of the new principal.

This last point raises intriguing questions about whether there were differences in the schools in regard to what might be termed their movement toward change and improvement and whether these differences were associated with differences in perceptions of the schools as satisfying. In recent years, there has been a reaction against the notion that improvements are most likely to occur in schools when the motivation to change and most of the ideas come from outside.[3] The contrary notion is that improvements are most likely to occur when those connected with schools—especially principals and teachers—become responsive to their own problems and needs and develop mechanisms for effecting continuous self-improvement.[4] Responsive schools maintain a state of readiness to respond to problems, set priorities, and use alternative ideas appearing to be useful, whatever their source.[5]

One of our analyses showed that 18 of the schools in our sample could be divided into two groups of more and less renewing schools, nine in each group. The two groups were separated, first, on the basis of the answers teachers gave to an interview question about whether changes had occurred in the school during the last three years and whether these appeared to be significant. This initial selection was then cross-checked against a series of questionnaire items which asked whether there was continual evaluation of programs, examination of alternatives, a search for new ideas, and a willingness to take a chance on a new idea. With the schools now separated on criteria pertaining to capacity for renewal, our researcher looked for associations between this capacity and other characteristics—teachers' personal characteristics (e.g., age), their beliefs about teaching, their control and influence over the circumstances of teaching, and aspects of both the staff decision-making process and the principal's leadership.

Congruent with other studies, this analysis revealed little relationship between personal characteristics of teachers and a school's classification as more or less renewing. It did show, however, that teachers in the schools identified as more renewing perceived their schools to be solving their problems, to provide appropriate conditions for them to do their job, and to have staffs capable of doing what needed to be done. In effect, the more renewing schools were perceived more generally by their teachers as taking care of their business. Teachers in these schools also were less likely to perceive inadequate resources and assistance as problems. Included in their perception of a school capable of doing its business was the perception of a principal who was open and supportive in his or her relations with the staff.

There was a substantial but not complete overlap of the schools identified as more or less renewing and those I have identified as more or less satisfying. This incomplete overlap could be partly the result of my having included data on satisfaction from teachers, students, and parents, whereas the attempt to differentiate between more and less renewing schools drew only on teachers' perceptions. The overlap was particularly close at the less renewing end of the scale. It appears that the less satisfactory schools are more consistently so, and consequently easier to identify.

One set of satisfying schools conspicuous for its absence among the more renewing schools is Dennison. The very small Dennison Junior/Senior High showed up monotonously at the top, virtually in a class by itself, on most of the characteristics discussed earlier. The elementary school ranked in the top quartile on more than half of the sets of characteristics, just slipping out of the most satisfying group overall. But as I examined the data, I had a feeling that the Dennison staffs were "coasting." They enjoyed exceedingly small classes— 11 teachers for an enrollment of 61 students at the secondary level and 4 teachers for 48 students in the elementary school. The quantity and variety of instructional materials and equipment were above average for our sample. The array of curricular offerings at the secondary level was surprisingly large for such a small school. But the variety of learning activities—low for schools generally—was very low at Dennison at all levels. Although the amount of affect and positive feedback demonstrated by teachers and the amount of student initiation in the classroom were low throughout, I expected something better at Dennison secondary. It was not there; indeed, Dennison was on the low side on all these instructional indices. It is worth noting, too, that teachers' professionalism—postcredential studies, participation in professional training programs, membership in professional organizations, and reading professional materials—was low. Professionalism was the only set of personal data regarding teachers found to associate with more renewing schools, admittedly at a modest level.

The Dennison schools had everything going for them by way of parental education, family income, community support, and absence of bureaucratic structures. And the teachers certainly were doing a creditable job by conventional standards. But our data do not suggest that these schools took advantage of their circumstances to be in the forefront of improvement. There appears not to be, dangling before advantaged schools, an image of ways of schooling going beyond the conventional. The Dennison schools appear to be prime examples of schools satisfying their several constituencies but not appearing to perform as well as their circumstances warrant.

CHARACTERISTICS OF MOST AND LEAST SATISFYING SCHOOLS

It is fair to say that on most things there were only shades of difference between schools. But we must remember that each set of differences was made up of many elements or groups of elements, each thought to contribute in some important way to the whole. Again we see that a series of many small differences constitute noticeable variations when viewed together. Further, these shades of difference increase in magnitude and often become significant when one school is compared with another in the sample perceived to be least like it. It was for this reason that, after separating the three schools perceived by teachers, students, and parents to be most satisfying from the three or four perceived to be least satisfying, I attempted to arrange them into similarly separated clusters on other characteristics.

Table 8-1 lists the three schools at each level scoring highest on the several indices of satisfaction described earlier and the four senior high and elementary schools and the three junior highs coming out as least satisfying. (For classification purposes the junior and senior high divisions of Dennison appear as usual with the senior high grouping.) The schools in each group are not listed in their actual order of ranking for satisfaction.

TABLE 8-1
The Most and Least Satisfying Schools

	Senior High	Junior High	Elementary
Most satisfying	Dennison Euclid Woodlake	Euclid	Euclid
		Vista Rosemont	Vista
			Palisades
Least satisfying	Newport Manchester Fairfield Bradford	Newport Manchester Fairfield	Manchester Fairfield Bradford Crestview

Rather, I have arranged the list so that it is easy to see when schools of the same triple are in the same group.

Every school listed in Table 8-1 as a member of the most satisfying group on the indices of satisfaction emerged more favorably than every school in the least satisfying group on the set of characteristics comprising perceived curriculum relevance, academic ambience, violence and fear, quality of the educational program, academic apathy, and accessibility of counselors. All but one of the most satisfying schools, as compared with the least satisfying schools, were perceived by teachers to be more gratifying workplaces. This set of characteristics was made up of staff problem-solving processes, teachers' influence over their teaching decisions, staff cohesiveness, teachers' influence over schoolwide decisions, and the principal's leadership. Almost uniformly, the students in the most satisfying schools reported more rewarding classroom climates. In only one of the most satisfying and two of the least satisfying schools did this pattern fail to hold up.

The data on students' perceptions of the school climate at the secondary level support the general picture of a somewhat more academic ambience in the most satisfying schools. With the exception of one of the most satisfying and two of the least satisfying schools, students in the most satisfying schools, in answering our questions on aspects of their school climate, perceived somewhat greater student interest in teachers and classes and somewhat less student preoccupation with sports and friends and, further, saw these aspects in a favorable light. Also, they were more likely to participate in extracurricular activities.

In addition to having more positive views of their workplace, teachers in the most satisfying schools tended to score somewhat higher on the indices of teachers' professionalism. And at both elementary and senior high levels, with the exception of one senior high, teachers in these schools perceived themselves to be spending more time on instruction and less on routines and controlling behavior in the classroom. There was a trend in this direction for junior highs, but it was not as consistent.

Two other patterns are worth noting. With only four exceptions out of the entire group of 20 schools divided into the two groups, parents in the most satisfying schools perceived themselves to have more contact with teachers and more knowledge of their school. Except at four schools, all secondary, the absentee rate was greatest among the least satisfying schools. And although we would not want to generalize from only one case, community responses to schools perceived as unsatisfying may take a very concrete and dramatic form. In 1981 the schools in one of the triples consistently in the least satisfying group were faced with closure as a result of the community's repeated refusals to support school tax increases. It may just be that when schools are not seen as satisfying places, children are more likely to stay home and adults more likely to refuse to pay the bills of schooling.

Some of the major areas in which no marked differences between the least and most satisfying schools showed up are noteworthy. Analysis of teachers' personal characteristics—such as age, experience, reasons for entering teaching—and views of what is important in teaching and learning revealed only the trend toward greater professionalism among teachers in the most satisfying schools. Most of these characteristics are not amenable to much modification by the school environment. Similarly, there were no clear trends with respect to the clustering of students with differing self-concepts or aspirations. Presumably, these are heavily influenced by factors outside of schools. And, of great importance, pedagogical differences, which were not extensive to begin with, did not differentiate schools in the most and least satisfying clusters except to some degree at the senior high level. Here the differences revealed for the most satisfying schools such things as less time on preparation and cleanup, fewer quizzes, more enrichment, less student and teacher nontask behavior, and less teacher time spent monitoring students and routines—what we picked up in the "snapshots" of classroom activity. There was no differentiation between the two groups of schools in regard to the basic modes of instruction—the dominance of teacher initiation of activity, telling and questioning, correcting students' oral responses to the teachers' questioning, addressing the total class, and so on.

Let us imagine, now, that we have studied two additional triples—six schools—and analyzed the data as we went along, but only now have juxta-posed these data with the data on the 38 schools constituting the sample described throughout. Suppose it turns out that the senior high schools in these two additional triples are quite different. One clearly fits in the cluster of most satisfying schools; the other matches the characteristics of the least satisfying groups. Without having the data, since these two schools were deliberately omitted from the sample, you are asked to compare them. Could you do it? I believe you could do so quite accurately.

My descriptions of "most" and "least" have been relative, as these words imply. In the ensuing descriptions, I shall insert from time to time some non-relative data gleaned from the groups of most and least satisfying high schools in our sample in order to add some specificity. The composite picture of each school described resembles the composite picture of most or least satisfying schools in our sample.

The new school in the most satisfying group is Mayberry Senior High School. Teachers, parents, and students gave it a good grade—averaged out, a solid B+. More than half of those in all three groups of respondents per-ceived Mayberry to be emphasizing the goals they believed to be most important. They came up with a short list of problems perceived to be of some seriousness—drugs and alcohol, student misbehavior, and lack of interest on the part of some of the parents and students. Curricular prob-lems or inadequacies were not included. Very few perceived teachers as not caring about students, or that average students were not receiving enough attention. Nor were many students viewed as not caring about learning.

Some students chose "nothing" as their response when asked what they liked best about their school, but the percentage was small (less than 2%). Clearly, athletes and good-looking students dominated in the popularity polls; nonetheless, nearly one student in five chose smart students as the most popular. Almost every student at Mayberry participated in extracur-ricular activities.

Apparently Mayberry was a pretty satisfactory place to be a teacher or administrator. Violence and fear were not issues of teacher, student, or parent concern. The principal viewed the teaching staff as competent. The teachers perceived her to be supportive of them, to have considerable authority, and to exercise that authority. They viewed themselves as having a voice in school-wide decisions and as virtually autonomous in their classroom decisions. They perceived themselves and their colleagues to be doing a good job in the class-room. And they viewed their school as a place where the necessary business of keeping school is attended to.

Perhaps the generally positive views of their school held by Mayberry students were generated to a considerable degree in the classroom. At any rate, many of them viewed their teachers as trying to make the class enjoyable, as listening to them, and as not ridiculing them or hurting their feelings. They generally knew what was expected of them, saw themselves as getting corrective feedback, and understood the words used by their teachers. Further, they tended to see their teachers as fair, as not having favorites, and their fellow students as helpful and not excessively competitive. Most saw themselves and their peers doing what was expected of them. Overall, the classroom was not an unpleasant place to be.

Parents who sent their adolescent boys and girls to Mayberry appeared to have rather easy access to teachers and to be quite well informed about school programs and activities. The balance of power regarding school decisions was rather to their liking. The teachers and principal appeared to have a good deal of power and each group said their own was about as it should be. The superintendent kept a low profile, as the teachers and principal thought he should.

Inside the classrooms, the teachers appeared to be very much in charge. They lectured a lot, now and then directing a question to the class as a whole. The answer given, they went on to the next point. Students were often in a listening posture; engagement in reading and writing assignments usually emerged from the period of listening; and in nonacademic classes added to these activities was frequent practice involving some kind of physical activity. The class structure appeared to take care of discipline; teachers spent little time seeking to control classes. Although most classes were rather pleasant, unmarked by student outbursts or scolding by the teacher, there was not much fun and laughter either. The students were reasonably attentive and appeared not to be as bored as an observer might expect.

Things were different at Boxwood Senior High School—some of them quite a bit different. The overall grade (of about C–) was dragged down particularly by the students' grading of their school. Only about a sixth of the teachers perceived Boxwood to be emphasizing the goals they thought to be most important. Overall, for teachers, students, and parents, the congruency between goals preferred and goals perceived as stressed was less than 25%. Boxwood's leadership would not have been able to get a clear sense of direction by attempting to respond to the direction of the differences between these preferences and perceptions. Students would have emphasized even more what appeared to be a heavy vocational program; teachers would have opted for greater stress on the personal; parents would have shifted the balance toward a heavier academic emphasis.

Whereas teachers, students, and parents at Mayberry listed as serious only two of the three problem areas they identified, the three groups came up with 25 such at Boxwood, many of them repeated by each of the groups: student behavior (at the top on all the lists), drugs and alcohol, student and parent interest, or rather lack of it, the quality of teaching (even teachers identified this one) and administration, staff relations, and the curriculum. Parents' dissatisfaction with the curriculum reappeared in the low satisfaction index derived from checking their views of curricular relevance and quality in the subject fields. Many students perceived there to be teachers who didn't care much about students, saw average students not getting enough attention, and saw the school regarding as not very important students who did not plan to go to college. Some of these views were shared by their parents, and even many teachers had negative views about their peers' treatment of students. Likewise, all three groups perceived there to be a high level of apathy about learning. All groups expressed concern over violence and fear in the school environment. The percentage of students perceiving teachers to be doing a good job and students getting a good education was low.

Nearly 20% of the students surveyed checked "nothing" as the one best thing about their school. Over 80% chose athletes or good-looking students as the most popular. Since almost 10% chose gang members, only about 10% of the first choice were left to spread over the other categories including "smart students." A third of Boxwood High's students participated not at all in the extracurricular activities.

Students' views of the classroom environment often were very negative. Many saw their teachers as unfair, not interested in them, derisive of some students, having favorites, not making much effort to create enjoyable classes, and frequently talking down to them. They often perceived classmates as less than helpful and as noisy and argumentative in the classroom. Although most said that they did what was expected of them, their overall compliance with the teacher was lower than at Mayberry. Classroom experiences appeared to be much less enjoyable and free from dissonance than was the case for Mayberry students.

Teachers, too, viewed their work environment as less than ideal. They viewed the principal as neither competent nor supportive. Indeed, the picture coming through from a variety of sources is of nobody in charge. The principal, on the other hand, saw the competence of teachers and staff relations as part of the problem. Teachers agreed that there was a problem in staff relations and in effecting schoolwide decisions of any kind. They perceived their own role in school decisions to be low, just as they viewed the principal not to have a strong hand. Although most appeared to be in charge of their classroom decisions, many were dissatisfied with the amount of time they were forced to spend in controlling students' behavior. Also, many were less than satisfied with the teaching job being done by peers.

Parents' views of sources of power in decision making strengthened the growing impression of nobody in charge, of a school needing to come to grips with its problems. Many had not spoken with their children's teachers during the year; many felt ill-informed.

Inside classrooms, teachers initiated almost everything, as at Mayberry. But somewhat more time was spent in preparing for what was to follow, cleaning up and other routines, and in teachers seeking to control student behavior. There appeared to be less lecturing and questioning and more monitoring of students' reading and writing activities, perhaps to assure the control teachers value. Teachers spent a considerable amount of time at their own desks. The tone of classrooms in Boxwood was low-key, as at Mayberry, but there was often an edge of tension, of keeping tight control to assure the maintenance of stability. And there was very little fun and unbridled laughter here either.

DISCUSSION: THE PROBLEM OF IMPROVEMENT

Schools differ; *schooling* is everywhere very much the same. Schools differ in the way they conduct their business and in the way the people in them relate to one another in conducting that business. But the business of schooling is everywhere very much the same.

There are phenomena which together constitute schooling. These come together commonly in all schools, with only modest variations in the configurations. Consequently, there is a sameness about schools just as there is a sameness about post offices or hospitals. The buildings are surrounded by open space and flat ground, usually devoid of trees, boulders, hillocks, and ravines. Sometimes this open space is covered with concrete or asphalt; sometimes it is not. The urban schools of Chicago, London, and Hamburg look more alike than do the urban schools of Chicago and the schools of the surrounding suburbs. But we still recognize them all as schools—places where schooling occurs. The highly visible similarities are what lead us to conclude, erroneously, that schools are everywhere the same.

It takes a great deal more probing to discover the more significant and probably more persistent ways in which schooling is everywhere the same, and if we stop too soon in this probing, we may never discover the ways that schools differ. We usually do stop too soon, largely out of ignorance, and so we fail to realize that the differences in schools are not in the regularities of schooling, but in the ways individual schools relate to them. These differences show up in the perceptions of those most affected by them—the principal, teachers, students, and parents associated with the school. The discovery of these school-to-school differences gives us some hope, perhaps unjustified, that even the persistent characteristics of schooling can be modified.

These regularities of schooling have emerged repeatedly in preceding chapters. I summarize here some of the most important ones. Among the most visible is the way subject matter is packaged, arrayed, presented, and tested. Variations are initially as consistent as the overall characteristics are common. In the three early elementary grades, more than in the later grades, there is some emphasis on learning skills and facts in the context of some other experience, less dependence on textbooks and quizzes, and use of a wider range of teaching practices. The teacher who sits at her desk most of the time, monitoring children and not involved actively with them, stands out as different. Teachers in the first three years do more to help children relate to the material being learned. But these differences between levels of schooling are in degree, not kind, and stability of curricular expectations and emphases and of instructional practices becomes increasingly apparent from the fourth grade on.

In secondary schools, the differences built into the system are between the academic and nonacademic subjects. Teachers of the arts, physical education, and vocational education lecture less and demonstrate more; encourage their students a little more to participate in selecting learning activities; engage students more actively in physical doing and performing; and give fewer written quizzes. Again, the differences are in degree; what goes on in these three fields most of the time is more like mathematics, English, science, and social studies than one might expect.

Also, in secondary schools there are built-in accommodations for students of differing accomplishments. These differences are accommodated in upper, middle, and lower tracks. The variations in content, pedagogy, and student-teacher relations characterizing the tracks are similar from school to school.

Some teachers lecture and question students less than others; some characteristically sit most of the time at or on their desks monitoring seatwork; some use small group discussions regularly; some resort to films almost monotonously. But such idiosyncrasies fit within the conventional. Rarely does one find a teacher who has abandoned lectures, quizzes, textbooks, workbooks, and written exercises in favor of learning organized almost exclusively around observations of things outside of schools, projects requiring small group collaboration, and primary documents—with the reading, writing, and dialogue emerging out of such activities.

Common, too, is the deliberate sustaining of a socialization process believed essential to the conduct of schooling. Very deliberate in the primary grades, this process is fully established by and rarely questioned after the upper elementary grades. The dominant role of the teacher, limited opportunity for student-initiated activity, and quiet passivity of the class group become virtues to be reinforced. Deviation may be tolerated but it is neither condoned nor rewarded. Usually the socialization process, as powerful among teachers as among students, simply discourages or ultimately suppresses deviation.

This process of socialization into group mores is not, however, for purposes of cultivating the power of the group. Quite the contrary. The rewards are for *individual* accomplishment. Students, like 30 berry pickers proceeding side by side down the rows, work individually side by side on the same tasks. From time to time they turn in their buckets and are rewarded on the basis of the teacher's perception of the quality and quantity of what the buckets contain. The evaluative scales used, however, are more vulnerable to subjectivity than are the scales used to weigh berries.

It is the extracurriculum of team sports and student government and so on, not the regular academic program, that provides opportunity for working toward shared goals, contributing to group solutions, achieving through a division of labor, and experiencing success as a member of a group. But the extracurriculum too is relatively narrow and constrained by convention and, in sports, competition; not all students participate.

More visible than these regularities of schooling are the schoolwide organizational arrangements and conventions that support them. Paramount among these is the age-grade structure. Subject matter is arranged by grades; each grade is to take up two semesters, or an academic year. To this is added at the secondary level and sometimes at the elementary level a further division into subjects, each in turn delivered up in periods of from 30 to 60 minutes per day, one or more days per week.

This structure not only retains the characteristics summarized, it virtually negates any changes in them. The age-grade division encourages a short-term view of what is to be learned—topics and facts rather than basic concepts and relationships; focus on what can be acquired in a week or semester and then measured rather than the long-time maturation of intellectual capabilities; observing rules rather than becoming increasingly self-disciplined. The division into subjects and periods encourages a segmented rather than an integrated view of knowledge. Consequently, what students are asked to relate to in schooling becomes increasingly artificial, cut off from the human experiences subject matter is supposed to reflect. This artificiality increases as students grow older and more aware of the complexities with which they must cope. For many, schooling becomes increasingly irrelevant.

Over the years, these ways of schooling have proved to be extraordinarily resistant to change, encouraging the view that "nothing changes; there is only the appearance of change." Whether or not schooling has changed over time is partly a matter of perspective. There have been modifications. Years ago we stopped screwing desks to the floor and screwed them instead to slats, three to the slat. Later we introduced desks, chairs, and tables that could be moved about at will. But most of the time they remained in rows. Teachers maintained that the custodians insisted on this to assure a clean sweep between the rows. Increasingly, however, it became clear that this programmatic regularity helped sustain the behavioral regularities of frontal teaching.[6]

One could draw up a quite impressive list of additions to and modifications of programmatic regularities. But schools have been stubbornly resistant to those more deviant ones designed to break down the prevailing structures—the elimination of grade levels (nongrading), teaching cooperatively rather than alone (team teaching), the elimination of walls between rooms (open space classrooms), the utilization of large blocks of time (so as to accommodate an integrated core curriculum), or the provision of varied periods of time for differing subjects (modular scheduling). Each of these points toward changing the behavioral regularities of teaching and learning. Since the precise nature of these behavioral changes rarely is made clear (and since, indeed, programmatic changes often are obscure), proposals to make fundamental changes usually create threat and insecurity in the culture of the school. Instead of facilitating improvement, an innovation tends to arouse all those mechanisms that protect conventional practices. Reformers rarely understand all this and tend to place the blame at the feet of principals who guard the gates and incompetent, recalcitrant teachers who cannot comprehend the new and better ways to keep school. But replacing all the principals and teachers tomorrow would change only the actors. The play would go on as before.

In spite of the sameness of schooling, however, seeing one school is not seeing them all. Schools do differ, not in their programmatic or behavioral regularities, but in the ways the humans in them, individually and collectively, cope with these regularities and relate to one another. The principal, for example, encourages teachers to participate in decisions pertaining to the school's business. What both principal and teachers are largely unaware of is that the degrees of freedom for conducting this business are very limited. Those in schools are so much a part of what schooling is that they perceive what is as what should be. Why change? But there are more and less satisfying ways to arrange parent-teacher conferences, conduct staff meetings, schedule library usage, monitor playgrounds and lunchrooms, distribute supplies, and report tardiness. These become the decision-making areas in which teachers seek a voice. They become important to individuals far beyond their significance in schooling.

Classrooms differ—not in their behavioral regularities, but in the atmosphere of concern established by the teacher. It is somewhat easier, apparently, to establish and maintain a satisfying classroom ambience when the ambience of the school as a whole is supportive of the classroom effort. The support is needed to help ease or lubricate but not change the behavioral regularities. Indeed, everyone would be surprised if the autonomy so valued by teachers were used to deviate markedly from what is and, therefore, should be.

In college-level teaching, I sometimes divided the class into small discussion groups. Occasionally we became so preoccupied in our discussions that we failed to hear the period's closing bell and the clamor of the incoming class outside the door. Once—but only once—we forgot to rearrange the chairs. "Mr. Goodlad," said the incoming instructor haughtily, "do whatever foolish things you wish during your class period, but when it's over, please arrange the furniture in the way it is *supposed* to be."

This chapter has revealed some of the differences between more and less satisfying schools. The implications for developing schools that are more satisfying for those associated with them are reasonably clear. And there is now an ample literature on how principals and teachers might work together to create a more satisfying workplace, and that literature includes attention to the human factors which this chapter suggests create fundamental school-to-school differences. Similarly, we have seminal research and guidelines not only on some of the requisites for more satisfying classroom learning environments but also on how to attain them. The research on change has illuminated past follies and some promising alternatives.[7] Getting schools that are more satisfying for those associated with them appears to be an attainable goal well worth the effort. I address myself to it in the succeeding chapter.

What the foregoing discussion of differences between schools makes us painfully aware of, however, is that these more satisfying schools are not likely to differ markedly from less satisfying schools in programmatic and behavioral regularities. Further, if we use only the criterion of achievement test scores to determine the quality of schooling generally and only criteria of teacher, student, and parent satisfaction to determine the quality of the local school, there will be no incentive to change these regularities. The curricular and instructional emphases of the schools in our sample give me no cause to celebrate the kind and quality of education being provided for the nearly 35,000 students in the schools we studied. And yet the level of satisfaction with the curriculum was quite high, even in the less satisfying schools.

The point to be made is that for the regularities of schooling to change a critical mass of the persons and groups constituting our society must first see the need. This means that larger numbers of people in addition to those closely associated with schools must detach themselves sufficiently from their cultural surroundings to recognize other possibilities for schools than those now prevailing. This will not be easy. Is it possible?

Schools do not take on emphases unless they receive rather clear messages to the effect that these emphases are wanted. Then they respond, over time, with varying degrees of effectiveness. There is at present no strong pressure to change the ways schools conduct the business of schooling. Indeed, current ways appear appropriate to some popular perceptions of what schools are for—as represented, for example, in the back-to-basics movement. The broad expectations of parents appear not to guide school policy and practice. There appears to be limited public awareness of the need for greater stress on a wider range of behaviors and therefore on the kinds of pedagogical approaches relevant to their cultivation. Teachers get a glimpse of these other possibilities in their professional preparation programs but insufficient experience with them to offset the traditional ways they were taught in schools and colleges. Consequently, the teaching profession itself exerts little pressure toward alternatives. Advances in other fields come about primarily because of expansion in the relevant knowledge and the acquisition of this knowledge by professionals. But teaching is as yet a weak profession, not firmly established on strong underpinnings of biological, sociological, and behavioral knowledge.

It appears to me that the most satisfying schools in our sample are in a reasonably good position to effect some of the curricular and pedagogical improvements our data suggest are badly needed. Their clients appear to be quite satisfied; the principals and teachers have much of the autonomy they need for effecting change. Missing, it appears, are the kinds of encouragement and support for change that must come from the larger context. Why do anything differently when the need to do so is not pressing, when present shortcomings have not been diagnosed, and when the nature and demands of alternatives are not at all clear?

It is my belief that data of the kind discussed here help create necessary discomfort regarding many aspects of schooling. It is my further belief that similar data for the local school would be an impetus for improvement. But the less satisfying schools described are not sufficiently in charge of their own destiny to build agendas from these data and subsequently to take action. They are not healthy organisms. They simply are not good candidates for tackling the difficult tasks of curricular and pedagogical reform. The first step is for them to become more effective in their conduct of present business and in the process to become more satisfying places for those associated with them. They need data about their present condition and considerable support and encouragement in the needed process of renewal.

The more satisfying schools, on the other hand, are at a stage of greater readiness for more fundamental improvement. But little is likely to occur unless the larger system helps create an awareness of need, assists in the diagnosis, and provides support relevant to this specific diagnosis of the individual school. The critical error in past efforts to effect change and innovation has been to assume that those in remote places, with funds to disperse, have known best what is wrong and what to do about it.[8] Whether or not we actually have learned any useful lessons from past failures remains to be seen.

Back to the questions of whether it is possible for us to see schooling as it is, whether we can be sufficiently uncomfortable about what we see to want fundamental improvement, and whether we can envision and advance other possibilities. If the answers to these questions are "no," at least we can address the task of creating rather satisfying schools with the knowledge that they are attainable. But we are unlikely to stop there. At an accelerating pace, students of schooling are providing us with insight into this complex enterprise, and in the process revealing the misleading simplicity of past diagnoses and solutions. Slowly, we are giving up our "villain" theories in the realization that the regularities of schooling transcend the individuals caught up in them.

The loss of ignorance is an essential step in all of our efforts to create and maintain institutions which sensitively and effectively serve humankind. We have been slow to gain the knowledge essential to understanding schooling and enlightening our conduct of schools. But there are encouraging signs of a quickening pace. As our understanding of schooling increases, both the pressure and our ability to improve schools will become greater. This belief motivated A Study of Schooling.

This concludes the presentation and analysis of data on the 38 schools studied. Subsequent chapters are devoted to agendas and strategies of school improvement and to the development of other possibilities for educating both in and outside of schools. These agendas and strategies are as relevant, I believe, to private schools as they are to the public schools from which our data were obtained. Some new data are introduced but for the purpose of illuminating the process of improvement rather than that of understanding schools.

Chapter 9

Improving the Schools
We Have

Much can be done over the short run to improve the schools we have. There is no need to await the development of grand designs or completion of all the studies currently under way. The urgency of the need to improve our schools dictates the importance of a short-term agenda. To some of its elements I now turn.

The data presented in preceding chapters are compelling. To the degree the schools we studied are representative, the agenda of school improvement is formidable. It includes clarification of goals and functions, development of curricula to reflect a broad educational commitment, teaching designed to involve students more meaningfully and actively in the learning process, increased opportunities for all students to gain access to knowledge, and much more. Significant improvement will come about not by tackling these problem areas one by one, but by addressing all or most of them as a system.

An assumption underlying what follows, however, is that schools beyond our sample exhibit *in varying degrees* the problems appearing most consistently in our data. Thus some readers may prefer to stop here, summarize for themselves the most critical problem areas, and set forth what they believe to be the needed improvements. It is more productive to get some common agreements on an agenda for school improvement than to lose sight of the central problems in debating any one set of proposed solutions, including mine.

Although most of the agenda to evolve in what follows grows out of findings presented in Chapters 2 through 8, not all of it does. We did not study the whole of schooling, nor did I present all the findings. In organizing and synthesizing the data so as to illuminate major themes, many interesting but not obviously related findings were left unused. In going through the many tables and accompanying analyses not used and especially in reading responses to open-ended questions which remain largely unanalyzed, I gained impressions which may be as trustworthy as those derived from data treated systematically and incorporated into the themes of this book. It would be virtually impossible to drop these impressions by the wayside even if I sought now to remain entirely with the data presented to readers.

Also, A Study of Schooling emerged from an immediately preceding study of educational change and improvement that my colleagues and I conducted in collaboration with 18 schools and their constituent 18 districts. Whereas A Study of Schooling was directed toward the substance of what goes on in schools, the previous study sought to gain insight into processes of improvement. I draw on its findings quite extensively in what follows.[1] Also I draw on my experiences with other inquiries into schools and a host of associations as student, teacher, administrator, teacher educator, consultant, and frequent observer.

WHO IS TO MAKE WHAT DECISIONS?

One of the most popular ideas about school improvement to emerge in recent years is that parents should participate much more actively in making decisions. Supporting opinions range from the rather vague notion that parents should have more power to the specific one that they should set up their own schools.

The concept of greater parent participation and involvement has natural appeal. There is evidence to suggest greater client satisfaction with PreSchool Playgroups in England[2] and cooperative nursery schools in the United States[3] which are run jointly by parents. The so-called Free School Movement, flourishing in the United States during the 1960s, saw small groups of seemingly like-minded parents setting up and sometimes teaching in their own schools.

There is, however, a considerable degree of unrealistic romanticism about parents taking over schooling. The founders of free schools frequently found themselves in apparently irreconcilable ideological disputes. As new schools appeared, others with a life history of just a few years or sometimes only months closed.

At the opposite end of the organizational spectrum, we find the American public school system. Surrounding its development has been the belief that schools should do much more than reflect the parochial values and beliefs of a few families or a neighborhood—that they should introduce young people to a much broader array of viewpoints. Indeed, Joseph Schwab argues rather convincingly that the school fails in its function unless it exists in a state of productive tension with the home: home and family create a press of one ethnic identity, one religion, one social class; the school presses toward a common identification with diversity and a sense of homogeneity which encompasses and integrates diverse elements.[4] From this sense of school function emerged the concept of the common school. Schools created to assure reinforcement of only one set of values or to serve only my race, my neighborhood, and my economic class fail in this function.

The debate over public schools as we have known them versus parent-run schools has had an either-or tone, and this has led, I believe, to an unfortunate and unproductive polarization of views. It stems in part from superficial interpretations of what parents want. Polls and surveys show that they would like a greater say in the affairs of their schools. But this does not mean that parents want to take over the schools. Some do, but most don't. Rather, they want to be kept informed in as clear a fashion as possible, especially about their children's progress and welfare. Further, they want the decisions and those who make them to be visible. They would prefer to leave the running of the school to the principal, and the classrooms to teachers and, if possible, to hold them accountable. Holding one's neighbors accountable leads to tensions most people would prefer to avoid.

Our data reflect this point of view. Most parents perceived the important decisions, even for their own school, to be made by the superintendent and board—a perception shared by principals and teachers. Most would shift more power to the local site, away from district superintendents, board members, and both state and federal lawmakers. Most would increase the decision-making role of parents, parent associations, and lay advisory councils. But they would not elevate their authority above the professional individuals and groups or the board.

Principals and teachers concurred in the desire for a rebalancing of power toward greater decentralization and localism. It is fascinating to note that principals put themselves before teachers and teachers put themselves before principals in the preferred authority structure. The preferred order for teachers was themselves first, followed by the principal, the superintendent, and then the board. Principals placed themselves in the top slot, followed by teachers, the superintendent, and the board. The superintendents and board members queried in regard to this issue would place themselves in one or the other of the two top decision-making roles they perceived themselves already holding. All would elevate somewhat the individual and collective roles of parents.

There is nothing in these data to suggest to me that the parents in this very diverse sample were seeking to take over their schools. They placed themselves and their organized groups below the top four in the preferred hierarchy. But there is a message: most of the parents we surveyed would take power from the more remote, less visible, more impersonal authorities heading the system and place it in the hands of the more visible, more personally known, close-at-hand staff of the school and parent groups close to the school.

The wish for this kind of shift in power comes through clearly for our sample. It implies the significance of the school as the unit for improvement and those associated with the individual school as the persons to effect change. It does not imply, I think, that it would be wise to dismantle completely the educational system, leaving tens of thousands of schools to float free from all external directives and restraints. Some of these undoubtedly would become stars in the constellation of schools, but most, I fear, would fall victim to fad, fashion, orthodoxy, incompetence, and local politics. And there would be gross inequities in the school-to-school quality of the education provided beyond those currently existing. Further, the tantalizing vision of freedom would soon become obscured in a blizzard of financial rules, regulations, and paperwork coming from outside. If only to correct local variability in ability to support schools, the state will continue to provide most of the money. This means the use of measures designed to secure some accountability for the use of funds, whatever the structure of schooling.

Again, an either-or approach to this structure—either no system or a highly centralized, bureaucratic one—gets us nowhere. Rather, authority and responsibility must be differentiated and distributed across the system. The central purpose of doing so is to stimulate and support local efforts to provide good programs for the students in each school. The following recommendations are designed to move us toward an appropriate balance in authority and responsibility.

First, the state should back away from its current tendency to focus on principals, teachers, and individual schools in its efforts to assure accountability. Rather, the state should hold the district accountable for communicating the state's goals for education in schools, developing balanced curricula in each school, employing qualified teachers, providing time and resources for local school improvement, and assuring equity in the distribution of these resources. It is reasonable for states to assess the way districts conduct their business. But to seek to monitor from remote state capitals the activities and performance of individual schools and teachers is unrealistic and ultimately damaging. This is a district responsibility. It has not proved feasible for states to assess the consequences of legislation directed at individual schools and their personnel. Further, because much of it is inappropriate for some schools, it is quite possible that such legislation has done as much harm as good.

State officials, including the governor, should be held accountable for articulating a comprehensive, consistent set of educational goals for schools. Current expectations for schools constitute a hodgepodge, resulting from accumulations of piecemeal legislation. New legislation takes little or no account of existing requirements in the education code. In fact, most legislators are virtually ignorant of these requirements and the potential impact of new bills on the finite time and resources of schools.[5] Principals and teachers often are caught in a paralytic inertia created by the bombardment of changing and often conflicting expectations.

The goals articulated should be subsumed under a limited number of categories, as are those presented in Chapter 2. They should be updated for emphasis and content relevance periodically—perhaps every four years at the beginning of each governor's term of office. The list should be endorsed as a composite whole and be declared off-limits to piece-by-piece whittling away by legislation and political log-rolling. The relative stability and slow, deliberate revision of the state goals for education in schools would give us some hope of developing and refining over time a means of assessing the fit between these goals and conditions designed for their attainment. These conditions include not only curricula and teaching in schools but also the resources provided by states and school districts.

The intended net effect of these recommendations is a common framework for schools within which there is room for some differences in interpretation at the district level and for some variations in schools resulting from differences in size, location, and perspective. Clearly, state governments would play a leaner role than at present. They would have virtually no involvement in the specifics of instruction. But they would have increased concern for the conditions enhancing or hindering the development of effective, satisfying schools. And, accordingly, the state role would include assuring the production and dissemination of knowledge required for appraising assets and liabilities at all levels of the system.

A second set of recommendations pertains to district authority and responsibility. What I am proposing is genuine decentralization of authority and responsibility to the local school within a framework designed to assure school-to-school equity and a measure of accountability. Each school is to be held responsible for providing a balanced program of studies. Each school is to develop and present its program and accompanying planning document and budget to the superintendent through the principal. I recommend that program and budget be projected over a three- to five-year period, with an annual updating and review.

The superintendent and board should concern themselves primarily with the balance in curricula presented rather than exact school-to-school uniformity, with the processes employed in the planning effort, and with equity in the ultimate distribution of funds. They should avoid detailed specifications for local school planning, providing at most rather broad guidelines and consultative assistance. The essence of the district-school relationship is the review process, in which the principal presents and justifies the plans developed under his leadership. The superintendent, in turn, following appropriate consultation, should be free to allocate discretionary funds to support unusually creative efforts and to deny funds for failure to plan.

I believe that to invoke in these ways the principle of "every tub on its own bottom," or nearly on its own bottom, would go a long way toward developing schools that took care of their own business, rectified chronic problems, and communicated effectively with parents—characteristics of the more satisfying schools in our sample. Further, I envision that, in time, those associated with schools would become increasingly creative in designing alternative programs of instruction—something not characteristic of the schools in our sample. And finally, I believe that the potential for developing an increased sense of ownership on the part of those associated with the local school would be vastly enhanced.

A third set of recommendations regarding authority and responsibility pertains to individual schools. The guiding principle being put forward here is that the school must become largely self-directing. The people connected with it must develop a capacity for effecting renewal and establish mechanisms for doing this. Then, if drug use emerges as a problem, these mechanisms of self-renewal can be used to attack it. If children's reading attainments appear to be declining, improved reading will become a top priority item on the school renewal agenda. This approach to change differs markedly from starting out by bringing in innovations from outside the school. Only if present procedures appear to be failing and innovative alternatives appear to be needed and potentially useful are these tried. Existing processes involving the identification of problems, the gathering of relevant data, discussion, the formulation of solutions, and the monitoring of actions take care of both business as usual and change.[6] This is the self-renewing capability school personnel must develop if their place of work is to be productive and satisfying.

But this capacity is lacking in most schools, largely because the principal lacks the requisite skills of group leadership. Most new principals are plucked out of the classroom in June and plunged into the new job soon after. Little in the first area of experience prepares them for the second. Few beginning principals know how to prepare a year-long agenda for school improvement; some call faculty meetings only for announcements which could be delivered as effectively on the bulletin board or by a memorandum; very few know how to secure a "working consensus." Current on-the-job training for principals emphasizes their role in instructional improvement. Whatever merit this training may have, it does not usually include provision for developing the principal's capacity to lead in the solution of schoolwide problems.[7]

Consequently, I recommend that each district superintendent take as first order of business responsibility for selecting promising prospective principals and developing in them—and in present principals—the ability to lead and manage. In fulfilling this role, it may be necessary for the superintendent to draw upon expert assistance to provide the necessary training. There should be, waiting in the wings, a sufficient number of qualified persons to take over each principalship as it is vacated. The search for leadership in a district should be continuous. Unusually promising men and women should be chosen and provided with paid leaves for purposes of attending universities with outstanding programs in educational administration. A superintendent and board choosing a principal should look beyond local personnel for candidates and beyond their own resources in making the selection. The selection committee should include other responsible persons connected with the school for which the principal is being selected.

The principals of the district should constitute an organized group with time provided for continually updating their knowledge and skills. They should establish their annual agenda in consultation with the superintendent and a consultant chosen from outside the district. This agenda must include provision for the infusion of ideas from beyond the district—the concept of hearing drummers whose beat may convey deviant messages.

My picture of decentralization is not, then, one of schools cut loose, but rather of schools linked both to a hub—the district office—and to each other in a network. The ship is not alone on an uncharted sea, cut off from supplies and communication. But neither are decisions for the welfare of those on the ship the prerogative of persons in the hub or in charge of other ships. The principal is the captain with full authority and responsibility for the ship. But if reasonably wise and prepared for the post, he or she will make them in the company and with the counsel of others.

Indeed, it is essential that persons in addition to the principal be involved in decisions for the school's welfare. There should be, for example, some kind of policy and planning group chaired by the principal and including teachers, students, parents, perhaps a nonparent, and if possible, a representative from the district office. The group should be quite separate from the structure used to administer the school and from the usual processes of the faculty's deliberation over their immediate responsibilities. This body would be constantly alert to problems affecting the school as a whole, would identify the need for new policies, and would be responsible for final approval of the planning document and budget prepared for discussion by the principal with the superintendent. The specifics of the body's membership should not be mandated. Rather, school principals would be required to justify the procedures designed to assure widespread participation in the planning processes.

The budget of each school should include all costs and alternative plans for the use of funds. Because, even in the domain of allocating the funds spent on teachers, the individual school should be free to exercise some control. For example, anticipating the departure of two teachers, a remaining group of three primary teachers might recommend the addition of no regular replacements. Rather, they might want to employ, with the same expenditure of funds, five or six part-time individuals to work under their supervision. The result would be to reduce the number of fully qualified teachers but to increase the number of adults available to the children. A team-teaching project conceived and implemented in this way has a far greater chance of being successful than has one imposed on all schools from the central office.

Similarly, teachers should have a say in how the money allocated for materials is to be spent in their school. Indeed, they should have some funds to spend as they see fit. It should be acceptable, for instance, for a teacher to request and obtain six copies of each of five books rather than 30 of a single book for a particular class, if the request were subjected to appropriate internal review. This type of ordering usually is more expensive but frequently is more cost-effective.

Individual schools should have the authority and responsibility to develop long-term staffing plans, to be effected through judicious replacement of retirees and those teachers who go elsewhere. For example, an elementary school faculty might specify that the next teacher hired should possess, in addition to general teaching ability, a background in mathematics in order to round out a faculty representing a wide range of specialized backgrounds, each serving as a resource person to all other teachers but each assigned as a regular classroom teacher.

As I have suggested earlier, very little time is allocated specifically for school improvement. Some states and districts allocate days for staff development, but these almost always focus on the skills of individual teachers and usually draw them away from the school site. Our data revealed that the teachers in our sample rarely worked together on some school-based issue or problem. Consequently, schoolwide concerns frequently go begging. And yet these often are central to teachers', students', and parents' perceptions of the school and to the ability of teachers to conduct their classes. Allocations to district budgets should assume, then, the need to employ teachers for a minimum of 180 days of teaching and 20 days of planning and effecting school improvement. The additional salary payment would be a significant step toward improving teachers' annual income. The additional days should be used sparingly, if at all, for districtwide purposes. But the length of these days should be governed as firmly by district rules as is the length of teaching days. Further, individual schools should have some flexibility regarding the scheduling of these days, some perhaps favoring interspersing several weeks of teaching with a week of planning rather than concentrating all four weeks at one time of the year.

We should consider, also, my earlier suggestion that the hours of teaching be reduced. This would provide more time for planning—as well as working with individual students, reading students' essays, and so on. High school teachers have told me that they could reduce their weekly teaching time to 20 hours and still provide programs for as many students as are presently enrolled. Presumably, they have in mind different staffing patterns than now prevail and ways of helping students to be more self-directing. Why not let them try? Similarly, why not encourage elementary school teachers to experiment with alternative staffing plans?

The proposals made above open up, I believe, the opportunity for local schools to take on individual, even alternative characteristics within a framework designed to assure some accountability, the cost savings associated with the centralization of some but not all budgeting and other routines, and considerable equity. I can hear the mutterings of those professional administrators and board members who believe in tightly centralized control of program, staffing, budget, and other matters. But they should note the provisions for checks and balances as well as the possibilities for unleashing the creative energies of concerned principals and teachers who now feel overly constrained by "the system." And the potential for pleasing parents currently unhappy with remote control of their schools is no small consideration. To assume that the system of schooling we have or the system some people think we have is the one best system is to invite further disaffection and flight from it.

DISTRIBUTING TIME AND TEACHERS

There appears to be a formidable discrepancy between the goals for schooling summarized in Chapter 2 and curricular provision for their attainment in the schools we studied. The availability of time and classes—and therefore teachers—for the areas of knowledge and thinking implied is a necessary first condition for goal attainment. Averaged across schools, our data suggest a comprehensive curriculum, growing less so with progression from the elementary to the senior high school grades. But the curricula experienced by students in specific schools, out data indicate, do not reflect averages. The school-to-school differences we found were enormous. So were the differences between curricula experienced by students in the same school.

There are essentially two major arguments of justification for such variability: local option and individual differences among students. If local variations among the schools we studied resulted from the deliberate determination of policy, the processes of decision making involved escaped our attention. Further, my own probing into this possibility during visits to schools led me to the conclusion that gathering and examining the data relevant to decisions about curricular balance were rarely the concerns of superintendents, principals, guidance counselors, and teachers. Existing curricula resulted, I believe, not from careful local planning but from accretions of expedient decisions and omissions.

But even if the right to determine the major components of the curriculum is being carefully exercised—and I trust that some school districts are exemplary in this regard—how much variation can we afford? We live in a highly mobile society. Is it acceptable for some students to be almost illiterate in mathematics, American literature, and computer use simply because they happened to attend a school where little opportunity to attain such literacy was provided? I think not.

Of equal significance is the question of whether some students and not others should take certain courses because of perceived differences in students' learning abilities. Should differences among them be construed to mean omitting subjects such as mathematics? Again, I think not. Should alternatives be selected because some students might be more interested in something else? As Harry Broudy has so incisively asked, how can students be interested in something they know nothing about?[8]

If education in schools is to be effective, it is essential to make some provisions for individual student differences. These include pedagogical ones—more time for students who take longer, experiential activities designed to overcome difficulties with abstractions, summaries and reviews of work covered through use of a different medium of instruction, and so on. The *specifics* of content also can and should be varied. The principles of ecology can be learned as readily in the lakes and ponds of Indiana as in the tidepools of California. But I have difficulty accepting the omission of ecological concepts in the schools of any state. Students judged to be less able than some others have equal right to be exposed to such learnings.

Given much current practice regarding school improvement, the data on curricular variability presented earlier suggest that states should mandate specific requirements for all schools. Indeed, as I write, some states already are contemplating legislation and in some instances are using our data as justification. I urge caution. The consequences of some of the actions being proposed are as likely to be disappointing or even damaging as they are to be constructive. Let us look, then, at some promising alternatives to legislated mandate, some primarily applicable at the elementary level, some at the secondary level, and some equally applicable at both.

First, however, I want to reemphasize the states' positive responsibilities. States have a right and a responsibility to articulate educational expectations for schools. They have a further right and responsibility to call upon local districts to assure comprehensive, balanced curricula in each school. They have a responsibility, also, to conduct studies designed to reveal overall strengths and shortcomings and to disseminate the findings widely, without reference to specific schools. They have a responsibility to assess the costs involved in needed improvement and, to the degree possible, assure the needed resources. The states doing all of these things well would fulfill their accountability for curriculum development.

Time

In Chapter 5 we saw the curricular consequences of gross school-to-school differences in the amount of time available for learning and instruction. Elementary schools at the upper end of the range for time utilized allocated not only substantial time for mathematics and the language arts but also about an hour a day each for such subjects as science and social studies. But in those near the lower end, little time was left for these subjects after the mathematics and language arts allocations were made.[9] Children encountered marked curricular differences just because of the schools they happened to attend.

I suggested in Chapter 5 that 25 hours of instructional time each week, compared with an average of about 22.5 hours in the elementary schools studied, might be a reasonable target figure. However, establishing a uniform time utilization target probably would be less constructive than initiating a process of improvement in each school. A self-appraisal over a period of several weeks that produced awareness of a present average of 23 hours a week of time in an instructional setting at the fourth grade level might result in a decision to increase time for social studies, science, and the arts by an hour each per week, with a year being determined as a reasonable time for effecting the change. The effort might involve such things as the following: a collaboration between home and school in getting children to school on time each morning; more efficient procedures for getting children in and out of classrooms first thing in the morning, at recess, and at lunchtime; and less time for opening exercises and for final clean-up. There is some variation across the country in regard to the length of the school day. Some schools may find it necessary to increase this length, but the step should be taken only after adjustments such as those suggested have been made.

State and local mandates in this area should be avoided. Our data on time utilization already have gained attention in the press. As a consequence, I have received letters from conscientious teachers lamenting prompt but unwise administrative action. For example, one board ordered that recesses in all elementary schools be cut to 10 minutes from the present 15! The teachers, rightfully, were outraged because of an arbitrary decision not based on data pertaining to this particular school. An unwise action based on a newspaper report virtually eliminated the possibilities for the principals, students, teachers, and parents in each school themselves to assume responsibility for assessing the local condition and proceeding with whatever program of improvement appeared desirable. Much more than improved use of time probably would have been the result. We have seen that, overall, the more satisfying schools in our sample were perceived to be taking care of their problems. The more satisfied teachers saw themselves involved in making important decisions. Data not reported previously revealed a desire among many parents to be involved in more than funding drives and attending PTA meetings. Once effectively mobilized for school improvement, those associated with a school will go far beyond the task with which they began. *Developing the capability to effect improvements is more important than effecting a specific change.*

Furthermore, encouraging the development of self-renewing capability is more likely than mandates to stimulate creative ways to achieve desired ends. In the present case the purpose is not simply to increase instructional hours in local schools. Nor is it to assure unvarying uniformity in the weekly allocation of these hours to subjects. The purpose is to assure for boys and girls some reasonable measure of access to knowledge and the ways of knowing.

Some schools may find it preferable not to schedule the arts, for example, on a weekly basis or in balanced fashion each week. They may prefer to offer no art for three or four weeks and then to offer it for several hours each day during the fourth week. Given the probability that progress in the arts is best served by large blocks of time, this may be a highly defensible alternative. Or teachers may prefer to schedule a half-day each week for the arts and have their children study music, visual arts, drama, and dance by turns in four time blocks over the year. Such arrangements can satisfy a state or district directive that schools assure that all students have experience with the arts. This experience should not be stifled by prescriptions designed to assure uniformity.

And I repeat an earlier warning. If our interest is in quality educational experiences, we must not stop with providing *only* time. I would always choose fewer hours well used over more hours of engagement with sterile activities. Increasing the days and hours in school settings will in fact be counterproductive unless there is, simultaneously, marked improvement in how this time is used.

Teachers and What They Teach

It will take time and some unusually creative measures to correct curricular imbalances and assure that students will not be penalized simply because of where they happen to attend school. There are some eminently practical things that can be begun right now, however, and that depend for their success almost entirely on school-based initiative and both state and district support.

It is essential that school faculties initiate two kinds of planning processes not always under way. The first of these is a careful interpretation of the possible meaning and implications of state goals for education in schools. The second, to be carried out mainly in secondary schools, is an analysis of both the distribution of teachers to subject areas and the actual distribution of subjects, courses, and modes of thought in the curricula experienced by selected students.

The first of these processes includes two kinds of sustained discussion. One is schoolwide and involves the principal, teachers, students, and parents. It is designed to develop awareness of the depth of intellectual and other behaviors to be sought in students and the range of knowledge and human experience to be explored in the curriculum. There is no need to begin from scratch. The list of goals for education presented in Chapter 2 might readily serve as a basis for dialogue. The specific ways to organize and conduct these discussions should not be mandated. Various ways exist. The town of Ellensburg, Washington, for example, with the leadership of persons in the State University, used public forums, with community leaders addressing this list from their particular perspectives.[10]

The other kind of discussion involves the faculty (by departments or in small groups cutting across departmental lines in schools large enough to have departments) in developing understanding and appreciation of the kinds of learnings to be sought in their students. It is not enough for teachers of English to concentrate only on grammar or composition. They must consider how their subject might be used to promote critical thinking. They must consider, also, how classes in English might serve to address the personal and social development of young people. If the teachers of each subject do not address such goals, who in schools will? The purpose of all this is to infuse an awareness that education involves more than the memorization of facts and the refinement of motor skills.

The second planning process, proceeding simultaneously, involves the establishment of procedures for assessing curricular balance. Most secondary schools have the resources, particularly in the principal and guidance counselors, for making this assessment. The necessary information exists, and it needs only to be arranged and analyzed somewhat differently from common practice. It needs to be analyzed to provide, first, a graphic presentation of the distribution of teachers by subject fields or divisions, and second, a summary profile of the study programs of a random sample of the most recent graduating class. Both kinds of data are revealing and force the question: Are these the desired or even defensible distributions? The data on junior high school graduates now enrolled in senior highs would have the added benefit of serving to guide these students in planning their next years' programs.

It is encouraging to note that some states are recognizing increasingly the importance of such curricular assessments. The California State Department of Education, for example, has prepared a handbook directed to local boards and designed to stimulate interest and guide the process.[11] In my judgment, the handbook's list of 100 questions to be answered is overkill. Of greater use would be a short list of questions designed to guide collection of centrally important information. Michael Kirst has done us a service in developing a suggested priority list.[12] It is appropriate and important, I believe, for states to identify the need for curricular assessment, alert local districts to it, and provide guidelines for dealing with it. But mandating the specifics of the curriculum appears not to be a constructive state action.

The purposes in recommending these processes are to increase sensitivity to the present distribution of curricular resources and to stimulate adjustments. In many instances the data gathered will speak for themselves, lead to readjustments, and provide supporting justification. Future staffing will become a planned enterprise in line with needs for reallocation. Teachers of English, for example, who leave or retire will not necessarily be replaced by teachers of English. More rapid realignment can be effected by moving teachers from schools with excessive allocations in a field to schools with shortages in it.

THE CURRICULUM

At the time of writing these words, I am very much aware of growing national, state, and local concern with precollegiate curricula, particularly at the secondary level. The mood emerging appears to be toward greater specification of the subject requirements for high school graduation. By requiring more years of mathematics and science, for example, universities in some states already are sending a strong message to secondary schools. But these new requirements are designed to affect future enrollees in higher education—well below half of those students even anticipating college attendance—and not nearly the entire population of today's secondary schools.

However loosely coupled the system of schooling may be, it is nonetheless a system. Major changes in one part of it affect other parts. For example, the proposed curricular changes, if not accompanied by substantial improvements in pedagogy, could increase the high school dropout rate, already too high, especially for Latin Americans.[13] The quality of an educational institution must be judged on its holding power, not just on assessments of its graduates.

Curricular mandates and changes in the admissions requirements of universities affect the demand for teachers and have implications for teacher education—matters not easily or quickly adjusted. The National Education Association estimated at the beginning of this decade a 22% gap between demand for and supply of mathematics teachers. Simultaneously, the National Council of Teachers of Mathematics estimated that 26% of mathematics teaching jobs nationwide were filled by teachers with either no certification or only temporary certification in mathematics. This is not a new problem. In the early 1960s I worked with James B. Conant in his study of the education of American teachers.[14] Inquiring into the virtual nonexistence of prospective mathematics and science teachers in the preparation programs of Eastern universities, we were told that more were being prepared in the West. On the West Coast, we were told that there were, our respondents thought, more teachers being prepared in these subjects on the East Coast!

Curricular Balance

Difficult, sensitive decisions at the local level are essential to early, real progress in securing balance in the curricula of individual schools. It is essential that there be guidelines, but mere compliance with state mandates will assure such negative consequences as excessive expenditures of time on paperwork and encourage fraudulent behavior (such as converting social studies teachers to science teachers in name only).

What should be the nature of these guidelines? I reject university entrance requirements as well as state requirements of specific courses and years of study in each field, uniformly required for all schools. But also I have argued, and will argue below, for better balance among fields of study and greater commonness of study in these fields.

What follows is directed primarily to secondary education. This is not to remove elementary schools from our concern. There was imbalance in the elementary schools of our sample, much of it resulting from the substantial role allocated to the language arts and mathematics and the uncertain status of other subjects. There appears to be no need to reduce these emphases, however, if appropriate steps, as recommended, are taken to secure more time and the time is used for the neglected subjects.

The first and most important unit of attention in securing curricular balance is the student. Ironically, it is the individual's program of studies that has received least attention. I recommend that there be for each student a cumulative record showing studies completed, studies contemplated (tentatively, at least, for the complete span of years of the institution), and a comparison of the total program with an ideal prototype.

The categories of this prototype will be the same for all students. For specification of these broad categories, I go back to the recommendations of the Harvard report, *General Education in a Free Society*, discussed in Chapter 5. If we can agree on the importance of the "five fingers" of human knowledge and organized experience—mathematics and science, literature and language, society and social studies, the arts, the vocations—then it remains to determine the desired balance, acceptable degrees of variance among them, and the time, if any, to be left completely free for individual choice.

Regarding desired balance, I would not depart radically from the *averaged* data on the schools we studied, reported in Chapter 5, and would favor for the secondary curriculum the junior high over the senior high distribution. But I would not allow the freedom to produce the degree of school-to-school variability revealed by our data.

My preference would be for up to 18% of a student's program (over a given year or averaged for the secondary years) to be in literature and language (English and other), up to 18% in mathematics and science, up to 15% in each of the remaining three fingers, and up to 10% in physical education. A variation of up to one-fifth of the percentage of the program allocated to any of these categories would be acceptable. But I would stipulate that the maximum total for all five fingers plus physical education be not more than 90% of a student's program. The remaining 10% or more would be for individual choice—a guided choice but ultimately the individual's own. Clearly this mandatory 10% is realizable only when slightly less than the maximum allocation to at least one domain is utilized. A school planning group might decide to meet only minimal specifications in several domains, freeing up perhaps as much as 20% of a student's program for maximal use of the sixth, special-interest domain.

Within each of the other five domains, I would argue, about two-thirds of all students' programs would be common; the rest would be made up of selections from a limited array of electives, the array inevitably varying with the size of the school. The ultimate effect would be, of course, that all students would have experienced, by the time of graduation, a curricular core. I argue against a common set of topics constituting this core but for a common set of concepts, principles, skills, and ways of knowing.

The proposed framework leaves room for some local option regarding domains of more or less emphasis. It also leaves 10% or more of each student's program unspecified. The purpose of this portion of the curriculum would be to develop and refine an area of individual interest and talent development—linguistic (refining use of a foreign language, creative writing, etc.), artistic (sculpting, painting, playing a musical instrument, etc.), psychomotor (swimming, skiing, playing tennis, etc.), or cognitive (mathematics, physics, computer programming, etc.). Presumably, student preferences and initial stimulation frequently would arise out of the home environment, some other part of the school program, or observing a role model. This sixth domain may be the most significant of all in determining life-long commitments and accomplishments.

Just how much of the instruction in the sixth domain would be provided directly by the school is dependent largely on the school's setting, the resources available in the community, and like matter. I recommend that students be given vouchers with which to exercise their choice. A student might use all of his or her vouchers (a number sufficient, perhaps, for purchasing up to five hours of instruction each week) to employ a private tutor, fees being set according to a specified rate for participating instructors. Affluent families no doubt would supplement this instruction, but at least the opportunity for talent development would be extended beyond that currently available to poor families.

A gifted mathematics student no doubt would take the maximum number of math courses permitted by the curricular guidelines proposed above. Because of these guidelines, he or she would be assured of a reasonable exposure, most of it in common with other students, to the other domains of learning. The student might well expend the allocated vouchers on advanced work in mathematics by enrolling in college classes, seeking an approved internship with an electronics firm, and employing a tutor—all of this spread over a three-year period and worked out in consultation with the school's counselor. The need for small schools to offer advanced math courses for a handful of students would be eliminated, no doubt with some relief of the problem of teacher undersupply. I would not rule out the possibility of using the best prepared math teachers to meet the demand for specialized personnel in students' sixth curricular domain. But not all math teachers would meet the criteria set for instruction geared to talent development. These criteria and teaching methods should closely approximate those identified by Benjamin Bloom in his studies of the development of talented individuals.[15]

The question arises as to the degrees of curricular freedom to be allowed the student for studies in this domain. Given the greater structuring of the rest of curricular choice than now exists, the dangers of potential abuse quickly become apparent. The domain could become a kind of dumping ground for all those electives squeezed out of the other domains. Nonetheless, I would favor a rather long list of alternatives. I remind the reader that the sixth domain is in addition to an assured general education for all, given the guidelines.

The prime criterion in establishing the degrees of choice, it appears to me, is the learning demands of the area of personal preference. There must be almost unlimited opportunity for the individual to grow to the level of excellence required to hold an audience, as in artistic performance, or to be capable, ultimately, of instructing others in something that requires a substantial commitment of time and energy to study and practice. The person becomes, in effect, an expert in something not learned easily. The accompanying feeling of accomplishment is rewarding in itself and perhaps is transferable to motivation in other areas of endeavor—and certainly to appreciation of excellence in other fields. For humans not to experience this kind of satisfaction is a great loss.

Overall, the concept of the common school is preserved to a considerable degree in the foregoing. Simultaneously, because of the sixth domain, there are opportunities to achieve at least some of what is promised, for example, by magnet schools in the United States and sports schools in the People's Republic of China. Objections will come from those who believe in curricula characterized primarily by more options and electives.

I have argued earlier and elsewhere that the concern over individual differences in learning and interest, on which the appeal of electives primarily depends, is in part a misinterpretation of and an overreaction to these differences.[16] The data on individual differences, from my perspective, have more compelling implications for pedagogical than for curricular differentiation.

But this argument aside, I believe that what is proposed leaves substantial room for both school-to-school and student-to-student variability while still facilitating a certain economy of curricular offerings. First, there is a permissible 20% range in a student's studies within any of the first five domains. Second, only two-thirds of the curriculum in any of these domains need be commonly required. Admittedly, the choices for the remaining third are not to be unrestricted. A student might elect, for example, after meeting or while completing the common requirements in English, a course in Western, Eastern, modern, or medieval literature, but would not be permitted to substitute courses in another domain. Third, the sixth domain provides an opportunity for highly individual selection, albeit guided by certain principles, to satisfy personal interests. I believe that the proposed guidelines would assist schools in assuring for each student a balance among common curricular elements, rational choice from options in the five major curricular domains, and exercise of choice according to personal interests and abilities. I further believe that the proposed framework sets up some safeguards against the excessive selection of electives not appearing to lead very far.

Let me add here a strong affirmation regarding opportunities for corrective work. It is to be hoped that the application of mastery learning concepts and improved pedagogy will diminish the need for corrective work, but it will continue to be of concern for some time to come. My affirmation is this: whatever provisions for remediation in a domain of knowledge a school faculty deems necessary must be accommodated within the maximum time allocated to that domain in a student's program. The third or less not taken in common could be used by one student to take honors classes and by another to assure a higher level of mastery in an area of low performance—but in the same domain for both. School personnel will be tempted to use the sixth domain for remedial purposes. This simply must not be a permissible option. Slower students often are denied access to learning activities in other fields enjoyed by able students because of their remedial assignments. It is to prevent this corruption that I would place vouchers in the hands of students to be used to pursue the purposes of the sixth domain—in or out of school.

Early in this discussion of curricular balance I recommended that each student's overall program of studies, completed and projected for the several years of a unit of schooling (e.g., the senior high school) should be compared with an ideal prototype. Now I have put forward my conception of that prototype, including specification of the permissible degrees of freedom within it, and in the process have indicated that I believe all students' programs should in fact conform to it. Not everyone will agree with this prototype; indeed, the level of consensus may prove to be quite low. Nonetheless, the questions it raises are fundamental and, I think, cannot be ignored. Addressing them squarely should result in better curricula. I urge that the dialogue focus on the principles introduced; variations in the specifics might well occur. My proposed guidelines are designed to assure order and balance in each student's curriculum. They are not intended to restrict creativity in seeking ways to fulfill the intent—that is, to assure each student a curriculum balanced among the domains specified.

Curricular Contents

Our data on the instructional curriculum offered by teachers—topics, materials, and quizzes—suggested two kinds of curricular deficiencies in the schools we studied which have attracted the attention of philosophers and curriculum reformers for a long time. The first is the way in which the specifics designed to teach concepts, skills, and values become the ends rather than the means, obscuring the larger ends such as those set forth in our goals for schools.

Less definitive data pertaining to activities designed for improving curriculum and instruction suggest a second problem: lack of faculty attention to the *overall* curriculum of the local school. A Study of Schooling did not attempt to find out where sustained curriculum development work is under way in the United States. My own conclusion, as a long-term student of curriculum reform, is that there has not been intensive, sustained attention to the content of elementary and secondary education for some time. The large-scale curriculum projects flourishing in the 1960s have withered away. Curricula continue to be determined largely by the editorial staffs of publishing houses and the subject-matter specialists and writers chosen by them. Their products are influenced in a circular way by those who choose and use the textbooks. The results currently are drawing fire from many quarters, as they have periodically for years.

These two sets of problems—the confusion of ends and means and the hap-hazardness of curriculum development and improvement—are closely connected. The solutions likely to be effective, moreover, are not at all clear and are likely to be complicated; the time required to make significant progress undoubtedly will try our patience. When our patience is tried, we are inclined to do something other than beginning the necessary process of genuine improvement. Money and time often are wasted on what may appear to be obvious and logical but proves to be ineffectual.

The "obvious" and "logical" solutions to the schools' curricular inadequacies being bandied about today are those that were most frequently bandied about yesterday and the day before that. Essentially, they involve a "get tough" approach combined with a dose of elitism. Course requirements in basic subjects are to be extended; textbooks are to become "harder," with less watering down to the lowest common denominators of students' abilities. The elitism comes from the universities, which are primarily concerned with the qualifications of their prospective students, who represent a minority of those enrolled in secondary schools. There is an impatience with grass-roots processes of improvement, sometimes verging on contempt for notions such as alternative strategies for change, the need to recognize and deal with the power of the school culture, and the importance of a school's faculty "owning" a proposed innovation, conditions which students of the improvement process believe to be significant. Sometimes university administrators and professors place themselves in a stance of noblesse oblige, promising to make the schools a target of top priority for a while and set them right.

What they offer is what they think they can do best—namely, beef up those soft courses in the basic subjects. But what most schools need is not a somewhat lower-level replication of college courses, most of which, contends Professor Charles Muscatine of the University of California, Berkeley, do little more than teach students to take notes and memorize facts, "a very narrow range of skills to be teaching at such expense."[17]

What our data suggest to be the major shortcomings of the schools' subject offerings is the common failure of the learning activities to connect the student with "the structure and ways of thinking" characterizing the field, to use the jargon of an earlier period of curriculum reform. This deficiency has curricular as well as pedagogical origins. We found topics (magnets and batteries) and not concepts (energy) highlighted in grade-specific courses of study, reinforced in textbooks and workbooks, and further broken down into facts to be acquired for quizzes. The more important and lasting concepts and principles tend to be obscured except in the classes of those creative teachers who somehow manage to transcend most of the curricula and teaching they experienced in schools and colleges. But what these somewhat divergent teachers do—and we found some in our sample—generally is not reinforced by the surrounding environment. Rather, quite the opposite teaching behavior is reinforced by periodic back-to-basics movements.

University professors can and should make a contribution to remedying at least the curricular side of the problem. After all, they are the experts in their respective fields. But few are equipped by preparation, interest, perspective, or temperament to be very useful, even on the curriculum side, especially over the long term. The late Beardslee Ruml, an insightful student of higher education, questioned the ability of faculties to plan the general education programs of even their own colleges—and general education is mostly what elementary and secondary schools are all about. University professors are far more adept at the work of advancing knowledge than at that of humanizing knowledge, the central task of both curriculum development and teaching.

Two fundamental principles must guide the long-term effort to improve school curricula. First, the provision of general, not specialized, education is the role of primary and secondary education. Consequently, the answers to deficiencies must arise out of questions pertaining to what constitutes general education for all—not college entrance requirements, on one hand, and job entry requirements, on the other. Good general education is the best preparation for both.

Second, it always will be necessary to make judicious provisions for individual differences in the student population. Most of these should be pedagogical. But there also must be some modest curricular adjustments for students' future expectations, so long as these do not jeopardize their opportunities when they change their minds. There is, I believe, a good deal of flexibility in the curricular prototype already presented. Its opportunities for individual choice do not contradict the first principle of assuring general education for all students.

What, then, is a promising direction for addressing the contents and organization of school curricula? There are no clear, tested models. But there is much to be learned by going back to the curriculum reform efforts of the late 1950s and 1960s. The literature describing and analyzing this movement provides a good place to begin.[18] Major centers for curriculum development were established, initially in mathematics and the sciences—fields of much present concern—and funded primarily by the National Science Foundation. Activity spread to other subjects; other agencies, including philanthropic foundations, entered the funding picture.

Early collaborations involved primarily university professors and secondary school teachers. Inclusion of experts on human development and learning was stimulated by Jerome Bruner's book *The Process of Educa-*

tion.[19] The central focus was on developing new materials designed to do a significant part of the teaching job. Many teachers were brought into in-service workshops for both refining and learning how to use the learning materials, but their involvement tended to decline with the passage of time. And reform neglected many political aspects of change. With some exceptions, reformers regarded administrators, especially school principals, as potential blocks to, rather than partners in, curricular reform. A major shortcoming was that the movement never became linked to the structures and institutions preparing and certifying teachers. Consequently, there was no stream of incoming teachers knowledgeable in the new programs to pick up the momentum lost when the in-service teacher education programs—never encompassing more than a fraction of the teachers—declined and ultimately ceased.

These shortcomings aside, the curriculum reform movement of the 1950s and 1960s probably came closer than any previous one to both bringing together the necessary coalition of contributing groups and revitalizing teaching and learning. It is reasonable to assume that we might avoid the mistakes in designing a new era of improvement based on the principles and profiting from the experiences of this previous one.

Consequently, I recommend the creation of centers designed to give long-term attention to research and development in school curricula and accompanying pedagogy. Each center's sphere of activity should embrace an entire domain of knowledge, thought, and process. For example, there should be a center for research and development in arts education, not separately in the several divisions of the arts. The reason for this is that these centers must reflect the realities of finite resources (of time, for instance) in the schools. Elementary and secondary schools simply do not have the luxury of offering programs in music and dance to satisfy the expectations of specialists in these fields. What they need is a program likely to provide their students with some reasonable understanding, appreciation, and practice of the arts.

Because these centers will be addressing the full scope of the kindergarten-to-grade-12 curriculum and will be seeking to identify its organizing elements (the underlying principles, concepts, skills, etc.), to suggest creative ways of involving students sequentially in these elements, and to develop illustrative materials, the costs involved prohibit a proliferation of centers. One only in the nation for each domain might limit the necessary competition of ideas, but finances probably limit the number to two or three.

Although I favor a separate corporate entity for these curriculum research and development centers, some might be located in major universities. Each should have a small core of continuing staff members, preferably on indefinite leave from some other post. (Many excellent people are unwilling to cut themselves off permanently from school districts and universities but would take such leaves; this will help avoid the danger of getting second-level personnel seeking employment.) Most of those employed, however, will be specialists released from their employing institutions for periods of a very few years.

It will be necessary to seek creative ways of combining public and private sources of funding and rearranging spending patterns. The current federal movement is toward a research role and away from an interventionist role in education—a direction appearing to be in harmony with federal support of at least the research function of the proposed centers. Several major philanthropic foundations have interests that could be directed toward exclusive or cooperative support of such centers. For example, the Getty Foundation, with headquarters in Los Angeles, and the Ford Foundation, with headquarters in New York, might take advantage of their settings to create centers for education in the arts. The Hewlett and Packard Foundations, given their proximity to Stanford University and the University of California, Berkeley, might seek to broaden the base of the National (formerly the Bay Area) Writing Project, which seeks to improve teachers' skills in teaching writing, to include attention to the whole of English and the language arts. These centers would draw upon the nation's, not just the region's, resources in seeking to achieve excellence. Desperately needed are clarification of the respective roles of funding agencies and the elimination of much duplication.

The problem of putting together a comprehensive, general education program in the finite time available to each school still remains, however. I already have provided some guidelines for state, district, and local school exercise of responsibility in the necessary task. But these are insufficient. Needed is continuous, sustained attention to ways of creatively organizing curricula to assure balance for each student in his or her progression through the levels of schooling. The tasks include developing exemplary programs for schools of varying sizes; developing assessment systems to be used by the individual schools in determining current curricular excesses and shortcomings; and developing techniques for assessing and guiding the program of each student. Accomplishing such tasks requires the creation of centers staffed primarily by specialists in curriculum design working collaboratively and experimentally with school triples (elementary, junior, and senior high schools linked in sequence).

One such curriculum design center might be sufficient in a small state, but several might be required in a large one. Again, the funding might well involve the redirection and combination of public (primarily state) and private resources, especially from the corporate sector.

These centers would not develop curriculum materials. Rather, they would design ways of combining and alternating the domains of learning to assure curricular balance for each student. The contents of the domains would come primarily from the research and development centers through the materials of instruction based on their work. Presumably, publishing companies would be significantly influenced in their production of materials by the work of the several centers.

I do not see the combined costs of all centers as excessive. With annual budgets of from two to three million dollars each, ten curriculum development centers in the nation would require not more than 30 million—substantially less than the current budget of the National Institute of Education, for example. Some of the Institute's present research centers and laboratories might well be given the curriculum development focus. Presumably, there would continue to be need for centers inquiring into the techniques necessary to the evaluation of curricula and instructional programs designed to achieve educational goals. The state-based centers in curriculum design could be funded to a considerable degree by the redirection of money now scattered about in several small-scale curricular activities.

Let me conclude this section by stressing the need for all of the centers proposed to be divorced from the current governmental structure of schooling and education. What I am proposing is a network of semiautonomous centers, including the curriculum design centers, intended to infuse vitality and authenticity into the curricula of elementary and secondary schools. The political process of decision making involving states, districts, and local communities will continue to function, enlightened by the work of the centers.

Ability Grouping and Tracking

Preceding recommendations, if adopted, would push schools toward assuring a common core of studies as well as some individualization of emphases. They do not eliminate, however, arrangements within schools that would deny or impede access to this core for some students. These include certain invidious grouping practices, the worst of which is tracking.

As described in Chapter 5, the circumstances which tracking in secondary schools is intended to address have their beginnings in the primary grades. The common clustering of children in these first three grades into groups based on levels of perceived ability and attainment in reading and mathematics is an understandable response to teachers' need to cope with students' variability in readiness to learn. But this practice limits the opportunity for children in the lower groups to keep pace with their peers even before interclass grouping begins.

Although the conventions of teaching support this practice, it is possible to eliminate it or modify its effects through introducing teachers to alternatives. One of these is mastery learning which emphasizes a combination of large-group instruction and small-group peer tutoring. The class moves along together, with quizzes "that don't count" being used to identify the need for more time and with the teacher and peers who have achieved the specified level of mastery working with those who have not until mastery has been achieved.[20]

Similar techniques characterize the best of the Infant (Primary) Schools in England which enroll children in the first three years of the public school system. Rather than divide the class into three groups working at three different levels, teachers endeavor to keep the class moving along together. They frequently work with clusters of children, but these are likely to be heterogeneous, family (multi-age) groups with a common reading problem or requiring some direction for an upcoming activity. It is common to see, simultaneously, several groups of three children at different ages and varied attainment reading together, with the best reader in the group assuming responsibility for helping the other two.

One characteristic of these and similar approaches is that they legitimate and reinforce helping one another and working cooperatively as desired implicit learnings. This is in considerable contrast to much of what I have described as implicit in many classrooms we studied and is in harmony with some of the goals set for schooling in the United States.

These recommended means for securing a higher level of mastery and eliminating failure are effectively blocked when students of differing accomplishments are divided into separate classrooms rather than into groups within classrooms, as was sometimes done in the elementary schools we studied. When this so-called interclass grouping is used, the attainments of the most able students are lost as standards of excellence, as is the availability of these students as tutors. For those readers who worry that the progress of the most able will be retarded, let me remind you that teaching another is one of the most effective ways to acquire mastery. Further, research cited in Chapter 5 reports no significant advantages of interclass grouping for the most able but significant losses for the slowest learners.

Nonetheless, some parents, teachers, and school administrators discover interclass groupings from time to time and pay no attention to our past experiences with it. The continuation of this folly tempts me to urge its mandatory abolition so that ill-informed people will be forced to refrain from its use. Surely there are some areas in which we know enough to take such a stand. However, since we are as likely to get mandates in areas where we have little knowledge as we are to get them when a firm stand is warranted, I urge minimal use of mandates in general and continued use of the educative rather than the legislative process in seeking the abolition of this and other unwarranted school practices.

Tracking in secondary schools is another of these. But this practice is so embedded and has proved to be so intransigent that it is more likely to be settled by the courts than by persuasion. And since tracking appears to block the poor and disadvantaged from access to knowledge which might serve to advantage them, pressure to abolish it undoubtedly will find its way to the judicial branch of government. It is conceivable to envision a day when tracking will be prohibited, as is now the case in Sweden.

Tracking prevails in secondary schools for the same reasons that achievement and ability grouping prevail in elementary schools: it is perceived to be a logical and expedient way to take account of wide differences in students' academic attainments. In effect, however, it serves as an organizational device for hiding awareness of the problem rather than an educative means for correcting it. The decision to track is essentially one of giving up on the problem of human variability in learning. It is a retreat rather than a strategy. The difference in teachers' expectations for high track as contrasted with low track classes noted in Chapter 5 is evidence enough of capitulating to rather than addressing the admitted complexities of the problem.

Just as interclass grouping in elementary schools blocks use of the most promising ameliorative practices, tracking in secondary schools makes it virtually impossible to correct curricular and instructional deficiencies. The self-fulfilling prophecy set in motion in the primary grades is confirmed; low achievers remain low achievers.

The first corrective measure is agreement on a common core of studies from which students cannot escape through electives, even though the proposed electives purport to be in the same domain of knowledge. Many of the electives we found bore little or no relationship to the courses replaced. The second corrective measure is the elimination of any arrangements designed to group in separate classrooms on the basis of past performance students presumably enrolled in the same subject. Students should be assigned to classes randomly in a way that assures heterogeneity. Only in this way can we have some assurance that grouping practices alone will not lead to different subject matter, different expectations, and different teacher treatment of students. Students should not all be treated alike, but the variations should be based on teachers' deliberate judgment that this rather than that practice serves the student better. Classes of randomly assigned or heterogeneous students appear to offer the most equity with respect to gaining access to knowledge while still preserving the more advantageous content and teaching practices of the upper tracks. Exceedingly good pedagogy may be able to overcome some of the ill-effects of interclass grouping and tracking, but these practices represent a handicap almost too great to overcome.

INSTRUCTION

Transcending Conventional Wisdom

One of the most disturbing findings reported in preceding chapters is the narrow range of teaching practices used by the teachers in our sample, particularly at the secondary level. Although the schools varied quite markedly in many characteristics, the school-to-school variation in these practices was modest. Those staffs appearing to have developed considerable capability for resolving schoolwide issues and problems appeared not to have had comparable success in developing unusually stimulating teaching. They lectured, monitored seatwork, and engaged in activities requiring only rote learning about as much as did teachers in schools where many problems appeared to have gotten out of hand. Generally, the planned improvement of pedagogy did not appear to be an agenda item in the schools of our sample. And yet, the goals set for schools call out for varied pedagogical techniques.

Why? I have suggested three contributing factors, none of which is amenable to simple solution. First, there is no pressure in the surrounding society to change these practices. They reflect much conventional wisdom regarding how classes *should* be conducted. Second, this is the way teachers most commonly were taught from their elementary school days through college. Third, their teacher education programs were not of sufficient depth to transcend the conventional wisdom regarding the nature of teaching. Our data suggest that many of the teachers had been exposed to countervailing notions but not sufficiently to assure their use later.

There is a fourth contributing factor. One of the tenets of academic freedom is that teachers are to be left alone in their classroom to teach as they see best. This tenet is far more sacred at the college level than in the elementary and secondary schools. Nonetheless, temple rubbings from the heights of academe influence the lower levels of schooling and serve to support teacher autonomy in the classroom. But the press of the environment in and out of schools appears to curtail innovative use of it.

What should and can be done? One answer is "little or nothing," proffered not because it would be futile to try, but because things are as they should be. We simply should provide in-service opportunities to help teachers do better what they now do. Many school districts have used their supervisors and brought in outside teams of consultants to do precisely this.[21] One cannot quarrel with the apparent usefulness of this practice.

The problem remaining, however, is that these customary teaching procedures rarely provide opportunities for students to practice the full range of learning behaviors implied in our goals for education in schools. Recent analyses show that students are far more proficient in regurgitating facts and performing at the lower levels of cognition than in solving problems. Many can give short, written answers to questions but have difficulty writing a coherent paragraph. Some who have no difficulty recalling important dates and individuals cannot relate two events occurring in different places at the same time.

If the language of the goals summarized in Chapter 2 is to be taken seriously and not merely as pious rhetoric, schools are to do more than teach the fundamental mathematical operations of adding, subtracting, multiplying, and dividing. In addition, they should help students see the significance of the relationship between the hypotenuse and the other two sides of a right-angled triangle in constructing a flight of steps, for example. Teachers respond, with varying degrees of success, to the messages of expectations they receive. There is no need to go beyond the simpler levels of knowing if these are the ones preferred. Indeed, it may be dangerous to give up time to activities designed to respond to a broader conception of education instead of devoting all of it to meeting lesser expectations.

First, then, if we subscribe to the goals set for schools in state documents, the implications for the kinds of classroom activities required for their attainment should be made abundantly clear. Second, teachers must be provided ample opportunity to see and use techniques designed to elicit such things as problem-solving behavior, imaginative essays, and a clear grasp of how our government functions and compares with others.

Providing Exemplary Models

During the first half of this century, laboratory schools attached to such universities as Columbia, Ohio State, Chicago, and California (the Los Angeles campus) often were in the forefront of experimentation with programs and practices not yet established in the public school system. Units of work developed in the Laboratory Schools of the University of Chicago (where John Dewey worked out many of his philosophical views) became prototypes for thousands of visitors. The methods of Corinne A. Seeds at the University Elementary School at UCLA influenced generations of teachers and were incorporated into the messages of supervisors working out of the State Department of Education. The ideas of a few imaginative leaders in schools and school districts showed up in the literature read by educators in the form of the Berkeley Plan, the Pueblo Plan, the Dalton Plan, the Winnetka Plan, and so on. All of these included pedagogical procedures deviating markedly from the practices we found to be most characteristic of the classes in our sample.

Most of the university-based laboratory schools are now gone, victims in part of budget cuts but more often of their own inability to sustain the momentum of their founding mothers and fathers. Those remaining, with perhaps a few exceptions, are not at all clear on their appropriate function and are fearful of their futures.[22] A few schools, both public and private, are cited as exemplifying a rather carefully designed curriculum (e.g., New Trier), but rarely achieve visibility and influence in the vast forest comprising schooling today.

I see little prospect of reincarnating the laboratory school movement of the past. But I do perceive the possibility of creating in each state a network of district-based schools, specifically charged with the responsibility of developing exemplary practices extending beyond mere refinement of the conventional. A report in which I recommended such a plan for the State of California, in 1968, was politically untimely.[23] Perhaps the time is come to resurrect the idea with some hope of its adoption.

In several cities, magnet schools already have broken, in concept at least, with the tradition of one system of like schools with no parental choice among alternatives. Why not, then, schools whose special function is to serve as centers for developing practices not now established, practices involving some risk-taking and requiring special cultivation? Since many people have trouble with the word "experimental" when applied to the education of children, I suggest the word "key" as the designation for such schools—but let us not waste time over the name.* Because these schools must have the freedom to try out unfamiliar practices, perhaps described only in the educational litera-

---

*I draw the name from its use in designating exemplary schools in the People's Republic of China. These schools are often used to pioneer the implementation of new policies and sometimes cooperate with universities in conducting modest experiments. Some controversy surrounds their presence and designation because of the elitist connotations.

ture, the concept of choice is critical. For this reason I recommended in the aforementioned report locating them in heavily populated areas where more than one school is accessible to the residents.

It is essential to accept at the outset the necessity for these key schools to be set free from many of the conventions of keeping school. There must be an unabashed search for the very best teachers, from wherever they can be obtained, and the expectation that most will have a tenure of perhaps five years in a given school before going on to influence regular schools. I am assuming that teaching in key schools will be recognized as a career opportunity calling for superior qualifications and carrying with it greater prestige and a higher salary. This higher salary would go with teachers leaving key schools to become leaders for pedagogical improvement elsewhere. It is high time we created opportunities for gifted, well-prepared educators to move upward in their chosen profession without leaving the classroom.

For the most part, the key schools will develop programs and disseminate descriptions and evaluations of practices brought to a level of successful operation. It should not be part of their role, however, to implement these practices in other schools. This should be the responsibility of persons with expertise in effecting change who would work in separate demonstration schools designated to carry out precisely the implementation function. When experimental schools become also demonstration schools, the staff begins to feel that it has the answers. Why move on to something else when "the one best way" is now available? The innovative function of the school is sacrificed to the self-gratifying function of showing others "the way." Teachers should be released, however, to work for short periods of time with those seeking to implement exemplary practices in the designated demonstration schools. In general, visitors should not come to key schools for orientation to alternative practices, but to demonstration schools seeking to implement the work of the former.

Key schools should be linked to universities and to one another in a communicating, collaborating network. There simply are not in universities the resources for serving many schools on an individual basis. But one university might well provide to a network of a dozen or more key schools a comprehensive evaluative program and potentially powerful ideas emerging from research and inquiry. Principals and teachers would meet regularly to exchange information, address common problems, and counteract isolationism and apathy. And surely we are close to the time when each unit in a network would be connected to all the others and to those demonstration schools affiliated with it through responsive two-way video communication.

Employing Instructional Leaders

I recommend the employment of head teachers for units of schooling. The level of preparation I have in mind is highly successful teaching experience coupled with a doctorate in the field. Persons with such qualifications exist, as do the means for providing a continuing supply. Those with clinical rather than research inclinations would be encouraged to enter these head teacher posts instead of pursuing research careers in universities, a career route for which there currently is little demand.

It should be clearly understood that the head teacher position is a designated classification requiring special qualifications, not merely a reward for seniority in the system. Head teachers would be recruited in a nationwide search. The salary range would overlap the upper end of the existing scale for teachers and extend well beyond it. As with the posts in key schools, head teacherships would provide attractive career opportunities for educators not wishing to leave the classroom.

All head teachers would teach part of the time, occupying positions normally filled by regular classroom teachers. In addition, however, they would be expected to serve as role models to fellow teachers, provide them with in-service assistance, diagnose knotty learning problems, and so on. I envision them serving as heads of teaching teams made up of qualified full- and part-time teachers, neophytes in teacher preparation programs, and aides. To the degree that these head teachers served as clinical members of teacher education faculties (see the section on teacher education below), they would teach less in the classroom and be paid partially by the university or from some other source. The salary savings could then be used to employ aids or a part-time teacher. The number of head teachers employed would depend on the size of the school and the willingness of districts to make this kind of commitment to improved instruction.

I offer these recommendations as a counterproposal to the currently popular one that principals themselves be the instructional leaders in schools, acquiring the necessary specialized preparation, teaching pedagogical skills to the teachers, and evaluating teachers' performance. Certainly a principal should be keenly aware of the need to foster improvement of pedagogy and should make every possible effort to assure the availability of opportunities for teachers to improve. But I disagree with the more extended definition of the modeling and evaluating role of the principal for at least three reasons.

First, developing and maintaining a school that is first-rate in all the characteristics discussed in Chapter 8, as well as the planning processes recommended earlier in this chapter, is a full-time job. And so is the job of being both the role model for and the monitor of all teaching in the school. One or the other is bound to suffer when both are assumed by the principal. In the final analysis, the principal will be evaluated on his or her success in the former. Neglect of the latter already is showing up in cases reported to me and others of harassed principals quickly and routinely checking off the competencies of their teachers on forms provided for this purpose. One teacher told me of a principal who was so insecure in the process, for which he had limited preparation, that he checked off teachers' competencies in empty classrooms while teachers and children were gone for recess or lunch!

Second, it is naive and arrogant to assume that principals, who may or may not have been effective teachers, can acquire and maintain a higher level of teaching expertise than teachers engaged in teaching as a full-time occupation. The concept becomes particularly absurd at the secondary level, where presumably the principal who has attended some special institutes on teaching, necessarily for short periods of time, will have acquired teaching competence beyond that of the teachers of each of the diverse subjects. If this is a tenable assumption, then I fear that teachers' competence is below anything we have contemplated heretofore. I certainly would not want to put myself in such a posture of universal excellence!

Third, increasingly we are learning about the importance of trust in the principal/teacher relationship. It emerged as significant in our study of change and school improvement reported earlier in this chapter. And it was a factor differentiating more and less renewing schools in our sample. What are the chances of establishing a bond of trust between the principal and teachers if the principal is to be both evaluator and judge of these teachers? Very little, I fear. And yet the California legislature recently enacted into law essentially this procedure. If diligently carried out—an unlikely expectation, fortunately—it would virtually foreclose the schoolwide self-improvement process to which many past legislative enactments have been committed. The only models for evaluating teaching that have proved reasonably effective to date are those of peer review, as used by major universities. Administrators monitor the process and act on the recommendations coming to them, but they do not conduct the reviews.

The alternative approach I have recommended will go much farther, I believe, toward loosening up the hard knot of instructional improvement. It is far more likely to upgrade the competence of those likely to be teaching for years to come. Well-intentioned efforts to identify and remove incompetent teachers seldom have achieved their goal. Almost invariably we come back to the solution of trying to do better with those we have. The preceding recommendations concerning head teachers and their role are directed not only to this end but also to the ends of improving the quality of the workplace and providing incentives for attracting and keeping high quality teachers.

SOME ORGANIZATIONAL REARRANGEMENTS

My previous visits to schools, coupled with several of our findings, suggest we may need to examine and possibly rearrange some of the little-questioned conventions of schooling. Four of these are examined below, and proposals for change are presented. The four conventions are the isolation from each other of elementary and secondary schooling; the casual preparation and selection of school principals; the equally casual way most elementary schools are staffed; and the trend toward one large school rather than several small ones, particularly at the secondary level.

In the succeeding chapter I make a more radical proposal for restructuring the continuum of schooling, a suggestion which has implications for preceding recommendations and which bears rather directly on those to be made now. It is my assumption that with these more modest proposals out of the way, and perhaps some of them even accepted as reasonable and do-able, readers will be ready to consider more sweeping changes.

The Separateness of Our Schools

Elementary schools and the secondary school which graduates of the former probably will attend exist in virtual isolation from each other. The three schools of one of the triples in our sample sharing a common site might just as well have been in different towns, given the lack of communication and articulation among them. My comment to the junior high principal, "Some boys and girls might spend their entire period of schooling here—as many as a dozen years," presented to him a new perspective. So far as I was able to determine, continuities and discontinuities in the progression were not an agenda item for the three principals. Indeed, when they did come together to discuss problems, which was rare, the topics were those of sharing playground space, bullying of young children by older ones, the use of bicycle racks, and the like.

As one step toward improved continuity from level to level, I recommend the appointment of a person to serve as headmaster or headmistress over one senior high school and the junior high and elementary schools advancing their students to it.* Even though this person would be senior to the several principals, his or her authority would not detract from the usual authority and responsibility of the latter group. A principal would continue to be the person in charge of his or her school—providing lead-

*There are many possible variations on what I am proposing here, including one principal administering the entire sequence with an associate relating to heads or units (see later recommendations in this chapter) for purposes of curricular and instructional coordination.

ership to the teachers, relating to students and parents, developing long-range plans, etc.

The primary responsibility of the headmaster or headmistress would be to address matters of continuity and sequence in the curriculum, focus attention on each student's balance of studies, assure maintenance of a cumulative record of studies taken by each student from kindergarten through the twelfth grade, approve recommendations for accelerated progress of students from one unit of schooling to the next, and the like. These tasks begin to suggest the qualifications of the incumbent. The recommended background of formal preparation includes studies in curriculum planning, techniques of evaluating programs and students' progress, research methods, and the human and institutional management understandings derived from the behavioral sciences and commonly offered in the best graduate schools of management. Previous experience as a principal would be desirable but not required. My purpose here is in part to provide another opportunity for persons with outstanding credentials but not necessarily seniority in the system to enter positions of leadership. Such is necessary if new talent is to be attracted into the system and public credibility restored.

The group of headmasters and headmistresses would have qualifications very much like those sought in the associate superintendent for curriculum and instruction and would report directly to him or her. There is the possibility here of effecting savings in the superintendent's office of a big district by reducing central office supervisory personnel, whose services often are too disparate and too thinly spread to be effective. Also, this group would constitute a highly qualified pool of candidates should the associate superintendency become vacant.

My central intent is to have an appropriately qualified person devoting almost full time to the vital tasks of curriculum improvement and level-to-level articulation. Space limitations prevent me from detailing these tasks. One illustration is sufficient to suggest the possibilities. Our data revealed an almost monotonous repetitiveness in the mechanics of teaching mathematics from the upper elementary years into the junior high schools and even the first year of senior high. One must assume that essential diagnoses and remediations of students' deficiencies were not taking place or were inadequate. Many students apparently moved along, re-experiencing the pedagogy, textbooks, quizzes, and the like of a kind which previously had proved to be, at best, only modestly successful. We saw evidence of boredom and apathy. It would be the responsibility of the headmaster or headmistress, working with the head teacher of an upper elementary unit, for example, to address deficiencies at the precise level where these mathematical operations are first introduced. The coordination of the entire elementary and secondary curriculum by one person would enhance the prospect of this and many similar problems becoming more visible and consequently receiving corrective action.

Selecting and Preparing School Principals

In our earlier study of educational change and school improvement, we found that most of the school principals of the participating schools lacked major skills and abilities required for effecting educational improvement. They did not know how to select problems likely to provide leverage for schoolwide improvement, how to build a long-term agenda, how to assure some continuity of business from faculty meeting to faculty meeting, how to secure and recognize a working consensus, and on and on. Most were insecure in their relations with faculty and rarely or never visited classrooms. Some were hopelessly mired in paperwork, exaggerating the magnitude of the tasks involved in part to avoid areas of work where they felt less secure. Remedying these deficiencies became the major agenda item at monthly meetings of the entire group.

These were not substandard principals. Indeed, many of them were believed by their superintendents to be better than average in their leadership abilities. It is fair to assume, I think, that these shortcomings are widespread. Yet the principal increasingly is being viewed as the key person in school improvement.

One need not look far to find that in many districts the selection and preparation of those selected for this important post is, to say the least, casual. It simply is not established procedure in the educational system to identify and groom cadres of the most promising prospects for top positions, as is the case with IBM, for example. Rather, the selection process is one of looking over the possible prospects in late spring for a principalship to be filled a few months later. Often, short-sighted policies—usually promoted by present employees—restrict candidacy to persons presently employed in the district.

Two rarely practiced procedures, both referred to briefly early in this chapter, are basic to correcting this sloppiness and upgrading both the status of the principalship and the quality of those who aspire to it. First, there should be a continuous districtwide effort to identify employees with leadership potential. A first clue to this potential is recognition by peers. Such persons often are overlooked because they most frequently are identified with peer group interests and causes and thus come into negotiation or conflict with management. Superintendents and board members too often are unable to transcend considerations of potential loyalty and the absence of boat-rocking tendencies in return for the greater assets of intelligence, creativity, and courage.

Second, the district must be willing to make an investment designed to pay off in the future. There always should be candidates available for each vacated principalship who have been groomed for the post. Once identified as promising, potential candidates should be added to a list of persons scheduled for paid two-year study leaves, to be taken at a major university offering a carefully planned program. Leading to a special certificate or a degree directed to professional competence, these programs would balance academic study and one or more internships as an assistant principal. Schools of education would compete in the marketplace, as do schools of management, to build a reputation for quality of program, in contrast to using conformity with usually outmoded credentialling requirements as the mark of success. States have the right, if they so choose, to set licensing examinations, as they do in law and medicine, but quality of all school of education programs is more likely to be enhanced when curricula are planned separately from rather than governed by credentialling requirements.

School districts would be well advised—and perhaps should be required—to select, for posts available, from a pool of qualified applicants extending far beyond district lines. This procedure does not nullify the investment in selection and preparation. With all districts similarly engaged in the process, interest from investments would be shared.

Legislators prefer to select highly specific targets in seeking school improvement and the principalship often is seen as the bullseye. But some have allowed themselves to get caught up in the machinations of those incumbents who do not want to see anything changed. Legislating long lists of paper requirements and procedures for credentialling school principals sometimes is the unfortunate result. The status quo is reinforced.

More to the point of initially selecting and subsequently preparing better candidates for principalships are the procedures recommended above. States might well underwrite the costs involved by eliminating much of the cumbersome, costly machinery now required for accrediting programs and establishing fellowships for our future educational leaders. It would be difficult to suggest a better way to use public funds wisely.

Staffing Elementary Schools

Customarily, when a vacancy occurs on an elementary school staff, the district personnel office simply selects the next person from a general list of applicants. Rarely is the selection guided by some awareness of the patterns of expertise represented by the school's present faculty. Consequently, a school already well supplied with teachers whose academic preparation was heavily in English and the social sciences is as likely as not to receive still another person of similar background. If nobody on the staff has had extensive preparation in music, why not look for someone who has?

This will suggest to some readers an orientation toward a departmentalized elementary school. Not so. To the unrelenting advocates of departmentalization, on one hand, and the self-contained classroom, on the other, my response has to be, "A plague on both your houses." Surely there are creative ways to secure some of the advantages of both departmentalization and self-contained classrooms without the weaknesses of either. School staffs should be encouraged to seek such ways, drawing from the ample literature of alternative practices available, and to participate actively in spelling out the qualifications of prospective colleagues.

I briefly sketch one such alternative. A guiding assumption is that each elementary school will have a nucleus of fully qualified teachers. The teachers in this group will all possess the capability of teaching across the board in at least mathematics, language arts, science, and social studies. A second assumption is that each will also have some concentrated preparation in one of these or in some other curricular area. Further, an assessment of the nuclear staff should reveal such additional strength in the total group sufficient to assure at least one person with some degree of specialization for each curricular field—a generalist with supplementary strength in science, a generalist with supplementary strength in physical education, etc.

A third assumption is that the school will not in fact be departmentalized. Rather, each teacher will serve as a resource person in his or her domain of additional preparation. Initial assessment of teaching strengths may reveal some gaps and duplications. With the departure of a teacher in a duplicated field, the search will be for a person to fill a gap. Over a period of several years, it should be possible to build a well-balanced core faculty. If the turnover rate is low, it may be necessary to speed up the process by exchanging teachers with nearby schools.

A fourth assumption is that the nuclear faculty will be less than the total number of positions assigned the school. This assumption runs counter to common procedure. Almost all schools fill all positions with full-time, certified teachers. This practice sharply restricts the opportunities for providing both a well-balanced curriculum and the specialized resources needed to staff it. Given the present shortage of mathematics teachers, it is unlikely that all elementary schools will find even one qualified teacher with a reasonably extensive background in mathematics. Creative ways must be found to secure this and other needed resources. By leaving some positions open for part-time personnel, money is freed for employing non-certified college students, negotiating with computer firms for persons to teach computer literacy, hiring aides and tutors, etc. At the Corinne A. Seeds University Elementary School at UCLA, there are 22 full-time teaching positions, but not all of these are filled with full-time persons. The total staff of full-time and part-time personnel working with children often numbers more than 40.

A fifth assumption is that available staff will be organized into various-sized teams. Most states require that one member of a team be a fully certified teacher. But few, if any, specify limits to the size of the group under that teacher's general supervision. Consequently, opportunities open up for groups of 50, 75, 100, or more children to be taught by teams of full-time and part-time persons representing in sum the array of specializations required for the curriculum offered. Teachers-in-training might be included in such teams.

Team teaching has been tried in the past, especially during the 1960s, with varying degrees of success. Where plans were carefully laid and developed, participants expressed considerable satisfaction. But more often than not, the proposals were handed down from the top and were implemented without adequate preparation and understanding. Most fell apart. To focus on organizational arrangements, as usually was the case, is to misplace the emphasis.

What we are after is to secure the teachers needed to provide a balanced curriculum and simultaneously to organize these resources for maximum utilization. Given the imbalanced nature of teacher supply—as it has been, is, and probably will continue to be—school staffs must depart from conventional procedures in employing creative ways to secure and use available talent. Schools differ in their needs and in the availability of potential teaching resources. Principals and the recommended head teachers should take the lead in developing staffing plans appropriate to local circumstances.

Schools Within Schools

Most of the schools clustering in the top group of our sample on major characteristics were small, compared with the schools clustering near the bottom. It is not impossible to have a good large school; it simply is more difficult.

What are the defensible reasons for operating an elementary school of more than a dozen teachers and 300 boys and girls? I can think of none. One might put forward economic reasons, but I am unaware of supporting

data. Surely any arguments for larger size based on administrative considerations are far outweighed by educational ones against large schools. Headmistresses of British Infant Schools, enrolling five-, six-, and seven-year-olds,
are appalled at the size of many elementary schools in the United States. Most
regard 225 to 250 students as the maximum enrollment desired. These experienced former teachers spend little or no time in their offices. They are more
head teachers than administrators.

Conant suggested that a high school with 100 graduating seniors would be
sufficiently large to facilitate his recommended curriculum.[24] Some school
boards and superintendents concluded, apparently, that more would be better and pushed for school consolidation, usually accompanied by extensive
busing. Expansion in school size usually was accompanied by curricular expansion, the availability of more alternatives, and the teaching and course
resources necessary to tracking. I have difficulty arguing the virtue of any of
these, given our data.

Clearly we need sustained, creative efforts designed to show the curricular
deficits incurred in very small high schools, the curricular possibilities of
larger schools, and the point where increased size suggests no curricular gain.
The curriculum design centers recommended earlier might well provide
this service. The burden of proof, it appears to me, is on large size. Indeed, I
would not want to face the challenge of justifying a senior, let alone junior,
high of more than 500 to 600 students (unless I were willing to place arguments for a strong football team ahead of arguments for a good school, which
I am not). Given our data, I would not want to risk losing what Dennison
appears to have, with only 61 students in the junior and senior high schools
combined, for the assumed curricular advantages of consolidating with
another school—which in this as in many other instances would be quite far
distant. Admittedly, the low student-teacher ratio required to provide Dennison's surprisingly rich curriculum is costly, but substantial costs would be
incurred through consolidation.

Community leaders will argue, understandably, that little can be done to
create small junior and senior high schools, given existing facilities. Here is
where creative reorganization can achieve at least some of the advantages of
smaller schools. The idea of creating schools within schools is not new, but it
has had negligible impact on practice. Described simply, a school of, say,
3,000 students is divided into relatively self-contained smaller schools within
the existing buildings. The result might be six schools of 500 pupils each.
Most existing buildings lend themselves poorly to providing some spatial
identity for each school—or "house," to borrow a term quite commonly used
by private colleges. Ideally, some internal reconstruction should accompany
the recommended reorganization.

The central concept is that each house is to be characterized by its own curriculum, students, faculty, and counselors. For most activities, each house is self-sufficient. Obviously, there are potential gains from some house-to-house sharing—of the library (a significant gain over small schools on their own site), of gymnasia and other facilities for physical education, of the most expensively equipped laboratories, of vocational education centers, and the like. But each house uses these facilities separately, according to an overall schedule, not in company with students from another house. Some schoolwide activities are to be desired. The sixth curricular domain recommended earlier, for example, would provide students with opportunities to gain access to teachers from other houses and from outside the school.

The graded structure of American schooling leads one to think of houses organized horizontally across single grade levels. I recommend precisely the opposite structure—namely, houses organized vertically so that each contains students from all secondary grade levels, or, put differently, so that each student spends his or her entire junior or senior high school career affiliated with one house.

I argue this on curricular grounds and on the basis of students' personal welfare. First, the range of achievement among students coming into the tenth grade, for example, is wide, spreading over several grade levels. Mastery teaching may result in more students being at grade level but will not reduce the number performing above it. With several grade levels available to them in a single house, teachers have an enhanced opportunity to adjust the levels of work to students' present attainments. Given my recommendation for greater commonality in the curricular sequences through which students are to progress, students' individuality can be accommodated to some degree through placement in advanced courses, regardless of present age or grade placement. Requiring students to remain at grade level when they could readily master more advanced studies cannot be justified educationally. Slower students are not tracked into inferior content. They simply have more time and support in seeking to reach mastery of what is common for all while a few of their age-mates are accommodated in a class composed predominantly of older students. Such adjustments are particularly useful in the field of mathematics. The principles involved are those of continuous progress and nongrading.[25]

The argument regarding students' personal welfare arises out of pieces of data, some of them already reported, on the problems and preoccupations of those in our sample. Secondary school students were not relating strongly to their teachers even on academic matters. Most were preoccupied with peer group interests. Their teachers, by and large, were not relating to the personal concerns of their students. How could they, facing in succession so many classes of different students? There were evidences of teacher frustration over this and a considerable desire for greater emphasis on the personal goals of education. I spoke earlier to a disjuncture between students and teachers. Whether or not this can be overcome in a large school divided into small schools remains to be seen. Small schools provide a better answer, I believe. But schools within schools appear to offer some amelioration of the problems accompanying large size.

To cut down on school size without simultaneously attacking the problem of student-teacher contact is to do too little. An additional step is to assure the long-term association of a group of students and their teachers. The vertical organization of schools within schools would provide, under the present structure of secondary schooling, three or four years of continuity and, I believe, a reduction in both student alienation and teacher frustration.

Finally, each house would contain only a few teachers in each subject—too few to justify the usual designation of department heads. A more logical arrangement is a head responsible for the entire house, providing leadership to the whole, much as colleges have deans or provosts for the several units. Still another career opportunity opens up. We begin to see, now, increased possibilities for the kind of dialogue over goals and attention to a correspondingly comprehensive curriculum as recommended early in this chapter. We begin also to see increased possibilities for considering students as persons characterized by more than their performance in the subject-matter slices of the daily schedule.

TEACHER EDUCATION

Educators' interest in teacher education wanes when there is an abundance of teachers. A period of oversupply in most fields is now ending; a period of undersupply in many is beginning. The shortage in mathematics and the natural sciences has been chronic and promises to remain so. As I said in Chapter 6, the greater availability to women of careers in addition to teaching, nursing, secretarial work, and social work has been accompanied by a sharp decline in the percentage of women entering teaching. The number of men interested in teaching has been declining for years—in part because of the low status often given the profession and in part because of the increasingly large gap between the salaries offered and the income available in other fields.

It is unfortunate that interest in teacher education increases most often in times of shortage because attention of those who employ teachers is almost always focused then on increasing the supply at the expense of quality. Districts only recently picayunish in their attention to credentials are now advertising for essentially unqualified persons and simultaneously asking preparing institutions to abort their programs, at least temporarily. The only time to address quality, it appears, it when there is an oversupply, and that is when interest is at its lowest ebb. In teacher education, we seem always to be zigging when we should be zagging, or vice versa.

My recommendations are directed only to the matter of improved quality, regardless of supply and demand. Needless to say, some of them will be shot down precisely on the basis of arguments based on supply and demand. But in matters of professional preparation, supply and demand constitute a set of changing circumstances to be met *after, not before*, the nature of quality programs and incentives for entering them are addressed.

Incentives

Regarding incentives, the "flatness" of the profession—that is, the low ratio of salaries after ten years to beginning salaries—is a major deterrent to entering. Part of the responsibility for this state of affairs lies with the organized profession itself. Given the labor-intensive character of teaching, it simply is not economically feasible to pay attractive salaries to all who teach if "all who teach" is to mean "a certified teacher in every classroom," with class enrollment restricted to 25 or even 30 students. If this is to be the stand of the teaching profession into the indeterminate future, we might as well resign ourselves to a permanent state of low pay for teachers and the continuation of teaching as a marginal profession.

The alternative—never popular with teacher associations and organizations—is a deliberate distinction among various assisting and apprentice roles, more highly paid career teachers, and the head teachers described earlier. The essential ingredient is differentiation in salary corresponding with differentiation in function and accompanying preparation to perform a particular function. We could turn to several other service professions for models, but equally functional models for teaching have surfaced in the past.[26] Some models failed, in my judgment, because of overelaboration of these distinctions, given the difficulty of determining a hierarchical order of teaching tasks.[27] Just a few relatively clear distinctions are needed.

Also needed are clarity of and firm adherence to the entry routes. Mere completion of designated requirements should not ensure advancement to the next position. There must be a vacancy at the level sought, not just accommodation to reward the seniority of the candidate.

I shall be specific. Let us assume that one classification is "aide," with its own salary schedule. Progression beyond this classification on the basis of seniority is closed. The only route to becoming classified as a career teacher is for the aide to resign and enter an appropriate preparation program. The preparation program, let us assume, provides two classifications and two modest payment schedules: intern (during one of two years of preparation) and resident (for up to three years at a higher salary but one significantly below the beginning level for a career teacher). A resident cannot become a career teacher on the basis of seniority; the advancement occurs only when a position so classified becomes available in the school where the resident is employed or elsewhere. Current unavailability of such a position creates the temporary necessity of employment at a lower level in the system. Head teacher positions are open only to former career teachers who left their positions to complete an advanced (doctoral level) preparation program. They are not open to career teachers on the basis only of seniority. Within classifications, the usual opportunities for increasingly higher salaries would prevail. Career teacher salary schedules would overlap the bottom half of head teacher salary schedules, which in turn would overlap and even extend beyond principals' salary schedules (as is the case in universities, where salaries of the most distinguished professors frequently exceed those of deans and presidents).

Our data in Chapter 6 on why teachers enter teaching could be interpreted to mean that professional and idealistic values and challenging work are sufficient incentives. This interpretation would be incorrect, I believe. Of course we want teachers who want to teach, just as we want professionals in all fields who are attracted to the work. But this is insufficient incentive to assure a continuing supply of able people. Anticipated income always will be important. Not all people seek to enter the highest paid professions. Many would enter teaching if the possibilities of and requirements for ultimately earning a decent living were clear. Currently these conditions simply do not prevail.

Programs

I hope that future teachers will experience preparation programs of such length, depth, and quality that they will be effectively separated from most of the conventional ways of teaching. They will acquire and persist in using as practicing teachers a greater variety of methods designed to assure students' interest and accomplishment in learning. There is, however, little either in current practice or even in innovative stirrings to sustain this hope. Teacher education programs are disturbingly alike and almost uniformly inadequate.

The conventions to be broken and the traditions to be overcome in developing the needed programs are monumental. First, there is the general indifference of college and university faculties—even in those institutions recently "graduating" from classification as teachers' colleges. Their contributions seldom get beyond condemning schools of education and proposing for teachers more courses in the subject departments. These suggestions would make scarcely a dent in the problems of schooling revealed earlier. It is difficult to imagine a more useful activity for an undergraduate faculty than to set out to design the best general education for a future elementary school teacher. It is a general education that elementary teachers very much need—which, when defined, would look very much like the liberal education many of us would find appropriate for all college students. Such education precedes or accompanies professional preparation to teach. What college presidents are ready to lead their faculties in this significant task?

Second, there is the gap between the subject departments and schools of education that so often leads to students' lack of success in relating content and method. The problem is most serious in the major universities, where professors in the teaching of a subject have no clear home base. A professor in the teaching of science has little support in any of the science departments and is effectively cut off from scholarship in biology or chemistry or physics if located in the school of education. There are exceptions but they are few, the individual competence of faculty members sometimes transcending organizational limitations. One answer is for professors in learning and instruction within the school of education to team teach seminars in the teaching of mathematics, for example, with professors of mathematics. What prestigious university, likely to influence others, is ready to take the lead?

Third, the high expectations for research in leading universities tend to work against a commitment to teacher education by professors in the schools of education. Harry Judge, Director of the Department of Education at Oxford University, pinpoints the dilemmas of major graduate schools of education in American universities in a commissioned report to the Ford Foundation.[28] He quotes a fictitious dean stating that his school's commitment is to study teacher education, not work at it. The remark may startle us. But finding the time to teach and advise doctoral students and carry out a program of research virtually removes the possibility that professors in the major schools of education will devote much time to the demands of teacher education programs.

There are no easy solutions. One is to turn more research attention to teaching and the circumstances of teaching while simultaneously combining in the teacher education program the talents of research scholars with those of skilled practitioners from the schools who temporarily hold clinical appointments.[29] The needed orientation to research probably will come as professors of education increasingly transcend the research problems and methods of psychology, sociology, and the like in favor of those pertaining to policy and practice in schools. But research-oriented schools of education will be reluctant to allocate regular positions to clinical personnel. Consequently, it probably will be necessary to earmark positions for this purpose.

A fourth convention to be surmounted by most schools of education is the common practice of assigning student teachers to classroom teachers in schools selected somewhat casually for this purpose. If we are as worried about schools as popular opinion suggests and if most teachers teach as described in Chapter 7, why do we so automatically turn over to these schools and teachers those who are to learn from them? Surely such a practice assures perpetuation of the very things we want teacher education programs to change. The success of professional preparation, it seems to me, depends on the degree to which programs are able to separate beginners from the primitive or outworn techniques of their predecessors. If we were to set out to provide the most advanced preparation for future doctors, surely we would not intern them with those whose solution to every illness is bloodletting.

The direction for breaking out of this convention is, I believe, implicit in preceding pages. Teacher preparing institutions must join with school districts in identifying and subsequently working with schools to be designated as key and demonstration schools.[30] These are the schools targeted for innovation and change which I recommended earlier in this chapter. To them, outstanding career and head teachers are to be drawn. Beginning teachers are to be interned *only* in these schools. University faculty members oriented to research and development in school organization, curriculum, and teaching are to be provided with space in these schools and here carry on their scholarly inquiries, sharing their expertise with the school faculty. The head teachers and a few highly gifted career teachers will serve as clinical faculty in the schools of education. Here, too, resident teachers will spend time as junior members of the faculty, preparing for appointments as career teachers. Research, school improvement, in-service education of experienced teachers, and preservice teacher education will proceed hand in hand.

I am recommending a two-year program of professional studies and clinical experiences prior to a period of resident status in the hope that future teachers will actually experience, under guidance, the use of teaching methods not commonly practiced in schools. These they would encounter and analyze in the selected schools affiliated with universities for teacher education purposes, as described. During this internship part of their preparation, they would be called upon to demonstrate a full repertoire of teaching procedures, each designed to develop students' abilities in the range of goals we espouse. Presumably, these methods would be further refined and evaluated during the residency period prior to an individual's acquiring the designation "career teacher." This nation cannot continue to afford the brief, casual, conforming preparation now experienced by those who will staff its classrooms.

What I am proposing is a multidimensional approach to complex problems that have successfully defied assault. Promising but equally complex proposals, such as those of B. Othanel Smith, have aroused temporary interest but little action.[31] We do not take easily to many-part solutions, even when the problems are complex. But the relatively minor adjustments of the past have proven to be almost completely futile. Some have done little more than to rearrange or just retitle the same courses. What hope, then, have my recommendations?

The only hope I see lies in a reasonably broad coalescence of teacher education faculties around the growing realization that radical breakthroughs are needed. There are some present signs of this beginning.[32] But, ominously, there are stronger signs of school districts being willing to abort improvement efforts through offering teaching posts to woefully ill-prepared persons.

To break the recurring cycle, it will be necessary, I think, for private funding agencies to try one more time to provide monetary incentives, in this case for a few promising networks each comprising several key and demonstration schools and a central university. The criteria for selecting these include the strength of interested universities and their schools of education, their commitment to try, the quality of surrounding school districts, the bonds and potential for stronger bonds between the universities and the districts, the willingness of school boards to experiment with new structures and salary schedules, and the readiness of state officials to suspend existing certification and accreditation requirements for teachers and institutions.

Several of these networks collaborating across the land might be able to effect the necessary breakthroughs. The sums of discretionary funds required over a minimum of five years are quite substantial—probably necessitating a consortium of funding agencies. The effort will be a gamble. But if the gamble is not taken, I fear that future attempts to improve teacher education—and, subsequently, our schools—are doomed to repeat the puny, inadequate efforts of the past.

CONCLUDING COMMENTS

There are in this chapter dozens of suggestions and recommendations for improving the schools we have. Steps toward implementing them could begin immediately. Costs are involved, but they call more for rearranging the use of existing funds and time than for adding resources. Where additional money is required, the purpose usually is for attracting and holding able teachers and principals and for developing the finest teachers we can have, which is the intent of the networks described above.

The temptation now is to provide a simple list of all recommendations. This I resist. We are prone to making laundry lists of unconnected, simplistic solutions to complex problems. My proposals are not intended to be prescriptive. Rather, they are designed to illustrate directions and guiding principles for betterment. *And they are interconnected.*

The recommendations for states are intended to assure the clear articulation of a comprehensive set of goals for schools, the availability of alternative curricular designs and pedagogical procedures, continuing assessment of the condition of education in schools, and support for school improvement. They are intended, also, to impress upon state leaders the need to stimulate creative ways to organize and staff schools, develop teacher education programs, and eliminate the present "flatness" in teaching opportunities and salary schedules. States must be held accountable for what they do and do not do in these as well as other areas of responsibility, just as state legislatures are prone to hold teachers and administrators accountable for students' learning. This implies continuing evaluation, at state expense, of the impact—good and bad—of legislative initiatives in the educational arena.

The recommendations for school districts are intended to effect greater decentralization of authority and responsibility to the local school site. They are designed, also to stimulate long-range planning in each school, under the leadership of the principal and with assistance in self-assessment from the district office.[33] The inherent principle is "every tub on its own bottom," each with a strong link to the superintendent and to the other tubs in the system. The unit of improvement is the individual school. The major decisions regarding it are made there, where they are easily scrutinized by the school's patrons. The district prospers to the degree that its schools exhibit good health.

The recommendations for teacher education are intended to separate the preparation process from the customary ways of keeping school. This is a sharp departure from much conventional practice. One part of the future teacher's orientation is an immersion in behavioral and humanistic studies relevant to schooling and teaching. Another is guided observation and practice only in key and demonstration schools working in collaboration with the teacher preparing institutions. The education of beginning teachers, development of experienced teachers, and school improvement go hand-in-hand.

The recommendations for distributing time and teachers are intended to produce curricula of sufficient scope and balance to reflect the expectations of state goals. The curricular recommendations emphasize balance in the student's, not just the school's, program of studies. They provide for a common minimum in each domain of knowledge, some degrees of freedom for local option in each domain, some provision for either more advanced work or remediation in the domains of the curriculum common to all students, and assurance that all students, not just the most academically able, will have some opportunity for the development of special interests and talents.[34]

Recommendations for the elimination of ability grouping and tracking and for greater emphasis on methods of mastery learning seek greater equity in access to knowledge for all students. Similarly, the recommendations for improving instruction are intended to expand students' opportunities to learn.

The recommendations for research and development centers focused on curriculum design, on the content of the major domains of the curriculum, and on teaching and evaluation hold out the possibility of getting new models to guide planning and teaching. The prospects here for long-term funding from the private sector enhance the possibilities for innovation and for transcending the uniformity of schooling.

Among the recommendations most likely to lead us beyond conventional ways of conducting schooling are those for close articulation of our elementary, middle, and senior high schools, more rigorous selection and preparation of principals, alternative ways of staffing elementary schools, and the division of large secondary schools into smaller, semiautonomous units. These procedures address the flatness in opportunities and incentives for teachers and administrators. They invite innovations in the organization of schools, curricula, and collaborative teaching. Together, they challenge the conventions that characterize most schools and resist change. And they encourage longer, closer relationships among teachers and groups of students. Greater satisfaction on the part of both might well be the result.

Tomorrow's systems of education will evolve if present arrangements are dynamic. But if we dig in our heels, become defensive of what now exists, and engage in improvement only at the edges, the schools we have will atrophy. We will continue to educate our children, but not necessarily in better ways. Surely we can build from what we have, profiting from past experiences in the search for something better.

Chapter 10

Beyond the Schools
We Have

Futurists have a tantalizing way of describing the year 2001 as though being there has little to do with getting there. The future simply arrives full-blown. But it is the succession of days and years between now and then that will determine what life will be like. Decisions made and not made will shape the schools of tomorrow.

The recommendations of Chapter 9 challenge few of the conventions of schooling. The most radical, not new, are those directed to the lack of opportunities for advancement within teaching itself and to the organization of the conditions of teaching to correct this condition. They leave untouched many assumptions about schooling, especially that of the school's preemptive role in educating the young.

This chapter goes further, in the light of four conditions, all mentioned in previous chapters, that will affect schools whether or not we address their implications for the conduct of education and schooling. Not to address them would be to leave to the vagaries of omission what should be the subject of commission.

The first is a youth culture powerfully preoccupied with itself and made up of individuals much less shaped by home, church, and school than once was the case. How well suited to the young people of today is a school that hardened into shape during a previous era? Some of our data suggest a poor fit. Other studies and statistics on absenteeism, truancy, and interpersonal tensions—sometimes leading to violence—raise serious questions about the appropriateness of schools, as conducted, for many of the older students in attendance. But merely to remove the most troublesome may be to obfuscate the basic problems.

A second condition, to which our system of schooling has responded sluggishly, is the stunningly swift advance of technology in virtually all aspects of life. The end is not in sight. Persons who just a few years ago were operating elevators, attending to parking lots, and selling newspapers on the street corners have been replaced by buttons to push and boxes which respond to the insertion of plastic cards. Persons not replaced use special languages to instruct the computers on which we have become dependent. Television may be the closest thing we have to a common school. The schools, compared with other institutions, have responded very little to this technological revolution. But it is difficult to believe that schools can have a future apart from technology.

Third, in regard to vocational education the school may be, in the late twentieth century, where the home was in the late nineteenth. It became impossible, about a hundred years ago, for families to provide their children with the skills required for gainful employment in the emerging workplace. Similarly, it simply is not feasible today for schools to prepare specifically for the vast array of jobs available and increasing. To prepare youths for jobs whose requirements are obvious and relatively simple is to produce workers who will quickly become obsolescent. The requirements of a large segment of the workplace are obscure. The best preparation for work is general education. The specifics required for jobs are best taught by employers. Clearly, the future calls for better understanding and engineering of the relationships between education and work and between schools and the workplace.

Fourth, there will be no diminution in the need and our expectations for a highly educated society. Periodic disjunctures between the supply of and demand for highly educated workers raise the issue of creating an overeducated citizenry. But it becomes increasingly difficult to cope with the complexities of our society, let alone be successful in it, without the high degree of awareness, insight, and problem-solving ability that comes from education. It is difficult to envision a society of overeducated parents, voters, and workers.

However, a need to expand in the length and breadth of schooling does not necessarily follow from well-founded arguments regarding the critical importance of education. As I have said repeatedly, schooling and education are not synonymous, however much we link the two. The parents in our sample wanted for their children education in all areas of development. But they were given almost no options beyond schools for securing that education, and there are limits to what schools can do. Further, the drop in voters' approval of school bond initiatives from the 1960s through the 1970s attests to limits in our willingness to support schools.[1] Although many parents in our sample wanted more school services, many endorsed the view that they should not have to pay for them. So long as our expectations for education are comprehensive—as, again, they will continue to be—and we continue to equate schooling and education, there is little possibility that our schools will be satisfactory.

Hope for the future rests with our ability to use and relate effectively all those educative and potentially educative institutions and agencies in our society—home, school, church, media, museums, workplace, and more. In the process, presumably, the purposes and limitations of schools will become more clear. If our analyses are sound, less and less of what can be done better elsewhere will be done in schools. More and more of what is education in the most fundamental sense will become the central function of schools. The perspective in what follows is that schools are only part of a network of agencies and institutions educating the young. Once we begin to change schools significantly from what they are now, we pose challenges for the larger society—especially for higher education and the world of work.

RETHINKING THE CONTINUUM OF SCHOOLING

The organization of schooling appears to proceed as if we had no relevant knowledge regarding the development of children and youth. In fact, however, we have far more than we use. The addition of junior high schools and community colleges to the traditional hierarchy of elementary, secondary, and tertiary institutions, hailed initially as based on such knowledge, achieved only a few of the stated intentions—and these only mildly. The new institutions were quickly socialized into the norms and principles of the old. It is time to rethink the whole.

The modest rethinking that has occurred has been directed almost exclusively at the parts. It has been suggested that the four-year college be reduced to three years.[2] There are in existence some middle schools embracing upper grades of the elementary school and lower grades of the junior high school. The good intentions of these approaches can be realized, however, only within a restructured whole continuum of schooling.

Some Incongruities

In seeking to envision the desired direction for this restructuring, let us look at some incongruities in the present system. For one, the customary grade levels for beginning elementary school and completing secondary school don't jibe with compulsory attendance laws. A little-known fact is that the attendance laws of most states specify age 7 or occasionally even an older age as the latest for remaining out of school. Yet entry into the first grade shortly before or after age 6 is common practice. The legal leaving age in most states is 16. Yet graduation usually occurs close to one's eighteenth birthday. These practices fit fairly well a society with a parent at home with young children and a small percentage of the population going on to high school graduation.

Today things are different. There is a growing trend toward earlier entry into schooling and various kinds of less formal educational arrangements. The nation's kindergartens and first grades enroll approximately 93% of the 5-year-old age group. It is estimated that about 45% of 4-year-olds are in preschools of one kind or another.[3] It is difficult to keep track of the growing number of young children attending day-care centers. The practical need of parents to place their children in custodial settings offering some semblance of educational opportunity is buttressed ideologically by research into the importance of cognitive stimulation of the young. Reinforced by the theories and studies of Bloom,[4] Bruner,[5] and others, the federal government launched Head Start; some states seriously considered offering public schooling for 4-year-olds; and private foundations supported *Sesame Street*.

Almost simultaneously there was growing concern about the relevance of schooling for some of the older youths enrolled. One of several studies on adolescence, youth problems, secondary schooling, and work[6] noted the disruption of schools and classrooms by older, alienated students and recommended their removal by as early as age 14.[7] The report was vague on alternatives; it was directed more to the welfare of those interested in profiting from school experiences and failed to address the needed adjustments in the larger society.

Our data suggest the preoccupation of many adolescents in the sample with interests other than academic. Such statistics as are available suggest that shockingly large numbers of youths enrolled in secondary schools are absent for class periods or for days at a stretch. One school administrator said that it was not unusual for over 50% of the students supposedly in school to be elsewhere on a given day. To address ourselves only to those commonly classified as "incorrigible" is to obscure the possibility that secondary schooling and many of those it is supposed to serve are out of sync.

The problems of student disaffection with the ways of schools undoubtedly begin early. They become very apparent in the upper elementary grades and grow in visibility thereafter. There is a kind of upside-down relationship between adolescents' growing preoccupation with one another, participation in athletics, and experimentation with drugs, alcohol, and sex, and the school's lack of creativity in making academics attractive. The disjuncture between the two appears to be occurring at lower grade levels more than was the case several decades ago, perhaps in part because the age of the first menstruation has decreased by about two years during this century.[8] A corresponding shift downward in the age of attaining puberty has occurred for boys. These decreases, which have characterized all developed countries, have led in this country to proposals for returning to a four-year high school program in order to become more "socially appropriate."

Indeed, one does wonder about the appropriateness of secondary schools, as I have described some of them, both for the youths who graduate and for those who drop out of the eleventh and twelfth grades. Although not legally adults and, for the most part, lacking the maturity we ideally look for in adults, many of these young people have had experiences belonging more to the world of adulthood than childhood—some of them beyond the ken of both their teachers and their parents. I doubt that implementing all the recommendations of Chapter 9 plus comparable ones from many other sources would significantly increase the relevance of schooling for significant numbers of the oldest now enrolled. More drastic solutions are required.

An Earlier Beginning and Ending

I recommend that secondary schooling end and a completion certificate be awarded at the age of 16. This appeared to me to be a radical proposal until I heard Mortimer Adler expand on a recommendation that tertiary schooling be completed at that age with simultaneous awarding of the baccalaureate![9] My proposal now appears sufficiently modest to gain a serious hearing.

Regarding the lower end, I recommend that school begin at age 4. What is attempted over 12 years beginning at age 6 and ending at age 18 is now to be accomplished between the ages of 4 and 16. I have no hesitation in saying that the results will be as good or better than currently is the case. Expenditures will be less because public kindergarten will be included in the span of years. The extraordinary costs in developing curricula, in teacher frustration, in policing schools, and in monitoring absenteeism will be reduced. The costs to society in general will be less and the gains considerable. Children will be off to an earlier start, a condition which pays dividends in regard to their ultimate attainment and society's welfare. The costly prolongation of higher and professional education in the lives of young men and women will be reduced by two years. And we will have one of the greatest opportunities of all time to rethink what schools should be for.

Simultaneously, we will have an unusual opportunity to redesign the years beyond, a process that must include as participants the young graduates themselves.[10] What is to be society's responsibility to cadres of young people completing secondary education at the age of 16? I return to some suggestions later but leave to others the tasks of gathering the relevant data and tackling the exciting challenges of designing formal and informal educational possibilities for the 16- to 20-year-old group. I turn now to some possibilities for a precollegiate system embracing 12 years of schooling but serving an age group two years younger, overall, than that now enrolled.

Three Phases in the Redesigned Continuum

I propose that these 12 years be divided into three closely-linked phases of four years each. The first would be a primary phase beginning at age 4 and continuing through age 7, replacing two years of the present preschool—the second year of nursery school and kindergarten—and the first three grades. The second phase would be an elementary phase enrolling children from age 8 through age 11, replacing the present grades four through eight. The third would be a secondary phase for the 12- through 15-year-old group, replacing the present grades nine through twelve. Since these 12 years embrace what are now grades one through 12 and also include kindergarten and the upper year of nursery school, we are considering accomplishing in 12 years what now, for many children, spreads over 14. It is necessary to pick up, somewhere, the net difference of two years. I see this being done by clarifying the functions of each phase, installing quality controls, and assuring the fulfillment of these functions.

There are, I think, three noticeable "soft spots" in the current hierarchy. The first is the transition from so-called preschooling to the first grade, with or without kindergarten as the transition year. The perspective and practices of nursery school and kindergarten teachers are more child-oriented and less subject-oriented than those of primary teachers. Organizationally, public school kindergarten classes often are separated from the typically graded structure of elementary schools. In the eyes of many people, "real school" begins with the first grade. There are few if any adaptations in the first grade for boys and girls with nursery school and kindergarten experiences as differentiated from those without. The transitions from nursery school to kindergarten and to the first grade are bumpy for those enrolled throughout. Some children enter the first grade directly from home, without any association with preschools, and this can produce an even bumpier transition.

I believe it reasonable to assume, with these seams removed, that what is now accomplished by the end of the third grade (age 9) could easily be accomplished by the end of the proposed primary phase (age 8)—a saving of one year. The years from 4 to 8 are generally believed by specialists in child development to be unusually propitious for sound educational intervention.

The second soft spot, I believe, is in the substantial repetition and slow progression of subject matter in the upper grades of the elementary school and into the junior high years. Studies of child development suggest that the years from age 7 or 8 to 11 or 12 are relatively stable ones. The rapid growth of earlier years has slowed, as has the incidence of disease, and there appear to be available great resources of energy. Puberty is beginning for some girls and a very few boys, but for the most part, the onset is in the next age span. Further, this younger age period appears to be one of marked increase in brain weight.[11] Children appear to be moving into what Piaget called the stage of formal operations by about the age of 11.[12]

It appears reasonable to assume, then, that what is now accomplished in grades four through eight can be as well done in four years—the proposed second phase of schooling (age 8 through 11). We have now picked up the second year. By the age of 12, presumably, the educational accomplishments of boys and girls would compare favorably with those of their 14-year-old counterparts today.

This leaves us with a third phase for the 12 through 15 age group. Why four years of schooling for these four years in the life span? Why, indeed, when today's twelfth grade is a curricular soft-spot, with many able students simply coasting? My reasoning is that these are years of great change and stress for most young people. The onset of puberty, the growth spurt, and the struggle for self-understanding use up energy and create tensions with parents and other adults. It will be recalled from data presented earlier that junior and senior high teachers, somewhat more than elementary teachers, expressed awareness of the need for attention to the personal development of students. Intuitively, they apparently were aware of the personal problems being experienced by these young people.

Consequently, I would not attempt to do more academically in the four years of the third phase than is now done in the ninth through the twelfth grade. These are years in the life cycle characterized by marked spurts and regressions in development. The four-year span of schooling provides time for these to work themselves out, with academic accomplishment dragging for a time but then leaping ahead. With another spurt in brain weight apparently occurring and with the experience of puberty working itself out for most students, there appears to be an excellent opportunity to concentrate on learning during the years immediately preceding graduation.[13]

The Student Flow

I would have children begin on their fourth birthday. I would not quarrel with the practice of admitting together all those who became four during a given month. Although this is a quite common procedure for entry into preschools, some educators reject the proposal on the grounds that it connotes a close connection between age and ability to learn and encourages grade placement according to the former rather than the latter. On the contrary, I believe that this unfortunate interpretation would be minimized, at least in comparison with current practice. We assume a fit between being 6 and being ready for a predetermined first-grade curriculum. We should be asking, "What is the child ready for?"—a question that should guide educating throughout the school years. This question is more likely to be asked at the outset if entry into school and the beginning of a grade or school year do not occur simultaneously. And the significance of these artificialities is likely to fade subsequently.

A second argument for the proposed practice is based on equity. Current admissions policies often result in nearly a year's delay for a child almost but not quite 6. This year represents a sixth of the life span to date. A wait of a year for a child of 4 is a delay of a quarter of the life lived so far. It is difficult to make up the time lost, even for youngsters who take readily to the school environment.

The practice recommended creates the possibility of a warm welcome for the newcomers. They begin school with a birthday party. Then they become givers of parties for those who follow. We should do everything possible to make school a welcomed part of growing up.

The timing and rate of departure would approximate the timing and rate of entry—departure from the first phase at or near the eighth birthday, from the second near the twelfth, and from the third near the sixteenth. I am not completely ruling out some departures at ages younger or older than these norms. Departures from the third phase occurring throughout the year certainly would even out entry into whatever is to follow graduation from school.

Children beginning a primary school would enter, more or less randomly, one of up to three or, at the most, four nongraded, four-year units of not more than 100 children each. For each unit this means the entry and departure every year of 25 children—two or three out and two or three in each month. The tumultuous business of socializing 25 or so beginners each September is completely eliminated. Schooling immediately takes on a highly individualized character. It is a relatively natural, simple matter for teachers to become acquainted with just two or three children and their families at the time of admission. And the children come into a classroom environment already stabilized. Given these potential advantages, one begins to wonder why current practices have survived so long and have been so little questioned.

Given maxima of four units and 100 children per unit, the maximum enrollment of a primary school is 400. Needless to say, with population mobility, there must be degrees of freedom. Pending adjustments, enrollments might run a little higher or lower for periods of time. Schools located in resort areas such as Florida might decide to create a new unit exclusively for winter residents, sparing remaining units the disruption of temporarily swollen enrollments. But the very nature of the proposed system minimizes the problems created for the present one by the arrival of students not evenly spread over grade levels, resulting often in marked variability in class size.

Internal Organization

In keeping with the schools-within-schools concept described in Chapter 9, I recommend that each of the three phases be organized vertically rather than horizontally. Each nongraded unit of 100 children or less would contain the complete age span of the four-year phase. A cluster of teachers would be responsible for the entire group of boys and girls—a few coming and going each month—for the full spread of years. Again we see the possibilities for teachers and children getting to know each other well, for more individualization and intimacy in the learning process, and for peer teaching. This is in contrast to the practice of moving 25 or 30 children through a grade each year and then beginning all over again with a new group.

Following the proposals of Chapter 9, possibilities emerge for creative staffing arrangements. Assume the *equivalent* of four full-time teachers per unit of 100 children. Assume, further, that this roster would include a head teacher and at least one career teacher for each unit. This leaves up to two full-time equivalents for interns, resident teachers, aides, and other part-time personnel. A computerized learning system might take the place of one of these or be added. The lack of differentiated career opportunities in teaching is markedly reduced; the prospects for paid internships and residencies are enhanced.

This arrangement in no way contradicts the recommendation of Chapter 9 that elementary schools be staffed with a balance of specializations represented in the teachers. In a school of three units, it should be possible to include on the full-time faculty at least one teacher for each of the major domains of the curriculum, providing for the availability of specialized persons for the school as a whole. Of course, with the recommendations of Chapter 9 implemented, each of the full-time teachers would be able to teach all of the central academic subjects.

I am assuming giving to schools the responsibility for keeping all students in attendance and for developing programs to this end. This rules out the alternative of preparing some for early departure—by way of job-oriented courses, for example. Consequently, we are now dealing with a continuum of schooling in which, nationwide, enrollment remains almost constant. Children who enter at age 4 depart 12 years later at age 16.

Several alternatives emerge for organizing the continuum and the relationships among phases. One is to have three successive phases of equal enrollment. Since the maximum recommended size of the primary phase is 400 students, the size of each successive phase likewise is restricted to 400. We have seen some possible advantages to small high schools. It would be ideal for all three phases to be housed close together. With a headmaster or headmistress over the three phases and with head teachers for each unit (see Chapter 9), we begin to see the possibilities for carefully monitoring the progress of each student through 12 years of schooling. Just as boys and girls have periods of rapid and slow development on the average, individuals vary from the general patterns and require special adaptations and interventions.

Another alternative is for a single site to house the first two phases—a primary school leading to an elementary school. The graduates of two elementary schools would then go into a single secondary school of from 600 to 800 students.

Both of these alternatives eliminate the current junior high school and the abrupt transition of boys and girls into a departmentalized curriculum. Junior highs often are watered-down senior high schools, ill-adapted to the special needs of the age group. The ninth grade becomes part of the new third phase. The seventh and eighth grades become part of the new second phase—an elementary school, not a high school, characterized more by the values and practices we tend to associate with elementary education.

I would envision elementary schools organized internally similarly to the primary school pattern described. Units, or houses, of 150 or up to 160 students each might be a desirable arrangement for secondary schools. This would facilitate the range of teachers required for the self-sufficiency of each house and the desired more intimate association of the same teachers and students over a period of four years.

As recommended earlier for the primary phase, each unit at the elementary and secondary levels would be nongraded. This removes the cumbersome process of promoting or retaining each student a year and a grade at a time. Students normally spend four years in each unit. Some progress faster and accomplish more than others. Every effort is made to diagnose and remedy the deficiencies of those who progress more slowly. Progress in the more structured subjects such as mathematics is measured in increments of work mastered, not the time spent or topics covered in a grade. Difficult as it is to think in this way, it becomes easier as one aligns each decision of schooling with the basic philosophy. And after all, the learning we do outside of schools—where we spend the bulk of our lives—is not organized by years and grade levels. The criterion of worth becomes possession of the requisite knowledge and skills, not grades completed and marks attained in schools.

A note on the contemporary scene is in order. Cities all across the United States are closing schools because of declining enrollments. Almost the only criterion being used in making these decisions is whether the enrollment of school X or school Y has dropped to the point where many classrooms are going unused and the costs-per-pupil of maintenance, including heating or cooling, are increasing. But what a marvelous opportunity this is to consider rearranging the continua of schooling. Farsighted superintendents and school boards might begin the school structures of tomorrow by enrolling 4- and 5-year-olds in underenrolled elementary school buildings. Other adjustments involving underenrolled junior and senior high schools could then set in motion a process leading ultimately to a completely redesigned continuum embracing students from the age of 4 through the age of 15. During times of both decelerating and accelerating enrollments we are provided with unique opportunities to be creative. What may appear to the reader to be a radical proposal for restructuring schooling I offer as a serious alternative for transforming what we now regard as crises into the genesis of the schools we should and could have.

Programmatic Considerations

The foregoing proposal raises profound questions about what is to be taught and learned during each successive four-year period of schooling. The structure has been made quite specific; substance remains to be discussed.

Actually, the curricular questions to be answered are no different from the ones to be answered for the present structure of schooling. But we have seen in preceding chapters the degree to which the topics of instruction, textbooks, quizzes, grade-levels, and the like interlock. So much is assumed that the basic questions are rarely asked. A new structure focuses attention on them. And the radically different nature of the one proposed makes it difficult to transpose the present curriculum without effecting changes. Things previously locked into place become unlocked.

Specifying the programs of study for each of the three phases of schooling is a task going far beyond the scope of this book and the resources of the author. I provide here only some broad outlines. The specifics are best left to the creativity of teachers who have worked with the age groups involved and specialists in curriculum development. Accompanying research and evaluation should provide the necessary refinements and verifications.

The major function of the primary phase is to move the narcissistic 4-year-old from self-contemplation to a much broader awareness of one's relations to others and the larger environment. Robert Ulich referred to the process as self-transcendence.[14] Socialization into the interpersonal demands and group expectations of school is a necessary part. As less and less energy is required for self-identification in the group setting, more and more energy becomes available for acquiring the tools for expanding one's learning. Recall our data on primary children's perceptions of classroom activity (Chapter 4). They perceived a much larger proportion of classroom time to be devoted to socialization and controlling behavior than did their teachers or our observers. Obviously, the socialization process is important and places demands on their attention.

It is my belief that children's efforts to cope with the physical and social realities of the first grade often interfere with the academic learnings teachers have in mind. But nursery school and kindergarten teachers view social and personal development as goals calling for the use of time and the provision of activities. They are not "under the gun" to have children reading, spelling, and writing within a matter of months. Indeed, these are not goals at all. Rather, the teachers use games, dance, stories, building with blocks, and the like to develop awareness of space, weight, size, symbols, and relationships, which are forerunners of successful reading and mathematical operations.

In the plan I propose, these methods are coordinated to help 4- and 5-year-olds move from individual activity in a group setting to parallel activity and then to collaborative activity. Along the way, the abstractions of symbols and concepts increasingly are added to the concreteness of blocks, toys, and puzzles. There is no sudden entry into "school" as something different at age 6 from what it was at age 4 or 5. One begins to read as a natural progression from using symbols orally, to attaching symbols to objects, to connecting symbols visually. Increasingly, the acquisition of word-attack skills expands the child's ability to read as a form of experience in itself. The effect is that for most children the recognition and interpretation of the phoneme in graphic form is taken in stride. With this facility acquired to the satisfaction of the teachers, the child is ready to move from learning to read to reading to learn and the activities of the next phase of schooling.

A parallel development is to occur in the quantitative, mathematical area. The things which at age 4 are primarily the objects of individual and group attention for play and social development increasingly become the subjects of cognitive manipulation. The teacher encourages habits of counting things and dividing them into groups for purposes of sharing—all done quietly but "out loud." It is common in today's kindergartens to see youngsters performing, at a simple level, all of the fundamental operations of adding to, subtracting from, multiplying, and dividing in order to conduct normal processes of sharing. It is a natural step to connect oral numbers to these operations and then to move to the visual abstractions. Given these early experiences, why are children, later, often introduced to adding, subtracting, multiplying and dividing in a graded sequence, as though these were distinctively separate operations? Why not, with each increase in the size of the numbers introduced, proceed through all four operations simultaneously, as variations on a common theme, which they are? This is the way children encounter mathematical operations in schools of the People's Republic of China, for example. Since our children experience them this way in their early years, why not extend this concrete learning through a similar approach to the more abstract manipulation of symbols? An understanding of the four processes and ability to apply them to whole numbers appears to be a reasonable expectation for the primary phase of schooling, and this is a practical, reasonable approach to meeting it.

It is exceedingly important for there to be a continuous assessment of each child's progress as a thinking, social, reasonably self-assured person. The vertical organization of each unit of 100 children or less who stay together with approximately the same team of teachers over a period of four years facilitates a developmental view of the child and provides the necessary time for assessment, diagnosis, and relatively long-term interventions. The availability of a highly trained head teacher in each unit adds to the likelihood of sound diagnoses and subsequent programmatic adjustments. Much can be done to redesign the program of a 6-year-old appearing to be having difficulties so that progress in all areas is proceeding nicely by the age of 8. The present choppy, graded organization of schools is not conducive to the identification and redirection of developmental deficiencies and irregularities.

All phases have the function of providing maximally over time for each child's development in the goal areas discussed throughout this report. But the balance among goals is not necessarily the same for each phase. Vocational goals, for example, increase in importance beyond the primary phase. Learning the fundamentals of reading, writing, spelling, and quantitative operations is important for young children but must not be allowed to occur at the expense of a child's self-concept. Indeed, these learnings emerge as a natural aspect of development—the child progresses from visiting a landmark to making up stories about it; from telling stories to writing them; from writing his or her own stories to reading stories written by others. Clearly, the assessments of children's progress required for diagnoses and helpful interventions are far more comprehensive than those currently in use, which rarely go beyond tests of knowledge retention. Some pieces of the necessary assessment system are scattered about, but intensive work is required to bring them together and fill in the missing ones. This is appropriate work for the evaluation centers recommended in Chapter 9.

It is important that children come out of the primary phase of schooling into the elementary with a high level of confidence in themselves and a positive view of their ability to learn. They will have been under the watchful eyes of the same teachers, at least one of whom is highly prepared in techniques of diagnosis and remediation, over a four-year period.

They will not have experienced promotion or nonpromotion, since progress is to be continuous and not interrupted by such debilitating practices. So-called social promotion of children results in the accumulation of learning deficits and candidacy for the lowest tracks of secondary schools. Grade repetition rarely achieves its academic purposes while frequently increasing the feelings of self-doubt we found in many students perceiving themselves to be performing badly in schools. Schools must open up the desire to learn, not turn it off. They should not contribute to malfunctioning.

For reasons put forward earlier, children entering the elementary phase should be, as a group, as well prepared as children entering fourth grade in present schools. Like today's fourth-graders, they will vary in their developmental levels. They will have made up, so to speak, the equivalent of a year of academic work, in part because the customary disjunctures between early units of schooling will have been replaced by a single organizational unit. Diagnosis and corrective action should have eliminated a good deal of the malfunctioning that limits or interferes with learning in the upper elementary and junior high years. By now, we hope, the adjustment to peers, adults, and school is a reasonably healthy one, though ongoing, continuous appraisal should identify boys and girls who still are immature in this area and require special help. The physical growth of the earlier years has slowed; manual dexterity is well developed; skills of social interaction are surprisingly mature. The dislocations of puberty are still in the future for most children, especially the boys. There are no good reasons for failing to accomplish in the four years of the proposed elementary school what is now accomplished in five.

Whereas the primary phase emphasized the acquisition of academic, social, and physical skills, the elementary phase emphasizes their use. The relentless monotony of telling, questioning, textbooks, and workbooks which we found to be so characteristic of classes from the fourth grade up must be in part replaced by activities calling for student involvement in planning and in the collaborative execution of plans. A significant part of the day is to be spent in large and small group activities dependent upon cooperative, social behavior. Social goals parallel the academic in importance. All such activities are to be laced with academics—reading an array of books to find the answers to the problem or issue chosen for analysis; writing reports based on the information so acquired; planning and using an effective means of reporting the results to the entire class; preparing evaluation devices for determining the learnings acquired. Ample provision should be made for children to construct physical models—for example, of a port city with its provisions for sanitation, communication, transportation, and functional aesthetics. Children should create their own economies, based on sound economic principles; create their own plays, with due attention to the structure of drama; conduct mock courts, legislative sessions, and world peace organizations. In the process, they read, write, compute, and deal with the problems of people, their environment, and the relationships among them.[15]

These activities accompany more conventional approaches to learning; they do not completely replace them. However, the "new" activities are not supplementary. They are where inquiry begins; more conventional activities grow out of them. Students read to gain knowledge and then bring it to bear on the problems being pursued. This is what we do in "real life." School should not be made "unreal." A major problem of schooling is the degree of unconnectedness it often has with reality beyond school, even while those in it are living out the only lives they know. The resulting incongruity makes much of school meaningless, as was found in the follow-up of Project Talent mentioned in Chapter 7.

A major function of the elementary phase is to develop in boys and girls an awareness of a world of human experience, past and present and both close at hand and afar, most of which cannot be reached through direct participation. One must employ other means if understanding is to be achieved. Specifics of goal attainment rise out of this function so that this awareness becomes pervasive. The tools for reaching out to experience vicariously become essential and are integrated into one's personal development. The primary phase develops the requisite skills; the elementary phase sees to it that they are used in a wide range of activities in and out of classrooms.

It is essential that the elementary phase provide as part of its learning environment some of the activities characterizing the primary phase. There will be 9- and 10-year-olds who are not yet well coordinated physically. In this second phase of schooling, they should have opportunities for daily use of those balancing devices found in good kindergartens and primary classes. There will be children who need eye exercises requisite to the scanning of printed materials. When these activities are not labeled by grade level, there are no negative connotations regarding their natural use with older children who stand to profit from them. Teachers are not bound by graded conventions; they provide for learnings not adequately developed at an earlier time.

The next step in the upward progression is immersion in and acquisition of humankind's disciplined ways of knowing. Whereas students in the elementary phase will have revelled in the fruits of their own and others' inquiry, the secondary phase emphasizes the structures by which knowledge is organized and the processes of acquisition—from hunch and intuition to the posing of the question, problem, or hypothesis and subsequent clarification. The secondary phase is "the one period in the total program of formal schooling in which learners are to be exposed to all the major significant areas of human knowledge."[16] A guiding question becomes: "What *are* the significant areas of human knowledge and how can these be incorporated into a high school curriculum?"[17]

Since I gave considerable attention in Chapter 9 to the general framework for a curriculum balanced among the significant areas of human knowledge, I shall say little more here. It is important to point out, however, that the arts, which tend to be underemphasized, have played a significant role in history as a medium of expression and as a means of understanding human behavior and experience. To omit the arts in the secondary curriculum is to deprive the young of a major part of what is important in their education.

Given our findings, the danger in implementing my earlier recommendations for a balanced curriculum is that the results would be little more than a rearranging of what now exists. This is what frequently happened to Conant's recommendations. The curricular problems to be addressed will not be resolved through such juggling. The major deficiency, sharply revealed in Chapter 7, is that activities of the classroom, combining subject matter and pedagogy, scarcely provide for the learnings implied in our educational goals for schools. Many students successfully go through the motions of rote learning, pass the requisite tests, and move on to more of the same in college. What they have had little of, however, are encounters that connect them with the major ideas and ways of knowing that the fields of knowledge represent. Too often, they were "given" knowledge; they did not acquire it through genuine inquiry. Consequently, many of the activities recommended above for the elementary phase should be carried over into the secondary. More often, however, the activities of the secondary phase should be culminating activities through which students demonstrate their mastery, dexterity, and personal identification with the material of learning and begin to get a sense of style.

"Style is the ultimate morality of mind . . . the exclusive privilege of the expert," said Whitehead.[18] In the hope that students will begin to get a feel for style as he viewed it, I recommended in Chapter 9 that 10% or more of the secondary curriculum be devoted exclusively to the development of an area of interest chosen by the individual. And I recommended the use of vouchers to assure student access to teaching resources outside of schools.

Readers of Chapter 9 may have become uncomfortable with the possibility of crowding in the curriculum resulting from my desire to assure the inclusion both of fields sometimes neglected and of the sixth domain of individual choice. They may have been worried, too, about inadequate depth resulting from too little time for mathematics or foreign languages. I had in mind, of course, the four-year secondary phase proposed. It now becomes possible to provide for substantial involvement in the strategies of the several domains. The secondary phase is to accomplish academically what is now expected for grades nine through twelve. As I said earlier, to try to do more seems inadvisable because of the stresses of growing up that young people from 12 to 16 are experiencing. On the other hand, gone will be much repetition of earlier work in current ninth-grade classes, plus the curricular soft-spot of the twelfth grade. Given also the nature and expectations of the earlier phases and the continuity of the vertically organized units, or houses, of the secondary phase, I see little or no prospect of tomorrow's 16-year-old being any less well prepared academically than is today's 18-year-old. Indeed, I envision a substantially greater percentage attaining a level of general education basic to work, further schooling, citizenship, and personal functioning.

Some Common Elements and Principles

All three phases are to have some characteristics in common. First, they are to be of relatively small size. Although I have set top limits for school size at 800 students for the secondary phase and 400 for each of the lower two, my preference is for 600 and 300, respectively. And I believe that primary phase schools of only 150 boys and girls can be very satisfactory. Recent research summaries raise fundamental questions about the assumed cost and programmatic advantages of increased school size, especially when weighed against disadvantages such as increased anonymity of students and greater impersonality in the student-teacher relationship.[19] We need more studies into an array of correlates of school size.

Each phase is to be organized vertically into units of not more than 100 pupils at primary and elementary levels and 160 at the secondary. But there is no special magic in these figures. The idea is to create the smallest unit that can be maintained over four years with essentially the same core group of students and supporting adults. I can envision a highly effective, satisfying primary school of 180 children divided into three four-year vertical units of 60 students each.

Each unit is to be largely self-contained but to have access to common facilities—library, gymnasia, laboratories, clinics, etc. The head teacher of each unit is to possess advanced preparation in the curricular, instructional, and diagnostic needs of the unit. Head teachers are paid commensurately more than other teachers. They work together with the school principal as a core leadership team. Each unit also has access to consultative help from teachers serving other units in the school.

Approximately one quarter of each unit's total enrollment enters and departs each year, usually at monthly intervals. It is conceivable that a small percentage of students might be accelerated, leaving the unit a few months earlier than the norm, simply because the next phase appeared to more suitably and normally provide for their unusually advanced progress in all areas of development, not just the academic. However, the recommended practice is for individual deviations to be provided for within each phase. Thus it is essential that each unit maintain a continuous appraisal of children's personal, social, physical, and intellectual development. In addition, the phase of which each unit is part has a clearly defined and articulated major function, with subfunctions defined with sufficient clarity to guide appraisal of each child's current development and appropriate readjustment of his or her program. These functions and sub-functions are made clear to the students who are charged with responsibility not only for fulfilling them personally but also for assuring that all others in the unit do likewise.

Consequently, peer-group teaching is a dominant characteristic of all phases and their composite units. The older students help the younger—and, remember, there is a four-year age range among those comprising each unit, providing an excellent opportunity for teachers to use the best role models for assisting younger children. Students teach each other.

Since curricula are planned for the entire four-year continuum and not by grade levels, the spurts and pauses characteristic of growth are allowed to occur naturally and without the penalty of failing a grade because a lag occurred during the concluding months of a school year. Teachers are less likely to get caught up in the relentless process of covering certain topics by Thanksgiving, the end of the fall term, or the spring vacation.

Curricula are to be organized with a limited number of concepts, skills, and attitudes in mind for development. Topics are used to develop these progressively, with every possible pedagogical effort being used to emphasize the more fundamental learning each topic seeks to assist. Teachers have considerable freedom to select topics likely to interest the students, becoming more creative in this with the acquisition of experience. Every possible teaching technique is used to enhance understanding—direct experience, films, discussion, reading, bodily movement, writing stories, role playing, building models, etc. Students' learning is enhanced through interaction with computers. It is better to learn a few concepts well and to know how to apply them than to cover long lists of topics for purposes of recall. The search is for understanding and for the processes basic to acquiring this understanding.

A four-year perspective on fulfilling each phases's functions offers the hope that teachers will be willing to engage in activities requiring a longer time frame with a beginning, a middle, and an end. Head teachers will be called upon to assure students' involvement in all the modes of learning, not just listening, reading texts, and taking quizzes. They must take the lead in revealing and appraising the variety of teaching styles, learning modes, and curricula being experienced so that subsequent revisions provide a broad exposure for each student. Unless such assessment is built in, corrective action is unlikely to occur.

Each successive phase is to provide time for the development of individual interest and talent, in or out of school. A student might pursue excellence in a single area for the entire 12 years or might pursue a new one in each successive phase, while continuing to develop in the area or areas chosen earlier. Increasingly each student becomes a resource to others, vastly increasing the expertise available for instruction.

In preceding chapters, I have stressed the need for assessments of ongoing school curricula, instructional practices, and the like. Preceding pages address again and again the need for continuously appraising student progress in all areas of development. These two kinds of assessment require the identification of relevant criteria, the translation of these criteria into qualitative indices, the development of procedures for gathering information, data collection, and data interpretation. We do not yet have the necessary appraisal systems, although some modest beginnings exist.[20] Developing them is first-order business.

We now have available a significant tool, the microcomputer, to assist us. We are beginning to recognize that this invention must be as much a part of tomorrow's school for students of all ages as the pencil is of today's.[21] And it already is being used in some schools for a variety of managerial tasks, mostly pertaining to the storage and retrieval of demographic information. But the microcomputer becomes indispensable as we begin to think about developing and conveniently using the kind of appraisal systems recommended above. Not just teachers but students as well become users of information designed to assess students' programs and the need for improvement in developmental areas defined for each successive phase of schooling. A microcomputer in each unit, or house, becomes part of the management system needed to make usable the information on which individual diagnosis and sensitive guidance increasingly will depend. The marked acceleration in purchases implies the growing availability of this valuable resource.

TECHNOLOGY

Microcomputers, of course, are a new phenomenon in an area which writers have long been relating to our educational future. For decades they have predicted sweeping changes in the conduct of schooling as a consequence of startling advances in technology and their infusion into schools.[22] But we found little use of calculators, computers, or even the earlier forms of electronic aids such as films, filmstrips, and television. The technological revolution appears to be sweeping around schools, leaving them virtually untouched, even while purchasing microcomputers is becoming the "in" thing for school districts to do.

Now, however, some predictions of change can be made quite confidently, given present trends. Increasingly, school districts will maintain computer-based information systems to provide employees with detailed information to explain the difference between their gross and net wages, to compile information about administrators, teachers, and students, to store test information, and so on. Using desk consoles located in their offices, principals will be able to call up more information about the student body than they know how to use. At a slower rate of increase, two-way systems will provide face-to-face communication between district superintendents and the principals in the schools. And there will be more settings like Irvine, California, where teachers-to-be in the University of California employ two-way video to observe and raise questions about classroom practices in the nearby schools. For children and youths to become functionally literate in their understanding and use of computers will be recognized as a necessity, not a frill. The far-sighted philanthropy of the International Paper Company Foundation, for example, in funding the purchase of microcomputers for schools will be replaced by the purchase of computers as a normal part of expenditures for public schools. These and more uses of technological advances will occur until they become virtually standard practice. But the role to be played in the instructional process remains ill-defined. Technology increasingly will provide educational delivery systems, however, whether inside or outside of schools.

Visions of such developments have led to excessive rhetoric regarding the replacement of teachers and even schools by machines. What often has been lost in the rhetoric is the astonishing emergence of sophisticated, mobile, and easily used communication devices as shapers of our purchasing habits, banks of information, what we believe, and how we think. The radio and audio cassette do a great deal of this shaping, during the night through plugs in the ears of near-sleeping listeners, through the earphones of joggers, and in the small machines people of all ages carry everywhere. Television adds the visual to the auditory, providing another dimension to learning while leaving less to our imagination. For some of us, it is not just an opiate but verification of what exists and matters, of being here.

Yet when I talk to others about the educative role of television, one person in two thinks I am talking about what the letters E.T.V. once conveyed—that is, the use of television to teach and enrich the formal curriculum of educational institutions, as if only then does television teach. Television teaches all the time, even while it informs or entertains. What it inadvertently or deliberately teaches and how it influences our perceptions, habits, and orientation to learning increasingly are subjects of study. But most of the questions to which we need answers await attention. Some of these can be best answered by setting up procedures for studying the evolution and impact of television in countries that have had little of it.

As for this society, television may be, as I have already suggested, the nearest thing we have to a common school. But in pondering the fare offered and the sums of money invested in providing it, one easily becomes despondent. Free competition among the major networks has not provided much to enlighten the mind or free the human spirit. If television as now offered is becoming the new common school, we would be well advised to reinvigorate the old one.

This brings us to another deficiency in the curriculum of schooling. The classroom programs and materials we examined provided few signs of a school aware of television in the lives of its students. Schools are supposed to develop and refine tools of critical analysis. Once upon a time in our society, the family meal provided a forum for discussing dominant events, changing mores, and what was good or bad about them. Our goals for schools imply such a role for them today. In Chapter 7, I commented on the relative absence in schools of activities calling for inquiry likely to enhance students' insight into the world around them. Apparently, teachers have not received a strong message to provide for such learning. It appears to me that the development of critical abilities applied directly to newspapers, advertising, and all forms of television is as much the responsibility of today's schools as is the teaching of computer literacy. It need not be done by the regular teaching staff. The instructional resources are available in most communities.

Returning to the formal educative role of television, the dominant view of those who grew up in and dominate the industry is that the basic role of the medium is to inform and entertain, not to educate.[23] An alternative view is represented by many promoting cablevision, with its emerging promise of diversity and choice of programs. The possibilities for educating, whether in or out of schools, loom large in the thinking of leaders in this burgeoning field. Unfortunately, these educational possibilities have not been uppermost in the minds of educators. School districts, colleges, and universities so far have been conspicuously absent from the lists of applicants for available channels. The advent of cablevision is affecting and will affect schools, but the pace of use is likely to correspond to the snail-like pace of past school acceptance of technology in educational processes. Cablevision is more likely to mature as an informing, entertaining, and educating medium in its own right, side by side with tomorrow's schools.

The central point to be made is that the advent of technology has added to the array of educating agencies and institutions, rearranging what once was a triad of home, church, and school. Just how the products of technology have added to and taken away from the educational role of the traditional institutions is not yet clear. But we do know that any serious consideration of education beyond schools must encompass the educating being done and capable of being done by the new media of communication.

CAREER EDUCATION AND THE WORLD OF WORK

In his preface to a recent yearbook of the National Society for the Study of Education, Harry Silberman wrote the following:

> The separation of youth from adults is a product of the decline of the family and the separation of school and work. It is becoming increasingly apparent that the educational development of youth cannot succeed solely through the efforts of the schools. Learning must be enhanced through exposure of young people to a variety of opportunities to test themselves in the community and the workplace alongside supportive adults.[24]

I agree. Schools alone are neither sufficiently powerful to guide young people through the turbulent adolescent years nor sufficiently cosmopolitan to effectively link the worlds of school and work. Schools have a way of infusing everything they take on with the principles they employ in teaching and evaluating students' progress in English and mathematics. Although things are somewhat different in subjects such as the arts, physical education, and vocational education, these subjects too carry the baggage of the more academic subjects—often to the point of squeezing out the vitality these more hands-on fields appear to offer the young.

This impression grew and stayed with me in my visits to schools. For the most part, I was not impressed with the "shop" or hairdressing classes, for example. The leisurely pace, the clowning of students, the distance between ongoing activity and a customer to be satisfied, the absence of need to get out of each student enough work to justify wages, and the use of textbook-based quizzes as a measure of quality and a means of control appeared to separate the whole from the real world of work. I wondered if students were learning the very things likely to be detrimental to productivity. And I wondered how many alternative vocations were being opened up to these students. The fact that poor and minority students were disproportionately represented in vocational *training* classes did not escape my attention—an observation later supported by our data.[25]

In general, too, I was depressed by many of the jobs for which training was being provided and by the equipment available. Much of what I observed appeared anachronistic—training for the mechanical age recently jumped over by the technological. This is not surprising. Even though helped by federal monies, schools simply do not have the funds to keep up with advances in technology in even a few fields.

There is need for a much clearer delineation of what schools should and should not do, can and cannot do, in the vocational/career area. I argued earlier for vocational and career education for all students, regardless of their goals and scholastic attainments, and provided for this domain a place in the curriculum. And I have said that schools should get out of the business of providing sequences of courses directed toward training for specific jobs. They should assure a measure of technological literacy—especially in computers—and awareness of how economies function, some understanding of economic principles such as cost effectiveness, and a broad exposure to careers and work. The learnings involved constitute general education and, with those acquired in the other curricular domains, are the best preparation for productive, satisfying work.

From the early years on, schools should and can play a useful role in the development of a mature perspective on careers, career choice, and bases of career decision making.[26] As much as possible, career awareness should be provided in contexts through which individuals can envision themselves involved in the work and test the nature of their identification with it. Recent research suggests that simply being involved in a part-time job does not necessarily provide for all of the learning benefits frequently claimed to be associated with work experiences.[27] But preliminary evaluations suggest there is promise in experience-based career education involving close collaboration between secondary schools and the community.[28] Some 20,000 students in 150 communities, it appears, are variously involved in programs designated as experience-based and designed both to apply academic learnings to the workaday world and to teach students how to make informed career decisions.

Current efforts to use the workplace to provide direct experience with jobs and careers are part of a long evolutionary process based on desire to help students link school and work. The central thrust has focused on students not likely to enter colleges and on the more visible careers in the community, many of them requiring only short preparation programs. But today's young people know little of what goes on behind the smooth, shiny walls of buildings housing individuals engaged in work not easily imagined, let alone described, simply by observing these apparently inaccessible fortresses. Many know little or nothing about the careers and work of their fathers and mothers. Schools do little to help them comprehend. But those in the offices planning other buildings, negotiating advertising contracts, writing insurance policies, creating television scripts, and studying economic trends could help a great deal. Among other things, they could provide role models in addition to those of athletes and good-looking people showing up in our data.

What is called for, then, is a collaboration of school and elements of the workplace in assuring a broad career perspective for every student. This would occur primarily in the vocational/career domain of the curriculum and would replace training in and for specific jobs. Visits would be accompanied by extensive reading, writing, and discussion. Industrial, business, and professional representatives would participate in and out of classrooms. After careful examination, students would select sites for internship-type experiences in a limited number of vocations. School districts already experimenting with such approaches report the expected problems with logistics but usually note both readiness to participate on the part of adults and worthwhile learnings for students. Clearly, a high level of volunteerism is called for and this is what we must have if the community as a whole is to do what schools cannot do alone.

How much of this career education should be provided as part of general education in the third phase of schooling? I already have provided limits to the curricular domains in Chapter 9. Experience-based career education must come out of the vocational/career component. Since I had in mind that many of the instructional activities would be designed to provide *all* students with hands-on experiences with wood, metal, film, computers, and the like, there is limited time for what I have suggested above. Perhaps more extensive educative encounters with the world of work would be appropriate for a fourth phase, beyond the secondary school. To this possibility I turn in the next section.

In Chapter 6, I discussed the growing difficulties of providing a general education program to students of low-income families as they move upward into the senior high school years, citing the data on the three Rosemont schools. Parents appeared to appreciate the academic program; students expressed considerable satisfaction; the senior high teachers expressed rather high levels of frustration. As the students grew older, the need to become financially productive increased, as did the pressure to provide school-based vocational training. One secondary program, in particular, caught my attention. Some students not performing well previously in the junior high and planning to drop out at age 16 reported to me their excitement with the experience-based career program. They spent a substantial part of their time in a job and related community activities, supervised by school personnel, in school-based discussions of their experiences, and in academic classes scheduled specifically for them. But, as is so often the case, the program was available only to students diagnosed as potential drop-outs and not to all of these.

It seems to me that problems such as the above and the programs they sometimes spawn for a few students arise out of schools' concern about the two-year span of time between the school-leaving age of 16 and the school-graduating age of 18. Anxious not to dump out on the streets adolescents lacking employable skills, schools often begin vocational training early to assist in the 16-year-olds' transition to work or to keep them until graduation. There is a certain internal logic to all of this that is used to justify and sustain the practices. But there also are consequences of grave importance to individuals and our society. I discussed some of them earlier and will not repeat them here.

My recommendation, presented earlier, is to synchronize the leaving and graduating age so that they occur simultaneously at age 16, to provide 12 years of general education for all through three phases of schooling, and to provide for all some limited and carefully planned career education, as outlined, within this curriculum. The educational tasks allocated the schools in this redesigned continuum and with this younger student body appear to be reasonably focused and in line with what schools do best. The charge is to do them better, with a deeper understanding of what education is and a keener awareness of current discrepancies between current and desired school functioning.

A FOURTH PHASE IN THE CONTINUUM?

I have argued seriously for beginning and ending earlier what is now elementary and secondary schooling and for cutting two years from the combined length of preschool and precollegiate education. There remain the challenging tasks of clarifying alternatives for the 16-year-old graduates.

My recommendations have implied little regarding what might be done with the years beyond. One answer is "nothing." Some 16-year-olds would seek jobs—and they would carry with them high school graduation certificates, which few do today. Some would go to community colleges, some to four-year colleges and universities. The age of the undergraduate student population would drop, as would the age of entering professional and graduate schools—at a time when the length of professional preparation continues to increase. The resulting earlier entry into occupations and professions would increase the average person's earning years and provide a longer period of payment into social security, helping to bail out this sinking benefit of retirement.

It appears that my recommendations have some merit even if no other adjustments are made. But innovations rarely succeed when there are no facilitating adaptations in the surrounding context, and these will certainly be needed here and will not be easy. My recommendations will not be taken seriously, for example, by parents who perceive the prospect of their "children" being dumped unceremoniously into the workplace. Some adaptations must be made to win their support. On the other hand, one can readily conjure up the opposition likely to come from groups reluctant to make these and other necessary adaptations—labor unions, the sponsors and promoters of interscholastic and professional athletics, and segments of the higher education establishment, for example. Most important, unless the environments into which these young people go, the workplace and others, are more cognizant of their needs and more nurturing than are those now receiving 18-year-olds, the transitions for many will be abrasive to the point of permanent, personal damage. Surely we can do better.

Others have explored some of the possibilities for the 16-to-20 age group but almost invariably within the assumption of secondary school ending for most at 18. Arthur Cohen and Florence Brawer have analyzed thoughtfully the possibilities of the community college, an institution still seeking a definitive place in the formal hierarchy of institutions—not from the perspective of enrolling younger students but from the relevant perspective of the multiple roles this institution can and does play. Their chapter on career, compensatory, and community education is particularly relevant to the preceding discussion.[29] Willard Wirtz and his associates have provided us with a useful analysis of dilemmas and possibilities regarding the education and employment of young adults in their late teens and early twenties.[30] And Fred Hechinger, in an essay on the high school-college connection, describes the disjointed parts of American education that, in fact, fail to connect.[31] Periodically, over the years, thoughtful persons have proposed combinations of work, study, and service for youths and young adults.

I favor what would be essentially a fourth phase in the education/schooling continuum. It would be a combination of work, study, and service conducted within an educational ethos. Community colleges might well serve as home base, but they would be members of a partnership involving government, business and industry, human service agencies such as health and social welfare, and other kinds of educational institutions. The program would be heavily experiential in its orientation, with the more academic aspects arising out of guided experiences rather than the other way around. Individual and group counseling would constitute a major part of the program.

Built into the whole would be a concept of adult "volunteerism" far beyond what currently prevails. I have placed the word "volunteerism" in quotation marks because I have something more in mind. Although each of us would volunteer his or her area of contribution, the service expected of us would be comparable to jury duty on a continuing basis. We would be assigned interns, aides, or advisees in line with some predetermination of our competence to serve as a role model, mentor, or supervisor, just as individuals are accepted or rejected for specific jury duty. Many of us might find ourselves seeking new competencies or shedding off dubious habits in order to qualify for what would become regarded as one of our most significant obligations as citizens—the education of youth.

One of the objections voiced in the past to proposals of this kind is that they would interfere with or interrupt some part of the formal educational system. But with two years cut out of the precollegiate system and the tertiary system left in place, we have opened up two years between the proposed new third, or secondary, phase of schooling and the present structure of higher education. The recommended fourth phase might simply be slipped in between and fill those two years.

However, there are other alternatives. For example, there might be a single postsecondary year combining service, experience-based career education, work, and study for all. Then youths clearly committed to attending a four-year college or university would do so. Others would continue in the community college setting, combining various combinations of the first year as described above, preparing for vocations, or continuing in a balance of work and study. A major function of this fourth phase, whether of one or two years for all, is to ease the education-work transition, on one hand, and to strengthen the work-study-service combination as a desirable lifetime condition, on the other.

For those going on to higher education after a fourth phase of only one year, a reduction in the normal college years to three instead of four, as has been seriously considered by the Carnegie Commission on Higher Education, would make sense.[32] They would be prepared to enter graduate or professional schools at the age of 20. Faculties of the restructured three-year college would have a magnificent opportunity to rethink general education without the intrusion of specialized, professional preparation, all of which would become graduate. There is no doubt in my mind that a careful study of the present four-year undergraduate curriculum would reveal most of the corruptions we found in secondary schools. Those in institutions of higher education who are so critical of the lower schools would be well advised to look inward first.

It is not my intent to lay out here a detailed plan for the years beyond the recommended new continuum of primary, elementary, and secondary schooling. What I have proposed for these three phases goes a long way, I think, toward both providing a solid base of general education for work or further studies and eliminating much of the sorting and selecting of individuals and groups to which schools have contributed. Further, I believe that the system of schooling likely to emerge would be more free than is the case today from the special interests of professionalism—whether in academics, athletics, and health sciences, or engineering—and of business and industry. We would have a rare opportunity to plan the curriculum of each phase by deciding what is most desirable and feasible to learn at the successive stages of human development.

The years beyond provide a similar opportunity. It will not be grasped successfully, however, if the necessary inquiry takes place in segmented fashion, within each of the currently separated segments of secondary and tertiary education and divorced from the rest of the continuum. Success will depend on bold collaborations among old and new institutions—on the creation of healthy educational ecologies.[33] To this prospect I now turn.

TOWARD EDUCATIVE COMMUNITIES

The Greek word *paideia* does not translate easily into English. Whatever the definition, however, it evokes generative thoughts regarding the interplay between the development of mature, enlightened individuals and maximum cultural development. The community optimally educates. This educating is not merely instrumental to the attainment of goals. It is itself a good.

Visions of utopian societies educating through *paidea* have intrigued philosophers and educators throughout history. One characteristic of such societies is that education is part of the fabric, interweaving with politics, religion, economics, and family life. Education is no more confined exclusively to schools than is religion confined to churches, mosques, and synagogues. How can we move our own schools and our own society as a whole toward such educational conditions?

Some of the schools in our sample struggled against greater odds than others, such as larger size, less family capability to support their children's learning, poorer equipment and more limited supplies, less sensitive and supporting central administration, greater competition from outside forces such as the need for their students to become wage earners, and so on. Some struggled with problems of integrating markedly different groups of students. All were faced to some degree with problems of drugs, alcohol, and indifferent or recalcitrant students. And although we did not specifically study the problem, we know that the schools in our sample were affected variously by declining ability of their traditional allies, home and church, to mold the attitudes and behavior of the young. The school is not and cannot be an institution apart. Nor is it, nor can it be, the exclusive provider in a community's educational system.

There are essentially two major ways of viewing the school's role in this educational system. The first view is of a school extending its educational services beyond the customary hours and days, the age groups commonly enrolled, and the subjects traditionally taught. The school becomes a center for community education, recreation, and education-related human services. The second view is of a school more sharply delineating its own role and joining other agencies not only in clarifying their discrete functions but also in promoting collaboration. The school may be the only institution charged exclusively with the educational function, but the ability and responsibility of others to educate is recognized and cultivated. There is not one agency, but an ecology of institutions educating—school, home, places of worship, television, press, museums, libraries, businesses, factories, and more.

In the United States, the best known effort, probably, to pioneer and develop the school's broadened commitment to the community began during the 1930s in Flint, Michigan. Frank Manley used the schools as recreation centers to attack problems of juvenile delinquency. The concept moved from a program of recreation for children and youths to activities for all community members, over and above the regular school program.[34] Supported by the Mott Foundation, the Flint approach attracted and joined with similar interests to become a national movement. In 1972, the school board set two goals for the community's schools: "to help every citizen of Flint become the best person he is capable of becoming, and to help every neighborhood become the best community possible."[35]

These goals neatly state the essence of an ideal form of the community school. They do not necessarily negate or deny the concept of other institutions besides the school performing an educational function. The school, to the degree possible, deliberately extends its influence beyond the students officially enrolled for regular programs.

The second view necessarily encompasses both the reality and the potentiality of other institutions' educating. It neither denies nor specifies a broader community role for schools. Different kinds of institutions which educate or might educate exist in various relationships to each other. That is, an educational ecosystem exists. It may be in good, fair, or poor health. The first step toward healthier functioning is to bring the existence of this ecosystem to a level of consciousness. The second is to seek the best possible understanding of its nature. The third is to formulate policies, develop plans, and execute these plans for purposes of increasing the effectiveness of the ecosystem.

My purpose here is to raise the level of consciousness regarding this ecological view of each community's educational system. The implications are many. Should there be, for example, a commissioner of education and culture in at least the larger cities who chairs a council made up of key representatives of agencies whose educational role is most obvious? The superintendent of schools would be a member of this council but not necessarily the commissioner. The qualities and qualifications required of the commissioner do not necessarily coincide with those required of the superintendent of schools. Preparation for the post of school superintendent, while perhaps useful, would be neither required nor necessary.

The agenda for such a body would include attention to the need for parent education and where this might best be done; how to increase child-care opportunities for working families; how to improve the transition of children from home to school; what incentives to use in seeking experience-based vocational education for secondary school students; how to identify and legitimate agencies capable of assisting in developing individual talents; how to develop increased awareness of and accountability for the educational role performed by the media; how to bring optimal availability and quality of cablevision to home and schools; and a host of topics pertaining to relationships and collaborations. This local agenda suggests state and federal agendas for policy development. An incentive for business and corporate entities to expand their educational commitment might be, for example, tax rebates.

Communities vary widely in size, resources, cohesion, and other characteristics. Some have no schools; students are bused to a neighboring community or to a site having no single community identification. At the other extreme, sections of large cities exist as small enclaves with virtually every type of institution and agency within walking distance of all residents. Clearly, the components and therefore the nature of different educational ecosystems vary enormously. The most appropriate function to be performed by each component will differ from community to community. No single set of policies, guidelines, or practices will suffice.

It becomes quite reasonable, then, to envision appropriately different forms of schools resulting from deliberate decision making and subsequent utilization of school facilities for an array of purposes. All schools would perform the common educational functions and offer the core programs defined for them earlier. But, depending on the availability of additional educational resources, students would secure the talent development portion of their education at the school in one community but in a dozen or more places in another. Some schools would have no gymnasia or lunchrooms because appropriate facilities would be available close by; some would make such facilities within the school available to the entire community. Some schools would offer no education or other services beyond those of their commonly assumed responsibility to an age group; some would operate 24 hours daily, with three shifts of employees offering an array of educational activities for the entire community.

But at the heart of all schools would be the balanced educational programs I have described. The ecological perspective, properly understood and implemented, assures that schools will not take on functions or tasks likely to corrupt the general education they appropriately provide. Schools have muddied their proper roles to the point of obliterating them by taking on many things appearing to be good. Vocational *training is* necessary and desirable for most communities, but I have argued that schools should not do it. The superintendents and principals of schools in our sample allowing the vocational education program to consume 40% or more of the teaching force should be upbraided, not commended. Had they worked with business leaders to assure the availability of the training portion elsewhere (or even after regular school hours in the building), they might have produced a more balanced curriculum. Whether or not driver education produces better drivers is not the question to ask or answer in seeking to justify driver education in school programs. The proper question is whether it should be offered as part of the general education of all students during regular school hours. What will it displace? English? Mathematics? If we put the "should" question to this hard test, there is little likelihood of the answer to it being "yes." We ask schools to take on things better done elsewhere, if at all, because we are not accustomed to asking what knowledge is of most worth, are unaware that all decisions involve trade-offs and costs, or have not considered other alternatives. One of the most serious costs of schools doing things simply because they appear to be good or virtuous is the weakening of other institutions. Had we spent more time and resources strengthening the educative function of families instead of transposing more of it to schools, our society might be better off and our schools might be more effective and appreciated.

Although the elements of the community ecosystem often function apart and therefore dysfunctionally, each is affected by the others, for better or for worse. Indeed, one usually is so dependent on another that its room for change and innovation is sharply restricted. The total system may be uncoordinated, but drastic or often even modest changes in a part can and do disrupt the whole.

Few of the changes for schools I have proposed in Chapters 9 and 10—especially the latter—can occur without awareness and participation from the whole. There must be at least a partial conceptualization of the interconnected nature of things and some beginning steps toward the necessary collaborations. Cooperative functioning of agencies and institutions so far has proved to be difficult, in part because we have not recognized the urgency of the need and in part because as yet we have only a glimmer of the potential. And the necessary federal, state, and local policies are not yet on the books.

The idea of the educative community is chimeric, intriguing us and then dancing away. It has been with us for a long time. But it may be an idea whose time is come.

Collaborations

Increasingly, the concept of an ecology of educating institutions is being written about and discussed at national conferences.[36] Thought regarding the role of media has now gone beyond educational television, for example, to include television as it comes into our homes purportedly only to inform and entertain but simultaneously to educate implicitly. Hope Leichter has reminded us effectively that families, not just schools, educate—as they did before schools were available.[37] Networks in the arts all across this country educate in their own right as well as help the schools to educate in and through the arts. New configurations of educating institutions are being consciously formed.

Local, state, and national policies will be required to assist in the necessary, difficult collaborations. They are unlikely to create the educative communities of tomorrow full-blown. They can be useful for legitimating functions, creating incentives, and clearing roadblocks. Policies will help beginnings become a movement. The beginnings are likely to arise out of the felt needs of just one institution or of two institutions sharing some problems and turf in common—perhaps even disputing their interests in that turf. Some of us may have to give up some of the turf we cherish in seeking to create the future and not let it just happen.

During the decade of the 1970s—a decade dismally devoid of educational ideas—I became increasingly depressed over the noneducational agendas of educational leaders. Preoccupied with crises, they were forced to delegate or push aside central matters of curriculum development and school improvement. Worse, some school board members and superintendents forgot what is essential to their mission. Some appeared to enjoy jousting with heads of unions and special interest groups, even as they complained about it.

After addressing this phenomenon at several conferences and writing about it, I decided to initiate some action.[38] I wrote a letter to approximately twenty school superintendents and community college presidents located within a reasonably short drive of UCLA. Included among the superintendents were those in charge of the offices of public education serving school districts and community colleges in the four counties involved.

The letter repeated my theme of undue preoccupation of administrators with collective bargaining, desegregation, declining enrollments, vandalism, and the like, to the neglect of the centrally educational issues. I used preliminary findings from A Study of Schooling, then being sorted out by my colleagues and me, to suggest an agenda for improving education in schools. I went on to suggest some communitywide issues having educational implications which I believed neither they as educators nor the schools and colleges over which they presided could resolve alone. I sketched the possibilities of a collaboration involving their institutions, the newly created Laboratory in School and Community Education of the UCLA Graduate School of Education, and some educative and potentially educative agencies of the kinds listed earlier. It was not to be an end in itself. Rather, the collaborative entity envisioned was to become a vehicle for the reconstruction of schools and the educational system.

Not knowing how these other agencies might be quickly reached, fearing that too large and elaborate an undertaking would not get off the ground, and with only one associate able to free a little time to assist me, I chose to bring together only the superintendents, presidents, and a few colleagues. Aware of the common reluctance to give up turf, I tried to describe what I had in mind, approaching somewhat gingerly the concept of institutions in addition to schools constituting an embryonic collaborative network for the conduct of education in each community. I put forward three broad purposes: (1) to improve the quality and general effectiveness of existing institutions; (2) to develop an understanding of education as a communitywide rather than only a school-based activity; and (3) to develop new configurations of educational institutions including both the traditional ones and those of the media, business and industry, and cultural agencies. I had in mind that within such configurations we might join to create, for example, the redesigned continuum of schooling recommended in this chapter.

Today, the three broad purposes put forth then guide the activities of the organizational entity that evolved. Named *The Partnership*, this as yet unincorporated invention is characterized by both a structure and a set of emerging concepts which will shape its future. One of these is that accomplishing anything significant takes time. We refer to a ten-year commitment, a period stretching beyond the work years remaining for some of us. Another is personal responsibility and accountability. Each superintendent and president serves with me on *The Partnership's* Council; we may not delegate this leadership responsibility.

A third concept is that each of us on the Council is to take the lead in his or her own geographic area to fulfill the three purposes. None of us, individually or collectively, can do the work of another. We can encourage, share and review ideas, exchange resources through the network, and join forces, but the superintendent or president is in the best position to take the lead in mobilizing the resources of a community for educational renewal. Ultimately there may be a commissioner of education and culture chairing the local council of agencies, and the superintendent or president may or may not become that commissioner. As of now, however, most people tend to think of schools when they think of education and to expect the top school official to lead, for better or worse.

This is not the place to elaborate guiding concepts pertaining to the role of *The Partnership* in seeking and infusing new ideas; in selecting and shaping projects; regarding the research and development role of the university; in guiding the change process; and so on. Work below the level of Council members is under way—with school principals in some districts and with school and community groups in others; developing a rather different approach to teacher education, in collaboration with UCLA, in several; reexamining the secondary school program in others. It is generally anticipated that the findings and recommendations emerging from A Study of Schooling will add specificity to the agendas now being formulated. A good deal of stimulation stems from the Council, but a basic premise is that change will bubble up.

The Charles Stewart Mott Foundation has provided a grant for developing the Laboratory in School and Community Education at UCLA which includes in its provisions assistance in forwarding the work of *The Partnership*. But little of this money goes to direct support of a project. Rather, the grant makes it possible to bring to the Council awareness of changes in society having implications for education; to explore alternatives for the reconstruction of schools; to gather data regarding the nature of a problem; to collate research findings on an anticipated project area— to fill in where resources are needed but not readily available among members of *The Partnership*. It is anticipated that, soon, member institutions will contribute funds to retain a secretariat and that the collaboration as an entity will seek funds to supplement those of its members for the support of projects.

The major problem with an enterprise of this kind is the time required to accomplish something significant and, therefore, difficult. The proposals set forth on preceding pages provide an agenda for the balance of this century. *The Partnership* is not in itself a project, although it will generate many projects. The effort to stimulate thinking running counter to the familiar and comfortable dominates the early stages, as it should. We are not installing new ways of doing things; we are seeking at this stage to develop the capability to do old tasks more effectively, as well as to take on tasks only dimly envisioned. There are as yet no products to admire, no behavioral objectives to check off. It is not easy to convince philanthropic agencies to support self-renewing capability in our institutions and long-term reconstruction, rather than the customary production of "deliverables."

But *The Partnership* model provides part of the framework needed if we are to have any hope of evolving through improving the schools we have to creating the schools and systems of education we need. And although we are just beginning with our work, the idea of *The Partnership* is capturing the imagination of others. My only full-time colleague and I must express regrets in all but a few cases to those like-minded individuals and groups interested in creating similar enterprises in other parts of the country. The interest is sufficient to stimulate my thinking regarding the prospects of a network of such partnerships, each a tub on its own bottom but linked with the others, pursuing common goals—improving the schools we have, designing alternative versions based on some views held in common, and working toward educative communities. There is a yearning, apparently, to break out of this depression of the spirit and of creativity that has held us in its grip for too long.

Needed is a critical mass large enough to make a visible difference—a really sizable network of partnerships, if you will. Each partnership must be small enough to be conceptually and logistically manageable and large enough to include the essential components of the community arena—but no more. The network to which the partnerships belong must be a binding, communicating one sharing a reasonably common agenda. And there must be resources not normally available to the basic component parts.

To go beyond schools and seek educative communities and the educative society is a mind-boggling concept for many people. Some educators will embrace the concept as a kind of opiate to help them escape the problems of the present. As a people, we are not accustomed to delayed gratification; the setting of long-term goals and beginning to work toward them is frustrating. Nonetheless, creating the future begins with transforming the present.

If each of us begins with his or her part of the envisioned ecosystem—the piece we understand best and can control most easily—we may be able to shape the necessary evolution. To continue with the myth that schools alone can provide the education we need is to assure their continued insularity and probably their ultimate irrelevance. This need not be the scenario we follow.

CODA

Those of you who commenced to read on page one and continued have come with me a long way. We began with a query as to the effectiveness of schools. The data and arguments brought together to answer this question presented a divided picture.

On one hand, schooling for all at the elementary level has been extended to schooling for most through the secondary level. Instruction in reading, writing, spelling, and arithmetic has been expanded to include introduction to social studies, science, the arts, and vocations. There is justification for the self-congratulatory rhetoric at commencement exercises extolling the role of schools in developing a land so often equated with liberty, justice, and opportunity for all.

But as the image of a boundless future began to cloud over in recent decades, the image of the schools also became less clear. Their history was rewritten to show how they assured the provision of workers for the mines, railroads, and factories owned by those whose children began with a head start and profited most from the schools. Also, though the road from rags to riches was there, those who found their way to it most readily were white.

The judicial branch of government intervened to advance what the Constitution promises to uphold. People are not to be denied the benefits of schools because of color, race, or religion. The ideal still escapes us in practice, but the principle is clear and the attendance of many more black children and youths at integrated schools, their graduation, and their movement into the mainstream is a considerable accomplishment. Open the case book of our Native American and Mexican-American citizens and the gap between the ideal and reality widens again.

The recurring criticism of schools, however—whoever their clients—is that they do not adequately fulfill their primary function of educating. Here too the picture is a divided one. It is charged that schools neglect the basics and have abandoned traditional ways of teaching, but the data presented readers of preceding chapters suggest quite the opposite. Mathematics and the language arts dominate in the elementary schools we studied and are well represented in the curricula of the secondary schools. And the traditional procedures of telling, questioning, reading textbooks, performing workbook exercises, and taking quizzes were infrequently interrupted by so-called progressive methods of teaching and learning. If a predominance of rote learning, memorization, and paper-and-pencil activity is what people have in mind in getting the schools back to the basics, they probably should rest assured that this is where most classrooms are and always have been.

The data through which we have found our way attest to broader expectations for education, however, and presumably for schools. The goals emerging with this country's development, espoused by the states and endorsed by large percentages of parents, teachers, and students in our sample, imply not only curricular breadth but also pedagogy going far beyond that commonly demonstrated in the classrooms we studied.

The agenda suggested by the data presented will not be carried out by a little tinkering. Curricula and pedagogy appear not to reflect adequately the expectations implied in our goals for schools. There are inequities both among schools and within schools regarding students' opportunities to gain access to knowledge. There is much to be done in humanizing knowledge through curriculum development and creative teaching so that more and more students will make it their own. These are not new challenges. We have addressed them before; we will do so again. We have not concentrated sufficiently on this part of the agenda during recent years.

Unfortunately, current interest in curricular and instructional improvement does not appear to reflect either improved insight into what is wrong or remedies appropriately addressed to shortcomings. Tougher requirements for admission to universities will add certain courses to secondary schools but will not necessarily stimulate thought and action regarding what constitutes general education for all. The separation of pedagogical methods from curricular substance in both preservice and inservice programs for teachers is not likely to correct a prime curricular weakness we found in our data—namely, the organization and presentation of topics not clearly connected to the concepts, ideas, and modes of thought constituting major domains of knowledge. There are few signs that the joining of faculties in colleges of education and colleges of liberal arts necessary for remedying this weakness is likely to occur.

We have seen that the pedagogical variability and creativity required to engage the young in challenging encounters with knowledge tended to decline with upward progression through the schools of our sample. Paralleling this decline were the academic self-concepts of many students.

We saw that, simultaneously, peer-group interests and values having little to do with academic learning were becoming increasingly compelling. There seems to be an upside-down quality in schooling, with those procedures most likely to engage students in learning decreasing at the time their development increasingly is distracting them from school demands and expectations. The result is a disjuncture between what powerfully preoccupies adolescents and what secondary school teachers perceive their job to be.

We have to a large extent assumed that whatever is wrong with the schools will be corrected by shoring up eroded curricula and improving the skills of teachers. Also, we have assumed that teacher shortage is a waxing and waning condition which shifts somewhat predictably with changes in the economy and population growth. These assumptions are dangerous. Teachers find themselves confronting problems for which they are ill-prepared. Many in our sample see the need for schools to pay more attention to the personal educational problems and needs of students while the surrounding pressure often is for a more strictly academic or vocational orientation. The staff development activities in which they engage appear not to address problems perceived to interfere with their teaching role. Teachers are widely reported to be frustrated, burned out, uncertain as to what is expected of them, and suffering from low morale.

Salaries rose slowly during a period of increasing inflation. Increases are based more on seniority and course credits than merit. One cannot look ahead to a good salary as an incentive for continuing in the classroom. There is little to attract young people into teaching beyond a passion to teach—and the word is out that there is little encouragement for zeal. Teaching as a career has not been powerfully attractive to men for some time; it no longer is one of just a few options for women. Many of those persons coming into teaching today appear to be less well prepared intellectually and academically than their counterparts of an earlier time. And yet the demands of providing quality education are such that we need in every school at least a few teachers who are well prepared and highly gifted.

I have argued that there is very little hope of assuring the presence of such individuals in schools unless the "flatness" of the teaching profession is corrected. Several ways were suggested. All include differentiated salaries based upon differentiated roles calling for differing levels of preparation and based not at all on seniority. The organized teaching profession has fought such provisions for decades and has argued for a "qualified" teacher in every classroom and advancement through a salary schedule geared to years of service and course credits. The time has come for teacher preparing institutions and selected school districts to join in breaking out of this paralyzing mode. Chapter 9 took us into some of the possibilities.

The agenda for restructuring the schools we have is a demanding one. At its heart is the need for data of a contextual sort to guide the determination of priorities by planning groups of responsible parties at the school site level. Guidelines for local initiative in the curricular area must come from the state and from school districts. Opening up new career paths for teachers and creating new staffing patterns require policies not now on the books. There are many obstacles to be overcome in securing the appropriate participation of universities. For example, professors in research-based schools of education must learn to transcend the problems and paradigms of the academic disciplines if their work is to enlighten educational policy and practice. Some of the needed curriculum development, pedagogical experimentation, and evaluative inquiry requires the creation of new centers and institutes.

Were we to go in the opposite direction and close all public schools tomorrow, a bewildering array of substitutes would pick up the tasks of teaching children to read, write, and spell. Companies in the education business—especially those with electronic hardware and the software to go with it—would experience the bonanza many have dreamed about. It would be some time before any of these would make for millions of children and youths "the deliberate, systematic, and sustained effort to transmit or evoke knowledge, attitudes, values, skills, and sensibilities" some of us believe education to be and to require.[39] Would they ever? I very much doubt it. And it is equally doubtful that any of these companies would provide the benign, inexpensive baby sitting apparently required by active, working parents in our complex society. Indeed, I am sure that to meet these two needs—the day-to-day practical one and the idealistic but finally equally practical one—it would be necessary to recreate schools.

And besides, there is a more sensible alternative to closing the schools we have, an alternative likely to clarify what schools should and can do and simultaneously enhance the educating we need now more than ever before. I have dealt with it in this chapter. This alternative begins to emerge from considering that there are several institutions and agencies whose role always has been in part to educate and others that do so implicitly or secondarily while explicitly serving other goals. Radio and television are paramount among these, powerfully influencing our beliefs and habits. The computer vastly enhances the versatility of these and other educative and potentially educative devices. We have, in effect, not just an educational system of schools and school districts, but one made up of many different institutions and agencies. The possibilities of developing this system and managing it intelligently for the education of young and old alike are challenging. Community education becomes not just schools opening up their facilities and extending their resources, but an ecosystem of institutions and agencies conscious of their responsibility for developing the knowledge, values, skills, and habits of a free people.

Readers who left us in earlier chapters may have been discouraged over the gap between their conceptions of what education is and what many of the schools studied appeared to provide. I hope that those who continued began to see with me the possibilities for reconstructing schools, if we approach the challenge as most nations, including our own, have approached wars, for example—with the expectation of winning. Despite the formidable difficulties, I remain optimistic, perhaps because there is to me a contradiction in being simultaneously pessimistic and an educator. Whatever our individual experiences with a place called school, to think seriously about education conjures up intriguing possibilities both for schooling and a way of life as yet scarcely tried. And, indeed, education is as yet something more envisioned than practiced.

Afterword

The quarter century that began with the orbits of the Soviet Union's Sputnik I and II in fall 1957 and ended with the publication of *A Nation at Risk* in spring 1983 profoundly changed the role and status of the system of public schooling in the United States. It had little comparable impact on what Ted Sizer referred to in the Foreword of this book as the *grammar* of schools—the detailed ways and means of providing deliberate education.[1]

The nexus of public attention had been the loosely connected network of schools symbolized by the one nearby that young people attended—the *place* called school. But suddenly, in the alarm of a "foreign" satellite circling the earth a few miles overhead—with the poor dog Laika aboard Sputnik II—those schools rhetorically became the crucible for the science and mathematics necessary to the nation's continued, but now threatened, technological global superiority. Rightly, there was no accompanying rhetorical praise for the schools' assumed role when the U.S. space vehicle *Friendship 7*—with human being John Glenn aboard—orbited planet earth just five years later.

Absent the palpable image of potential space wars, the National Commission on Excellence in Education nonetheless managed to create in verbal technicolor the picture of a school system asleep, as though in the grip of a virus injected by a hostile country. The nation's assumed leadership in the global economy and its accompanying well-being were at risk.

When this dark cloud passed into memory in the 1990s, there were again, rightly, neither national nor local celebrations of a remarkable awakening of the schooling enterprise since our schools had neither caused our economic problems nor removed them. Yet the lack of supporting evidence for schooling's turbocharging our competitiveness in the infrastructure of the global economic and technological marketplace did not lessen the writing of scripts for such a role. The god of economic utility continued to provide the guiding narrative.[2]

The inflated expectations for schooling that characterized the late 1950s into the 1960s had tarnished in subtle ways the aura of romanticism kindled especially by the immigrants, now adults, who had been largely socialized by schooling into the American democracy. By the end of the 1960s, there was rapidly growing public realization that our system of schooling was an inadequate tool for achieving the goals former President Lyndon B. Johnson had put forward in his Great Society agenda: overcoming problems of illiteracy, unemployment, crime and violence, urban decay, and even war among nations.

Although these heady aims for schooling were little proposed or talked about during the 1970s into the early 1980s, citizens generally and parents particularly did not lose their affection for the school the local children attended. It was the place that gave particularization to the young. The neighbors' child was and still is referred to as a "third-grader" or "of junior-high age." And, of course, school had "created" childhood in Western civilization in the sixteenth and seventeenth centuries and had gradually extended it ever since. Today, school shapes the daily habits of most families with children and youths and the calendars of millions of the rest of us. The beginning and ending of each school year are extensively covered by the media. And few of us can resist the opportunity to talk nostalgically about schools we once attended.

The Elementary and Secondary Education Act (ESEA) of 1965 created an array of educational research and development centers and laboratories, some of which still exist. But the more local innovative work supported by Title III faded in the 1970s, as did many of the initiatives initially funded by private philanthropy. Money available for educational innovation lessened as money for evaluating existing improvement efforts increased. Accountability for results, especially as measured by assessment of academic achievement, increasingly became a requirement for continued project funding. The fingers of federal policy reached more and more into state and local district conduct of the schooling enterprise. Local dialogue over school affairs declined as educational debate, such as it was, increased in the legislative and executive chambers of state and federal governments.

For nearly a decade, beginning in the second half of the 1960s and continuing into the first half of the 1970s, colleagues and I were deeply involved with a collection of schools scattered across southern California that were committed to change and innovation. This consortium of 18 schools in 18 districts, known as the League of Cooperating Schools, provided a laboratory for the Research Division (which I headed) of the education arm of the Kettering Foundation—the Institute for Development of Educational Activities (|I|D|E|A|).

In the mid-1970s, we published the story of this work, particularly our research on the perplexing problems of effecting change in the deep structure of schooling, in a half-dozen books published by McGraw-Hill Book Company. We were, I think, only a little surprised by their disappointing sales. The enthusiasm for changing the conduct of schooling generated by the Elementary and Secondary Education Act had faded. Why read books on the subject? No winds were roughing the waters in which, deep down, were longstanding, little-addressed, fundamental problems of schooling. It was time to go fishing below the deceptively calm surface of the nation's system of schooling.

The ESEA did more than provide funds for educational research and development centers and local islands of innovation. It stimulated school districts to reach out for ideas—especially innovation that broke with well-established regularities of schooling. By the mid-1960s, the laboratory school at UCLA (which I directed) was well along with innovations such as nongrading, team teaching, and a variety of changes addressed to greater individualization of classroom learning. In the wake of the ESEA, busloads of teachers came to observe.

In conversations with visitors from all across the country, colleagues and I became acutely aware that most confessed that there was no infrastructure in their home schools for implementing things they had observed and liked. It would be difficult, most said, even to engage their colleagues in conversations that might lead to decisions and then collective action. There was neither time nor support for such in the context of schooling. More than occasional short meetings at the ends of highly demanding days of teaching would be required.

These were not the only teachers confronting this dilemma. There was at the time an ethos of ideas for change and interest in them. New ways of doing school and classroom business beckoned, but eluded clear focus. The implementation process was daunting; parents needed to be brought along. But there was and still is little to nothing in the abbreviated preparation programs of teachers and principals to help. And there was little then, and there is little still, to assist them in the in-service educational programs of most school districts. "Keeping school," not "changing school," is the systemic expectation. As Ted Sizer observed in the Foreword of this book, most people did not want a *new* day of schooling. They wanted a new dawn to an old day.

The literature of school change is now replete with studies and retrospective analyses of that rather heady era of unrequited educational promise and expectation.[3] Colleagues and I, stirred by the conversations with teachers and principals visiting our laboratory school, conducted our own probe. Thanks to the Fund for the Advancement of Education of the Ford Foundation, we had sufficient funds to support visits to a total of 260 classrooms, some selected randomly from across the country, some because of their high minority populations, and some because they had been identified as supposedly innovative. From other work, we had concluded that both the grammar of schooling and the cognitive processes of learning are well established early on, and so we decided to look deeply into practices in the first four years of school. Drawing from the extensive literature on childhood learning, we drew up a list of pedagogical principles and the practices we might reasonably expect to find ongoing in the classrooms we would visit.[4]

Three general conclusions, supported by enormous consistency in the data, predicted a large chunk of what other colleagues and I found later in the much more comprehensive study of the full length of elementary and secondary schooling reported in this book:

> Most of the schools visited were oriented to some generally accepted concept of what school is (a school is a school is a school) and not to an ongoing inquiry into either group or individual learning needs of specific children in particular communities. There was, in fact, a notable absence of total staff or small group dialogue about education in general or school plans and prospects. . . .
>
> . . . it would appear that neither pre-service nor in-service teacher education programs have provided them [teachers] with the precise pedagogical understandings and skills required for diagnosing and remedying the learning programs and needs of individual pupils. . . .
>
> . . . teachers are very much alone in their work. It is not just a matter of being alone, *all* alone with children in a classroom cell, although this is a significant part of their aloneness. Rather, it is the feeling—and in large measure the actuality—of not being supported by someone who knows about their work, is sympathetic to it, wants to help and, indeed, does help.[5]

These and more were precisely the kinds of generalizations we were drawing from our parallel experiences with the League of Cooperating Schools. And it was the problems these conditions appeared to generate and support that constituted the agendas of our collaborative work with the principals and teachers of the 18 schools. Recently, I had an opportunity to view, once again, the documentary film developed as this relationship progressed. One of the most moving testimonials to the value of this support came from a veteran teacher: "We knew that the |I|D|E|A| staff was there to help us and you did. You visited us; we called on you; we knew that you cared. This is the kind of support I needed and never had throughout my career."

It was to the infusion of promising ideas for change, some new and some old, and support in their implementation that the entire |I|D|E|A| organization was committed. It attempted to do so through a nationwide program named Individually Guided Education (IGE). For our part in the Research Division, we saw the necessity of having a detailed map of the existing schooling territory: mission, pedagogy, subject matter, instructional materials, provision for student diversity, assumptions regarding the learning process, characteristics and competencies of teachers, standards of conduct, assessment of student learning, relationships with parents, and more—in effect, the entire enterprise.

We could find no precedent for such a comprehensive, costly, time-consuming undertaking. Nor did we find in our search any comparable coming together around a common educational research purpose the array of philanthropic foundations that eventually joined the Kettering Foundation in providing the financial support. Nor had I up to then—nor have I since—lost so many hours of sleep over not having in hand or promised the many thousands of dollars needed for a new fiscal year about to begin.

During the years since the study was completed and reported on in preceding pages and elsewhere, I have spent many more hours pondering the question of why the findings and conclusions—neither refuted nor challenged beyond a few queries regarding presentation of some of the data—appear to have had so little impact on changing practices in the places called school. As Sizer observes in the Foreword, the patterns chronicled are still sweepingly familiar: "There is a sad, almost eerie relevance to the detailed specifics. . . ." Modest impact was not, I believe, due to lack of commendation, media and policymaker attention, or readers. Teachers and teacher educators tell me that the book has influenced their work. Twenty years out, it still sells and is quite often cited. This reissue will help to keep the book alive, but is not likely to produce the new dawning of an old day, let alone a new one.

In the pages that follow, I shall endeavor to do two things. The first is to revisit briefly some of the findings and conclusions that call out most clearly for a new day. These are not artifacts unique to A Study of Schooling. Sufficient attention has been addressed to many of them in studies and commission reports of the past to get them on the agendas, but not among the accomplishments, of school reform initiatives. That these have not been the accomplishments of reform is largely because of repeated, rather mindless, reliance on a narrow, linear input-output model of change. The complex mix of human interactions and contextual circumstances is such that ecological models embracing an array of factors—some negative, some positive—are necessary to effecting school change. The necessary processes are more like bringing a healthy garden along than watering a plant or eliminating a patch of weeds. Then, after taking inventory of some critical elements in this ecology, I address the troubling, daunting challenge of the renewal I believe necessary to a new day in and for our schools.

During the intervening years, much has been added to the source materials that guided the writing of *A Place Called School*. Only a year after its publication, for example, colleagues and I were planning a comprehensive, nationwide study of the education of educators.[6] Also, we were drawing from our past experiences with the League of Cooperating Schools and the study of change accompanying them in creating a network of school-university partnerships seeking the simultaneous renewal of schooling and teacher education—the National Network for Educational Renewal (NNER), which, today, is alive and well and cautiously growing.[7]

Out of both initiatives, built on concepts and principles from the earlier work, we created an agenda of mission, necessary conditions, and strategies of change for schooling and the education of educators in America—the Agenda for Education in a Democracy.[8] It guides the work of the NNER and is increasingly attracting the attention of other educational organizations, groups, and individuals who believe, with us, that we currently are headed down a path for schooling that is not readying the young in the breadth and depth of dispositions and attributes necessary for productive, satisfying lives in our transforming world—a path that puts our social and political democracy at risk.

I endeavor to recount the odyssey that brought me to the observations, conclusions, and recommendations of *A Place Called School* in a companion volume to its reissue. Entitled *Romances with Schools: A Life of Education*, it documents the thesis that the major problems and issues that accompanied the hardening into place of the deep structure of schooling early in the twentieth century are essentially the problems and issues confronting us in the twenty-first. The oft-repeated recommendations for "reform" have been very much the same and have largely ignored the accumulating body of knowledge regarding human development and cognition and its implications for learning, teaching, and the overall conduct of schooling.[9] As a result, the school we have—whether public or private—is growing more and more out of sync with both the young people it seeks to educate and their context.

What we repeatedly ask or tell this school to do is very much like what it already does. Our images of change are implanted with our memories of the past. The rhetoric calls for changes; the expectation is that these will be familiar. But if the process is continuous renewal, there will be no sudden dawning of an unfamiliar-looking new day. The new will simply replace the old as day follows night.

Again, as noted in Ted Sizer's analysis, *A Nation at Risk* was, indeed, a thunderclap. It was Sputnik III. Having been invited to address the commission as one of the so-called experts to be consulted, I had been kept aware of its progress. I began to fear that its publication before that of *A Place Called School* would so overshadow the latter as to make it almost invisible. My manuscript was still going through the editorial process when, in April 1983, the thunder reverberated from coast to coast. I had not anticipated that the consequences would be quite the reverse of what I had feared.

The media were hungry for more. But not for chapter after chapter of hard data. They wanted horror stories, or close to them, to support the thesis that the nation was in dire trouble because of schools remiss in their educating role. The education editor of the *New York Times*, Edward (Ted) Fiske, wanted something deeper, especially if it supported or added to the commission's recommendations. He kept checking with publishers regarding relevant publications in progress. He discovered mine when it was in page proofs and secured a copy of the whole. Time to its release date was short; he was on the phone daily, sometimes more than once, questioning me regarding page after page. He advised a more attention-getting opening and suggested the following: "American schools are in trouble. In fact, the problems of schooling are of such crippling proportions that many schools may not survive."

It was the only change or addition I made, and it was made reluctantly. But I was impressed by his argument. His review gained the front page. And, of course, it went out to and was reprinted in part or whole in the 800 or so newspapers that draw upon the *Times* for material. UCLA (from which I was on leave at the time) and our home telephone were swamped with calls. Most were from journalists whose primary terrain of reporting was other than schooling. I became acutely aware of how difficult it is to give very short answers to questions that innocently involved complex issues. I am sure the reporters were as frustrated as I was.

And I quickly learned that had *A Place Called School* preceded *A Nation at Risk*, it would not have come to Ted Fiske's attention and that of hundreds of other reporters. I cannot recall an event that so turned public attention to our system of schooling than did the commission's thunderclap. That so little substantive change occurred as a result of it undoubtedly was a disappointment to its members. It is a disappointment that I share, and to which I add mine over the limited impact to date of *A Place Called School* on the deep structure of schooling.

This is not to say that the reports were ignored. Both have been frequently cited.[10] There followed, however, no mobilization of human and material resources to create the dawn of a new day, or even the new dawn of an old one. This suggests that there is far more awry than our schools. Rather, there is something fundamentally amiss in the quick-fix, piecemeal, goal-inflated, and largely mandated approach that has characterized the school reform apparatus for decades. Nowhere else in the conduct of our affairs have we learned so little about so much. Ironically, the subject is education. Yes, our schools are in need of change, but there will be little more than tinkering and islands of innovation until we abandon some of our fundamental educational assumptions and the ways we try to effect renewal.

I turn to this matter later, but first let's revisit some of the findings, conclusions, and recommendations that precede it. If you read some time ago the original issue that ended with Chapter 10, I urge you to reread the concluding two chapters because I shall not repeat here the findings that led to the recommendations I made there.

The study that undergirds *A Place Called School* involved the collection of buckets of data from each school in a representative sample during a specific period of time. By contrast, the companion volume accompanying its reissue, *Romances with Schools*, reviews aspects of schooling and its context over more than seven decades. It is somewhat akin to an album and a diary in which a family's history was documented over the years. Writing an account of my own experiences and observations over these decades has provided insights I did not yet have in the early 1980s. What follows has been significantly influenced by this longitudinal perspective and my intensive relationships with the school-university partnerships of the National Network for Educational Renewal since the mid-1980s.

I am convinced that, were we to conduct the Study of Schooling today, the findings, conclusions, and recommendations would be much as they were before. There are several domains, however, where the need for change, for the end of various policies and practices, and for addressing omissions is more apparent and urgent. Heading this list are the mission of schooling and teacher education, the overall structure of schooling and its organizational straightjacket, the antiquated curriculum and teaching practices, severe inequality of educational opportunity, the custodial ethos of schooling, and parent-community relationships. In subsequent analyses, I blend some of these with other characteristics of schooling described in preceding chapters.

There is a profound paradox in this nation's orientation to the mission of its schools. We blame them for not doing what we should not ask them to do, impose upon them expectations best directed elsewhere, and fail to provide the resources necessary to performing well what most of us agree they should and can do. We give little thought to the most significant guidelines for determining the purpose of schooling: It should do educationally what the rest of society does not do or does not do well. By this criterion, instilling information should not be its primary function. And yet, given the fact that the progress of students and the success of schools are increasingly judged by tests primarily of information possession, we appear to be going down precisely the wrong road.

We do not even talk much about school mission beyond the platitudes of commencement speakers and, recently, self-proclaimed "education" politicians. School administrators interviewed in our Study of Schooling did not think there is much public agreement on what our schools are for. In our later Study of the Education of Educators, students nearing the end of their preparation programs could not remember much about discussing in their classes purposes beyond developing in the young basic literacy and intellectual skills. They thought that the idea of schools' preparing the young for responsible citizenship was interesting, but getting ready to manage classrooms dominated their thoughts. We found nothing about this broader public mission in the catalogs of institutions of higher education. Where else in our society but to schools and colleges might we look for assurance that our children and youths are being educated in democratic character?

Ernest Boyer and I, in our respective books published a few months apart in 1983 and 1984, reported from somewhat different analyses that there is high agreement among parents on wanting their children to gain more from school attendance than reading, writing, and arithmetic. They want and expect attention to personal, social, vocational, and academic development. Indeed, they agreed with their children and their teachers that the perceived high academic emphases might well be reduced a bit to give more to the personal and social.

In the United States of America, we are loosely but significantly bound together by a moral ecology grounded in concepts of freedom, equality, and justice for all. This ecology is best described and communicated as a social and political democracy. The public school has been a major part of the fabric holding it together. Our schools have played a major role in socializing immigrants into the American democracy from all segments of the world's people. In recent years, we have come more and more to assume that this encompassing moral ecology is secure, that it will take care of us. But it actually is frayed and—in highly visible places too long ignored—torn.

The time has long since come for us to make caring for our democracy the guiding mission of our schools. Instead of narrowing the primary responsibility of the educational workforce to raising test scores, we should be charging it with advancing this noble mission. There is at long last a growing restlessness among educators regarding the robotlike programming and minimalizing of their role in contexts growing ever more complex. They have been near silent too long. Many of the best, depressed to the point of leaving teaching or administration, become energized over the thought of being charged with providing in their schools a publicly supported apprenticeship in democracy. If we are to have good schools, we need such teachers. If we are to have a robust, renewing democracy, we need such schools.

This proposal is not new. Indeed, the history of the so-called common school is replete with references to its role in enculturating immigrants into the American democracy. And, yes, it did seek to provide the fundamentals necessary to functioning in the social and vocational marketplace in a less complex environment. But, beyond these, the apprenticeship in democracy has been more ritualistic than substantive. And it is difficult still today to muster a convincing argument that the conduct of schooling is democratic, in spite of the pious rhetoric that "it's all for the children."

Unfortunately, a somewhat cultlike advocacy of teaching democracy in the schools became a movement that coincided with, and was partly blamed for, a steady decline during the first half of the twentieth century in the proportion of the high school curriculum devoted to the traditional core subjects: English literature and composition, science, and mathematics. And history and geography were increasingly lost to "social studies."

This is not the place to delve into the accompanying controversy. The point to be made here is that productive, satisfying engagement in our democracy and the transforming world of which it is a part requires comprehensive education in the systems of knowledge and learning that undergird and guide such engagement. The challenge to the conduct of this education is to connect it to the world beyond schools where these systems are not mere replications of the curriculum within them.

This curriculum has been described by an insightful teacher as a nine-teenth-century artifact embedded in a twenty-first-century block of concrete. It is a rather intellectually impoverished inheritance from the scholarly disciplines that constitute the curriculum of the undergraduate college. When I was the director of the Center for Teacher Education at the University of Chicago years ago, I learned to my surprise that some of the professors teaching graduate courses in these fields wished that their students had received no previous instruction in them. "There would be less to undo," they said.

Even more to my surprise, I learned that attention to the structure of the discipline—that is, the elements that organize and structure the field to which new knowledge is added—is primarily a matter for doctoral seminars.[11] Is it little wonder, then, that elementary school teachers with only a smattering of academic background in the six or seven subjects they teach, derived from their high school and college studies, are ill prepared for the pedagogical challenge of their daily work? Or that the undergraduate majors of secondary school teachers rarely prepare them to excite students, even if they are teaching in those fields? Nonetheless, today's politically correct position is that the bachelor's degree with a major in an academic subject is sufficient preparation for teachers at both levels of schooling.

These circumstances should provide us with sufficient reasons for effecting major renewal in the curricula and pedagogy of both schooling and teacher education. But I add another reason for emphasis. A great deal has been learned about human cognition in the last two or three decades—and shamefully ignored in the education enterprise. Studies are increasingly showing a weak connection between school-based learning and its use in the arenas of daily living for which one would assume it to be relevant.

Ironically, high academic test scores do not predict greater use of what is tested; they only predict with considerable confidence continued high test scores. The correlation between these test scores and the personal and social attributes most parents expect schools to develop in the young is, not surprisingly, even lower than that between scores in such subjects as mathematics and science and students' ability to apply mathematical and scientific principles and concepts to problems outside of schools for which these are relevant. Equating high test scores with high-quality schools or well-educated human beings is an oxymoron—and one with dire consequences for this nation.

We do not need a massive body of behavioral science research to convince us that the frozen structure of schooling is out of sync with many of the developmental characteristics of today's students and their lives beyond schools. For one thing, it begins too late in childhood and lasts too long, extending adolescence into early adulthood. Those inquirers from the media attacked most my recommendation that public schools be available to all by the age of 4 and end at 16, the money saved by the years subtracted being used to enrich the education provided in the early years.

Many 4-year-old children of the affluent now attend so-called preschools; few of the economically poor do. This egregious inequity leaves millions of children behind educationally before they even begin to attend school. Most of these are in impoverished families that lack the educating skills and resources available to millions of children able to be in settings of intentional education. There is currently debate in high places about whether Head Start should be taken away from them. An argument for this is that there is insufficient evidence that Head Start contributes significantly to later academic performance in school. Is there evidence that the preschools of the affluent add significantly to the contribution of the home environment to school performance?

The Agenda for Education in a Democracy screams out for correcting what is so obviously morally wrong. Equality of educational opportunity means *for all*. We could make an enormous contribution to equity very quickly and easily by simply dropping the arcane practice of setting a date in late summer by which each child must be five years old in order to gain kindergarten admission. Those born a little late must wait another year. Children whose parents can afford the fee go to private preschools; those of the poor simply wait another year. So much for equity and justice!

In Chapter 10, I recommended not only providing (not requiring) schooling for all at age 4, but also welcoming each newcomer into attendance during the month of his or her birthday. Are our school policies so stuck in a deep pit of glue that they remain frozen in the past even in regard to a practice easy to change that would contribute so much to leaving no child behind?

The initiatives now directed to redesigning the upper years of the existing high school testify to malfunctioning structure: dual credit in the secondary school and community college for courses usually taught in the latter, advanced placement, rethinking the senior year because many students complete most of their graduation requirements in the junior year, and more. Why not just get rid of these dangling upper years instead of trying to fix them? It will take an inordinate amount of fixing to develop in a school structure meant for children and youths a culture appropriate for the education of young adults now attending high school.

The 17- and 18-year-olds enrolled in our secondary schools are busily trying to shed their adolescent skins and take on those they would like to have as adults. Why are we setting them up to be role models for enculturating their younger schoolmates into an ethos they would be pleased to leave behind? There are promising models of adult education available for our consideration; developing alternatives is not an overwhelming challenge, once we get our minds beyond longstanding befuddlements of policy and practice.

Beginning school during the month of their birthdays would bring young children into a stable classroom environment instead of the rather tumultuous one common to current practice. The first couple of weeks of the year often are unnecessarily stressful for both teachers and children—and frequently parents as well. Under the proposed plan, newcomers would be socialized into an already-functioning culture within a few days. And the teacher would have time to assess and establish a close relationship with the several newcomers instead of an entire new class. Each child would experience a welcoming and then become one of the welcomers.

Of major significance is that the myth of age-graded placement and progress fades away. Using academic achievement as the measuring stick, there is no such thing as a first-, fifth-, or tenth-grade class. One would need hundreds of 9-year-olds to select from in order to have a class of the same age at so-called grade level in all subjects. And math, science, and reading are not packaged by grade level either, at least not until we input them into school classrooms. For teachers to identify themselves and conduct their teaching as stewards of the fifth or any other grade is to move to the periphery most of the class. The egg-carton, graded structure of schooling we connect with the place called school is simply an adult convenience for classifying, tracking, assessing, advancing, and retarding the millions of students who move through it. It serves no sound educational purpose and should be left behind as an artifact of the school we had.

Increasingly, we are learning that educational attention to the personal, social, vocational, and academic purposes of schooling is enhanced when schools are small. In Chapter 8, I reported greatest parent, student, and teacher satisfaction in the smallest schools of our sample; greatest dissatisfaction in the largest. Now we are getting evidence that development in these domains is enhanced and alienation reduced when schools are divided into small, largely self-contained units.

, I recommend today smaller sizes than I proposed two decades ago. Each of the three distinctive four-year units—primary, middle, and senior in a continuum—would be capped at approximately 400 students. This appears to be about the point that any economic and curricular advantages of increased size begins to run out. These units would share the same site and some facilities. Having begun the first unit at different times, students would move smoothly from primary to middle to senior at different times.

A rich program of after-school activities also would be shared, with students of more advanced artistic, literary, athletic, and other attributes frequently serving as mentors. If the perceived loss of competitive team sports is the rub, let's just move them to the community where they once commonly were. Since school sports often continue undisrupted even during teacher strikes, they already appear to have a semi-independent status not yet matching that of the higher education version.

Teachers of teachers have told me over the years that they have carried on lively discussions in their classes regarding the proposals of foregoing chapters, particularly the concluding chapter entitled "Beyond the Schools We Have." But it appears that these sessions have provided a theater of the unlikely or impossible—a kind of fantasy departure from the schooling that prevails. There are now some encouraging stirrings of philanthropic interest in breaking through the encasing block of concrete, however. The Bill & Melinda Gates Foundation, in particular, sometimes in collaboration with other foundations, is cutting into it, especially in promoting small schools. Meanwhile, unfortunately, federal and state policy appears to be advancing a reform agenda that strengthens the concrete. Nonetheless, growing awareness of the need for a new day nourishes hope.

Hope for a renaissance in our system of public schooling, tied to confidence in the nation's future following World War II, reached a high level in the mid-1960s. President Johnson's Great Society program scripted a key role for the schools. The Vietnam War, the discouraging message of the Coleman Report regarding the schools' inability to overcome in students' learning the limited human capital in impoverished home environments, urban decay, the struggle for racial equality, and other issues sharply depleted the light of hope. The 1983 report, *A Nation at Risk*, rekindled it for a time.

The report contributed to shifting public perception of the nexus of power and responsibility for school improvement. President Reagan, who had entered office with the intention of eliminating the new Department of Education and whose interests in schooling were nowhere addressed in the report, was persuaded that education was high in the priorities of people nationwide. He should be cheerleader for state and local action. Most governors held education summits. I recall commiserating with Ted Sizer over coast-to-coast engagements in these as we wearily came together for one in California. We commented on the lack of new resources to support the crusade educators were expected to launch.

Lamar Alexander, coming on board as secretary of education during the administration of the first President Bush, called for cities to sign up for the education train trip toward "America 2000." Sometimes, the superintendents of schools were peripheral to the occasions. Precisely where the train was to go and what was to be discussed or done on board presumably were to be decided once under way.

There was much talk at state conferences of "systemic" reform, of having large city districts in particular choose which among various embryonic models of school innovation they might seek to scale up. A critic coined the metaphor of providing parachute drops to waiting schools. There was a growing ethos in policy circles of local schools eager for such. This expectation denied the research of Seymour Sarason and others regarding the receptivity of school culture to the penetration of proposed changes either not asked for or brought in without negotiation.

There was, however, a groundswell of interest among schools scattered across the country in joining networks of other schools for purposes of sharing progress in appealing innovative initiatives: the Coalition of Essential Schools founded and headed by Ted Sizer, James Comer's School Development Program, Carl Glickman's League of Professional Schools, the Galef Institute's Different Ways of Knowing, Henry Levin's Accelerated Schools Project, our own National Network for Educational Renewal joining schools and universities, and more. The ideas of a corps of intellectual leaders gained the attention of practitioners. Financial support came largely from philanthropic foundations.

This somewhat heady surge of the 1990s was neither an answer to the political-corporate call for school reform nor the product of a belated response of the federal government to implementation of the recommendations of *A Nation at Risk*. These sources of power had something quite different in mind: the development of criteria and measures for holding schoolteachers and administrators accountable for student performance.

In June 1999, the Institute for Educational Inquiry, located in Seattle, hosted in a nearby city, Bellevue, a national conference entitled "In Praise of Education." It assembled in one place representatives of 21 initiatives that met the Institute's criteria, their leaders, and an array of other key figures in the groundswell referred to above.[12] The place of meeting bubbled with excitement as participants shared their ongoing work and listened to panelists and plenary session speakers. For weeks afterward, callers to the Institute inquired into dates and other details regarding the next conference. It was not to be.

The small staff of the Institute was exhausted from putting the conference together. The fund-raising entailed for the conference was itself sufficient reason for keeping at a distance any thoughts about mounting a repetition. But, even if such had been planned for five years out, it would have been a shadow of the original. We hear little today of some of the initiatives assembled. Several are gone; most are struggling. Finding money for travel and living expenses would have been far more difficult. And the presentations and conversations would have been very different, much like conversations that take place today at conferences of schoolteachers and administrators: How do we hang on to what we and most parents believe we should be doing educationally for our students? Our school days are filled with readying for and taking tests. Yes, we believe in standards; yes, we believe in improving students' academic performance. But this should not mean endangering the breadth and depth of the curriculum and the joy in teaching and learning. How and when will we regain what we are losing? There is an enormous disconnect between politically driven school reform and educator-driven school renewal.

This downside of school reform eras may be more detrimental to the well-being of schooling than their repeated failure. Such eras, hailed rhetorically as the answer to things gone wrong and people performing badly, add to the public perception of a system malfunctioning. Teachers' belief in what they are doing is shaken. But there is rarely a script for the new grammar needed or support for effecting reform. The more intrusive the mandates, the more teachers are set adrift from their ideological and operational moorings.

They seek to get back to these moorings, once a reform movement has run its course, before they are ready to consider other ways. This does not happen overnight; usually, it takes years. Then they open up to ideas such as Howard Gardner's on several modes of intelligence.[13] These do not discredit their present ecologies of educational belief. They kindle revisiting, adding to, and perhaps modifying them.

This is the learning, renewing experience that so enriches life's journey. It characterizes the kind of groundswell of interest in innovation and change referred to above. What a shame it is that it commonly takes five or more years of recovering lost ground before the renewing cycle begins once more.

A powerful message comes through, a message that virtually every serious student of educational change has tried to deliver, with very little result. Schools and the intentional educating they carry on are sufficiently different from other enterprises in the nation's infrastructure and, indeed, from one another that there is no all-encompassing script for the guidance of their conduct. When this loose network of cottage industries is viewed as a system of interlocking parts and given a blood transfusion, the results are often comparable to injecting every patient who comes in off the streets with type AB blood. Help must begin with careful assessment of present institutional circumstances, characteristics, and need.

There is much talk of schools' and educators' resistance to change. Schools have been invaded over the past several decades by so many alien substances that their stewards have become cautious about giving entry even to potential friends. What is wrong with the system is not something that might have been imposed by an unfriendly foreign power. It is largely the result of trying to make tangible a system that exists only as an abstraction for linguistic convenience and policy determination in remote halls of power.

I have written in this book that our schools must be improved one by one. This belief has been enormously strengthened by my observation of and experience with policy and practice since these words were written.

This places a considerable burden on educators and the local context of their work and responsibility. We would be well advised to view parents, teachers, and students as an extended family and their school as a part-time home joined with other families and homes in a common democratic educational mission. It is the responsibility of state and federal government to monitor and assist in the conduct of this mission.

Colleagues and I have endeavored to provide a map of the conduct of this mission and an agenda for its advancement.[14] In Chapter 8 of this book, I have summarized conditions that appear to correlate with the good health of individual schools as evidenced by high satisfaction of parents, teachers, and students. These conditions correlate also, I believe, with the health of our democracy. This method of inquiry is very much like that of Robert Putnam and his colleagues, who studied over a considerable period of years the correlation of government and local social and civic engagement of the citizens in the northern and southern regions of Italy.[15] The northern sector has enjoyed for a long time both more citizen-participant governance and more civic engagement of the populace at the local level.

What obviously is missing in creating good, satisfying schools is the translation and transmission of knowledge and ideas based on solid inquiry of the kind that has guided those islands of innovation referred to earlier. The movement of the health fields to increased prevention of illness has provided useful information and stimulated millions of people to engage in healthful, renewing practices. But little of inquiry relevant to educational renewal gets beyond the pages of professional journals. Consequently, there is little shared by school board members, parents, administrators, teachers, and others in seeking to fulfill their supposedly common mission.

Advancing a common mission begins with the education of educators. There are too many paths to entry into the educational vocation and little convergence in the substance of preparation programs—no common cases as in law, no teaching hospitals as in medicine. The partner "teaching" school has attracted some attention, even among policymakers, but the necessary financial commitments have not followed. Teacher education is a sorely neglected enterprise. Commission reports have suffered the obscurity of most school reform reports, for much the same reasons.

The shortcomings of policy aside, much of the responsibility for generating, translating, and transmitting the knowledge and strategies necessary for school renewal rests with the professional sector of the educative community. Above all else, if the educational workforce is to gain professional legitimacy—a point of longstanding dispute—it must establish the legitimacy of its claims to academic knowledge relevant to practice.[16]

Schools of education must reach out in four critically important directions: to the public constituency that most of their graduates serve, to the academic disciplines, to the schools, and to the array of membership organizations representing millions of key players in the well-being of the thousands of schools scattered over this land. Since relationships with the first are so dependent on those with the other three, I turn to the latter.

Perhaps in part because of longstanding prestige deprivation, schools of education have not been aggressive in seeking to ensure for future teachers the general and specialized education in the arts and sciences they need for their future work. Ironically, schoolteaching is the only occupation that uses this subject matter as an instructional tool. Other professions set studies in the arts and sciences as prerequisites for admission to their schools but rarely revisit the disciplines for professional purposes. The revisitation of departments of education to these subject fields, primarily in regard to methods of teaching them, has brought down upon them the scorn of critics who blame schools of education for shortcomings in the academic background of teachers.

A large part of the knowledge required of teachers lies outside the academic boundaries of schools of education. It is high time that those schools wishing to stay in the business of teacher education put behind them their past quarrels with the arts and sciences to bring a chunk of the intellectual domain of the latter into the acknowledged professional domain of the nation's teachers. The arts and sciences schools have no pressing reason to solicit the necessary negotiation. The future of schools of education depends upon it.

Surely the time for partner "teaching" schools or professional development schools has come. It must not be allowed to pass us by. There is now a sufficient literature on the concept to support the conclusion that it could readily become part of ongoing practice were it to receive the necessary financial support.[17] With budgets seriously limited, neither school districts nor universities are stepping forward to pick up the costs. It is time for those policymakers to begin the time-consuming process of building the necessary resources into state budgets.

Colleagues advised me that advancing the idea of a center of pedagogy as both a concept and a place for bringing together the three sets of actors engaged in the initial preparation of teachers would be just another scenario of my imagination. However, the idea has been widely discussed—both negatively and positively—in some educational circles and implemented in several settings in the National Network for Educational Renewal, sometimes with different language.[18] Montclair State University was the first to announce the launching of one in its advertisement for recruiting a director.

Again, the problem of rearranging existing budgets in the absence of new money has proven to be a deterrent. More serious, however, is the issue of authority. Placing a center of pedagogy in a school of education or a college of arts and sciences frightens one or the other or both and confounds the image of equal partners. Further, partner schools appear to be left out in such an arrangement, or if included in some way, they are players of secondary importance. The concept of tripartite equity is essential to such a center's successful functioning.

The school of education has an exceedingly important political interest in external perceptions, particularly of state legislatures in the case of public institutions. If teacher education is conducted in a university setting but outside of the school of education, why should the latter exist? In the Venn diagram that accompanied the original proposal, the center of pedagogy occupied the circle of overlap where three ellipses came together, each representing one of the three equal partners: the school of education, the school of arts and sciences, and the clutch of teacher-educating partner schools. Given the support that exists for future teachers' having apprenticeships in school settings, perhaps a center coordinating the teacher education work of all of the partner schools as well as that of the collaborating university is the best political solution. It might well be the best operating alternative as well. The deterrent once again is the necessity for fiscal and budgetary arrangements that break with established patterns. Until general education, subject specializations, pedagogy, and the teaching apprenticeship are brought together under the authority of a single entity and a clearly identified composite faculty, it will be exceedingly difficult, probably impossible, to have coherent teacher education programs.

Every sector of the school-oriented educational community has an identifying organization: parents, school boards, administrators, teachers, guidance counselors, and more. They do not articulate a common mission other than that of educating the young. Entries in the pages of the book in which might be recorded instances of collaboration for improving this education are few. These organizations have been largely and conspicuously silent in the face of those intrusions into the system of schooling, referred to above, that create dissonance in the culture of local schools.

There are encouraging signs of change, stimulated in some of these organizations by the serious dropout rates of teachers in their beginning years—up to a third in the first three to five years—and the increasing signs of stress in teachers and administrators.[19] Joined in common purpose, these organizations could sustain and support educators throughout their entire educational careers and make a huge reduction in chronic problems of shortage and turnover.[20] Periodic announcements of several organizations collaborating are rarely followed by reports of significant accomplishments.

More quietly and with clear purpose, a dozen of the largest of these organizations have joined in creating the Learning First Alliance. The proposed work is close to that entailed in strengthening the knowledge base relevant to curriculum and pedagogy at the level of the local school and sharing it with school board members and parents. The group recognizes the close relationship among good schools for everyone, the well-being of our social and political democracy, and the need to advance an educational mission of ensuring democratic character in the young.

This is not an inconsequential development. Nor does it usher in still another era of short-term, hyped-up school reform, with accompanying intrusions of troublesome eduviruses. The alliance's developing agenda is the proper work of its member organizations and all those others that represent segments of the education community. Dare we hope that the hard work of bringing in the dawn of a new day for the place called school has begun?

Notes

CHAPTER 1

[1]Charles E. Silberman, *Crisis in the Classroom*. New York: Random House, 1970.

[2]Robert M. Hutchins, "The Great Anti-School Campaign," *The Great Ideas Today*, p. 54. Chicago: Encyclopaedia Britannica, 1972.

[3]James S. Coleman, *Equality of Educational Opportunity*. Washington: Government Printing Office, 1966.

[4]John W. Gardner, *Self-Renewal: The Individual and the Innovative Society*. New York: Harper and Row, 1965.

[5]Christopher Jencks et al., *Inequality*. New York: Harper and Row, 1973.

[6]For further analysis and discussion of this point, see Christopher J. Hurn, "Theory and Ideology in Two Traditions of Thought About Schools," *Social Forces*, Vol. 54, No. 4 (June 1976), pp. 848–864.

[7]As quoted in Lawrence A. Cremin, *The Transformation of the School*, p. 252. New York: Vintage Books, 1964.

[8]Stephen K. Bailey, "Political Coalitions for Public Education," *Daedalus* (Summer 1981), p. 32.

[9]Diane Ravitch, "Forgetting the Question: The Problem of Educational Reform," *The American Scholar* (Summer 1981), p. 332.

[10]George H. Gallup, "The 13th Annual Poll of the Public's Attitudes Toward the Public Schools," *Phi Delta Kappan* (September 1981), p. 37.

[11]Thomas F. Green, *Predicting the Behavior of the Educational System*, p. 108. New York: Syracuse University Press, 1980.

[12]See, for example, Samuel Bowles and Herbert Gintis, *Schooling in Capitalist America*. New York: Basic Books, Inc., 1976.

[13]Herbert J. Walberg (ed.), *Educational Environments and Effects*. Berkeley, Calif.: McCutchan, 1979, p. 354.

[14]Herbert H. Hyman, Charles R. Wright, and John Sheldon Reed, *The Enduring Effects of Education.* Chicago: The University of Chicago Press, 1975.

[15]Herbert H. Hyman and Charles R. Wright, *Education's Lasting Effect on Values.* Chicago: The University of Chicago Press, 1979.

[16]Harold Hodgkinson, "What's Right with Education," *Phi Delta Kappan* (November 1979), p. 160.

[17]Census Bureau, *Educational Attainment in the United States.* Washington, D.C.: U.S. Government Printing Office, 1981.

[18]Robert L. Ebel, "What Are Schools For?" *Phi Delta Kappan* (September 1972), p. 7.

[19]Edward Zigler and Jeanette Valentine, *Project Head Start.* New York: Free Press, 1979.

[20]*NAEP Bulletin*, pp. 1–2. Denver, Colo.: Education Commission of the States, April 29, 1981.

[21] Malcolm B. Scully, "Drop in Aptitude-Test Scores is Largest on Record," *Chronicle of Higher Education* (September 15, 1975), p. 19.

[22]Ibid., p. 2.

[23]C. H. Edson, *Why Scholastic Aptitude Test Scores Are Falling*, p. 9. Eugene, Oregon: Oregon School Study Council, University of Oregon, 1976.

[24]John C. Flanagan, *Perspective on Improving Education: Project TALENT's Young Adults Look Back.* New York: Praeger, 1978.

[25]John Raven, *Education, Values and Society*, p. 192. London: H. K. Lewis, 1977.

[26]Ernest House, *The Politics of Educational Innovation.* Berkeley, Calif.: McCutchan, 1974.

[27]Seymour Sarason, *The Culture of the School and the Problem of Change.* Boston: Allyn and Bacon, 1971. (Revised 1982).

[28]John I. Goodlad, *The Dynamics of Educational Change.* New York: McGraw-Hill, 1975.

[29]Michael Rutter and others, *Fifteen Thousand Hours.* Cambridge, Mass.: Harvard University Press, 1979.

[30]Lee J. Cronbach, "Beyond the Two Disciplines of Scientific Psychology," *American Psychologist* (February 1975), pp. 116–127.

[31]Educational Development Center, Inc., *American Schools: Today and Tomorrow* (A summary of eighteen key research projects). Newton, Mass.: Educational Development Center, Inc., 1981.

CHAPTER 2

[1]For a discussion of the decline of this coalition and its effects, see Stephen K. Bailey, "Political Coalitions for Public Education," *Daedalus* (Summer 1981), pp. 27–43.

[2]Ronald G. McIntire, "The Development of a Conceptual Model for Selection of Optional Educational Programs in an Elementary School," unpublished doctoral dissertation, University of California, Los Angeles, 1976.

[3]Lawrence A. Cremin, *Traditions of American Education*, p. 12. New York: Basic Books, 1977. For elaboration of this configuration and the component parts, see Lawrence A. Cremin, *American Education: The Colonial Experience*. New York: Harper and Row, 1970.

[4]Joseph J. Schwab, "Education and the State: Learning Community," *The Great Ideas Today*, pp. 234–271. Chicago: Encyclopaedia Britannica Inc., 1976.

[5]Lawrence A. Cremin, *The Transformation of the School*, pp. 122–123. New York: Alfred A. Knopf, 1961.

[6]For purposes of comparing these concepts with those that guided provisions for free public schooling throughout the second half of the nineteenth century and well into the twentieth, see James S. Coleman, "The Concept of Equality of Educational Opportunity," *Harvard Educational Review*, Vol. 28, (1968), p. 11.

[7]For further analysis, see Ernest R. House, *The Politics of Educational Innovation*. Berkeley, Calif.: McCutchan Publishing Co., 1974.

[8]Ralph W. Tyler, *Basic Principles of Curriculum and Instruction*. Chicago: University of Chicago Press, 1949.

[9]For an intriguing glimpse into what a global education program in schools might look like, see Lee and Charlotte Anderson, "A Visit to Middleton's World-Centered Schools: A Scenario," in *Schooling for a Global Age* (ed. James M. Becker). New York: McGraw-Hill, 1979.

[10]John I. Goodlad, *What Schools Are For*, p. 16. Bloomington, Ind.: Phi Delta Kappa Educational Foundation, 1979.

[11]Myron J. Atkin, "The Government in the Classroom," *Daedalus*, Vol. 109, No. 3 (Summer 1980), pp. 85–97.

[12]For a compelling analysis of bureaucratic rationality applied to the improvement of educational practice, see Arthur E. Wise, *Legislated Learning*. Berkeley: University of California Press, 1979.

[13]For a comprehensive discussion of what is required, see Don Davis (ed.), *Communities and Their Schools*. New York: McGraw-Hill, 1980.

CHAPTER 3

[1]John I. Goodlad, M. Frances Klein, and Associates, *Looking Behind the Classroom Door*. Worthington, Ohio: Charles A. Jones, 1974.

[2]C. Wayne Gordon, *The High School as a Social System*. Glencoe, Ill: The Free Press, 1957.

[3]Particularly the work of James S. Coleman, as represented especially in *The Adolescent Society*. Glencoe, Ill: The Free Press, 1961.

[4]James B. Conant, *Slums and Suburbs: A Commentary on Schools in the Metropolitan Area*. New York: McGraw-Hill, 1961.

[5]Thomas F. Green, *Predicting the Behavior of the Educational System*. Syracuse: Syracuse University Press, 1980.

[6]Carnegie Council on Policy Studies in Higher Education, *Giving Youth a Better Chance*. San Francisco: Jossey-Bass, 1979.

[7]Robert L. Ebel, "The Failure of Schools Without Failure," *Phi Delta Kappan*, Vol. 61 (February 1980), pp. 386–388.

[8]National Commission on the Reform of Secondary Education, Frank Brown (Chair), *The Reform of Secondary Education*. New York: McGraw-Hill, 1973.

[9]Benjamin S. Bloom, *Stability and Change in Human Characteristics*. New York: John C. Wiley, 1965.

[10]Benjamin S. Bloom, *All Our Children Learning*. New York: McGraw-Hill, 1980.

[11]Freeman Butts, "Educational Vouchers: The Private Pursuit of the Public Purse," *Phi Delta Kappan*, Vol. 61, No. 1 (September 1979), pp. 7–9.

CHAPTER 4

[1]David E. Wiley and Annegret Harnischfeger, "Explosion of a Myth: Quantity of Schooling and Exposure to Instruction, Major Educational Vehicles," *Educational Researcher*, Vol. 3 (1974), pp. 7–12.

[2]Torsten Husén (ed.), *International Study of Achievement in Mathematics: A Comparison of Twelve Countries*, Vols. 1, 2. New York: John Wiley and Sons, 1967.

[3]Ibid.; and Alan C. Purves, *Literature Education in Ten Countries: International Studies in Evaluation II*. New York: John Wiley and Sons, 1973.

[4]See, for example, Benjamin S. Bloom, "Time and Learning," *American Psychologist*, Vol. 29 (1977), pp. 682–688; J. McKinney, J. Mason, K. Perkerson, and M. Clifford, "Relationship Between Classroom Behavior and Academic Achievement," *Journal of Educational Psychology*, Vol. 67 (1975), pp. 198–203; and B. V. Rosenshine and D. C. Berliner, "Academic Engaged Time," *British Journal of Teacher Education*, Vol. 4 (1978), pp. 31–36.

[5]Harvey A. Averch et al., *How Effective Is Schooling?*, p. 171. Englewood Cliffs, N.J.: Educational Technology Publications, 1974.

[6]Benjamin S. Bloom, "The New Direction in Educational Research: Alterable Variables," *The State of Research on Selected Alterable Variables in Learning*, pp. 10–12. Chicago: Department of Education, University of Chicago, 1980.

[7]See, for example, Michael J. Dunkin and Bruce J. Biddle, *The Study of Teaching*. New York: Holt, Rinehart, and Winston, 1974; Jacob. S. Kounin, *Discipline and Group Management in Classrooms*. New York: Holt, Rinehart and Winston, 1970; Donald Medley, *Teacher Competence and Teacher Effectiveness*. Washington, D.C.: American

Association of Colleges of Teacher Education, 1977; B. Rosenshine and N. Furst, "Research on Teacher Performance Criteria," in B. O. Smith (ed.), *Research in Teacher Education*. Englewood Cliffs, N.J.: Prentice-Hall, Inc., 1971; David L. Silvernail, "Teaching Styles as Related to Student Achievement," in *What Research Says to the Teacher*. Washington, D.C.: National Education Association, 1979. ERIC ED 177 156; Larry Fedigan, "School-based Elements Related to Achievement: A Review of the Literature." Edmonton, Canada: Alberta Department of Education, Minister's Advisory Committee on Student Achievement, 1979. ERIC 181043; and B. Rosenshine, "Enthusiastic Teaching: A Research Review," *School Review* (August 1970), pp. 499–514.

[8]Benjamin S. Bloom, *All Our Children Learning*. New York: McGraw-Hill, 1981.

[9]One such study concentrates on how 764 children aged 11 and 12 spent the seven hours from 3 P.M. to 10 P.M.; see Elliott A. Medrich et al., *The Serious Business of Growing Up*. Berkeley: University of California Press, 1982.

[10]John I. Goodlad, M. Frances Klein, and Associates, *Looking Behind the Classroom Door*. Worthington, Ohio: Charles A. Jones, 1974.

[11]Philip W. Jackson, *Life in Classrooms*. New York: Holt, Rinehart, and Winston, 1968.

[12]B. Othanel Smith et al., *A Design for a School of Pedagogy*. Washington, D.C.: U.S. Government Printing Office, 1980.

[13]For a description of this approach, see John I. Goodlad, *The Dynamics of Educational Change: Toward Responsive Schools*. New York: McGraw-Hill, 1975.

[14]Mary M. Bentzen and Associates, *Changing Schools: The Magic Feather Principle*. New York: McGraw-Hill, 1974.

[15]Paul Berman and Milbrey Wallin McLaughlin, *Federal Programs Supporting Educational Change, Vol. VIII: Implementing and Sustaining Innovations*. Santa Monica: The RAND Corporation, 1978.

CHAPTER 5

[1]See, for example, Thomas J. LaBelle, "Cultural Determinants of Educational Alternatives," pp. 29–48, and Val D. Rust, "Alternative Futures in Education," pp. 143–163, in John I. Goodlad et al., *The Conventional and the Alternative in Education*. Berkeley, Calif.: McCutchan, 1975.

[2]James S. Coleman, "The Concept of Equality of Educational Opportunity." *Harvard Educational Review*, Vol. 38 (1968), pp. 7–22.

[3]Basil Bernstein, *Class, Codes and Control, Vol. 3: Towards a Theory of Educational Transmissions* (2nd ed.). London: Routledge and Kegan Paul, 1977.

[4]Report of the Harvard Committee, *General Education in a Free Society*. Cambridge, Mass.: Harvard University Press, 1945.

[5]Ibid., p. 102.

[6]Ibid., passim.

[7]James B. Conant, *The American High School Today*. New York: McGraw-Hill, 1959.

[8]Mortimer J. Adler, "The Disappearance of Culture," *Newsweek*, Aug. 21, 1978, p. 15.

[9]Glen Heathers, "Grouping," in Robert L. Ebel (ed.), *Encyclopedia of Educational Research* (4th ed.). New York: Macmillan, 1969, pp. 559–570; also, John I. Goodlad, "Some Effects of Promotion and Nonpromotion Upon the Personal and Social Adjustment of Children," *Journal of Experimental Education*, Vol. 23 (June 1954), pp. 301–328.

[10]John I. Goodlad and Robert H. Anderson, *The Nongraded Elementary School* (revised edition), p. 36. New York: Harcourt, Brace, Jovanovich, 1963.

[11]Melvin L. Barlow, "The Challenge to Vocational Education," *Vocational Education*, p. 4. Sixty-fourth Yearbook of the National Society for the Study of Education, Part I. Chicago: University of Chicago Press, 1965.

[12]Barlow, op. cit., p. 2.

[13]Randall Collins, *The Credential Society*, p. 16. New York: Academic Press, 1979.

[14]Report of the Harvard Committee, op. cit., p. 102.

[15]See, for example, Samuel Bowles and Herbert Gintis, *Schooling in Capitalistic America*. New York: Basic Books, 1976; also P. Bourdieu and J. Passeron, *Reproduction in Education, Society and Culture* (translated by Richard Nice). Beverly Hills, Calif.: Sage Publications, 1977; M. F. D. Young, *Knowledge and Control*, London: Collier-Macmillan, 1971.

[16]Wellford W. Wilms, *The Unfilled Promise of Postsecondary Vocational Education: Graduates and Dropouts in the Labor Market*. Report to the National Institute of Education, 1980 (mimeo).

[17]Bruce Gunn, "The System is the Answer," *Florida School Administration*, Vol. 2, No. 3 (April 1979), pp. 30–35.

[18]See, for example, Caroline H. Persell, *Education and Inequality: A Theoretical and Empirical Synthesis*. New York: The Free Press, 1977.

[19]See, for example, W. R. Borg, *Ability Grouping in the Public Schools*. Madison, Wis.: Dembar Educational Research Services, 1966; and Warren Findley and Marian Bryan, *Ability Grouping—1970* (ERIC Document No. ED 048382). Athens: College of Education, University of Georgia, 1970.

[20]W. Schafer and C. Olexa, *Tracking and Opportunity*. Scranton, Penn.: Chandler Publishing Co., 1971.

[21]K. L. Alexander, M. Cook, and E. L. McDill, "Curriculum Tracking and Educational Stratification: Some Further Evidence." *American Sociological Review*, Vol. 43 (1978), pp. 47–66.

[22]J. Rosenbaum, *Making Inequality: The Hidden Curriculum of High School Tracking*. New York: Wiley, 1976.

[23]Thomas F. Green, *Predicting the Behavior of the Educational System*. Syracuse, NY: Syracuse University Press, 1980.

[24]John I. Goodlad, M. Frances Klein and Associates. *Looking Behind the Classroom Door*. Worthington, Ohio: Charles A. Jones, 1974.

[25]Torsten Husén, *Social Influences on Educational Attainment*. Paris: Organization for Economic Cooperation and Development, 1975.

[26]S. M. Lipset, "The Ideology of Local Control," in C. A. Bowers, I. Housego, and D. Dyke (eds.), *Education and Social Policy: Local Control of Education*, pp. 21–42. New York: Random House, 1970.

[27]For a summary of attendant conditions, see Benjamin S. Bloom, *All Our Children Learning*, pp. 153–175. New York: McGraw-Hill, 1981.

CHAPTER 6

[1]James S. Coleman et al., *Equality of Educational Opportunity*. Washington, D.C.: U.S. Government Printing Office, 1966.

[2]Christopher Jencks et al., *Inequality*. New York: Basic Books, 1972.

[3]For instance, see M. Dino Carelli and John G. Morris (eds.), *Equality of Opportunity Reconsidered: Values in Education for Tomorrow*. Third European Colloquy for Directors of National Institutes in Education, Hamburg, September 1978. Lisse: Swets and Zeitlinger, 1979.

[4]Dorothy M. Lloyd, "The Effects of a Staff Development In-service Program on Teacher Performance and Student Achievement." Unpublished Doctoral Dissertation. Los Angeles: University of California, 1973.

[5]Thomas Sowell, "Patterns of Black Excellence," *The Public Interest* (Spring 1976), pp. 26–58.

[6]National Education Association, *The American Public-School Teacher 1965–66*. Washington, D.C.: Research Division, 1967.

[7]Ibid., p. 100.

[8]Dan C. Lortie, *Schoolteacher*, p. 94. Chicago: University of Chicago Press, 1975.

[9]See, for example, Lee Braude, *Work and Workers*. New York: Praeger, 1975; Louis E. Davis, Albert B. Cherns, and Associates (eds.), *The Quality of Working Life*, Vol. 1, 2. New York: Free Press, 1975.

[10]L. J. Wehling and W. W. Charters, Jr., "Dimensions of Teacher Beliefs about the Teaching Process," *American Educational Research Journal*, Vol. 6 (1969), pp. 7–30; Marvin Sontag, "Attitudes toward Education and Perception of Teacher Behaviors," *American Educational Research Journal*, Vol. 5 (1968), pp. 385–402; P. Ashton et al., *The Aims of Primary Education: A Study of Teachers' Opinions*. London: Macmillan and Co., 1975; N. Bennett, *Teaching Styles and Pupil Progress*. London: Open Books, 1976.

[11]See, for example, Mary M. Bentzen and Associates, *Changing Schools*. New York: McGraw-Hill, 1974.

[12]See, for example, Kenneth A. Tye and Jerrold M. Novotney, *Schools in Transition*. New York: McGraw-Hill, 1975.

[13] See, for example, Gary A. Griffin, "Levels of Curricular Decision-Making," in John I. Goodlad and Associates, *Curriculum Inquiry: The Study of Curriculum Practice.* New York: McGraw-Hill, 1979.

[14] Lortie, op. cit., p. 114.

[15] Garth Sorenson and Cecily F. Gross, "Teacher Appraisal: A Matching Process," Occasional Report No. 4. Los Angeles: Center for the Study of Evaluation, University of California, April 1967; Frank Dyer, "Teacher Role Expectations of a Secondary School Staff." Unpublished Doctoral Dissertation, University of California, Los Angeles, 1966.

[16] Robert D. Hess and Virginia C. Shipman, "Early Experience and the Socialization of Cognitive Modes in Children," *Child Development,* 36 (1965), pp. 869–886.

[17] Philip Jackson, *Life in Classrooms.* New York: Holt, Rinehart and Winston, 1968.

[18] Willard Waller, *The Sociology of Teaching.* New York: Russell and Russell, 1961.

CHAPTER 7

[1] For a comprehensive analysis of secondary school social studies texts, see Frances Fitzgerald, *America Revisited.* Boston: Little, Brown and Co., 1979.

[2] Arthur Jersild and Ruth J. Tasch, *Children's Interests and What They Suggest for Education.* New York: Bureau of Publications, Teachers College, Columbia, 1949.

[3] Judith V. Torney, "Psychological and Institutional Obstacles to the Global Perspective in Education," *Schooling for a Global Age* (ed. James M. Becker), p. 84. New York: McGraw-Hill, 1979.

[4] The President's Commission on Foreign Languages and International Studies, *Strength Through Wisdom: A Critique of U.S. Capability.* Washington, D.C.: The White House, November 1979.

[5] See for example, Jerome J. Hausman (ed.), *Arts and the Schools.* New York: McGraw-Hill, 1980.

[6] Melvin L. Barlow, *The Unconquerable Senator Page: The Struggle to Establish Federal Legislation for Vocational Education.* Washington, D.C.: American Vocational Education Association, 1976.

[7] Roger G. Barker and Paul V. Gump, *Big School, Small School.* Stanford, Calif.: Stanford University Press, 1964.

[8] The Kincaid Elementary School in Georgia, for example. See Henry W. Hill and Associates, *Goodlad–Theory into Practice.* Atlanta, Ga.: Canterbury Press, 1982.

[9] Seymour Papert, *Mindstorms,* p. 5. New York: Basic Books, 1980.

[10] Kenneth A. Sirotnik, *"What You See Is What You Get: A Summary of Observations in over 1000 Elementary and Secondary Classrooms."* A Study of Schooling Technical Report No. 29. Los Angeles: Laboratory in School and Community Education, Graduate School of Education, University of California, 1981.

[11]John C. Flanagan (ed.), *Perspectives on Improving Education: Project Talent's Young Adults Look Back.* New York: Praeger, 1978.

[12]Progressive Education Association, *Thirty Schools Tell Their Story.* New York: Harper and Brothers, 1943.

[13]American Education Fellowship Commission on the Secondary School Curriculum, *Science in General Education, Language in General Education, Mathematics in General Education, Literature in General Education, The Social Studies in General Education, The Visual Arts in General Education.* New York: Appleton-Century Co., 1940.

[14]See Gary A. Griffin, "Levels of Curricular Decision-making," and Robert M. McClure, "Institutional Decisions in Curriculum," in John I. Goodlad and Associates, *Curriculum Inquiry.* New York: McGraw-Hill, 1979.

[15]D. H. Kerr, "The Structure of Quality in Teaching," *Philosophy and Education* (ed. J. F. Soltis), p. 79. Eightieth Yearbook of the National Society for the Study of Education. Chicago: University of Chicago Press, 1981.

[16]John I. Goodlad (with Renata Von Stoephasius and M. Frances Klein), *The Changing School Curriculum.* New York: Fund for the Advancement of Education, 1966.

[17]Doreen G. Nelson, *Manual for the City Building Educational Program.* Los Angeles: The Center for City Building Educational Programs, 1974.

[18]Marilyn L. Kourilsky, *Beyond Simulation: The Mini Society Approach to Instruction in Economics and Other Social Sciences.* Los Angeles: Educational Resource Associates, 1974.

[19]Stephen K. Bailey, *The Purposes of Education,* p. 61. Bloomington, Ind.: Phi Delta Kappa Educational Foundation, 1976.

CHAPTER 8

[1]Careful studies of schools of different sizes reveal differences between large and small schools in matters that would appear to affect satisfaction quite markedly. Students in small schools participate more broadly in the life of the school, are more likely to be known by teachers, and are less likely to be left out of activities. It appears to be more difficult in small schools for the more extreme peer group values to take hold. See R. G. Barker and P. V. Gump, *Big School, Small School.* Stanford, Calif.: Stanford University Press, 1964.

[2]Michael Rutter and others. *Fifteen Thousand Hours.* Cambridge, Mass.: Harvard University Press, 1979.

[3]See Arthur E. Wise, *Legislated Learning.* Berkeley: University of California Press, 1979.

[4]See Mary M. Bentzen and Associates, *Changing Schools: The Magic Feather Principle.* New York: McGraw-Hill, 1974.

[5]See John I. Goodlad, *The Dynamics of Educational Change: Toward Responsive Schools.* New York: McGraw-Hill, 1975.

⁶I am indebted to Seymour Sarason not only for the concept of regularities—programmatic and behavioral—but, especially, for his insightful analysis of the consistent, unchanging elements of school culture. See Seymour B. Sarason, *The Culture of the School and the Problem of Change* (2nd ed.). Boston: Allyn and Bacon, 1982.

⁷See, for example, P. Berman and M. W. McLaughlin, *Federal Programs Supporting Educational Change (Vol. VIII: Implementing and Sustaining Innovations)*. Santa Monica, Calif.: The RAND Corporation, 1978.

⁸Ernest House, *The Politics of Educational Innovation*. Berkeley, Calif.: McCutchan, 1974.

CHAPTER 9

¹For a summary of findings and recommendations, see John I. Goodlad, *The Dynamics of Educational Change*. New York: McGraw-Hill, 1975.

²See Norma D. Feshbach, John I. Goodlad, and Avima Lombard, *Early Schooling in England and Israel*. New York: McGraw-Hill, 1973.

³See John I. Goodlad, M. Frances Klein, Jerrold M. Novotney, and Associates, *Early Schooling in the United States*. New York: McGraw-Hill, 1973.

⁴Joseph J. Schwab, "Education and the State: Learning Community," *The Great Ideas Today*. Chicago: Encyclopaedia Britannica, Inc., 1976.

⁵Henry W. Hill, "Societal Decisions in Curriculum," in John I. Goodlad and Associates, *Curriculum Inquiry*, pp. 101–127. New York: McGraw-Hill, 1979.

⁶For further elaboration of these processes, see Mary M. Bentzen and Associates, *Changing Schools*. New York: McGraw-Hill, 1974.

⁷The importance of developing this capacity is well demonstrated in our work with The League of Cooperating Schools. See John I. Goodlad, *The Dynamics of Educational Change*, op. cit., 1975; and the experiences of the League of Cities in the Arts reported in Jane Remer, *Changing Schools Through the Arts*. New York: McGraw-Hill, 1981.

⁸Harry S. Broudy, "A Common Curriculum in Aesthetics and Fine Arts," *Individual Differences and the Common Curriculum* (Gary D Fenstermacher and John I. Goodlad, eds.), Eighty-first Yearbook of the National Society for the Study of Education, Part I. Chicago: University of Chicago Press, 1983.

⁹Findings in a comprehensive survey of time use in Minnesota schools are very similar. See Harlan S. Hansen and Richard D. Kimpston, *An Educational Contradiction: Is What Schools Say They Teach What They Really Teach, and What They Reinforce Through Testing in the Elementary Schools?* Minneapolis: College of Education, University of Minnesota, 1981.

¹⁰Using an earlier version of our analysis of state goals, as contained in John I. Goodlad, *What Schools Are For*. Bloomington, Ind.: Phi Delta Kappa Educational Foundation, 1979.

[11]California State Department of Education, *Curriculum Review Handbook* (second draft). Sacramento, 1981.

[12]Michael W. Kirst, "Policy Implications of Individual Differences and the Common Curriculum," *Individual Differences and the Common Curriculum* (Gary D Fenstermacher and John I. Goodlad, eds.), Eighty-first Yearbook of the National Society for the Study of Education, Part 1. Chicago: University of Chicago Press, 1983.

[13] For detailed statistics, see *Final Report of the Commission on the Higher Education of Minorities*. Los Angeles: Higher Education Research Institute, 1982.

[14]James B. Conant, *The Education of American Teachers*. New York: McGraw-Hill, 1963.

[15]Benjamin S. Bloom and Laura A. Sosniak, "Talent Development vs. Schooling," *Educational Leadership* (November 1981), pp. 86–94.

[16]John I. Goodlad, "The Common Curriculum in Concept and in Practice," *Individual Differences and the Common Curriculum* (Gary D Fenstermacher and John I. Goodlad, eds.), Eighty-first Yearbook of the National Society for the Study of Education, Part I. Chicago: University of Chicago Press, 1983.

[17]Quoted in Anne C. Roarck, "Lack of Funds for California Colleges May Be a Blessing in Disguise," *Los Angeles Times* (January 31, 1982), Part IV, p. 6.

[18]Regarding some of the movement's underlying concepts and assumptions, see G. W. Ford and Lawrence Pugno (eds.), *The Structure of Knowledge and the Curriculum*. Chicago: Rand McNally, 1964; for descriptions and analyses of major projects, see John I. Goodlad (with Renata von Stoephasius and M. Frances Klein), *The Changing School Curriculum*. New York: Fund for the Advancement of Education, 1966; and regarding the federal role, see the first 73 pages of *Educational Evaluation and Policy Analysis*, September-October 1981.

[19]Jerome S. Bruner, *The Process of Education*. Cambridge, Mass.: Harvard University Press, 1960.

[20]For additional information, see especially Chapter 8 in Benjamin S. Bloom, *All Our Children Learning*. New York: McGraw-Hill, 1981.

[21]The techniques developed by Madeline Hunter and her colleagues at the University Elementary School of the Graduate School of Education, University of California, Los Angeles, have been widely used to help teachers control their classrooms, sustain students' attention, organize their presentations more effectively, and so on. See, for example, Madeline C. Hunter, *Prescriptions for Improved Instruction*. El Segundo, Calif.: TIP Publications, 1976.

[22]For a recent review of the laboratory school scene, see *UCLA Educator*. Los Angeles: Graduate School of Education, University of California, Winter 1980.

[23]John I. Goodlad, "Instruction," in *Citizens for the 21st Century: Long-Range Considerations for California Elementary and Secondary Education*, pp. 443–485. Sacramento, Calif.: State Committee on Public Education, 1969.

[24]James B. Conant, *The American High School Today*. New York: McGraw-Hill, 1959.

[25]See, for example, John I. Goodlad and Robert H. Anderson, *The Nongraded Elementary School*. New York: Harcourt, Brace, 1959; and John I. Goodlad, *Planning and Organizing for Teaching*, Project in the Instructional Program of the Public Schools. Washington, D.C.: National Education Association, 1963.

[26]For example, see Francis S. Chase. "The Schools I Hope to See," *NEA Journal* (March 1957), pp. 164–166.

[27]John A. Brownell and Harris A. Taylor, "Theoretical Perspectives for Teaching Teams," *Phi Delta Kappan* (January 1962), pp. 150–157.

[28]Harry G. Judge, *American Graduate Schools of Education*. New York: Ford Foundation, 1982.

[29]For a discussion of clinical appointments, see James B. Conant, *The Education of American Teachers*. New York: McGraw-Hill, 1963.

[30]For a discussion of the school-university relationship, see John I. Goodlad, "The Reconstruction of Teacher Education," *Teachers College Record* (September 1970), pp. 61–72.

[31]B. Othanel Smith, *A Design for a School of Pedagogy*. Washington, D.C.: U.S. Department of Education, 1980.

[32]Hendrik D. Gideonse, "The Necessary Revolution in Teacher Education," *Phi Delta Kappan* (September 1982), pp. 15–18.

[33]Regarding the design of a comprehensive assessment system for schools, see Kenneth A. Sirotnik and Jeannie Oakes, "A Contextual Appraisal System for Schools: Medicine or Madness?" *Educational Leadership* (December 1981), pp. 164–173.

[34]While these recommendations are in the spirit of those put forward by members of the Paideia Group, they do not go as far toward curricular commonality for all students. See Mortimer J. Adler, *The Paideia Proposal*. New York: Macmillan, 1982.

CHAPTER 10

[1]The percentage of school bond initiatives passed in the United States dropped from 72% in 1962 to 47% in 1972 and either remained level or dropped in successive years. See National Center for Educational Statistics, *Bond Sales for Public School Purposes*. Washington, D.C.: U.S. Government Printing Office, 1978.

[2]Carnegie Commission on the Future of Higher Education, *Less Time, More Options: Education Beyond the High School*; a special report and recommendations by the Carnegie Commission on Higher Education. New York: McGraw-Hill, 1971.

[3]U.S. Department of Education. National Center for Education Statistics. *The Condition of Education, 1981 Edition*, pp. 10 and 26.

[4]Benjamin S. Bloom, *Stability and Change in Human Characteristics*. New York: Wiley, 1964.

[5]Jerome S. Bruner, *The Process of Education*. Cambridge, Mass.: Harvard University Press, 1960.

[6]These studies and reports included Edgar Z. Friedenberg, *Coming of Age in America*. New York: Vintage-Random House, Inc., 1970; Panel on Youth, Science Advisory Committee to the President, *Youth: Transition to Adulthood*. Chicago: University of Chicago Press, 1974; and Carnegie Council on Policy Studies in Higher Education, *Giving Youth a Better Chance: Options for Education, Work and Service*; a report with recommendations. San Francisco: Jossey-Bass Publishers, 1979.

[7]The National Commission on the Reform of Secondary Education, *The Reform of Secondary Education*. New York: McGraw-Hill Book Company, 1973.

[8]Stanley M. Garn, "Continuities and Change in Maturational Timing," in Orville J. Brim and Jerome Kagan (editors), *Constancy and Change in Human Development*, p. 124. Cambridge, Mass.: Harvard University Press, 1980.

[9]At a meeting of the Association of Chief State School Officers in Colorado Springs, August 1981. For this and other recommendations, see Mortimer Adler, *The Paidea Proposal*. New York: Macmillan, 1982.

[10]For a perspective on general education, see Carnegie Foundation for the Advancement of Teaching, *Common Learning*. A Carnegie Colloquium on General Education. Washington, D.C.: The Foundation, 1981.

[11]See Herman J. Epstein, "Growth Spurts during Brain Development: Implications for Educational Policy and Practice," in Jeanne S. Chall and Allan F. Mirsky (editors), *Education and the Brain*, p. 344. Seventy-seventh Yearbook of the National Society for the Study of Education, Part II. Chicago: University of Chicago Press, 1978.

[12]Roger A. Webb, "Concrete and Formal Operations in Very Bright Six- to Eleven-Year Olds," *Human Development*, 17 (1974), pp. 292–300.

[13]Epstein, loc. cit.

[14]Robert Ulich, *The Human Career: A Philosophy of Self-Transcendence*. New York: Harper and Bros., 1955.

[15]For a discussion of alternative possibilities for the elementary phase of schooling, see Bruce R. Joyce, *Alternative Models of Elementary Education*. Waltham, Mass.: Blaisdell, 1969.

[16]Lawrence W. Downey, *The Secondary Phase of Education*, p. 79. New York: Blaisdell, 1965.

[17]Loc. cit.

[18]A. N. Whitehead, *The Aims of Education and Other Essays*, pp. 19, 20. New York: Macmillan, 1929.

[19]John Ainley, et al., *Resource Allocation in the Government Schools of Australia and New Zealand*. Melbourne, Australia: Australian Education Council, (in press).

[20]Edith A. Buchanan, "From Institutional to Instructional Decisions," in John I. Goodlad and Associates, *Curriculum Inquiry: The Study of Curriculum Practice*, pp. 151–176. New York: McGraw-Hill, 1979.

[21] For a fascinating foray into the possibilities, see Seymour Papert, *Mindstorms*. New York: Basic Books, 1980.

[22] See, for example, W. C. Meierhenry, "The Impact of Technology on Curriculum," in Lois V. Edinger et al. (eds.), *Education in the 80's: Curricular Challenges*. Washington, D.C.: National Education Association, 1981; James Koerner, "Educational Technology: Does It Have a Future in the Classroom?" *Saturday Review of Education*, May 1973; J. Ellul, *The Technological Society*. New York: Vintage, 1964; and Joy Senter, "Computer Technology and Education," *The Forum Educational* (Fall 1981), pp. 55–64. Also, *Phi Delta Kappan* devoted its issue of January 1982 to the computer in education.

[23] For views of well-known figures in the entertainment industry, see *UCLA Educator*. Los Angeles: Graduate School of Education, University of California, Fall/Winter 1977/78.

[24] Harry F. Silberman (ed.), *Education and Work* (Eighty-first Yearbook of the National Society for the Study of Education, Part II), p. xi. Chicago: University of Chicago Press, 1982.

[25] Jeannie Oakes, *Limiting Opportunity: Student Race and Curricular Differences in Secondary Vocational Education* (Technical Report No. 28, A Study of Schooling). Los Angeles: Laboratory in School and Community Education, Graduate School of Education, University of California, 1981.

[26] For an excellent summary of current views of this development, see Edwin L. Herr and Stanley H. Cramer, *Career Guidance Through the Life Span: Systematic Approaches*, pp. 100–101. Boston: Little, Brown & Co., 1979.

[27] Ellen Greenberger and Laurence D. Steinberg, *Part-time Employment of In-school Youth: An Assessment of Costs and Benefits*. Irvine: University of California, June 30, 1981 (Mimeo).

[28] National Institute of Education, *A Comparison of Four Experience-Based Career Education Programs*. Washington, D.C.: U.S. Department of Health, Education and Welfare, 1976.

[29] Arthur M. Cohen and Florence B. Brawer, *The American Community College*. San Francisco: Jossey-Bass, 1982.

[30] Willard Wirtz, *The Boundless Resource*. Washington, D.C.: New Republic Book Co., 1975.

[31] Fred Hechinger, "The High School-College Connection," in *Common Learning*, pp. 115–128. Carnegie Colloquium on General Education. Washington, D.C.: Carnegie Foundation for the Advancement of Teaching, 1981.

[32] Carnegie Commission on the Future of Higher Education, *Less Time, More Options: Education Beyond the High School*, op. cit.

[33] For elaboration of this ecological concept as applied to education, see John I. Goodlad, *The Dynamics of Educational Change: Toward Responsive Schools*. New York: McGraw-Hill Book Co., 1975; Lawrence A. Cremin, *The Genius of American*

Education. New York: Vintage Books, 1966; and Urie Bronfenbrenner, "The Experimental Ecology of Education," *Teachers College Record* (December 1976), pp. 157–204.

[34]Jack D. Minzey, "Community Education and Community Schools," in *Communities and Their Schools* (ed. Don Davies), p. 271. New York: McGraw-Hill, 1981.

[35]Ibid., p. 272.

[36]For example, the *1981* annual conference of the American Educational Research Association.

[37]Hope Jensen Leichter (ed.), *The Family as Educator*. New York: Teachers College Press, 1974.

[38]John I. Goodlad, "Educational Leadership: Toward the Third Era," *Educational Leadership* (January 1978), pp. 322–331; and "Can Our Schools Get Better?," *Phi Delta Kappan* (January 1979), pp. 342–347.

[39]Lawrence A. Cremin, "Further Notes Toward a Theory of Education," *Notes on Education*, Vol. 4 (1974), p. 1.

AFTERWORD

[1]Sizer credits the source of the "grammar" of schooling to David Tyack and Larry Cuban, *Tinkering Toward Utopia: A Century of Public School Reform*. Cambridge, Mass.: Harvard University Press, 1995.

[2]For elaboration of the degree to which this narrative now drives educational policy and to an increasing degree practice, see Neil Postman, *The End of Education*. New York: Vintage, 1996.

[3]See especially Michael Fullan, *Change Forces*. New York: Falmer Press, 1993. For a superb analysis of the central problems of changing the culture of the school, see Seymour B. Sarason, *The Culture of the School and the Problem of Change*. Boston: Allyn & Bacon, 1971 and 1982.

[4]For an elaboration of these principles and expectations, see John I. Goodlad, M. Frances Klein, and Associates, *Behind the Classroom Door*. Worthington, Ohio: Charles A. Jones, 1970.

[5]Goodlad, Klein, and Associates, *Behind the Classroom Door*, pp. 78–79, 93–94.

[6]Reported in a trilogy: John I. Goodlad, Roger Soder, and Kenneth A. Sirotnik (editors), *The Moral Dimensions of Teaching* and *Places Where Teachers Are Taught*, and John I. Goodlad, *Teachers for Our Nation's Schools*. San Francisco: Jossey-Bass, 1990.

[7]Described and with lessons learned in Kenneth A. Sirotnik and Associates, *Renewing Schools and Teacher Education: An Odyssey in Educational Change*. Washington, D.C.: American Association of Colleges for Teacher Education, 2001.

[8]John I. Goodlad, Corinne Mantle-Bromley, and Stephen J. Goodlad, *Education for Everyone: Agenda for Education in a Democracy*. San Francisco: Jossey-Bass, 2004.

[9] John I. Goodlad, *Romances with Schools: A Life of Education*. New York: McGraw-Hill, 2004.

[10] Two other major treatises on schooling covered much of the ground tilled in *A Place Called School* and received widespread attention: Ernest L. Boyer, *High School*. New York: Harper & Row, 1983; Theodore R. Sizer, *Horace's Compromise*. Boston: Houghton Mifflin, 1984.

[11] A flurry of interest in organizing and teaching school curricula around the structure of the disciplines, even for the youngest pupils, was stimulated in the 1960s by the Woods Hole Conference of scholars and the accompanying book by Jerome S. Bruner, *The Process of Education*. New York: Vintage, 1960. Other treatises followed; see especially Phi Delta Kappa, *Education and the Structure of Knowledge*. Chicago: Rand McNally, 1964. Some of the principles and concepts were incorporated into the curriculum development projects, rather handsomely supported by the federal government and private philanthropy, that thrived for a time without much changing the nineteenth-century deep curricula structure of schooling. See John I. Goodlad, *School Curriculum Reform*. New York: Fund for the Advancement of Education, 1964. Lee Shulman's good work on content-specific pedagogy in the 1990s revived interest in this genre of curriculum inquiry, but the curricula of practice sank deeper into the outmoded patterns that are alive and well today.

[12] See Kathleen L. Florio, *Twenty-One Educational Renewal Initiatives*. Seattle: Institute for Educational Inquiry, 1999.

[13] See Howard Gardner, *Frames of Mind*, New York: Basic Books, 1983, for an interesting journey into his thinking.

[14] Goodlad, Mantle-Bromley, and Goodlad, *Education for Everyone*.

[15] Robert D. Putnam, *Making Democracy Work: Civic Traditions in Modern Italy*. Princeton, N.J.: Princeton University Press, 1993.

[16] For an analysis of the ways professions establish claims of legitimacy regarding the exercise of their work, see Andrew Abbott, *The System of Professions*. Chicago: University of Chicago Press, 1988.

[17] See, for example, Richard W. Clark, *Effective Professional Development Schools*. San Francisco: Jossey-Bass, 1999; and Russell T. Osguthorpe et al. (editors), *Partner Schools: Centers for Educational Renewal*. San Francisco: Jossey-Bass, 1995.

[18] Robert S. Patterson, Nicholas M. Michelli, and Arturo Pacheco, *Centers of Pedagogy: New Structures for Educational Renewal*. San Francisco: Jossey-Bass, 1999.

[19] John I. Goodlad and Timothy J. McMannon (editors), *The Teaching Career*. New York: Teachers College Press, 2004.

[20] National Commission on Teaching and America's Future, *No Dream Denied: A Pledge to America's Children*. Washington, D.C.: National Commission on Teaching and America's Future, 2003.

Index

Since all references are conveniently grouped by chapters immediately following Chapter 10, only authors and titles specifically cited in the narrative are included in the index.

About the Author

JOHN I. GOODLAD began his teaching in a one-room, eight-grade rural school. Since then, he has taught students in every grade above, including the doctoral level, and held an array of professorial and administrative positions. After earning the B.A. and M.A. degrees at the University of British Columbia in his native Canada, he completed studies for the Ph.D. at the University of Chicago, and subsequently, over the years, was awarded honorary doctoral degrees by twenty colleges and universities in the United States and Canada. His three dozen books and an array of other publications, many of them addressed to the role of public schools in advancing democracy and developing democratic character in the young, have contributed significantly to his receiving awards from various organizations devoted to educational research and policy.

CPSIA information can be obtained
at www.ICGtesting.com
Printed in the USA
FSHW020705010820
72438FS